The Critical Heritage Series

GENERAL EDITOR: B. C. SOUTHAM, M.A., B.LITT. (OXON)
Formerly Department of English, Westfield College, University of London

For list of books in the series see back end paper.

MILTON 1732-1801

THE CRITICAL HERITAGE

Edited by
JOHN T. SHAWCROSS
Professor of English, City University of New York

LONDON AND BOSTON: ROUTLEDGE & KEGAN PAUL

First published 1972
by Routledge & Kegan Paul Limited
Broadway House, 68-74 Carter Lane
London EC4V 5EL and
9 Park Street
Boston, Mass. 02108, U.S.A.
Copyright John T. Shawcross 1972

ISBN 0 7100 7261 9

Printed in Great Britain by
W & J Mackay Limited, Chatham
and set in 11 point Bembo 1 point leaded

General Editor's Preface

The reception given to a writer by his contemporaries and near-contemporaries is evidence of considerable value to the student of literature. On one side we learn a great deal about the state of criticism at large and in particular about the development of critical attitudes towards a single writer; at the same time, through private comments in letters, journals or marginalia, we gain an insight upon the tastes and literary thought of individual readers of the period. Evidence of this kind helps us to understand the writer's historical situation, the nature of his immediate reading-public, and his response to these pressures.

The separate volumes in the *Critical Heritage Series* present a record of this early criticism. Clearly, for many of the highly productive and lengthily-reviewed nineteenth- and twentieth-century writers, there exists an enormous body of material; and in these cases the volume editors have made a selection of the most important views, significant for their intrinsic critical worth or for their representative quality—perhaps even registering incomprehension!

For earlier writers, notably pre-eighteenth century, the materials are much scarcer and the historical period has been extended, sometimes far beyond the writer's lifetime, in order to show the inception and growth of critical views which were initially slow to appear.

In each volume the documents are headed by an Introduction, discussing the material assembled and relating the early stages of the author's reception to what we have come to identify as the critical tradition. The volumes will make available much material which would otherwise be difficult of access and it is hoped that the modern reader will be thereby helped towards an informed understanding of the ways in which literature has been read and judged.

This volume, covering the second period of Milton criticism, complements Professor Shawcross's earlier account in *Milton: The Critical Heritage* (1970) which surveyed the period 1628 to 1731.

B.C.S.

Contents

Period of Alleged Plagiarism, Some Analysis, Praise, and Dispraise (1741–51)

Period of Defence and Analysis (1752–73)

Period of Praise and Some Detraction (1774–1801)

CONTENTS

Acknowledgments

The author and publishers would like to thank the following for kind permission to reproduce the works cited, or extracts from them. All possible care has been taken to trace ownership of the selections included and to make full acknowledgment for their use.

Laterza and Sons, Bari, for *Prefazioni e Polemiche*, Giuseppi Baretti, ed. Luigi Piccioni; Macmillan and Company Ltd for *The Works of Thomas Gray*, ed. Edmund Gosse.

Introduction

I

During the years before 1732 the criticism which has to this day been directed toward John Milton and his works was being established. Positively, he was seen as a major epic and religious poet, whose versification was well adapted to subject and form; a great classical humanist, whose continuance of tradition was highly commendable; and a sublime poet whose ideas were philosophically uplifting and democratic. Emphasis lay on *Paradise Lost*, with glances at the minor poetry but with little attention being paid to the two other major poems or the prose, except for Milton's significance as a historian. Negatively, he was seen as a rebel in literary, political, and social matters; a poet whose verse, language, and literary form stultified the course of poetry often through deleterious influence on others; a dour man whose ideas were reprehensible. Such adverse criticism derived from antagonism to Milton the man, the anti-Royalist, the antiprelatical, the 'divorcer', as well as Milton the breaker of tradition whether in form or in versification, and Milton the blasphemer. The sources were Milton's life, some of the prose, and *Paradise Lost*. Milton seems seldom to have been read completely, and too frequently from biased angles.

Among the clichés inherited from the period before 1732 were Milton's near obscurity before 1688 when the fourth edition of *Paradise Lost* was published through subscription, assigned usually to the impetus of Lord Somers; the Latinity of his language and verse—that is, in *Paradise Lost*; his combining of the greatness of Greece (Homer) and of Rome (Vergil); his preference for *Paradise Regain'd* over *Paradise Lost*; and the error of including the allegory of Sin and Death in the epic. Critical approaches which were established during the contemporary or near-contemporary period of Milton's life include personal attack as a means of literary criticism (see, for example, Richard Leigh's *The Transproser Rehears'd*, 1673, pp. 41–3); extensive scholarly annotation (see Patrick Hume's notes to *Paradise Lost* in 1695); source-seeking (see Voltaire's advancement of Andreini's *Adamo* as inspiration for *Paradise Lost* in 1727); comparison or contrast with other (generally classical) achievements in epic form, versification, and decorum; examination of inconsistency of poetic greatness alongside political culpability (see Addison's statement in 'An Account of the Greatest English Poets', 1694); examination of religious truths offered by *Paradise Lost* (see such approving comments as Roscommon's in 'An Essay on Translated Verse', 1685, and such disapproving statements as Charles Leslie's in *The History of Sin and Heresy*, 1698); and examination of the sublimity of the ideas and the verse (see the numerous discussions of John Dennis from 1696 to 1729). One form of praise can be seen in the numerous imitations of Milton's verse and subject matter, and his reputation can be evaluated by the numerous quotations from the works in poetry of the period as well as in a variety of prose works and by the numerous allusions to him or his works. Perhaps too it should be noted that Milton's *Literae Pseudo-Senatûs Anglicani Cromwellii* was placed on the Roman Catholic Index of books on 22 December 1700; Paolo Rolli's translation of *Paradise Lost* was to be listed on 21 January 1732; and in Spain and other provincial sees *Defensio prima* was prohibited sometime before 1747 (although this has not previously been noted).[1]

On the eve of 1732, despite some adverse evaluation, John Milton was an exemplar of sublime thought presented through sublime expression, whose greatest work towered above anything else written in England and rivalled the magnificent epics of the ancients. His poetry was imitated, adapted, quoted. To evidence the validity of a thought or a style of writing or a use of language an author employed excerpts from Milton, and that was sufficient; to evaluate another's work the touchstone was *Paradise Lost*. His fame was spreading on the continent, primarily through the rise of translations and encyclopedic notices, and his poetry, at least, was readily available in England to the increasing population. Milton's verse had begun its move to becoming a universal standard of excellence, an expression of authority, a pattern for imitation, and a source for poetical licence.

The present volume of criticism from the period of 1732–1801 attempts to supply both well-known and outstandingly influential examinations of Milton's works and representative samples from less known authors who perhaps better typify the general educated reader's reaction. The plethora of materials available for this period—and their length—makes excerpting and selection mandatory and difficult. It is hoped that the items reprinted here offer a sample of all the materials a reader might expect. The year 1732 ushers in a phase of textual criticism not previously encountered in Milton study, although it had become frequent in classical study and for Shakespeare. Its mixture of intent—positive and negative—and its result—again both positive and negative—epitomizes the kind of ambivalence that Milton has constantly experienced at the hands of both his admirers and his detractors. By the end of the period, with the publication of Henry John Todd's variorum edition, the charted study and evaluation of Milton had so clearly been laid down that the succeeding years saw a 'classic' evolved with its attendant non-reading by the general public (except as schoolboy exercise) and lack of vitality. It is easy to see why Sir Walter Raleigh called *Paradise Lost* a monument to dead ideas, and that deathly hue elongated its shadows over Milton's other works. David Masson's still indispensable biography some six decades later placed poet and work in a magnificent mausoleum for a reading public who could not shake off the spectre of Milton as the last great mind of the Renaissance. Recent years have finally shown—though some seem blind to such dawning light—that Milton was also one of the first great minds of the modern and continuously contemporary world. The final piece included in this collection, written sometime after 1801 and before 1809, Henry Boyd's discussion of the fallen angels, reflects the tone of definitive statement which controls much of future criticism while it deals with substance leading to both disparagement and praise, argument and nodding assent, the old and the perpetually new views of Milton's message to the world.

II

In 1732 the poetic works of Milton were before the general reading public in England through numerous editions by the important publisher Jacob Tonson and numerous reprints of the edition with a life by Elijah Fenton. These were usually offered in two volumes with various illustrations by various hands, one containing *Paradise Lost,* one containing all the other poems and often *Of Education* since it had appeared in the second edition of the minor poems in 1673. The prose works were available in the 1698 three-volume edition carrying John Toland's 'Life' and thus often referred to as 'Toland's edition'. There were other printings of the works or of individual works, both poetic and prose, though these were less widely known. Through the eighteenth century numerous further issues or editions indicate the popularity that Milton enjoyed. Some of the so-called editions, however, such as Thomas Newton's or John Baskerville's (which gave Newton's 'Life' and used his texts), were really re-issues using older plates. The format ranged from small books with small print to large, meticulously composed folio volumes. Along with Shakespeare, Milton was given variorum treatment, the most important being those by Thomas Newton in 1749 (*Paradise Lost*) and 1752 (the remaining poems), Thomas Warton in 1785 and 1791 (the minor poems), Charles Dunster in 1795 (*Paradise Regain'd*), Todd in 1798 ('Comus') and 1801 (*The Poetical Works*). Early on, the texts usually reprinted were those in Tonson's editions, and sometimes those in Fenton's; both were textually inaccurate. During the remainder of the century it was Newton's texts which prevailed, although restudied versions also appeared from time to time. The first separate edition of 'Comus' in English since 1637, aside from adaptations, was published in Glasgow in 1746; the next was Todd's in 1798. The first separate edition of *Paradise Regain'd* was published in London in 1779; it next appeared separately in 1790 in Philadelphia, in 1793 in Alnwick, and in 1795 in Dunster's edition. The first separate edition of *Samson Agonistes* in English appeared in Bell's Library in 1796, with an illustration of a frenzied stage Samson. See Appendix (*c*) for a listing of important editions during 1732–1801.

John Dryden was not the only one who wished to 'improve' *Paradise Lost*, and Richard Bentley was not the only one who found faults in it. John Hopkins re-did Books I and II in rhyming couplets in 1699; George S. Green's *A New Version of Paradise Lost. In which the Measure and Versification are Corrected and Harmonised; the Obscurities Elucidated; and the Faults, which the Author Stands Accused of by Addison and Other of the Criticks, Are Removed* (Oxford, 1756) offered a revised first book; the hymn-writer John Wesley brought the poem into more usual rhythms in *Paradise Lost Improved* (1763); and *The First Six Books of Paradise Lost* were *Rendered into Grammatical Construction* by James Buchanan (Edinburgh, 1773). Other similar redactions exist, for example, a paraphrase entitled *The Recovery of Man: or, Milton's Paradise Regain'd. In Prose* (1771). The lack of perception of achievement, the assumption of 'correctness', and the gross effrontery of some of the writers of the Restoration and eighteenth century are certainly well attested by a study of the treatment of Milton at their hands. Indeed, the current volume makes quite clear the relationship between criticism and the age, and the insubstantiality of the belief that literary criticism is ever absolute.

A number of translations of the poems into Latin and Greek were made, possibly to increase the reading public beyond England but primarily as *tours de force*. Naturally, the most frequent was *Paradise Lost*, beginning with J. C.'s *Paradisus Amissa*, a Latin verse translation of

Book I, in 1686. William Hog produced the three major poems in Latin verse in 1690, *Paraphrasis Poetica in Tria Johannis Miltoni, Viri Clarissimi, Poemata, viz. Paradisium Amissum, Paradisium Recuperatum, et Samsonem Agonistem*; this was reprinted in Rotterdam in 1699. Hog followed these translations with 'Lycidas' (*Paraphrasis Latina, in Duo Poemata . . . alterum a Clieveland*) in 1694 and 'Comus' (*Comoedia Joannis Miltoni, Viri Clarissimi*) in 1698. T. P. (apparently Thomas Power) rendered Book I of the epic into Latin verse in 1691; Charles Blake, part of Book V in *Lusus Amatorius* in 1694; Matthew Bold, Book I in 1702 and 1736; William Tilley, some time before 1709; Robert Pitt, various parts in 1719; Samuel Say, part of Book I in hexameters *c.* 1736, though not published until 1745; Joseph Trapp, the full poem in two volumes in 1741 and 1744 respectively; John Theobald, part of Book IV *c.* 1750; and William Dobson, the full poem in two volumes in 1750 and 1753 respectively. (See also Glass's *Samson Agonistes*, 1788.) W. R. put 'Il Penseroso' into Latin in 1741, and Christopher Smart did 'L'Allegro' in 1752 (with frequent republication in Smart's poems). In Greek are Richard Dawes's 1735 version of Book I of *Paradise Lost*; Thomas Stratford's 1770 version also of Book I with Dobson's Latin; and Thomas Denny's 1779 rendering of Books I–IV. George Glass produced *Samson Agonistes* as a five-act drama in 1788 in both Greek and Latin, and J. Plumptre a Greek 'Lycidas' in 1797. We should note too that Milton's Italian sonnets were twice put into English, once by John Langhorne in *Milton's Italian Poems Translated and Addressed to a Gentleman of Italy* (1776) and once by Aaron Hill in *Works* (1779). In addition 'Mansus' was translated by Joseph Sterling in his *Poems of the Rev. J.— S.—* (1789). William Cowper's translations of the Italian and Latin poems were finally published by William Hayley in 1808.

The complete prose was re-edited in a scholarly two-volume edition by the antiquarian Thomas Birch in 1738; it was re-issued in slightly revised form by Richard Baron in 1753. This edition was standard until 1806 when Charles Symmons produced a new text. Although *Of Education* was also readily available in many of the poetry volumes (and in a 1723 English translation of Tannequi Lefevre's *A Compendious Way of Teaching Ancient and Modern Languages*, which was frequently re-printed), it did not appear in England in a separate edition until 1751, the first since 1644. *Areopagitica* was graced with a preface by James Thomson in a separate edition in 1738, the first also since 1644, except for two late seventeenth-century adaptations; Baron offered a separate *Eikonoklastes* in 1756, the first since 1650; and *A Treatise of Civil Power* and *The Ready and Easy Way* appeared in 1790 and 1791 respectively, the first separate editions since 1659 and 1660. *The Tenure of Kings and Magistrates* had been adapted in 1689 for a contemporary political context as *Pro Populo adversus Tyrannos*, but a slightly abbreviated text from Dublin in 1784 was otherwise the first separate edition of this tract since 1650. Because of its subject of tithing, *Considerations Touching the Likeliest Means* had appeared in 1717, 1723, and 1743, and became the first American edition of a Miltonic work when published in Philadelphia in 1770 under the title *An Old Looking-Glass for the Laity and Clergy*. Another edition came out of New Haven in 1774. (The poetry first appeared in an American edition out of Philadelphia in 1777.) Some works like *Of Prelatical Episcopacy* (1641) have not to date had a separate edition since the first, or like *Of Reformation* (1641) have had only a twentieth-century scholarly edition. In all, Milton's works were easily obtainable in English or original Latin by any interested person during the eighteenth century, and this fact helps account for the spread of his reputation and the overwhelmingly numerous allusions and imitations in the byways of publishing history—the many magazines with their unsolicited contributions and letters, and the miscellanies of amateurish and dreary poetry and prose.

On the continent Milton's works were also becoming available, although many countries had to rely on originals. Ernst Gottlieb von Berge had translated *Paradise Lost* into German verse in 1682; this may have been based partially on Theodore Haak's unfinished manuscript translation of about two years before. A new prose version by Johann Jacob Bodmer in 1732 set off much controversy and discussion among *literati*. Johann Christoph Gottsched, who had discussed such matters as prosody and the mythological elements in *Paradise Lost* in 1730, found himself embroiled in argument with Bodmer, Johann Jacob Breitinger, Conrad Effinger, and others over the accuracy of translation, Milton's sublimity, the nature of epic, etc. The translated or summarized criticism of Addison, Voltaire, Rolli, and de Magny also frequently supplied a springboard for the airing of German views on these subjects. The controversy raged during 1740–55, with numerous critiques, letters, and general articles in periodicals of the period. There is an interesting poem by W. J. C. S. Casparson entitled *Johann Christoph Gottsched, an Herrn Johann Jacob Bodmer in Zürich* (1770), which satirizes the argument and contains an allusion to Milton on p. 6. Reprints of Bodmer's translation appear throughout the century, although other versions, first printed in 1752, 1760–3, and 1792, also supplied a growing reading public. The influence of *Paradise Lost* on German letters is quite obvious in Frederick Gottlieb Klopstock's poetry, like *Messias*, 1751–73 (a fact cited in introductions to German and translated editions), and *Die Tageszeiten* (1757) and *Die Schöpfung der Hölle* (1760) by Friedrich Wilhelm Zachariä, the verse translator of *Paradise Lost* in 1760–3. *Paradise Regain'd*, *Samson Agonistes*, 'Lycidas', 'L'Allegro', and 'Il Penseroso' were available in a German prose version by Simon Grynaeus in 1752, as well as the 'Nativity Ode' in verse. Otto Heinrich von Gemmingen's 'L'Allegro' and 'Il Penseroso' were printed in Mannheim (with facing English texts) in 1782; other versions appeared in 1789–92. According to John W. Good in *Studies in the Milton Tradition*, a translation of *Of Education* was apparently included in 1752 and 1781 editions of poetry; I do not find it, however, in issues of those dates of Grynaeus's translations.

A French version of *Paradise Lost* was in print by 1729, based on Raymond de St Maur's (Nicholas François Dupré's) prose translation done in 1727 and revised by C. J. Chéron de Boismorand. This version was repeatedly reprinted; it includes a translation of Fenton's 'Life' and of some *Spectator* papers. Pierre de Mareuil's *Paradise Regain'd*, 'Lycidas', 'L'Allegro', 'Il Penseroso', and the 'Nativity Ode' were added to the 1730 three-volume edition of St Maur, along with 'Une Dissertation critique sur le Paradis perdu' by Constantin de Magny (a pseudonym), which had been published in Paris the year before, and an imitation called 'La Chute de l'Homme' by M. Durand. Other translations of *Paradise Lost* appeared originally in 1754–5, 1772, 1777, 1778, 1784, and 1786. In 1731 *Lettres critiques à M. le Comte sur le Paradis perdu et reconquis* by Bernard Routh were published, but it was Voltaire's 1727 English essay on epic poetry (almost immediately translated), which he later revised and put into French (1732), that caused the most discussion, primarily because it castigated the French for their lack of epic achievement. Paolo Rolli answered these remarks in 1728, and Giuseppi Baretti in 1753. Baretti's rebuttal of the full essay was reprinted in Paris in a French version as late as 1777. Routh's *Lettres* were reprinted in a 1753 Amsterdam edition of St Maur (*et al.*). A life of Milton, Addison's critique, and original comments on *Paradise Lost* and epic accompany Louis Racine's 1754–5 translation; this is reprinted later in the century.

The influence of Milton on French letters, however, is less apparent than on German. There are adaptations like Madame Marie Ann du Boccage's *Le Paradis terrestre* (1748), and the reference to *Paradise Lost* in Voltaire's *Candide* (chapter 25) is well known, as is perhaps the allusion in Rousseau's *Émile* (book v, part iv). But such discussions as those in Charles Rollin's *De la manière d'enseigner et d'létudier les belles-lettres* (1740), Abbé Jean-Bernard Le Blanc's *Lettres sur la itérature anglaise et française* (1747), and Abbé Charles Batteux's *Cours de belles-lettres* (1747–50), four volumes, are generally unknown to students of Milton. Le Blanc was translated into English in 1747, and Batteux's work reappeared in 1764 as *Principes de la littérature*. Voltaire's works, it should also be remarked, are filled with allusions and comments; particularly significant items will be found in a footnote to chapter 3 of *Essai sur les moeurs et l'esprit des nations*, in chapter 34 of *Siècle de Louis XIV*, in article 23 of *Fragmens historiques sur l'Inde*, in *Dictionnaire Philosophique* under 'Epopée', 'Marie Magdelene' (on blank verse), and 'Samson', in no. 9 of the *Lettres Chinoises, Indiennes et Tartares*, in his 'Lettre à l'Academie Française' (25 August 1776), and in no. 153 (1740) of *Recueil des lettres. Of Education*, translated by Le Blanc, was published by C. de Nonney de Fontenai in *Lettres sur l'éducation des princes* in 1746. An edition of *Areopagitica* by Count Mirabeau, entitled *Sur la liberté de la presse*, was available in 1788, 1789 (twice), and 1792, and J. B. Salaville's *First Defense* (*Théorie de la Royauté d'après la doctrine de Milton*) was published twice in 1789 with a preface on Milton perhaps by Mirabeau; it reappeared in 1791 and 1792 with a different title and without the preface. In general the French are concerned with *Paradise Lost* and its epic qualities, and with teaching methods and political ideas. The Miltonic influence on Chateaubriand at the very end of the century (1797) can be seen in his poem 'Milton et Davenant' and in the early nineteenth in his *Essai sur la littérature anglaise* and *De quelques imperfections en Paradis perdu*.

Only *Paradise Lost* and 'L'Allegro' appeared in Italian in the eighteenth century, the latter in a 1785 translation by Testa Domenico. Two early manuscript versions of the epic, which were known to other scholars and poets, were Lorenzo Magalotti's *c.* 1713 and Antonio Salvini's *c.* 1721. The most available translation was Paolo Rolli's, Books I–VI of which first appeared in London in 1729 and then in complete form in 1735. It was republished on the continent from 1740 onward. Rolli also translated Addison's papers in 1742. In 1794 a translation of Book I into Italian verse by Felice Mariottini included Fenton's 'Life' and Addison's criticism; the full poem appeared in 1796. Rolli, writing in England, also revised 'Comus' as a play, printed in 1737 in Italian and English, and defended epic writers, particularly Milton, against the strictures of Voltaire in 1728. Allusions and brief comments exist in Italian letters, but no really significant criticism was published.

Translations of the poetry into other languages continued through the century, although little criticism ensued in those countries. We find *Paradise Lost* translated into Dutch in 1728 (by Jacob van Zanten), in 1730 (in a paraphrase by L. Paludanus, that is, Lambertus van der Broek), and in 1791–2 (by Jan Hendrick Reisig). The *First Defense* had immediately appeared in 1651, but not thereafter; the only other prose work translated into Dutch was *Of Education* by Pieter le Clercq early in the eighteenth century. (This will be found with a translation of George Savile's *New Year's Gift: Nieuwjaaregift aan de Jufferschap . . . Waar agter gevoegd is een Brief, over de Opvoeding van Jonge Heeren, van den vermaarden Heer John Milton, n. d.*) *Paradise Lost* was put into Danish in 1790 by Johannes Henricus Schønheyder, who produced a *Paradise Regain'd* in 1792. No translation of any of the poems into Spanish was apparently published in the eighteenth century, although such translations are mentioned by commentators. An imitation by Felix José Reinoso, *La Inocencia perdida*, did appear in 1799. The two epics are found in Portuguese in 1789 and 1792 (both by José Amara da Silva) respectively. Russian versions of *Paradise Lost* were executed *c.* 1745 (by A. G. Stroganov), 1777 (by Vasili Petrovich Petrov), 1778 (by Ivan Greshishchev), 1780 (by A. Podobedov), and 1785 (by Serebrennikov Amvrosii). The two epics appeared in Polish in 1791 and 1792 (both by Jacek Idzi Przybylski), and in Hungarian in 1796 (both by Sándor Bessenyei). A Manx rendition of *Paradise Lost* was produced in 1796 (by Thomas Christian). Many of the above were reprinted in subsequent years. Translations of sections were also made and published. Some of the prose, of course, was in Latin, and so translations were not considered necessary for the educated reading public on the continent.

III

The eighteenth century saw two new developments in the use of Milton's poems: stage adaptations and musical renditions. Although Dryden's *The State of Innocence* had been written around 1673–4, it had apparently not been performed and its music has not survived. Paolo Rolli produced a three-act verse presentation from 'Comus' entitled *Sabrina, a Masque* (1737), preluding, as it were, the great success which John Dalton's 1738 version was to experience. This play, performed and printed repeatedly during the century, was called 'Comus', and the acclaim which it received was so loud that we today know Milton's 'A Mask' by that title even though it misrepresents Milton's poem, its subject, and its thesis. As has often been said, calling the masque 'Comus' is like calling *Paradise Lost* 'Satan'. 'Comus' focuses on the Lady and Comus, and her rescue by Thyrsis and Sabrina; it also employs the character of Euphrosyne reciting lines from 'L'Allegro'. Accompanying the play was music newly written by Thomas Arne; the words and music were immediately published in 1738 and often thereafter. The Dalton–Arne version has been presented a few times, with favourable notices, within recent years in England and the United States. A quite different revision of the masque in two acts was made by George Colman in 1772 and acted at the Theatre-Royal in Covent Garden. The latter part of the century saw both versions on the boards and in repeated printings, although Colman's is more frequent. Songs of the Dalton–Arne version were also published separately and included in recitals. For example, a performance of 'Sweet Echo' is recorded in Boston in the *Independent Chronicle, and Universal Advertiser* for 28 February to 4 March 1799 (vol. xxxi, no. 1873). Prologues and epilogues to 'Comus' were also written independently by various hands and often used in stage performances, for example, Samuel Whyte's 'Prologue' and Henry Grattan's 'Epilogue'; see Joshua Edkins (ed.), *A Collection of Poems, Mostly Original, By Several Hands* (Dublin, 1789).

The most celebrated music associated with Milton's texts was (and is) George Frederick Handel's. His settings of 'L'Allegro' and 'Il Penseroso' using an adaptation by Charles Jennens were first printed (text only) in 1740 along with a non-Miltonic third section: *L'Allegro, Il Penseroso ed Il Moderato. As Set to Musick*. Numerous printings of words or of music, or of words and music, appear sometimes complete, sometimes without 'Il Moderato', sometimes as only individual songs. The alteration of *Samson Agonistes* by Newburgh Hamilton, with lines interpolated from the 'Nativity Ode' and 'At a Solemn Music', appeared in 1742 as: *Samson. An Oratorio. Alter'd from the Samson Agonistes of Milton. Set to Musick by Mr. Handel*. This gave only the text, but *Songs from Samson an Oratorio*, also 1742, gave both the words and the music. Further printings are frequent, particularly in collected editions of Handel's works, sometimes as songs or oratorios, sometimes as orchestrated music for specific instrumental groups. But two other works also employed Milton's texts, though few today seem aware. *A New Occasional Oratorio. As It Is Perform'd at the Theatre-Royal in Covent-Garden. The Words Taken from Milton, Spenser, &c. And Set to Musick by Mr. Handel* (1746), composed the year before, has a text by Thomas Morrell drawn partially from Psalms 1–8. *Jephtha, an Oratorio. Or,*

Sacred Drama. As It is Perform'd at the Theatre-Royal in Covent-Garden. Set to Musick by Mr. Handel (1758), composed in 1751 and published earlier in collections of Handel's works, uses a text by Morrell which includes (on p. 4) a passage from the 'Nativity Ode'. Probably in 1790 appeared a collection of *All the Favourite Oratorios Set to Music by Mr. Handel*, to which was added *The Hymn of Adam and Eve; the Music of* [which was] *Selected from the Most Celebrated Italian Composers*. An edition of *Handel's Songs* in the 1790s also includes Alexander Balus's appropriation from the 'Hail wedded love' passage of Book IV. Samuel Arnold, a most important editor of Handel's works as well as composer in his own right, put together *Redemption: A Sacred Oratorio Selected from the Great, and Favourite Works of Mr. Handel* (1786); it includes a section from Handel's *Samson* but also a passage directly drawn by Arnold from *Paradise Lost*.

In France, Alexandre Tanevot created *The Tragedy of Adam and Eve* (1765) out of *Paradise Lost*, and in England Benjamin Stillingfleet reworked the epic into an oratorio with music by John Christopher Smith in 1760. The title page of the printed text reads: 'As it is Perform'd at the Theatre-Royal in Covent-Garden. Altered and Adapted to the Stage from Milton'. Richard Jago published his 'Adam: or, the Fatal Disobedience. Compiled from the *Paradise Lost* of Milton. And Adapted to Music' in 1784 with his *Poems, Moral and Descriptive* (pp. 217–66). It includes a preface and remarks 'To the Composer', but no music is known. A German rendering by a Mr Lidley or Liddell, then put back into English, became the basis for Haydn's *The Creation* in 1798, first performed in 1799, and first printed in 1800. Frequently copied out into magazines and poetic collections, the morning hymn of Adam and Eve from the fifth book was also set to music, first by John Ernest Galliard in 1728 and then by Philip Hart around 1729. An edition of words and music of the Galliard version in 1773 also gives 'The Overture, Accompanyments & Choruses Added by Benjn. Cooke Mus. D. Organist of Westminster Abbey'. (See also the version included in Handel's works noted before.) We should also remark the influence of the epic on Thomas Arne's oratorio *Abel* (1755); the 'Hymn of Eve' from it was sometimes published separately.

'*Lycidas*': *A Musical Entertainment, As it is Performed at the Theatre-Royal in Covent-Garden. The Words Alter'd from Milton. By W*[illiam] *Jackson* (1767) was first performed on 4 November 1767, but the music has apparently not survived. Michael Christian Festing set 'A Song on May-Morning' for the Academy of Music in London in 1740, as did

Carl Barbandt in 1759: *A Song. For June the 10th. 1759. Mr. Barbandt's Yearly Subscription of New Music to be Delivered Monthly* [no. 4]. And David Garrick created a cento called *The Fairies. An Opera. Taken from A Midsummer Night's Dream, Written by Shakespear. As it is perform'd at the Theatre-Royal in Drury-lane. The Songs from Shakespear, Milton, Waller, Dryden, Lansdown, Hammond, &c. The music composed by Mr. Smith* (1755); it employs three passages from 'L'Allegro' and one each from *Paradise Lost* and 'Arcades'. His *A Midsummer Night's Dream. Written by Shakespeare; With Alterations and Additions, and Several New Songs* (1763), a revision of the former, includes appropriations from 'L'Allegro', 'Comus', and *Paradise Lost*.

Discussions of music during the eighteenth century frequently cite Milton's works or their various settings. Charles Avison in *An Essay on Musical Expression* (I cite the revised third edition of 1775) quotes from *Paradise Lost* IV, from Handel's setting of 'L'Allegro', from 'Il Penseroso', and from *Paradise Lost* II. Sir John Hawkins in *A General History of the Science and Practice of Music* (1776) has much to say about Milton in the five volumes, including reprints of the sonnets to Lawes and Lawrence, a discussion of John Milton Sr's 'O Had I Wings Like to a Dove' with the full text and music, a printing of Lawes's 'Sweet Echo' from his holograph manuscript, and discussions of Handel, Hart, and Galliard, with the text and music of Galliard's 'Morning Hymn'. Charles Burney's *An Account of the Musical Performances in Westminster-Abbey, and the Pantheon . . . In Commemoration of Handel* (1785), the music and text of which performances were also printed separately, his *A General History of Music, from the Earliest Age to the Present* (1776–89), and *Dr. Karl Burney's Nachricht von Georg Friedrich Händel's Lebensumständen* (Berlin and Stettin, 1785) frequently allude to or quote from Milton. The *General History* includes a printing of Milton's father's 'Thou God of Might'.

IV

Reputation can be gauged by other items besides editions, translations, adaptations, and specific criticism. Biographical treatment, allusions, illustrative (sometimes authoritative) use, and imitations tell us much about the pervasiveness of an author's renown among ordinary readers. Biographical encyclopedias, like or based upon Pierre Bayle's from the 1690s onward, flourished during the eighteenth century. Representative is the edition of *A General Dictionary, Historical and Critical: In which a New and Accurate Translation of that of the Celebrated Mr. Bayle is Included* by John Peter Bernard, Thomas Birch, and John Lockman, published in ten volumes from 1734 to 1741. The entries under which Milton is discussed or quoted are 'Adam', 'Addison', 'Andrewes, Lancelot' (a reference to 'Elegia tertia'), 'Ariosto', 'Blackall, Offspring' (controversialist with Toland), 'Blount, Charles' (adapter of *Areopagitica* in 1679), 'Chaucer', 'Coke, Edward', 'Cromwell', 'Davenant', 'Dryden', 'Echard, Laurence' (the historian), 'Le Fevre', 'Hobbes', 'Marvell', 'Milton' (VII, 567–88; published 1738, additions to Bayle's account apparently having been produced by Birch), 'Morus', 'Oldenburg', 'Parker, Samuel', 'Philips, John', 'Prior', 'Rawlegh, Sir Walter', 'Roscommon', 'Spenser', 'Toland', and 'Wagstaffe, Thomas' (controversialist over *Eikon Basilike*); in addition Vol. X notes the adverse criticism of Milton as person, thinker, and poet in Louis Moréri's dictionary of 1704 and corrects errors therein (pp. 513–15).

Lives reprinted, quoted, or referred to frequently were Wood's (1691–2), Phillips' (1694), Toland's (1698), Fenton's (1725), Richardson's (1734), Newton's (1749), Johnson's (1779), and Hayley's (1796), the last being the most influential for the authors and artists of the Romantic period. Aubrey's notes were published in the *European Magazine*, xxviii (1795), 184–6. Excerpts from Richardson's, Johnson's, and Hayley's lives are included here as Nos 8, 66, and 82. Succeeding lives, of course, added new facts, such as the existence and significance of the Trinity MS., first discussed in print by Thomas Birch in the introduction to his edition of the prose in 1738. But many repeat certain stories over and over, such as Milton's long neglect and his preference for *Paradise Regain'd* over *Paradise Lost*. The former also crops up, typically, in such incidental places as the *True Patriot*, 5 November 1745, no. 1: 'Of all mankind, there are none whom it so absolutely imports to conform to this golden rule [of fashion] as an author; by neglecting this, *Milton* himself lay long in obscurity, and the world had nearly lost the best poem which perhaps it has ever seen'; or Abbé Le Blanc's *Letters* (1747): 'In this country, even more than in ours, the fate of a book often depends upon those who protect it. *Paradise Lost*, which is at present the honour of the English Parnassus, was not known in the author's life time. He had no friends but those of CROMWELL, whose views were more to subdue their country than to make arts flourish. It was Mr. ADDISON that drew MILTON out of the oblivion which his party had caused him to fall into in the reign of CHARLES II.'[2] Or the same thought appears in Henry Fielding's *Covent-Garden Journal*, 7 March 1752: 'The truest Brilliants often lie overlooked and neglected on the Booksellers Shelves, while the most impudent Counterfeits are received, admired, and encouraged. Milton himself (I am ashamed of my Country when I say it) very narrowly escaped from the Jaws of Oblivion; and, instead of shining for ever with those great Lights of Antiquity in whose Constellation he is now admitted, was like to have been bundled up with those *Ephemeran* insect Authors, of whom every Day almost sees both the Birth and the Funeral'; or William Shenstone's 'Essay on Men and Manners: On Writing and Books': 'The national opinion of a book or treatise is not always right—"est ubi peccat"—Milton's *Paradise Lost* is one instance. I mean, the cold reception it met with at first'.[3] The latter cliché (drawn from Toland's misreading of a remark by Phillips) occurs throughout the century, as in a note to Thomas Enort's 'Lines on Collins the Chichester Bard', *European Magazine*, xxxii (1797), 415.

Interesting items related to Milton's biography which appear during the century include the following. A frequently cited sonnet alleged to be by Milton and etched on a church window was quoted by Alexander Pope in a letter to Jonathan Richardson, dated 18 July 1737.[4] The influence of Forest Hill, Oxford (from which Milton's first wife's family came and where he was purported to have lived), on 'L'Allegro' was discussed (erroneously) at length by Sir William Jones in a letter to Lady Spencer, dated 7 September 1769.[5] His connection with Cromwell is recalled (usually favourably) in biographies of the Protector like John Banks's *A Short Critical Review of the Political Life of Oliver Cromwell* (1769), where we read such an encomium as 'Milton, the great Milton, was Latin secretary: a man that might have done honour to the mightiest monarch, to the most polite and learned court, in the best of ages' (p. 188). But see David Hume's summary of Milton the public man in No. 51 below. *A Biographical History of England* (1779) by James Granger pulls together and discusses portraits of Milton in II, 5, 295–6; III, 87, 92–3; and IV, 33–7, 67. Philip Neve wrote *A Narrative of the Disinterment of Milton's Coffin, in the Parish-Church of St. Giles, Cripplegate, on Wednesday, 4th of August 1790; and of the Treatment of the Corpse, During That and the Following Day* (thirty-four pages) and expanded it almost immediately to fifty pages. Besides William Cowper's poem given here as No. 77, the disinterment evoked the anonymous 'Milton's Ghost. An Elegy'.[6]

Allusions to Milton seem to occur everywhere and in all kinds of circumstances. Some that suggest the breadth of Milton's reputation and its nature follow. A most usual occurrence is in poetry wherewith the poet contemplates fame, or the power of verse, or the guidance and inspiration of Milton; for example, Thomas Gray's allusion in 'The Progress of Poetry'[7] or William Cowper's in 'The Task'.[8] Examples occur in little-known poems as well: James Hammond, Elegy xiv (1732);[9] Nicholas James, 'The Poet's Fate. Written at Christmas 1735';[10] N. Eliot, 'The Atheist' (1770).[11] The remarks of Lady Bradshaigh to Samuel Richardson (in a letter dated 28 July 1752) are worth quoting since they deal with Milton's views on divorce:[12]

I never read Milton's Treatise upon Divorces, but have heard it much condemned, as a thing calculated to serve his own private ends. Though, divorces may be thought allowable by those who do not think polygamy so. But whatever he may have written is of no great consequence, since I will stand and fall by the law of nature.

A letter from Andrew Eliot of Harvard College to Thomas Hollis, dated 10 December 1767, reflects the way in which the Colonies came to know Milton and presents what one hopes was a recurrent reaction:[13]

I am particularly obliged to you for *Milton*'s prose works. They who consider that very great man only as a poet of the first rank, know less than half his character. He was every thing. I have often read detached pieces of his, and shall never be weary of his *Defensio Populi Anglicano*, &c. I have been told, that Salmasius fell into a languishment upon reading that book; he must have been without sensibility, if he long survived it. I blush to own that I have never gone through the whole of these prose works. I have lost a great deal. Perhaps my pleasure is the greater now. *Milton* wrote Latin so well, that it seems a pity he should be read in any other language. But his sentiments are so just, and his attachment to liberty so firm, that he ought to be open to every Englishman.

Indeed, references in American writing are more than many might expect: Uzal Ogden cites Milton in *The Theological Preceptor: or Youth's Religious Instructor* (New York, 1772), pp. 32–3 n.; a letter from John Adams to James Warren, dated 3 January 1775, refers to and quotes from *Paradise Lost*;[14] Peter Oliver talks of Milton and quotes from *Paradise Lost* in 'Origin and Progress of the American Revolution' (1781);[15] and Nathaniel Emmons makes frequent reference in his sermons,[16] to cite only a few representative items.

Allusions appear in unexpected places: Richard Brocklesby's *Reflections on Antient and Modern Musick, with the Application to the Cure of Diseases* (1749), p. 77 (there is also a six-line epigraph from 'Arcades' on the title page); John Armstrong's *The History of the Island of Minorca* (1752), p. 21 (with a quotation from *Paradise Lost*); *The Rise and Progress of the Present Taste in Planting Parks, Pleasure Grounds, Gardens* (1767), pp. [3], 9–10, 30; John Witherspoon's *A Letter From a Blacksmith. To the Ministers and Elders of the Kirk of Scotland* (Leith, 1766), p. 59 (with quotation of *Paradise Lost* III, 493–6); and Samuel Richardson's *Clarissa Harlowe* (1747–8; eight allusions) and *The History of Sir Charles Grandison* (1753–4; five allusions). In all, Milton was well known, and a symbol of a sublime poet, an important thinker on many issues, a republican; or his works furnished subjects, characters, points of view, language. Although there is a concentration on some aspects of biography and on specific works (specific poems, that is), at times other items supply the allusion, suggesting an almost full range of knowledge about Milton and his works by a wide reading public. We ought to note these as representative: Catharine Macaulay discussed Milton's ideas drawn largely from *Areopagitica* in *A Modest Plea for the Property of Copy Right* (Bath, 1774), pp. vii, 18, 22–6; James Barry was concerned with Milton's pictorial imagination in *Paradise Lost* in *An Inquiry into the Real and Imaginary Obstructions to the Acquisition of the Arts in England* (1775), pp. 111–20; and Henry James Pye frequently cited Milton in *A Commentary Illustrating the Poetic of Aristotle, by Examples Taken Chiefly from the Modern Poets* (1792).[17] Two of the most interesting allusions, however, occur in the engravings of William Hogarth. One entitled 'Gulielmus Hogarth', dated March 1749, depicts a book identified as Milton's works.[18] The other, entitled 'Beer Street' and dated February 1751, shows a book labelled 'Lauder on Milton'.[19]

Quotations from Milton's works also seem to appear everywhere. They are used as epigraphs to volumes or articles, for illustration of thought or language, as simple asides, and often in others' poetry. A few interesting appearances are the following: Benjamin Franklin quoted the Morning Hymn in 'Articles of Belief and Acts of Religion', part i, dated 20 November 1728;[20] the *American Magazine or a Monthly View of the Political State of the British Colonies* (Philadelphia) for January 1741, in its 'Plan of the Undertaking', employs Milton's translation from Euripides prefixed to *Areopagitica*, p. viii; *The Preceptor: Containing a General Course of Education* (1749), published by Robert Dodsley, frequently cites *Paradise Lost* as material for exercises;[21] John Duncombe placed a clearly snide quotation from *Samson Agonistes* (ll. 982–5) on the title page of his poem *The Feminiad* (1754); lines from Milton's 'Fifth Ode of Horace' grace Mary Singleton's (that is, Frances Brooke's) periodical the *Old Maid*, no. 16, 28 February 1756; a repeated source for allusive quotations for the numerous books on education was Milton's tract, as in John Jebb's *Remarks Upon the Present Mode of*

Education in the University of Cambridge: To which is added, a Proposal for Its Improvement (Cambridge, 1773); Thomas Jefferson quoted Milton often in his Commonplace Books (1764?–72? and 1774–6?);[22] *The Trial of Elizabeth Duchess Dowager of Kingston for Bigamy, Before the Right Honourable the House of Peers, in Westminster-Hall, in Full Parliament* (1776), amazingly, evoked the judge to cite *Paradise Lost* III, 686–9 (p. 107); Vicesimus Knox, an important enough figure in Milton studies around the turn of the century, quoted *Paradise Lost* XI, 637–711, in an appendix to his translation of Erasmus's *The Complaint of Peace: With a Digression, on the Folly of Kings in Unlimited Monarchies* (1795).[23]

To supply illustration of their contentions or to offer example, authors often cited Milton's ideas and language, and usually in terms of their authoritativeness. If one finds example in Milton, then it must be correct! We see this in John Constable's *Reflections upon Accuracy of Style. Containing the Chief Rules To Be Observ'd for Obtaining an Accurate Style* (1734);[24] in John Upton's *Critical Observations on Shakespeare* (1746), which is designed to confute revisions of Shakespeare's text; in Thomas Warton's *Observations on The Faerie Queene of Spenser* (1754), which explains Spenser's language, imagery, and allusions through their occurrence in such other writers as Milton; in *A Dictionary of the English Language* (1755), compiled by Samuel Johnson, where citations occur on almost every page of the two volumes; in *The Youth's Instructor in the English Tongue or, The Art of Spelling Improv'd* (Boston, 1768), by Henry Dixon *et al.*, where a quotation from *Paradise Lost* on pp. 134–5 is the springboard for a discussion of blank verse; and in Benjamin Stillingfleet's *Principles and Power of Harmony* (1771), in which concepts of harmonious sound are illustrated by the 'Nativity Ode', 'The Passion', 'At a Solemn Music', 'L'Allegro', and *Paradise Lost*.[25] A different kind of illustrative use is shown in William Massey's *Corruptæ Latinitatis Index: or, A Collection of Barbarous Words and Phrases, Which are found in the Works of the Most Celebrated Modern Writers in Latin* (1755), for Milton's Latin is found to be faulty in form and quantity.[26] Compare Charles Burney's remarks on Milton's Greek verses (no. 78 here); Burney criticizes them adversely in almost every instance because the forms and quantities do not agree with his view of the Greek language. Massey and Burney typify the eighteenth-century attempt to define language into absolute categories, the doctrine of 'correctness' according to rules.

It has often been said that imitation is a high form of praise, and if so, Milton was profusely praised in the eighteenth century. Poems 'in the style of Milton' or 'in Miltonicks' or just 'in imitation of' the author or a work abound. By 'the style of Milton' was meant blank verse, some Latinate construction, and the 'sublime' language of *Paradise Lost*; by 'Miltonicks' were meant tetrameter couplets as in the companion poems. Or the influence is seen in imitative titles, some of which parody but with admiring humour. The following indicate the nature and variety of the imitative poems: E. C.'s 'Gin, A Poem, in Miltonick Verse';[27] William Shenstone's 'Eve's Speech in Milton, Upon Her Expulsion out of Paradise';[28] Moses Browne's 'Eclogue V: Renock's Despair. An Imitation of MILTON's "Lycidas"';[29] Elizabeth Singer Rowe's 'A Description of Hell. In Imitation of Milton';[30] *L'Allegro ed Il Penseroso in Sonno: or, The Power of Sleep. An Ode*;[31] Thomas Godfrey's 'Pastorals, I', an imitation of 'Epitaphium Damonis' in English;[32] William H. Roberts's *A Poetical Essay on the Existence of God* (part i), *A Poetical Essay, On the Attributes of God* (part ii), and *A Poetical Essay, On the Providence of God* (part iii);[33] *The House of Commons: or, Debates in St. Gyle's Chapel*;[34] Richard Jago's 'Psalm 104th Paraphrased in Imitation of Milton's Stile';[35] *The Demos in Council: or 'Bijah in Pandemonium. Being a Sweep of the Lyre, in Close Imitation of Milton.*[36] The closeness of William Mason's 'Il Pacifico' and 'Il Bellicoso' to Milton's companion poems will be seen in the following excerpts from the latter:[37]

> Hence, dull lethargic peace,
> Born in some hoary beadsmen's cell obscure;
> Or in Circaean bower,
> Where manhood dies, and reason's vigils cease;
> Hie to congenial climes,
> Where some seraglio's downy tyrant reigns;
> Or where Italian swains,
> 'Midst wavy shades, and myrtle-blooming bowers,
> Lull their ambrosial hours,
> And deck with languid trills their tinkling rhymes!
> But rouse, thou god by furies, drest
> In helm, with terror plumed crest,
> In adamantine steel bedight
> Glistening formidably bright,
> With step unfix'd and aspect wild;
> Jealous Juno's raging child,
> Who thee conceiv'd in Flora's bower . . .
> And when my children round me throng,
> The same grand theme shall grace my tongue;
> To teach them, should fair England need
> Their blood, 'tis theirs to wish to bleed;

And, as I speak, to mark with joy
New courage start in every boy;
And gladsome read in all their eyes,
Each with a future hero rise.
These delights if Mars afford,
Mars, with thee I whet my sword.

Aside from the foregoing kinds of imitation, titles were also influenced by Milton's works. As an example, the following direct appropriations of the title of Milton's brief epic are particularly interesting since the poem has so often been overlooked in criticism: *Paradise Lost and Paradise Regained by the Wonderful Works in God. In Verse* (Newark-upon-Tyne, 1720?); J. Lawrence, *Paradice Regain'd: or the Art of Gardening. A Poem* (1728); H. T., 'Paradise Regain'd', *The Christians Magazine, or a Treasury of Divine Knowledge,* ed. William Dodd (April 1761), pp. 188–9; G. Kellingworth, *Paradise Regained: or the Scripture Account of the Glorious Millennium* (1772); A. B., *Paradise Regain'd: or, The Battle of Adam and the Fox* (1780); William Thompson, 'Paradise Regained: To a Friend', *The Works of The British Poets,* ed. Robert Anderson (1795), x, 396.

V

Milton criticism from 1732 to 1801 may be divided into four periods dominated by certain critics or concerns. But such divisions are specious, for the seventy years of the eighteenth century move through all the areas of Milton criticism explored in the years prior to 1732. A topical view of Milton criticism during these periods is more meaningful than a strictly chronological one, and so as we note these periods let us also observe that their concerns continue later, and prior critical issues may rear up again.

The first period, ushered in by the textual criticism of Richard Bentley in 1732 and coloured by specific charges of Arianism, is generally negative, a tendency observed in the criticism of Voltaire and John Clarke in the years immediately preceding. Not that the praise and celebrity outlined in previous sections of this Introduction did not balance such negativity, but the period is overshadowed by the spectre of Bentley, though the religious criticism had little lasting effect at this time. And this is also not to say that the adverse criticism was not answered resoundingly: it was; or that positive criticism unrelated to either of these two concerns did not emerge: it did. But looking back, it is the iconoclastic tone that one usually remembers.

19

Actually, the critical approach which Bentley's edition of *Paradise Lost* presented had been announced by him before 1732 and had been rejected by various commentators, although he was not to be dissuaded. As early as 5 March 1730 a letter from Bentley (signed 'Zoilus', referring to a Greek grammarian and textual critic) appeared in the *Grub-street Journal*, no. 9, discussing needed emendations for the epic. This evoked adverse editorial comment in issue no. 12 (26 March 1730) and a letter from 'Philarcheus' plus additional editorial discussion in no. 25 (25 June). Bentley's nephew Thomas was also in disagreement with him about the emendations being proposed and apparently had tried to deter him from his project, but to no avail. An unpublished holograph letter from the nephew to Bentley's later critic Zachary Pearce, dated 20 April 1731, discusses the emendations and comments on the state of publication of the edition which appeared finally in January 1732.[38] During this year a general discussion on editing Milton was printed in no. 82 of the *Journal* (29 July 1731), followed by three epigrams on Bentley in no. 99 (25 November) and no. 100 (23 December). The first was in Latin; this is given in English as 'An Imitation' in no. 100:

> Just ready to be torn by Critics paws,
> Mild flames had sav'd me from fierce B—ys claws:
> But snatch'd from those by hands severely kind,
> To MILTON's dismal fate I'm now consign'd.

Below this is printed an 'Epigram occasion'd by seeing some Sheets of Dr. B-t-ly's Edition of MILTON's *Paradise Lost*':

> Did MILTON's Prose, O CHARLES, thy Death defend?
> A furious Foe unconscious proves a Friend.
> On MILTON's Verse does B-t-ly comment?—Know
> A weak, officious Friend becomes a Foe.
> While he but fought his Author's Fame to further,
> The murd'rous Critic has aveng'd thy Murder.

Bentley was a well-known Latin scholar whose revisions of texts (for example, of Horace) have been accepted, even in modern editions. Primarily he corrected defective metric quantity and made astute conjectures for *lacunae*, meaningless words, etc. Approaching Milton's text from the same point of view—that lines not equating a metric which he thought they should have and words or phrases not relating what he thought was meant should be emended—Bentley proposed a number of changes, apparently convinced himself that there were further and more egregious kinds of errors, and finally offered a text which slashingly (to use Pope's epithet) rewrote the epic. One has the feeling in his introduction and some of the notes (extracts of which appear here as No. 1) that the attempts to dissuade him from his enterprise clouded his judgment so much that he lost all control of reason and reasonableness. One feels that he moved to a point of defending his earlier suggestions about Milton's text and thus himself rather than continuing to present the fruits of a careful and scholarly examination of a text such as he would in his edition of Manilius. To justify the wholesale assault on words, lines, and passages, Bentley conjectured that an editor had intervened between Milton's manuscript and the first edition, thus falsifying the text. Aside from the errors he found (which seem to have grown in quantity as well as nature and length as he lavished his labours on the poem), the hypothesis of an ignorant editor arose from the fact of Milton's blindness. But Bentley's discussion of editions, publishers, and the relationships with *Paradise Regain'd* is erroneous, built on misinformation or misinterpretation and a lack of scholarly investigation. (Cf. comments in No. 2.)

The *Grub-street Journal* advertised the edition in no. 106, 13 January 1732, and noticed its publication in no. 108, 27 January. Indignant criticism immediately appeared. In the latter issue of the aforementioned journal was a letter from J. T. (perhaps Milton's publisher Jacob Tonson) on the emendations, and a further letter from the same correspondent appeared in no. 113, 2 March, both reproduced here as No. 2. This same issue of the *Journal* printed a letter from A. Z. (plus editorial comment), here given as No. 3, who corresponded again in no. 116, 23 March, where another epigram on Bentley was also printed. Two issues later, on 6 April, the editors of the *Journal* (Richard Russell and John Martyn) wrote up their reaction to the controversy—it also is anti-Bentley—and a letter from Zoilus (that is, Bentley) in confutation of the antagonists followed. A. Z. produced another letter, which preceded two more and a poem on Bentley, in no. 125, 25 May. Further examination of the emendations by the editors was offered in no. 131, 6 July, in which another poem on Zoilus appeared. And still additional editorial comment was forthcoming in no. 137, 17 August, and no. 146, 19 October. The former issue also printed an approving letter from 'Philo-Bent'. Lewis Theobald, although he criticized Pope's edition of Shakespeare, also found commendable results in Bentley's work (see No. 6), but not David Mallet. See his poem 'Of Verbal Criticism' (1733), subtitled, 'An Epistle to Mr. Pope Occasion'd by Theobald's Shakespeare and Bentley's Milton'.

The main argument against Bentley's edition, however, is that of the Reverend Zachary Pearce. *A Friendly Letter to Dr. Bentley. Occasion'd by His New Edition of Paradise Lost. By a Gentleman of Christ-Church College, Oxon.*, had probably been generally thought out before the edition actually was issued in January 1732. It is sixty-four pages long. This was expanded into three parts printed separately but with continuous pagination—*A Review of the Text of Milton's Paradise Lost: In Which the Chief of Dr. Bentley's Emendations Are Consider'd, and Several Other Emendations and Observations Are Offer'd to the Public. Part I. Containing Remarks Upon the First Four Books* (1732), basically 152 pages; *Part II. Containing Remarks on the V, VI, VII, and VIIIth Books* (1732), pp. 153–287; and *Part III. Containing Remarks on the IX, X, XI, and XIIth Books. To which is added An Appendix to the Whole* (1733), pp. 289–389, with appendix, pp. 390–400. Excerpts from this *Review* are here given as No. 7. Bentley's critics pointed out his misinformation, his errors in reading and understanding *Paradise Lost*, his lack of knowledge of certain words or concepts, and his illogical suppositions and conclusions, as well as accusing him, by implication at least, of a nefarious purpose to reduce Milton's fame. Some of the antagonists also err in knowledge and most evidence that they did not understand the structure and intention of the poem as we today hope we do. The controversy rears up in critical asides throughout the century, as in John Upton's *Critical Observations on Shakespeare* (1746), *passim*. Upton argued against revisions of Shakespeare's text through the use of explication and analogues; quite naturally then he was not favourable to Bentley's efforts with *Paradise Lost*. An anonymous poem (No. 40) shows that it was not a totally dead issue even in 1751. The advent of Bentley was not a phenomenon for the eighteenth century: it is a good example of the attention paid to doctrines of correctness and the amazing self-assurance which so many commentators exhibit.

One correction proposed by Bentley is universally accepted: 'Soul' for 'Fowle' in VII, 451; and another, which is the basis for the question in Jonathan Richardson Jr's letter to Pope (No. 4), 'swelling' for 'smelling' in VII, 321, has sometimes been approved. For the most part, however, the positive effect of Bentley on Milton scholarship was to take readers back to a study of the text and its meaning, as we can see in Warburton's notes (No. 17), and this in turn combined with the discussion of Milton's versification in *Paradise Lost*[39] to elicit numerous investigations of style, language, and verse in the succeeding years.

Study of the text and its meaning during the century often specifically took the form of explications of words or passages. Three items from the period of 1732–40 extracted in this volume reflect this kind of attention although not necessarily as a direct result of Bentley's assault. Richard Meadowcourt (No. 5) produced the first study of a single poem, other than Addison's *Spectator* papers on *Paradise Lost*, with his remarks on *Paradise Regain'd* (1732). Jonathan Richardson realized the need for *Explanatory Notes and Remarks on Paradise Lost* (1734), although extracts here (No. 8) present other concerns of that volume. And added to John Jortin's remarks on Spenser (1734) were a number of annotations for the brief epic (No. 9) and some for *Samson Agonistes*. But explicatory works continue to appear in other periods; for example, James Paterson's *A Complete Commentary, with Etymological, Explanatory, Critical and Classical Notes on Paradise Lost* (No. 23) appeared in 1744, and Thomas Newton's and others' annotations are gathered in the variorum editions of 1749 and 1752 (representative notes for *Paradise Lost* are given as No. 33). In the final period of the century we find Thomas Warton's work on the minor poems (1785), William Cowper's unfinished comments on *Paradise Lost* (1791–2), Charles Dunster's extensive restudy of *Paradise Regain'd* (1795), and Henry John Todd's new variorum of *The Poetical Works* (1801). Excerpts of these are given as Nos 69, 79, 81, and 90. The study of text yielded a better understanding of Milton's meaning and unwittingly assured the reading public that Milton's text was at least verbally accurate (with few exceptions, that is, if any).

Attention to language also led to indexes for *Paradise Lost: A Verbal Index to Milton's Paradise Lost: Adapted to Every Edition but the First* appeared in 1741; Newton's word index was included in his edition of 1749; and William Dodd's *A Familiar Explanation of the Poetical Works of Milton* in 1762 consisted primarily of 'Explanatory Notes on the Poetical Works of Milton, Alphabetically Digested'.

Style, which depends largely on language and language use, was analysed by Francis Peck in *New Memoirs of Milton* (1740), given here as No. 18. Even Milton's prose style was described by William Godwin in 1797 (No. 85). Among those studying the language were Richard Hurd in 1749 (No. 30), Edmund Burke in 1756 (No. 50), Hugh Blair in 1759–60 (No. 53), and Lord Monboddo in 1774–89 (No. 61). The foregoing, like John Dennis before them, praise Milton's use of language and sublime achievement, but during the negative period when Bentley was most prominent George Lord Lyttelton commented quite differently:[40]

[H]ard words and affected phrases are no more necessary in this sort of metre, than in rime; and . . . , if Milton himself had been more sparing of them, he would not indeed have appeared so great a scholar, and therefore perhaps might have pleased the ladies less; but he would have been a good deal finer writer, and not have spoiled the style of so many of his successors, who have chosen to imitate him chiefly in this point.

Daniel Webb (1762) specifically explored Milton's imagery (see No. 58), and an anonymous writer (1796–8), Milton's similes (see No. 84).

Earlier Milton's remark on the verse of *Paradise Lost* and the contrast of its blank verse with the heroic couplet, standard for the times, generally evoked antipathy. That antipathy recurs importantly in the eighteenth century in four articles by Samuel Johnson in the *Rambler* (1751), given here as No. 42. But the results of close attention to text (as well as the significance of aesthetics to the eighteenth-century world) brought forth a number of major examinations of Milton's versification, which contravene such rejection. It is regrettable that so few modern critics of Milton seem to have been aware of these examinations. William Benson in 1739 (No. 16), Edward Manwaring in 1744 (No. 21), James Harris in 1744 (No. 22), John Mason in 1749 (Nos 31 and 32), and Lord Kames in 1762 (No. 57) paid particular attention to this subject. Their work is analytic, as are Thomas Gray's comments from around 1760 (No. 55). In the midst of the Bentley aftermath the 'Remarks on the Numbers in the Argument to *PARADISE LOST* Written in the Year 1737' by the poet Samuel Say emphasize the variety of Milton's metric and suggest that part of Bentley's error was attempting to make it conform to an unalterable mould:[41]

MILTON has shown us, in the very Entrance of his POEM, tho' probably without Design, what an endless Variety of Numbers we are afterwards to expect, in a kind of Verse, consisting only of Five Feet and Ten Syllables, for the most part.

Of the Twenty-six Verses in the Argument, or Invocation, there are hardly two that are like one another in every Respect; much less any two that stand near each other. . . .

This is one Reason why MILTON abhorr'd, and avoided Rime.

There is undoubtedly a Pleasure which Rime gives to the Ear, but a Pleasure which soon grows Stale upon us, and breeds satiety, as Every larger Work will presently discover.

We can now turn to the second topic of this period from 1732 to 1740. The question of Milton's Arianism first erupted through the remarks of John Toland in his 'Life', for Toland was a strong adherent of such anti-Trinitarian and non-Christian views as Socinianism. To Milton were vaguely transferred the charges levelled at Toland, and it is against this background that Jonathan Richardson wrote of Milton's religious beliefs (see No. 8). (Warburton criticized Toland's 'falsification' of Milton's character and ability, although he did not get into the religious question even when putting Milton down; see No. 10.) Biographers without delving into the question incidentally review Milton's precepts; and Edward Gibbon in 1761 (see No. 56), in a position not too far from those who some years before had charged him with Arianism, indicates what is going to be a problem for twentieth-century critics of Milton's God.

In 1738 and 1739 a controversy over Arianism in *Paradise Lost* was carried on in the magazines. A letter from 'Theophilus' printed in the *Gentleman's Magazine*, viii (March 1738), 124-5, contended that the epic corrupted man's religious ideas through the presentation of God and his host, and this he labelled 'the *Arian* principle'; see No. 11. He objected to what he called ridicule and puns and heathenism, and to the figure of Satan. Some of his criticism has strangely been echoed in the twentieth century. These arguments were unacceptable to 'Philo-Spec.' because of the need for invention and because of Milton's presentation of abstruse doctrines such as free will and redemption (*GM*, viii [April 1738], 201-2); see No. 12. He commented further in *GM*, viii (June 1738), 288-90 (mispaged as second set of numbers; actually 296-8). A commentator in the *Daily Gazetteer*, referred to in *GM*, viii (August 1738), 417, demanded examples of what Theophilus had called Arian (see No. 13), and in rebuttal of Philo-Spec. Theophilus takes up each point, quoting Addison against him, and concludes that many things in the poem 'bear no good Aspect towards Religion' and might better be called 'the *Romance of the War in Heaven, and the Fall of Man*'. (See *GM*, ix [January 1739], 5-6, and No. 15 here.) Though not related to this controversy, the comments of Richard Hurd on Milton's invention (see No. 41) should be compared with Philo-Spec.'s remarks, and his discussion of romance in Milton's works (see No. 59) should be set alongside the foregoing rebuttal. Arianism in *Paradise Lost* meant for the mid-eighteenth century a discrepancy between the God of man's faith and the view given in the poem; one was 'truth', the other, 'fiction'. Yet many learned their Bible at the hands of Milton.

The question was to be little discussed after 1739[42] until the publication of *De Doctrina Christiana* in 1825, when, as if for the first time, the possibility of Milton's having subscribed to anti-Trinitarianism arose.

William Ellery Channing's review of Charles Sumner's translation discussed Milton's character and writings in the *Christian Examiner and Theological Review*, iii (1826), 29–77, and concluded from his application of the statements in the prose work to *Paradise Lost* that Milton could be called an anti-Trinitarian. 'But we have no desire to identify him with any sect' (p. 62). The reaction of Todd may have been duplicated in many readers: the revision of his fourth variorum in 1842 registers shock and disbelief and acceptance and discomfort. Todd did not want to accept Arian influence on *Paradise Lost*, and yet he could not deny its tenets in *De Doctrina Christiana*. The poem and its author had fallen irretrievably in his judgment. But Zacharias Conrad von Uffenbach had reported the rumour of this 'systema theologiæ' which was Arian in content in 1754.[43] He added that the whereabouts of the manuscript was unknown.

While the work of Bentley on the text of *Paradise Lost* has almost totally been discarded today, questions of the validity of text remain. The questions, however, have been raised over such accidentals as spelling, punctuation, italicization, and the like, but answers seem incapable of absolute definition. The controversy over Milton's alleged Arianism moved into a quite different path in 1825, but it is more lively today than it was in either the eighteenth or the nineteenth centuries. Part of the problem lies in the language of *De Doctrina Christiana* (and particularly its translation) and part lies in what is defined as orthodox, Arian, Subordinationist, etc. The contention that *Paradise Lost* is or is not an Arian document depends also on whether one understands its literary devices as *literary* devices (a point made in the eighteenth century) or as philosophic theory.

VI

Although the second period to be considered, 1741–51, evidences praise and analysis as well as some dispraise, as we have already seen, the period is dominated by charges of alleged plagiarism brought by William Lauder, and therefore by attention to sources. Through the continuing comparison of Milton with Homer and Vergil in *Paradise Lost* and through the extensive annotations of Patrick Hume onward, sources for Milton's poetry were repeatedly being suggested for language, versification, similes, imagery, ideas, characterizations, and narrative elements. At the beginning of this period an anonymous pamphlet was published, entitled *An Essay upon Milton's Imitations of the Ancients, in His Paradise Lost. With Some Observations on the Paradise Regain'd*

(1741), included here as No. 20. Attempts to assign this to Lauder seem far-fetched. It does not pull together previous suggestions, nor does it 'cover' its subject very well, but it is representative of the kinds of parallels which were frequently offered. Shortly before this, for example, Elizabeth Cooper suggested 'Piers Plowman' as source for PL XI, 477–92 (which is mis-cited),[44] and an F. T. wrote of Milton's borrowing from various Latin and Greek writers in a letter to the *Gentleman's Magazine*, ix (July 1739), 359–60. The search continued well after the period now under discussion, as we note from the following: Mary Singleton (i.e., Frances Brooke) printed a letter in the *Old Maid*, no. 12 (31 January 1756), from a T. W. alleging indebtedness to Beaumont and Fletcher in 'Il Penseroso'; Francis Fawkes cited Gawin Douglas's 'The Description of May' as source for PL VII, 438 ff.;[45] and an anonymous commentator in the *European Magazine*, xii (1787), 313 and n., argues for Milton's debt to a sonnet of Petrarch in the proem to PL III.

The question of sources is specifically represented here (other than as part of the Lauder controversy) by various excerpts. Giuseppi Baretti rejected Voltaire's argument that Andreini's *Adamo* was the source for *Paradise Lost* (1753; No. 44), although William Hayley was to revive the argument (1796) and William Cowper was to be convinced of its validity. Thomas Holt White, not so much urging sources, examined analogues to *Paradise Lost* (1786; No. 72). Philip Neve mentioned a number of sources for various poems in 1789 (see No. 76); Todd reviewed influences upon 'Comus' in 1798 (see No. 86); and in 1800 Charles Dunster analysed Milton's use of Du Bartas, through Joshua Sylvester's translation (see No. 89). James Beattie has well summarized the attitude that has prevailed towards Milton's extensive learning and its employment in his work (see No. 62): 'Milton was one of the most learned men this nation ever produced. But his great learning, neither impaired his judgment, nor checked his imagination.'

This period of the eighteenth century, however, has a distinctly negative flavour for Milton's reputation because of William Lauder's allegations that Milton had plagiarized his epic primarily from Jacopo Masenio's *Sarcotis*, Hugo Grotius' *Adamus Exsul*, and Andrew Ramsay's *Poemata Sacra*. These first charges are here reproduced from the *Gentleman's Magazine* (1747) as No. 26. Lauder had contributed an elaborate preface to *Poetarum Scotorum Musae Sacrae* (1739), two volumes, and a life of Arthur Johnston, a Scots poet writing in Latin. The volumes included much Latin poetry by Johnston as well as paraphrases of the Bible by William Hog, Latin translator of Milton's three longer poems,

'Lycidas', and 'Comus'. A controversy ensued upon Lauder's evaluating Johnston a better poet than the important Scots author George Buchanan. Lauder's attempt to draw Alexander Pope into the controversy on his side elicited only a scathing couplet in *The Dunciad* (1742; iii, 111–12), comparing Johnston unfavourably with Milton—an unfortunate ploy, as it turned out for Milton. Lauder used Pope's lines to justify the low sales of his volumes and passed his invective on to Milton. His charges of plagiarism were immediately rebutted in the same journal (of which Samuel Johnson was an editor) by various people[46] including Richard Richardson (No. 27). These in turn called forth comment by Lauder (No. 28). Richardson reprinted and expanded his remarks in *Zoilomastix: or, a Vindication of Milton, from all the Invidious Charges of Mr. William Lauder. With several new remarks on Paradise Lost* (1747). A complete revision by Lauder (No. 36) with a preface by Samuel Johnson (presented as if by Lauder; see No. 35) was published as *An Essay on Milton's Use and Imitation of the Moderns in His Paradise Lost* (1750). Samuel Johnson's part in this pamphlet has been deplored by his adherents, of course, and explained as human gullibility, done in by an antagonism to Milton the man. Yet it should be remembered that Johnson himself was consciously perpetrating a hoax in passing off his work as Lauder's. Johnson's biographer Sir John Hawkins, appropriately exercised by this unconscionable part in the controversy, criticized him (see No. 74), although Arthur Murphy was not thus moved (see *An Essay on the Life and Genius of Samuel Johnson, LL. D.,* 1792). Defences of Milton appeared in James Kirkpatrick's preface to *The Sea-Piece A Narrative, Philosophical and Descriptive Poem. In Five Cantos* (1750), pp. xxii–xxvi; 'Philalethes', *Pandæmonium: of a New Infernal Expedition, Transcrib'd to a Being Who Calls Himself W. Lauder* (1750); *Furius: or A Modest Attempt Towards a History of the Life and Surprising Adventures of the Famous W. L. Critic and Thief-Catcher . . . in a Letter from an Honest North-Briton to His Friend in London. To which is added, Some Remarks on the Passages Adduced by Furius with Intent to Prove the Said Milton a Plagiary* [1751?]; Robert Lloyd's 'The Progress of Envy' (1751);[47] and *Das Neueste aus der anmuthigen Gelehrsamkeit* (Leipzig, 1752), ii, 260–75, 341–52, 438–45, 620–6, 831–9, 913–23 (a general review of the controversy).

But Lauder had interpolated parts of Hog's translation of *Paradise Lost* into his quotations of Masenio and Staphorstius as Richardson argued in the *Gentleman's Magazine*, xx (December 1750), 535–6, although the letter is dated 28 January 1749.[48] John Douglas, however, produced the major statement of proof of Lauder's deceptions and forgeries. *Milton Vindicated from the Charge of Plagiarism, Brought Against Him by Mr. Lauder, and Lauder Himself Convicted of Several Forgeries and Impositions on the Public* (1751), actually 1750, given as No. 37, was revised into *Milton No Plagiary; or, A Detection of the Forgeries Contained in Lauder's Essay on the Imitation of the Moderns in the Paradise Lost* in 1756. Johnson obtained a confession of guilt from Lauder and, we are told, he dictated *A Letter to the Reverend Mr. Douglas, Occasioned by His Vindication of Milton. To which are subjoin'd Several Curious Original Letters from the Authors of the Universal History, Mr. Ainsworth, Mr. MacLawrin, &c.* (1751), in which volume are also presented passages interpolated into Masenio, testimonies (praising Lauder's earlier scholarly work rather than praising his allegations as implied), and a postscript; see No. 38. Then in a further pamphlet, *An Apology for Mr. Lauder, in a Letter Most Humbly Addressed to His Grace the Archbishop of Canterbury* (1751), given as No. 39, Lauder repeats his reason for the fraud: Milton had become too much the centre of idolatry and imitation in the poetic world. A few years later, in 1754, Lauder tried to recoup his lost character, curiously by raising again the issue of Milton's alleged insertion of Pamela's prayer in *Eikon Basilike*, in *King Charles I. Vindicated from the Charge of Plagiarism Brought Against Him by Milton, and Milton Himself Convicted of Forgery, and a Gross Imposition on the Publick* (cf. Douglas's first title); but history has remembered him not as a scholar but as a forger.

One footnote to the controversy was the appearance in 1757 of the works of Masenio. Lauder had promised publication in July 1750 under the title of 'Delectus Auctorum Sacrorum Miltono facem prælucentium'; this appeared in two volumes in 1752–3. The fuller French version of Masenio and the controversy was: *Sarcotis. Carmen. Auctore Jacobo Masenio S. J. Editio Altera Cura & Studia J. Dinouart* (Coloniae Agrippinæ: Parissiis, 1757); the book contains the Latin text followed by a French translation, and discussion and reprints of the controversy extracted from *Le Journal étranger* and the *Gentleman's Magazine*.

Every now and then one runs across someone who has heard something about 'Milton's plagiarism' ('Things most definitely attempted before in prose and rhyme', as one person quipped), but not enough, and a lurid light is cast over Milton's fame and achievement. Positively, though, the effect of Lauder on Milton scholarship was a further seeking out of analogues and sources, most notably Du Bartas, and the significance of Grotius has finally been recognized.

VII

In the years 1752–73 previous topics for discussion of Milton and his works continued to be aired in the form of defence against adverse critics and in analysis of poems, language, versification, style, etc. These twenty-two or so years do not take a new turn in Milton criticism or offer any single dominant concern; they are a pulling together and a development, generally but not quite always favourable. Defences of Milton against Voltaire and Lauder appear; and *Paradise Lost* remains the most significant single work for the period. Joseph Warton discussed Milton's paradise in 1753 (No. 46); the epic qualities of the poem are central to William Mason's remarks on Milton's achievement in 1756 (No. 49) and William Wilkie's often unfavourable ones in 1757 (No. 52); the poem was discussed by Hugh Blair in 1759–60 (No. 53), and it underlies the comments of Burke, Gray, Gibbon, Kames, Webb, and Hurd previously mentioned, as well as those of Lord Lyttelton in 1760 (No. 54). Three items printed here from earlier years, not previously mentioned in this Introduction, are likewise concerned with *Paradise Lost*; see Nos 14, 24, and 25. Perhaps a good representative comment for the age is Theophilus Cibber's:[49]

The British Nation, which has produced the greatest men in every profession, before the appearance of Milton could not enter into any competition with antiquity, with regard to the sublime excellencies of poetry . . . [T]he ancients had still a poet in reserve, superior to the rest, who stood unrivalled by all succeeding times, and in epic poetry, which is justly esteemed the highest effort of genius, Homer had no rival. When Milton appeared, the pride of Greece was humbled, the competition became more equal, and since Paradise Lost is ours; it would, perhaps, be an injury to our national fame to yield the palm to any state, whether ancient or modern.

Yet one of the most interesting analyses contemporary with the Lauder period a few years before is Charles Batteux's:[50]

S'il s'agit de faire naître l'admiration, d'étonner l'ame, de l'élever; il faut que les obstacles présentés au héros soient d'une difficulté extraordinaire à surmonter, qu'ils demandent une force plus que naturelle; & que cependant succès & la joie. C'est une grande vertue qu'on donne à admirer: si elle échouoit, elle seroit plus digne de pitié que d'admiration. . . . [E]nfin Satan dans le *Paradis perdu* de Milton triomphe du premier homme. Car c'est lui qui est le héros assurément. S'il ne l'étoit pas, & que ce fut Adam, le dénouement seroit tragique, & nullement épique: & s'il étoit tragique, toutes les machines surnaturelles qui sont employées dans ce poëme seroient des roues inutiles; puisque le merveilleux n'a nul rapport à la pitié, & qu'il n'est point fait pour l'exciter. C'est donc le Diable qu'on nous donne à admirer dans le *Paradis perdu*. L'objet est singulier; mais il faut en juger comme d'une idée de peintre, c'est-à-dire, par l'execution plutôt que par le fond même du sujet. D'ailleurs, s'il ne cause point l'admiration, il cause du moins l'étonnement.

Adherents of Satan as hero have not apparently been aware of this 1747–50 comment. The important statement by William Godwin in 1793 (see No. 80) has only once in a while been given its due attention, and none seem to take into account Henry Boyd's view (see No. 91) written somewhere in the midst of the Romantic period's development of the so-called Satanic hero.

Other poems, however, were having attention paid to them in the years 1732–73, and continued in the last quarter of the century to attract increased criticism. Meadowcourt's examination of *Paradise Regain'd* in 1732 and Jortin's attention to that poem and *Samson Agonistes* (1734) are comparatively early. At the beginning of the second half of the century William Shenstone commented on elegy with ideas deriving from 'Lycidas' (1754; No. 47), Joseph Warton analysed the 'Nativity Ode' (1756; No. 48), and Hugh Blair turned to the companion poems, among others (1759–60; No. 53). Samuel Johnson's two *Rambler* papers on *Samson Agonistes*, published just before in 1751 (No. 43), evoked criticism finally from Richard Cumberland in 1785 (No. 71) and William Mickle in 1788 (No. 75). Johnson's strictures derived from his conception of dramatic form and from the breaking of classic rules of characterization, versification, and treatment. In 1753 William Mason was also to air his views of this drama which influenced his own work so much (see No. 45). John Penn's alteration of the play and few 'observations' (1798) indicate that attention was being paid to the work (see No. 87), but altogether we recognize that the eighteenth century did not understand the play or appreciate its achievements. Even the praise is not really analytic or discerning; it is largely generalized statement to counter negative views.

The last quarter of the century saw outstanding criticism of Milton, most of it little known today: Lord Monboddo on language (1774–89; No. 61), Richard Richardson on the twin poems (1779; No. 63); Francis Blackburne on Milton's politics (1780; No. 67), Hayley on *Paradise Lost* and other works (1782 and 1796; Nos 68, 82, 83); Thomas Warton's introductions and notes to the minor poems (1785; No. 69); John Scott on 'Lycidas' (1785; No. 70); Philip Neve on several poems (1789;

No. 76); and Todd on 'Comus' (1798; No. 86). To these we may add Thomas Holt White on the sonnets (1786; No. 73) and Thomas Green on the three major poems (1799–1800; No. 88). Perhaps it is the close analysis of Milton's works that differentiates this period from the prior one.

Alongside these commendations are the ambivalent evaluations of Samuel Johnson, whose views, though important in the period, do not dominate it. Earlier criticism on 'Comus', versification, and *Samson Agonistes* all attest to Johnson's dislike of Milton as person and 'regicide' and, by extension, of his work. Remarks in *The Lives of the Poets* (see Nos 64, 65, 66) illustrate the same bias, while also making clear his admiration for certain poems—'Comus', 'L'Allegro', for example—and his analysis of literature through a rule-conscious eighteenth-century aesthetic. The categorization of literature and its subject, treatment, form, and language, controls many evaluations of literature in these years and is a main point of revolt for the Romantics who will follow soon. Johnson simply did not like Milton's experimentation and 'new' approaches. He is not the only critic against Milton (for example, in 'Lycidas') on grounds of prescription; compare someone like Wilkie or some of White's views of the sonnet. Indeed the sonnet which after Milton seems almost to have died as a form until the Romantics—with the notable exceptions of such 'Miltonists' as Thomas Edwards, Thomas Gray, William Lisle Bowles, and Thomas Warton—is an example of the kind of Miltonic achievement that could not garner approbation with many in the eighteenth century. But perhaps the diametrically opposed realization that we reach in reading Johnson's criticism with our hindsight is that he and other of the critics astutely hit on critical questions which still plague us, while on the other side they are so blind to Milton's structure and form, intention and artistry. While one cannot ask the past to be the present, we must none the less be amazed at the frequent lack of insight, particularly in view of a number of incisive perceptions. And though much comment seems to arise from the critical bias of the times, yet we can also see a growing change in these same regards, perhaps aided by our documented closer reading and by appreciation of Milton's attention to form and imagery and intention.[51]

Johnson's 'Life' did not sit well with William Cowper (see a letter to William Unwin, dated 31 October 1779),[52] or with Francis Blackburne, whose *Remarks* (1780) show his sense of indignant affront at Johnson's uncomplimentary reading, or with R. Potter in *An Inquiry into Some Passages in Dr. Johnson's Lives of the Poets: Particularly His Observations on*

Lyric Poetry, and the Odes of Gray (1783), pp. 3–4, 17, 19–20, 29. See also the final remarks of Lord Monboddo's analyses reprinted here as No. 61. On the other hand, Arthur Murphy in his biography (1792) presents an *apologia* for Johnson's censures (pp. 179–86).

As the century ends, Milton is more entrenched in the position he held in 1732: he is still the exemplar of sublime thought and expression, he is widely imitated and quoted, and he is employed as authority for ideas and language or for poetic licence. His status in these areas can be seen in the following remarks in the same year as *Lyrical Ballads* was published, favourable toward Milton but highly critical of the less talented whose inadequacies forced the need to usher in the 'new' poetry. These remarks are part of an anonymous mentor's 'Hints to a Young Author'. After advising 'L'Allegro' and 'Il Penseroso' as guide for 'local poetry', the writer says,[53]

In your poem, I must think (in Phillips) you have set a wrong model before you, and this seems to be its principal fault. Miltonian verse, through the slavish adherence of imitators, too often swells from the true sublime into turgid bombast. . . .

Milton's taste, formed by a perfect knowledge of the works of antiquity, led him to imitate their stile of verse, as given by their best poets, Homer and Virgil. His skill in music, his own good ear, and perfect command of language, gave his verse an harmonious variety and cadence, which Phillips is not equally skilled to attain.

The differences between the earlier and the later estimates of Milton lie in the more widespread reputation in England and the growth of his fame on the Continent and in the colonies. They lie not in kind but in depth and in universality. What is to follow in the nineteenth and twentieth centuries will develop these concepts further, rediscover them, and ultimately lead to what we hope today is a more valid view of Milton the man and the artist. There are still those who derogate both, and questions of Milton's God, of his alleged Arianism, of his Satanism, of his biography, of his significance as a prose writer and thinker continue, along with varied opinions and analyses of such works as *Paradise Regain'd* or *Samson Agonistes*, the Latin or Italian poems, and *Areopagitica* or *The Ready and Easy Way*. For the end of the eighteenth century, however, the following poem by a lesser poet may sum up the prevailing attitude towards Milton, drawn as it is from *Paradise Lost* while playing underneath its surface upon the significance of his work to theologic thought and to political philosophy:[54]

Ode to Milton
Addressed to the Lord Bishop of London

Hail, happy bard! with glorious thoughts inspir'd!
Immortal themes thy lofty judgment fir'd,
Thy soul with sweet celestial strains was won,
While secret powers led thy fancy on;
In tuneful bands cherubs around thee hung,
And lent new graces as the poet sung.

Oh thou, poetic prince of graceful ease,
Whose seraph notes ev'n savage minds can please;
In the smooth numbers of thy verse we stray,
Thro' sable mazes to eternal day;
Where on the rosy beams of bliss we soar,
And the sweet plains of paradise explore.

Still as we read, our sense is more refin'd,
A glow of rapture animates the mind,
Impress'd with beauties rising to our view,
With eager haste the pleasing tracks pursue.
First of thy race that trod the hallow'd ground,
And gain'd the top of Sion's sacred mound,
Or dar'd with soul sublime attempt the lyre,
Light by the mystic torch of gospel fire.

Had the Almighty king, enthron'd in state,
Reveal'd the hidden mysteries of fate;
Unfurl'd the clouds, unveil'd th' expanded sky,
And stood confus'd a god to mortals eye:
Descending deign'd, in voice celestial rare,
The wond'rous story of the fallen pair,
A secret long to angels knowledge given,
Lock'd in the bosom of the blest in heaven;
In Milton's phrase, the sov'reign Lord of Grace,
Had taught the sacred facts to human race.

No more shall Pagan poetry decoy,
Our riper judgment to the seats of Troy,
To Greece and Rome such mortal themes belong;
More perfect truths beam forth in Milton's song.
How poor that painter's skill, how unrefin'd,
Who drew the meditating poet blind!
His thoughts beyond weak nature ne'er aspir'd;
He knew not Milton's light to Heav'n retir'd!

As round the world the lamp of Phoebus plays,
In diff'rent quarters darts refulgent rays,
To eastern climes he moves in awful plight,
And bursts in floods of glory on their sight;
So Milton's orbs, eclips'd to human eye,
Blaz'd in meridian flame beyond the sky;
His lamps of light in higher regions burn'd,
From earthly sparks to heav'nly glory turn'd!

NOTES

1 See, respectively, *Appendix ad Indicem Librorum Prohibitorum Vero, & Accurato Alphabetico Ordine Disposita ab anno 1681. Usque ad mensem Junii inclusivè 1704* [Romae: Camerae Apostolicae, 1704], p. 347; *Appendix Novissimae Appendici ad Indicem Librorum Prohibitorum a Mense Maii MDCCXVIII. Usque ad totum mensem Julii MDCCXXXIX* (Romae: Camerae Apostolicae, 1739), p. 506; and *Index Librorum Prohibitorum, Ac Expurgandorum Novissimus. Pro Universis Hispaniarum Regnis Serenissimi Ferdinandi VI. Regis Catholici, Ultima Editione* (Matriti: Emmanuelis Fernandez, 1747), II, 686.

2 Letter 75, p. 129.

3 *The Works in Verse and Prose, of William Shenstone, Esq.* (1765), 2nd edn, II, 154. The essay was first published posthumously in 1764.

4 See George Sherburn, ed., *The Correspondence of Alexander Pope* (Oxford, 1956), IV, 80–1. The sonnet is given, among other places, in a letter to the editor [William Dodd] of the *Christians Magazine, or A Treasury of Divine Knowledge*, iii (June 1762), 283.

5 See John Shore, Lord Teignmouth's *Memoirs of the Life, Writings, and Correspondence of Sir William Jones* (1804), pp. 67–9.

6 See [John Almon, ed.], *An Asylum for Fugitive Pieces in Prose and Verse* (1785–9), IV, 123–5.

7 Written 1754; ll. 95–102 quoted from *Poems by Mr. Gray* (1768):
> Nor second He, that rode sublime
> Upon the seraph-wings of Extasy,
> The secrets of th' Abyss to spy.
> He pass'd the flaming bounds of Place and Time:
> The living Throne, the saphire blaze,
> Where Angels tremble, while they gaze,
> He saw; but blasted with excess of light,
> Clos'd his eyes in endless night.

8 Written 1784; from book iv, ll. 709–17, quoted from *Poems* (1800), ii, 175–6:
> Then Milton had indeed a poet's charms:
> New to my taste, his Paradise surpass'd
> The struggling efforts of my boyish tongue
> To speak its excellence. I danced for joy.
> I marvell'd much that, at so ripe an age
> As twice sev'n years, his beauties had then first
> Engag'd my wonder; and, admiring still,
> And still admiring, with regret suppos'd
> Thy joy half lost because not sooner found.

9 *Love Elegies. Written in the Year 1732* (1762), p. 28.

10 *Poems on Several Occasions* (Truro, 1742), p. 90.

11 *The Atheist. A Poem* (Birmingham, 1770), p. 27.

12 *The Correspondence of Samuel Richardson* (1804), VI, 198.

13 *Massachusetts Historical Society. Collections*, Vol. 34 [Vol. 4 of Series IV], (1858), pp. 412–13.

14 See Charles Francis Adams, ed., *The Works of John Adams, Second President of the United States* (Boston, 1854), IX, 354.

15 See Douglass Adair and John A. Schultz, eds, *Peter Oliver's Origin & Progress of the American Revolution. A Tory View* (Huntington Library, 1961), pp. 36, 93–4.

16 See *A Sermon Preached at the Installation of the Reverend David Avery* (Providence, 1786), p. 23; *A Discourse, Delivered November 3, 1790, at . . . Franklin* (Providence, 1790), p. 8; *A Discourse, Delivered, September 3d MDCCXCII* (Worcester, 1793), p. 19; *The Dignity of Man* (New York, 1798), p. 26.

17 See pp. xiv, 92, 97, 163, 209, 210, 311–12, 415–16, 418, 470–4, 478–84, 512, 562, 563.

18 See Ronald Paulsen, ed., *Hogarth's Graphic Works* (New Haven, 1965), II, Cat. no. 181, in fourth state of engraving, plate 193.

19 See ibid., Cat. no. 185, in second and third states of engraving, plates 197 and 198.

20 See John Bigelow, ed., *The Works of Benjamin Franklin* (New York, 1904), I, 24–5.

21 See pp. 32–3 (The Morning Hymn), 360, 363–4, 365, 368, 369, 371, 372, 384, 389, 393, 394, 396.

22 See, first, Gilbert Chinard, ed., *The Literary Bible of Thomas Jefferson, His Commonplace Book of Philosophers and Poets* (Baltimore, 1928); there are thirty quotations from *Paradise Lost*, pp. 134–40, and eighteen from *Samson Agonistes*, pp. 164–8. And, second, Gilbert Chinard, ed., *The Commonplace Book of Thomas Jefferson, a Repertory of His Ideas on Government* (Baltimore, 1926);

there are a quotation from *Paradise Lost*, p. 98, and summaries and quotations from *Reason of Church Government* and *Of Reformation*, pp. 384–5.

23 See appendix iv, 'Quotations, Tending to Promote Liberality, Peace, and Philanthropy', pp. 175–6.

24 See pp. 14–17, 92, 125–6, 141–2, 176–7.

25 See pp. 40, 110, 141.

26 See pp. 10, 16, 19, 27, 28, 36, 37, 41, 43, 51, 52, 55, 58, 59, 67, 68, 70.

27 *London Magazine*, iii (December 1734), 663, a parody following the lead of John Philips's 'Cyder'.

28 *Poems Upon Various Occasions. Written for the Entertainment of the Author, and Printed for the Amusement of a Few Friends, Prejudic'd in His Favour* (Oxford, 1737), pp. 40–1.

29 *Poems on Various Subjects. Many Never Printed Before* (1739), pp. 70–83.

30 *The Miscellaneous Works in Prose and Verse of Mrs. Elizabeth Rowe* (1739), I, 49–52.

31 Anonymous, published 1742.

32 Nathaniel Evans, ed., *Juvenile Poems on Various Subjects* (Philadelphia, 1765), pp. 22–5.

33 Published 1771; imitations of *Paradise Lost* exist throughout the poem.

34 Anonymous, published 1780; a parody of Belial's speech during the Council in Hell is found on pp. 7–9.

35 Undated holograph manuscript (three pages) in the Berg Collection, New York Public Library.

36 Anonymous, published in Boston, 1799.

37 John Almon, ed., *The Fugitive Miscellany . . . Part the Second* (1775), pp. 104–10.

38 The letter will be found in the Alexander Turnbull Library, Wellington, New Zealand, in a copy of Bentley's edition. I am indebted to Miss Kathleen A. Coleridge for this important item, which has not previously been noticed.

39 See the discussion and excerpts (e.g., from Dryden and Rymer) in the earlier volume of *Milton: The Critical Heritage*.

40 George E. Ayscough, ed., *The Works of George Lord Lyttelton* (1776), I, 396.

41 Samuel Say, *Poems on Several Occasions: and Two Critical Essays. viz. The First, on the Harmony, Variety, and Power of NUMBERS, whether in Prose or Verse. The Second, on the Numbers of Paradise Lost* (1745), 'Essay the Second: on the Numbers of *Paradise Lost*', pp. 143, 162.

42 A book on Arianism brought forth a reference to Milton and his introduction of God into *Paradise Lost* by a reviewer in the *European Magazine*, xxv (1794), 40.

[43] *Herrn Zacharias Conrad von Uffenbach Merkwürdige Reisen durch Niedersachsen Holland und Engelland* (Ulm and Memmingen, 1753-4), III, 585.

[44] *The Historical and Poetical Medley: or Muses Library* (1738), pp. 17-18.

[45] *Original Poems and Translations* (1761), p. 252 n.

[46] In vol. 17, by R. A. (February 1747), 58; Miltonicus (February 1747), 67-8; Philo-Milton Petriburgensis (March 1747), 145; W. B. (June 1747), 278-9; Y (August 1747), 395—a poem given here as No. 29; C. B. (September 1747), 423-4. The controversy emerges from time to time thereafter. See also a comment by Goronwy Owen, the Welsh poet who was strongly influenced by Milton, in a letter to Richard Morris, dated 1748; see Robert Jones, ed., *The Poetical Works of Goronwy Owen* (*Goronwy Ddu o Fon*) *With His Life and Correspondence* (1876), I, 20.

[47] See *Poems* (1762), pp. 206-21.

[48] The editors of the *Gentleman's Magazine* (Samuel Johnson was among them) withheld publication of Richardson's letter and others because 'we could not . . . admit a suspicion of so gross a forgery, and in copies which came through our own hands, we concluded that the lines in question were in *Masenius*, &c. and that Mr *Hog* had thence copied them to save himself the unnecessary trouble of translating *Milton*.' The reason for finally publishing Richardson's letter was Douglas's book (cited here next) and Lauder's admission of the charge. The naïvely damaging editorial comment suggests further duplicity from Johnson.

[49] *The Lives of the Poets* (1753), II, 108.

[50] *Principes de la littérature. Nouvelle édition* (Paris, 1764), II, 206-8 (under Characteristic iv, chapter vi). My translation of the passage follows: If it is a question of what creates admiration, astounds one's sensibility, and exalts it, the obstacles confronting a hero must be extraordinarily difficult to surmount; they require a more than natural strength, and still the hero triumphs over them. Thus will the denouement of the epic essentially be successful and joyous. This is the outstanding quality that brings one to admiration; if it fail, it will have been more deserving of pity than of admiration. . . . In short, Satan in Milton's *Paradise Lost* triumphs over the first man. For it is he who is assuredly the hero. If he were not, and the hero was Adam, the ending would have been tragic and in no way epic: and if it were tragic, all the supernatural machinery that was used in the poem would have been useless devices, since the marvellous has no relationship with pity, and it is not created in order to excite pity. It is therefore the devil whom we are presented with to admire in *Paradise Lost*. The view is curious; but it is necessary to judge it like a painter's conception, that is, by the execution rather than by the essential point of the subject. Moreover, if it does not bring about admiration, it begets less astonishment.

[51] Channing's remarks on Johnson are interesting: 'He did not and could not

38

appreciate Milton. We doubt whether two other minds, having so little in common as those of which we are now speaking, can be found in the higher walks of literature' (*Christian Examiner and Theological Review*, iii [1826], 55).

52 Thomas Wright, ed., *The Correspondence of William Cowper Arranged in Chronological Order, with Annotations* (New York, 1904), I, 164–5.

53 '"Hints to a Young Author", By a Gentleman, Late of Eton College, Selected from a private Correspondence', *European Magazine*, xxxiv (1798), 171.

54 Mary O'Brien, *The Political Monitor: or Regent's Friend* (Dublin, 1790), pp. 49–51.

Note on the Text

The materials printed in this volume follow the original texts; any alterations are indicated in headnotes or by ellipses. Most quotations from Milton's works have been omitted, their presence in the original being shown by a bracketed reference.

Original footnotes are indicated by a star (*), dagger (†), etc.

PERIOD OF TEXTUAL AND
RELIGIOUS CRITICISM

1732–40

---

1. Bentley's emendations to *Paradise Lost*

1732

Extracts from Richard Bentley, ed., *Milton's Paradise Lost. A New Edition* (1732), *passim*.

Richard Bentley (1662–1742) was well known for his discussion of Latin and Greek dramatists, *Epistola ad Millium*, and his proof of the spuriousness of *Epistles to Philaris*. After critically revising the texts of Horace and Terence, he turned to *Paradise Lost* and set off a heated controversy on the accuracy of the text. At least one of his alterations is universally accepted ('Soul' for 'Fowle', 1667; 'Foul', 1674; VII, 451), and another ('swelling' for 'smelling' in VII, 321) continues to appear from time to time.

Preface [pp. a₁–a₄]

'Tis but common Justice, to let the Purchaser know what he is to expect in this new Edition of *Paradise Lost*.

Our celebrated Author, when he compos'd this Poem, being obnoxious to the Government, poor, friendless, and what is worst of all, blind with a *Gutta Serena*, could only dictate his Verses to be writ by another. Whence it necessarily follows, That any Errors in Spelling, Pointing, nay even in whole Words of a like or near Sound in Pronunciation, are not to be charg'd upon the Poet, but on the Amanuensis.

The Faults therefore in Orthography, Distinction by Points, and Capital Letters, all which swarm in the prior Editions, are here very carefully, and it's hop'd, judiciously corrected: though no mention is made in the Notes of that little but useful Improvement.

41

Our Poet, in thousands of Places, melts down the Vowel at the end of a Word, if the following Word begins with a Vowel. This Poetical Liberty he took from the *Greeks* and *Latins*: but he followed not the former, who strike the Vowels quite out of the Text; but the latter, who retain them in the Line, though they are absorp'd in the Speaking. . . .

In this Innovation our Poet has shewn both his Judgment and Resolution; who durst do Right against Custom, having no body to precede him, nor any yet to follow him. By this, he in some measure amended the Hollowness and Emptiness of our *English* Verses, which in Cases of Nouns, and Moods and Tenses of Verbs must cram in *of, to, from*, &c. and *have, will, may*, &c. where *Greek* and *Latin* only change the last Syllable, as *numeri, numero; legit, leget, legat*: which generally makes one *Latin* Verse æquiponderant to two *English*. . . . But then this Excellency in *Milton's* Verse brought one Inconvenience with it, That his Numbers seem embarass'd to such Readers, as know not, or not readily know, where such Elision of Vowels is to take place. To remedy which, through this whole Edition such Vowels are mark'd by an Apostrophe; as II. 1021.

> So He with difficulty' and labour hard
> Mov'd on, with difficulty' and labour He.

As also, where he gives a Tone to some Words, different from the present Use; those are mark'd here with an Accent, as *Aspéct, Obdúrate, Féalty*, &c.

These small Improvements will be found in the present Text, which challenges to be the Truest and Correctest that has yet appear'd: not ONE Word being alter'd in it; but all the Conjectures, that attempt a Restoration of the Genuine *Milton*, cast into the Margin, and explan'd in the Notes. So that every Reader has his free Choice, whether he will accept or reject what is here offer'd him; and this without the least Disgust or Discontent in the Offerer.

But more Calamities, than are yet mention'd, have happen'd to our Poem: for the Friend or Acquaintance, whoever he was, to whom *Milton* committed his Copy and the Overseeing of the Press, did so vilely execute that Trust, that *Paradise* under his Ignorance and Audaciousness may be said to be *twice lost*. A poor Bookseller, then living near *Aldersgate*, purchas'd our Author's Copy for ten Pounds, and (if a Second Edition follow'd) for five Pounds more: as appears by the original Bond, yet in being. This Bookseller, and that Acquaintance who seems to have been the sole Corrector of the Press, brought forth their First Edition, polluted with such monstrous Faults, as are beyond Example in any other printed Book. Such as among many Hundreds are these following:

Book Line.

I.	91	Into what pit *for*	To what depth
	259	Not built	No Butt
	590	Gesture	Stature
	662	Understood	Underhand
II.	352	An Oath	A Nod
	517	Alchymie	Orichalo
	683	Front	Form
	801	Vex	Hem
III.	96	Faithless	Hapless
	131	First	Fraud
	534	And his Eye	As his Eyes
	664	Favour, him	Favourite
IV.	293	Severe	Serene
	555	Ev'n	Heaven
	879	Transgressions	Transcursions
	945	Distances	Discipline
V.	172	Thy greater	Creator
	173	Eternal	Diurnal
	215	Embraces	Branches
	711	Eye	He
VI.	162	Destruction	Instruction
	332	Nectarous	Ichorous
	356	Ensigns	Onset
	513	Subtle Art	Sooty Chark
VII.	15	Thy temp'ring	Thee tempting
	160	Chang'd	Chain'd
	373	Longitude	Long Career
	451	Fowl	Soul
VIII.	158	Light	Nought
	417	In degree	Indigent
	559	Loveliest	Forehead
	591	Is judicious	Unlibidinous

IX. 5 Venial   Mensal
     318 Domestic   Pathetic
     458 Angelic   Adamic
     815 Forbidder safe   Forbidder's Eye

X. 329 Rose   Rode
     647 To the Ages   Out of Ashes
     728 Eat or drink   Act or think
     805 Dust   Just

XI. 51 Gross   Dross
     212 Fear   Film
     276 Tender   Tending
     299 Wound   Stound

XII. 53 Spirit   Speech
     177 Fill   Foul
     554 End   Extent
     601 For   Come.

But these Typographical Faults, occasion'd by the Negligence of this Acquaintance, (if all may be imputed to That, and not several wilfully made) were not the worst Blemishes brought upon our Poem. For, this suppos'd Friend, (call'd in these Notes *the Editor*) knowing *Milton*'s bad Circumstances . . . thought he had a fit Opportunity to foist into the Book several of his own Verses, without the blind Poet's Discovery. This Trick has been too frequently plaid; but especially in Works publish'd after an Author's Death. And poor *Milton* in that Condition, with Three-score Years Weight upon his Shoulders, might be reckoned more than half Dead. See Instances of such spurious Verses; which the Poet, had he known of them . . . would have thrown out with a Fork; I. 197, 251, 306, 357, 486, 575, 580, 717, 763. II. 530, 609, 635, 659, 670, 1019, 1023. III. 35, 381, 444, 535, 574, 597. IV. 250, 256, 267, 294, 323, 499, 705, 714, 983. V. 261, 269, 285, 378, 395, 415, 458, 648. VI. 574, 826. VII. 391, 463, 481, 490. VIII. 24, 575, 628. IX. 15, 77, 167, 386, 439, 504, 522, 1058. X. 16, 524, 559, 578, 731, 818, 840. XI. 8, 130, 387.

And yet a farther Misfortune befell this noble Poem, which must be laid to the Author's Charge, though he may fairly plead *Not Guilty*; and had he had his Eye-sight, he would have prevented all Complaints. There are some Inconsistences in the System and Plan of his Poem, for want of his Revisal of the Whole before its Publication. These are all first discover'd in this Edition; as I. 39, 170, 326. II. 78, 456, 969, 997,

1001, 1052. III. 556. IV. 177, 381. V. 176, 200. VI. 55. X. 601. But though the Printer's Faults are corrigible by retrieving the Poet's own Words, not from a Manuscript (for none exists) but by Sagacity, and happy Conjecture; and though the Editor's Interpolations are detected by their own Silliness and Inadvertencies cannot be redress'd without a Change both of the Words and Sense. Such Changes are here suggested, but not obtruded, to the Reader: they are generally in this Stile; *It* MAY *be adjusted thus; Among several ways of Change this* MAY *be one*. And if any Person will substitute better, he will deserve every Reader's Thanks: though, it's hoped, even These will not be found absurd, or disagreeing from the *Miltonian* Character. . . .

Upon the View of what has here been said, such Reflexions, as these following, must necessarily arise in an attentive Reader.

First, he'll be throughly convinc'd, That the Proof-sheets of the First Edition were never read to *Milton*: who, unless he was as deaf as blind, could not possibly let pass such gross and palpable Faults. Nay, the Edition, when publish'd, was never read to him in seven Years time. The First came out in 1667, and a Second in 1674; in which all the Faults of the Former are continued, with the Addition of some New ones.

If any one fancy this *Persona* of an Editor to be a mere Fantom, a Fiction, an Artifice to skreen *Milton* himself; let him consider these four and sole Changes made in the second Edition, I. 505. V. 638. XI. 485, 551. These are prov'd here in the Notes, every one of them to be manifestly for the worse. And whoever allows them to be worse, and yet will contend they are the Poet's own, betrays his Ill Judgment, as well as Ill Nature. But now if the Editor durst insert his Forgeries, even in the second Edition, when the Poem and its Author had slowly grown to a vast Reputation; what durst he not do in the First, under the Poet's Poverty, Infamy, and an universal Odium from the Royal and triumphant Party? Add to this a farther Confirmation; That when *Milton* afterwards publish'd his *Paradise Regain'd* and *Samson Agonistes*; that Edition is without Faults; because He was then in high Credit, and had chang'd his old Printer and Supervisor.

There's another Reflexion, which the Reader must needs make. What a wonderful Performance, will he say, was this *Paradise Lost*? that under all these Disadvantages could gradually arise and soar to a national Applause and Admiration? How many Thousands would depress and vilify the Poem, out of Hatred and Detestation of the Poet; who they thought deserv'd Hanging on a Gibbet? What native, unextinguishable Beauty must be impress'd and instincted through the Whole, which the

Defoedation of so many Parts by a bad Printer and a worse Editor could not hinder from shining forth? . . . But I wonder not so much at the Poem it self, though worthy of all Wonder; as that the Author could so abstract his Thoughts from his own Troubles, as to be able to make it; that confin'd in a narrow and to Him a dark Chamber, surrounded with Cares and Fears, he could spatiate at large through the Compass of the whole Universe, and through all Heaven beyond it; could survey all Periods of Time from before the Creation to the Consummation of all Things. This Theory, no doubt, was a great Solace to him in his Affliction; but it shews in him a greater Strength of Spirit, that made him capable of such a Solace. And it would almost seem to me to be peculiar to Him; had not Experience by others taught me, That there is that Power in the Human Mind, supported with Innocence and *Conscia virtus*; that can make it quite shake off all outward Uneasiness, and involve it self secure and pleas'd in its own Integrity and Entertainment.

Nor can the Reader miss another Reflexion; How it could happen, that for above 60 Years time this Poem with such miserable Deformity by the Press, and not seldom flat Nonsense, could pass upon the whole Nation for a perfect, absolute, faultless Composition: The best Pens in the Kingdom contending in its Praises, as eclipsing all modern Essays whatever; and rivaling, if not excelling, both *Homer* and *Virgil*. And it's likely, he'll resolve it into This Cause; That its Readers first accede to it, possess'd with Awe and Veneration from its universal Esteem; and have been deterr'd by That from trusting to their Judgments; and even in Places displeasing rather suspecting their own Capacity, than that any thing in the Book could possibly be amiss. Who durst oppose the universal Vogue? and risque his own Character, while he labour'd to exalt *Milton*'s? I wonder rather, that it's done even now. Had these very Notes, been written forty Years ago; it would then have been Prudence to have suppress'd them, for fear of injuring one's rising Fortune. But now when Seventy Years *jamdudum memorem monuerunt* [have long since taught what to remember], and spoke loudly in my Ears,

Mitte leves spes & certamina divitiarum;
[Discharge your false apprehension; send forth the challenges of your wealth]

I made the Notes *extempore*, and put them to the Press as soon as made; without any Apprehension of growing leaner by Censures, or plumper by Commendations.

[Notes]

I, 13

Some Acquaintance of our Poet's, entrusted with his Copy, took strange
Liberties with it, unknown to the blind Author, as will farther appear
hereafter. 'Tis very odd, that *Milton* should put *Rime* here as equivalent
to *Verse*, who had just before declar'd against *Rime*, as *no true Ornament
to good Verse, but the Invention of a barbarous Age, to set off wretched Matter
and lame Meeter*. I am persuaded, this Passage was given thus:

> Invoke thy aid to my adventrous WING,
> That with no middle flight intends to soar
> Above th' *Aonian* Mount; while I PURSUE
> Things unattempted yet in Prose or SONG

Let's examin the Particulars: WING, the properest here of all Metaphors,
which is justified and prov'd by the following Words, *Flight*, and *Soar*.
So

III, 13. Thee I revisit now with *bolder Wing*.

And IX. 45. Damp my intended *Wing*.

Nor let it be objected; that in the IX, the Wing is *intended* by the Poet,
but here the Wing it self *intends*. For that is an allow'd Figure, and
frequent in the best Writers. So II. 727.

> O Father, what *intends* thy *Hand*, she cried.

And 738 [ll. 736–8].

I, 197

These *four* Lines from the Fables I am unwilling to believe *Milton*'s. He
compares *Satan* here to a Whale, so big as to be mistaken for a Promon-
tory of Land. What need then of these fabulous Monsters, vulgar and
known to the lowest Schoolboys, which make the sentence to lag, and
the Sense to dwindle? To be in the *Den of Tarsus*, doth not make *Typhon*
the bigger: and *Briareos* Four Syllables, for *Briareus* Three, . . . cannot
be justified. . . . Lastly, to call a Whale *the Sea-beast*, what stuff is it?
I leave them therefore to the Reader, content to set a Mark upon them,
as supposing them, and more hereafter of this sort, *spurious*; and a knowing by other Passages, that our Poet, blind, and then poor and friendless,
had frequently foul Play.

II, 1023

This and the Ten Verses following, I could wish would be counted
spurious. In Book the Xth, from Verse 285 for a Hundred and more, he

describes Poetically and pompously this same *Bridge* and *Intercourse*; as a thing untouch'd before, and an Incident to surprise his Reader. Why then is it here anticipated, in a few Lines passable indeed, but dry and jejune? Let the Lines themselves be approv'd; yet it must be allow'd, it is wrong Conduct and want of Oeconomy for the Whole Poem. Besides, in this particular Place, it's a mere Parenthesis, crowded in betwixt Verses, that long to be close together: [ll. 1021-2, 1034-5]. Perhaps I shall have some Votes to accompany mine, that this too among so many others is an Interpolation.

III, 444

I wish for the Poet and Poem's sake, that the Reader could be of my Opinion, That all this long Description of the outside of the World, *the Limbo of Vanity*, was not *Milton*'s own, but an Insertion by his Editor. There's nothing either of His Spirit or Judgment seen in it: in its several Parts it abounds with Impertinencies, which shall be taken notice of in their Order: in the Whole, 'tis a silly Interruption of the Story in the very middle, which ought to have been continued. . . .

VII, 321

A mere Mistake of the Printer: The Author gave it,

> Forth crept the SWELLING Gourd.

As Propertius;

> Caeruleus Cucumis, tumidoque Cucurbita ventre.

Those that stifly maintain, that SMELLING was *Milton*'s Word, and interpret it the *Melon*, seem not to attend, that he had the Word *Smelling* two Lines before, and would not have doubled it so soon again: and that he does not name here any particular Plant, but whole Tribes and Species; the Vine, the Gourd, the Reed, the Shrub, the Bush, the Tree. *Gourds* are as numerous a Family, as most of the other; and include the *Melon* within the general Name; which though it smells, it swells likewise.

VII, 451

A most shameful Fault here, to have gone through so many Editions. The Author gave it:

> Let th' Earth bring forth SOUL living in her kind.

So the Scripture, *living Soul. Fowl* were created the Day before this.

IX, 1058

The Editor, of whom we have heard nothing for more than twenty Pages, grew quite impatient of staying longer; and seems to have thrown this Line in at mere Random:

> He cover'd, but his robe
> Uncover'd more.

What could the Man design by it? *Adam* had no *Robe* yet; and without one how could he *cover*? Nonsense outragious!

XII, 648

If I might presume, says an ingenious and celebrated writer,[1] *to offer it the Finallest Alteration in this Divine Work*. If to make one small Alteration appear'd to be so *Presumptuous*; what censure must I expect to incur, who have presum'd to make so many? . . . The Gentleman would eject these two last Lines of the Book, and close it with the Verse before. He seems to have been induc'd to this, by a Mistake of the Printer, THEY *hand in hand*; which Reading does indeed make the last Distich seem loose, unconnected, and abscinded from the rest. But the Author gave it, THEN *hand in hand*: which continues the prior Sentence,

> Some natural tears they drop'd, but wip'd them soon:
> THEN hand in hand.

Nor can these two Verses possibly be spar'd from the Work; for without them *Adam* and *Eve* would be left in the Territory and Suburbane of Paradise, in the very View of the dreadful faces. . . . They must therefore be dismiss'd out of *Eden*, to live thenceforward in some other Part of the World. And yet this Distich, as the Gentleman well judges, *falls very much below the Passage foregoing*. It contradicts the Poet's own scheme; nor is the Diction unexceptionable. He tells us before, that *Adam*, upon hearing *Michael's* Predictions, was even *surcharg'd with Joy*, v. 372; was replete *with Joy and Wonder*, 468; was in doubt, whether he should *repent of*, or *rejoice in his Fall*, 475; was *in great Peace of Thought*, 558: and *Eve* herself *not sad*, but *full of Consolation*, 620. Why then does this Distich dismiss our first Parents in Anguish, and the Reader in Melancholy? And how can the Expression be justified, *with wand'ring Steps and slow*? Why *wand'ring*? Erratic Steps? Very improper: when in the Line before, they were *guided by Providence*. And why *Slow*? when even *Eve* profess'd her Readiness and Alacrity for the Journey, 614. . . .

---

[1] Addison in *Spectator*, no. 369.

And why *Their Solitary Way*? All Words to represent a sorrowful Parting? When even their former Walks in Paradise were so solitary, as their Way now: there being no Body besides Them Two, both here and there. Shall I therefore, after so many prior Presumptions, presume at last to offer a Distich as close as may be to the Author's Words, and entirely agreeable to his Scheme?

> THEN hand in hand with SOCIAL steps their Way
> Through *Eden* took, WITH HEAV'NLY COMFORT CHEER'D.

2. Anonymous reactions to Bentley's beliefs

January, February 1732

J. T., two letters, *Grub-street Journal*, no. 108 (27 January 1732), dated 21 January 1732, and no. 113 (2 March 1732), dated 26 February 1732.

Possibly J. T. was Jacob Tonson, Milton's well-known and important publisher during the late seventeenth and early eighteenth centuries.

> *Here studious I unlucky Moderns save;*
> *Nor sleeps one error in its father's grave.*
> *Dunciad,* B. I.

To Mr. Bavius, Secretary to the Grubean Society.
Sir,
I always imagined, that MILTON made use of an Amanuensis, for no other reason but because he was blind himself. But his late learned Editor has assigned three other substantial reasons for this; namely, because he was *obnoxious to the Government, poor, and friendless*, Pref. pag. 1. These circumstances, at first sight, seem to be such as would rather oblige a man to write his own copy himself; and none, but a person of an uncommon way of thinking, could have alleged them in proof, that a Poet *dictated his verses to be writ by another.*

However, from this manner of writing them from his mouth, it is certain, that many *errors in spelling*, and *pointing*, must needs have creeped into the first copy; and highly probable, that *even in whole words of a like or near sound*, one word was sometimes written down for another. These errors, being followed and augmented by those of the Printer in the first impression, received still an additional increase in the succeeding editions. The like has happened to many other English books, in prose, as well as in verse, which have borne several editions, the last of which are generally the most incorrect; insomuch that in some of them it is necessary to have recourse to the first, as to a manuscript, to discover the true original meaning of the Author. This observation was made to the Public, not long ago, in relation to Mr. CHILLINGSWORTH's *Safe guide*, &c. and I fear it may be justly applied to many other pieces. Which incorrectness is, I believe, chiefly owing to the inadvertency, and sometimes ignorance of Printers, who frequently undertake the correction of English books themselves.

And if this be the case of the prosaical pieces, that of the poetical must necessarily be much worse; which even a learned person is not capable of correcting, unless he have likewise a taste for Poetry, and somewhat of a poetical Genius himself.—Of this our learned Editor being throughly sensible, to prepare his readers for a more candid reception of his Emendations of *Paradise Lost*, assures them, in VIRGIL's words, 'That he has verses by him of his own composing, that some Pastors call him a Poet; but that he does not believe them.'

> *Sunt & mihi carmina; me quoque dicunt*
> *Vatem pastores: sed non ego credulus illis.*

Now altho' this has been hitherto so great a secret to the world, that they never entertained the least suspicion of any such thing: yet I doubt not, but they will not only believe the two former parts of the Doctor's affirmation, but will likewise readily join with him in the last part, and not presume to differ in this point from the faith of so great a Divine.

Many of these *typographical errors* are obvious to a diligent Reader; who will not be surprized at them, if he consider the two sources above-mentioned, from which they must necessarily flow. But there are besides many other *blemishes* in this Poem, which no man ever discovered, or even suspected, till our Learned Editor took it in hand. MILTON himself was guilty of many *slips and inadvertencies*, which *cannot be red[r]essed without a change both of the words and sense. There are* likewise *some inconsistencies in the very system and plan of his Poem*. Pag. 4. To these, he declares, the *Author may fairly plead Not guilty*, because he had lost his *eye sight*; which it seems is as necessary to draw *the plan* of an Epic Poem, as of a magnificent Palace. For these *inconsistencies in the plan* are declared to have happened *for want of his revisal of the whole before its publication*. Where by the word *revisal*, is meant, not a *mental revisal*, (which the Author must necessarily have often made) but an *ocular*; it being said immediately before, that *had he had his eye-sight, he would have prevented all complaints*.

But what is worst of all, the Author's *suppos'd Friend*, the first *Editor* of this Poem, *knowing* MILTON's *bad circumstances, thought he had a fit opportunity to foist into the book several of his own verses, without the blind Poet's discovery*; which the learned Doctor has now first *detected by their silliness and unfitness*. Pag. 3, 4.—To this perhaps it may be objected, that the Editor had little temptation to this piece of infidelity; and that the danger was very great of a discovery, unless the Poet had been *as deaf as blind*. But this is fully answered by the learned Doctor in the next page, where he tells us, *That the proof-sheets of the first Edition were never read to* MILTON: *nay the Edition, when published, was never read to him in seven years time.*—And this rascally Editor, being thus incouraged by the success, had the impudence to *insert* more of *his forgeries, even in the second Edition, when the Poem and its Author had slowly grown to a vast reputation.* Pag. 5. So that he, not only in the Poets *bad circumstances*, but even in his good, *thought he had a fit opportunity to foist into his book several of his own verses*; and consequently there was no security against such a villain.

If it be asked, What proof the Doctor has brought of the truth of these two pieces of Secret History, 'That this Poem was thus interpolated,' and 'That the Author never heard it read in seven years'? As to the first, he says, *the Editor's interpolations are detected by their own silliness and unfitness*; and as to the second, *an attentive Reader will be throughly convinc'd of it.* The latter of which he corroborates by *a farther confirmation; That when* MILTON *afterwards publish'd his Paradise Regain'd, and Samson Agonistes: that edition is without faults; because he was then in high credit, and has chang'd his old Printer and Supervisor.* Thus this blind Author, who, when the first edition of his *Paradise Lost* was printed, having *threescore years weight upon his shoulders, might be reckoned more than half dead*, could not prevent the errors of that edition; nor being *grown to vast reputation seven years* afterwards, could not prevent the propagation of those errors in the second; being at last got in to *high credit*, and grown older, revived on a sudden, *chang'd his old Printer and Supervisor*, and *published* his Paradise Regain'd *in an edition without faults*. This account may seem strange to vulgar apprehensions: but every thing is wonderful, which relates to this wonderful man—Thus much for this learned *Preface*, the foundation of all the succeeding criticisms: and if I see this letter in your next Journal, it is probable I may send you some instances of the *sagacity and happy conjecture* of this Great Critic, in his alterations of the first Book.

I am, Sir, your most humble servant,

Jan. 21, 1732. J. T.

> —*Many monstrous Forms in sleep we see;*
> *That never were, nor are, nor e'er can be.*

Sir,

Since I wrote the Letter concerning Dr. B's *Preface* to his *Paradise Lost*, published in your 108th *Journal*, I have met with several observations of others, and made some more myself upon that *Preface*.—At the beginning of my letter I took notice, that besides MILTON's *blindness*, the Doctor had assigned three other reasons why he made use of an Amanuensis, which could proceed only from an uncommon way of thinking, viz. because he was *obnoxious to the Government, poor*, and *friendless*: all which circumstances I find since directly contradicted.* To the first it has been answered, That after the Act of oblivion, having obtained a full protection from the Government, he appeared as much in Public, as formerly. To the second, That tho' whilst he was Latin Secretary to the Parliament, and the two Protectors successively, he did not amass a very large fortune, which he had so good opportunities of doing; yet no one, who pretends to give any account of his life, says, that he was poor or indigent. To the third, That his friends procured him a pardon, and a full protection from the Government, and a License for the printing of the first edition of his *Paradise Lost*. All which seems to amount to a full disproof of his *bad circumstances*; and to shew, that he was neither *obnoxious to the Government*, nor *poor*, nor *friendless*.

As a confirmation, I suppose, of the badness of MILTON's circumstances, the Dr. tells us, p. 3. That a *poor Bookseller, living near Aldersgate, purchas'd the Copy for ten pounds, and (if a second edition follow'd) for five pounds more.*—†In answer to this, it has been affirmed, that this *poor Bookseller* was Mr. SIMMONS, a Citizen of London, and Common Council-man, who died worth some thousands.

From the many supposed errors in the first edition of this Poem, the Doctor assures us, p. 5, that *an attentive Reader will be thoroughly con-*

---

* *Milton Restor'd. Pref.*
† *Ibid.*

vinc'd, That the proof-sheets were never read to MILTON. Which, tho' a thing very strange and improbable, is immediately followed by a positive assertion, which is much stranger, and even incredible: *Nay, the edition, when publish'd, was never read to him in seven years time.* In proof of which he adds, *The first came out in 1667, and a second in 1674; in which all the faults of the former are continued, with the addition of some new ones.*—But this I find contradicted by a person of a great authority, the Doctor himself; who in his note upon B. xi. 485, has these words, MILTON *made but two additions,* (in the second edition) *both proper and genuine;* (certainly *genuine* if made by him) *three verses in the beginning of the* viii *Book, when he divided one Book into two; and five in the beginning of the* xii, *when he divided another Book into two. The first edition comprised all in ten Books.* Let any one judge, whether MILTON could make these alterations and additions, without hearing the Poem *read to him;* and whether is more probable, that it was *read* in the manuscript copy, or in the printed edition.

To prove that this Poem was corrupted and interpolated by the Editor, the Doctor in the same page of his *Preface* brings an argument, by way of *confirmation,* which very much invalidates both this, and the preceding assertions. For, having asked, *If the Editor durst insert his forgeries even in the second edition, when the Poem and its Author had slowly grown to a vast reputation; what durst he not do in the first, under the Poets poverty, infamy, &c.* He subjoins, *Add to this a farther confirmation; That when* MILTON *afterwards publish'd his Paradise Regain'd and Samson Agonistes, that edition is without faults; because he was then in high credit, and had changed his old Printer and Supervisor.*—In which sentence, the word *afterwards* plainly referring to the *second edition* of *Paradise Lost,* mentioned in the sentence foregoing, we are informed, that the first *edition* of *Paradise Regain'd,* &c. is *without faults,* because MILTON *was then in high credit, and had changed his old Printer and Supervisor,* who *printed* and *supervised* both the first and second edition of his *Paradise Lost.* According to this account, the first edition of *Paradise Regain'd* must come out some time in 1674, the year in which, as the Doctor tells us above, the second edition of *Paradise Lost* was published: for the Author died in that very year. Now, supposing this account to be true (which it is not) the distance of time between the publications of the second edition of one, and the first of the other Poem, a distance perhaps of a few months, is too inconsiderable, for any great advancement of the Author's *credit* and reputation, and the change, supposed consequent thereupon, of his *old Printer and Supervisor.*—Nor will it be of any advantage to the Doctor's argument, to give this sentence a forced construction, by supposing he knew that the first edition of *Paradise Regain'd* was published in 1671, and consequently that he designed the word *afterwards* should referr to the first edition of *Paradise Lost*, which appeared, according to his account, four years before, in 1667. For if MILTON *was in high credit, and had changed his old Printer and Supervisor* in 1671; would he not three years afterwards, in 1674, when his *credit* must needs have risen still *higher*, have employed his new *Printer*, or at least his new *Supervisor*, in publishing the second edition of *Paradise Lost*? Is it at all probable, that he should take so much care of his *Paradise Regain'd* and *Samson Agonistes*, (two Poems inconsiderable in comparison of the other) as to send those abroad into the world, the very first time, *without faults*; and should so entirely neglect this grand Work, which had gotten him such *a vast reputation*, as to send it forth a second time, *polluted with* more than all the *monstrous faults* of the first impression? So that let us take this which way we will, and suppose that the first edition of *Paradise Regain'd* came out either in 1671, or in 1674; either before, or after the second edition of *Paradise Lost*; this is so far from proving the *insertion of forgeries* by the *Editor* in this second edition, that it makes such an *insertion* still much more improbable, and almost impossible.

The real truth of the matter is this: The first edition of *Paradise Lost* was published, not in 1667, as the Doctor affirms, but in 1669; the first of *Paradise Regain'd* in 1671; and the second of *Paradise Lost* in 1674. Which makes it very surprising, and even astonishing, that the Doctor should pretend to draw arguments from the different times of the publication of these editions, and yet not know when two of them were published.

I am, Sir, your most humble servant,

Feb. 26, 1732.   J. T.

3. Anonymous criticism of Bentley

March 1732

A. Z., letter, *Grub-street Journal*, no. 113 (2 March 1732), to which are added notes by an editor (Richard Russell or John Martyn).

Sir,

I have not as yet read any *Remarks on Dr.* BENTLEY's *Milton*, except the few that have been published in your *Journal*. I indeed am engaged in making some myself, and therefore avoid being led into other mens notions.* If I find any willingness in you to receive my Letters, I may, perhaps, at my leisure, send you my thoughts concerning that extraordinary performance. As I perceive a great part of it to be founded on the supposal of an Editor, who altered, added to, and corrupted MIL-TON's text, I shall at present set myself to overturn that main pillar of the Doctor's structure.

This Critic, to prove the reality of his imagination, relies chiefly on the following argument, thus expressed in his *Preface. P.* 5. *If any one fancy this* persona *of an Editor to be a meer fantom, a fiction, an artifice to skreen* MILTON *himself; let him consider these four and sole changes made in the second Edition.* I. 505. V. 638. XI. 485, 551. *These are proved here in the Notes, every one of them to be manifestly for the worse. And whoever allows them to be worse, and yet will contend, they are the Poet's own, betrays his ill judgment, as well as ill nature.*

I own myself one of them that take this Editor to be *a fantom, a fiction, an artifice*; and am willing to be determin'd by these passages, which the Doctor appeals to. But why are these called the *sole changes made in the second Edition*, when the Doctor confesses in his notes, P. 364. that MILTON made two additions, three verses in 'the beginning of B. VIII. and five in the beginning of B. XII?' He cannot distinguish between *additions* and *changes*: for most of these *changes* imputed to the Editor, are only *additions*. But let us turn to them in order.

---

* Tho' this ingenious Gentleman is unwilling to be *led into other men's notions*, yet, after he has written his own, I wish he would compare them with those of others. By this means, if he have insisted upon the same things too largely, he may contract his Reflections; if too briefly and obscurely, he may inlarge and illuminate them.

B. I. 504. MILTON, speaking of the nightly insolence of the *sons of Belial*, says,

> Witness the streets of Sodom; and that night
> In Gibeah, when hospitable doors
> Yielded their Matrons to avoid worse rape.

This was afterwards alter'd (either by MILTON or his Editor) to

> —*when* the *hospitable* door
> Expos'd a Matron, *to avoid worse rape.*

Dr. B. affirms *the first Edition* to be most *agreeable to the Scriptures. Gen.* xix. LOT, to save the two Angels from the outrage of the men of Sodom, *offers* them his two daughters, but did not *yield* them; for they were not accepted. Neither were they *Matrons,* but *Virgins* (which this Editor opposes to each other in his note on B. IV. 501.) *Judges* xix. An *Ephraimite* sojourning in *Gibeah,* entertain'd in his house a Levite, with his Concubine or Wife (for the text calls him her *Husband*) who were distress'd for lodging; but at night certain sons of Belial beset the house, and demanded the man, with the same vile intent, as the men of Sodom before-mention'd. To save him, the master of the house *offers* them his own daughter (not a *Matron,* but a *Virgin*) and the stranger's *Wife* or *Concubine.* It is not mentioned, that the Maiden was *given up* to them, tho' *offered*; but only the *Concubine,* whom they barbarously abused. So that in Sodom two *Virgins* (no *Matron*) were *offered* only, not *yielded*; in Gibeah two were *offered,* a *Virgin* and a *Matron,* but only the *Matron* said to be *yielded.*★ I think no one can doubt, which of the editions is most agreeable to *Scripture*; neither can it be doubted but that MILTON alter'd the passage, to make it more *agreeable to Scripture.* Besides, the *doors yielding* THEIR *Matrons,* implies, that the *Matrons* belonged to the house; whereas the *Matron* exposed in *Gibeah* was the stranger's wife; therefore MILTON, in his second edition, corrected this oversight also. Yet Dr. *B.* wonderfully asserts, that *two Matrons were yielded and offer'd in each place.*—He adds another feeble objection to the reading in the second edition, that *the streets of Sodom are called on to witness nothing at all.* Yes, they are called on to *witness* to the *insolence* and drunkenness of *the sons of Belial,* mentioned but just before: but there is no necessity for the Poet to specify their particular actions in *Sodom,* tho' he might the more re-markable one in *Gibeah.*

★ The Author of the *Review of the Text of Milton's,* &c. p. 35. justly observes, that 'Yielded was here changed, by M. into *Expos'd*; because the Levite's wife was not only *yielded,* but put out of doors, and *expos'd* to the men's lewdness'.

Next let us consider B. V. 637. where, describing the repast of the Angels, MILTON (or rather RAPHAEL) said in the first edition:

> They eat, they drink, and with refection sweet
> Are fill'd, before th' all-bounteous King.—

It is probable the Author, upon farther consideration, might judge this to be a more proper description of an human feast, than of an angelic banquet in the presence of God, and for this reason might afterwards change it thus:

> On flours repos'd, and with fresh flourets crown'd,
> *They eat, they drink, and* in communion *sweet*
> Quaff Immortality and Joy, secure
> Of surfeit, where full measure only bounds
> Excess, *before th' all bounteous King.*—

It would be no wonder if the description of an angelic repast could not stand the test of a cool philosophical examination: but let us hear this Editor's objections. He has nothing to say against the first of these verses, and therefore may fancy himself very cunning in giving it us, as tho' it were in the first edition. Nor does *communion* instead of *refection* offend him: but concerning *Quaff Immortality and Joy*, he asks, *Whether the liquors here, that the Angels quaff, produced their Immortality?* and whether *they were not possessed of it before?* To these idle questions I answer, that (tho' according to MILTON, Angels require food) the word *Quaff* is here used in a metaphorical sense which is easier to be comprehended, than expressed. In *communion sweet* they are transported with the possession of *immortality and joy:* which may signify immortal joys, according to the Scripture idiom, which MILTON lov'd to imitate.—But *secure of surfeit* may, without any violence or contrariety to MILTON's manner, be referr'd to *they eat, they drink:* tho' they have *piles of food* (says *Raphael*) *flowing nectar, fruit of delicious vines,* they are *secure of surfeit, where* plenty and *full measure* do not lead to, (as with mankind) but *only bound Excess;* prevent it, stop its approach. This is intelligible enough: and as to the questions concerning MILTON's *theory of Angels,* they are already answer'd by MILTON in this Book; That Angels have the lower faculties of man, and require food, v. 407, &c. that they eat heartily, v. 436; and that they *suffice nature with meats, and drinks, but do not burden it,* v. 451. As for the propriety of his theory, let MILTON himself be answerable for it; and let the Doctor raise a cloud of dust about it: I am contented to have proved this passage in dispute to be agreeable to it, and not unworthy of MILTON.

The next passage to be considered is, B. XI. 485. MICHAEL tells ADAM, a little before, that he will shew him *a monstrous crew of dire diseases*, v. 474. and the Author says *immediately a lazar house appear'd to him, wherein were laid numbers of all diseas'd*; which he then proceeds to reckon up, and names *eleven sorts*, says this Editor; perhaps there are more. However, MILTON forgot among these to reckon up any of the kinds of *madness, consumption,* or *plague,* and therefore in his second edition bestows these three verses on them:

> Daemoniac phrensy, moping melancholy,
> And moon struck madness, pining atrophy,
> Marasmus, and wide-wasting pestilence.

Good lines, which even this Critic can find no fault with but only with the place of them: MILTON, says he, *had named eleven sorts; enow for a Poem, if not too many.* I answer, that *seventeen* sorts, if well express'd, are not at all too many, when we are prepar'd to expect a *monstrous crew, and numbers of all diseas'd*: and these last inserted are of as great consequence as any. Indeed, considering the year when this Poem came out, 1669, it seems strange that the Author should on this occasion omit to mention the plague, the terrible effects of which he must have been a witness of. But it is not unlikely, that this work might be finished before the plague, and its publication prevented by the confusion in the following years. If this was the case, 'tis no wonder this omission was supplied in the second edition. But still the Dr. says, he should not have brought in *phrensy, and melancholy, and lunatic madness, for shapes of death*; because they *are exempt from pain and sickness, and often attended with long life.* This Gentleman, 'tis to be hoped, is free from *madness* himself; else he would have known it to be attended with sever *pain*, either in the fits or intervals, as *melancholy*, I believe always is with *sickness*. But there is no need, that these should be brought in for *shapes of death*, but for *diseases* produced *by intemperance*, as this Editor must have seen at v. 472. But what he said was thought more to his purpose; tho' even in that he was mistaken: for tho' they are often attended with *long life*, do they not *kill* at last? and are not *heart-sick qualms, stone, asthmas*, and other diseases here mention'd, often attended with *long life*? nay, does not MILTON himself, to aggravate those evils, say the same, v. 491?

> —Over them triumphant death his dart
> Shook; but delay'd to strike, tho' oft invok'd
> With vows, as their chief good, and final hope.

We have now but one passage to examine, and that will not create us much trouble. ADAM, speaking of the *combrous charge* of life, says, B. XI. 550.

> Which I must keep 'till my appointed day
> Of rendring up.

To which, in the second edition, is added,

> —and patiently attend
> My dissolution.

This Critic is forc'd to confess, that it is *a very good sentence*, and he finds no fault with the expression; but condemns it, as not *suiting the context*, and *contradicting* what ADAM said before. I allow, that what ADAM said before *shews rather some impatience to be rid of the combrous charge of life*: and this latter part of his speech shews the same thing, not contradicting his former *impatience*, but declaring, with some regret, what is his duty; not saying what he desires to do, but what he *must*. Tho' I am tir'd of life, and would chuse to resign it, yet, says he, *I must keep it 'till my appointed day*: to which he now adds another part of his duty; I must not only barely abstain from self-murder, but must, moreover, *patiently attend my dissolution*. Very good sense, beautiful expression, sound divinity, and properly inserted. ADAM gives much the same instructions to EVE, upon her proposal of killing themselves, B. X. 1016. and the following verses.*

But the *Dr*'s main objection against this addition is, that it *gives* MICHAEL *three syllables, which the Author had here and elsewhere pronounc'd with two only*. It may be worth while to give a full answer to this, not to justify this passage (which does not now require it,) but to expose the trifling cavils of this Critic in several other places. The truth of the matter is this: MILTON (whether out of negligence, or design to vary his numbers, I will not determine) makes URIEL, GABRIEL, MICHAEL, RAPHAEL, and such words, sometimes two syllables, and sometimes three. The learned *Dr.* possessed with the spirit of alteration, when he meets these words with three syllables, by some change or other contracts them into two, for this wise reason, because MILTON

---

* A Gentleman at Oxford, who sent us a letter dated Feb. 13. and subscribed R. S. defends this passage, by giving the same explication of it, more at large, and subjoins the same observation about MICHAEL, RAPHAEL, &c. The Author of the *Review of the Text of Milton's*, &c. p. 56. observes, that FAIRFAX, in the Argument of B. IX. of his *Tasso*, and elsewhere, makes MICHAEL three syllables. I find it likewise of two in Stanz. 58 of that Book.

always gives them in two. See note on B. XI. 466. A mighty ingenious proof this: I find these words in a dozen places to consist of three syllables, and reduce them to two, because MILTON *always* does! At B. II. 294. the Editor was not grown to so much boldness: MICHAEL is there first mentioned, and is given with three syllables: he alters it, but says only *our Author generally pronounces* MICHAEL, RAPHAEL, &c. *with two syllables*; tho' afterwards he takes courage, and says *always* instead of *generally.* In B. XI. 235. RAPHAEL has three syllables in all former editions: but the *Doctor,* to make it two, inserts *as,* which makes *nonsense; and that the nonsense may not be imputed to him, very honestly says nothing of the change he has made, nor does he print it in a different character from the text. Yet still, with all his *sagacity,* he has overlook'd some of these sad faults. B. III. 648. URIEL is left untouch'd with three syllables, tho' it has but two six lines afterwards. ITHURIEL is (I think) mention'd but thrice in the whole Poem. B. IV. 788, and 868, it has four syllables; and 810, but three. I have, upon this occasion, taken the trouble to look over the whole Poem; and tho' it is but a dull conclusion of a letter, will present you with an index of the places, where these words are used with a different number of syllables, from what this Editor affirms them to be always used with.

MICHAEL, 3 syllables. B. II. 294. VI. 202, 411. XI. 466, 552. XII. 466.

GABRIEL, 3 syllables. IV. 865.

URIEL, 3 syllables. III. 648. VI. 363.

RAPHAEL, 3 syllables. V. 561. VI. 363. VII. 40. VII. 40. XI. 235.

ITHURIEL, 4 syllables. IV. 788, 868.

---

* Mr. R. S. gives a like instance in B. IV. 865.

To whom their Chief
Gabriel from the front thus call'd aloud.

On which the Doctor makes this note: *A word is dropp'd here out of his verse: for* GABRIEL *is but of two syllables: I believe he gave it,*

Gabriel from *th' other* Front thus call'd aloud.

He speaks to UZZIEL *and his Party, that had wheel'd southward.* v. 782.

But GABRIEL and UZZIEL were now met, and had now joined their two parties, in the *western Point,* as appears from the verses immediately preceding, which speak of ITHURIEL and ZEPHON leading Satan whom they had seized.

Now drew they nigh
The western Point, where those half rounding guards
Just met, and *closing* stood in *squadron join'd*
Awaiting next command.

So that, as the Author of the *Review,* &c. says p. 145. '*The Front* was the Front of the whole Band of Angels.'

I hope, Sir, you will publish this, that it may be seen on what foundation Dr. BENTLEY's grand scheme of an *ignorant, pragmatical, corrupting
Editor*, is raised. I am your humble servant.

A. Z.

4. Richardson Jr on an emendation for *Paradise Lost*

November 1732

Jonathan Richardson Jr, letter to Pope (November 1732), from
The Works of Alexander Pope, ed. Whitwell Elwin and William J.
Courthope (1886), ix, 499–500.

Jonathan Richardson the younger (1694–1771) was the son of the
painter (see No. 8). His own essays into portraiture and independent literary activities were not distinguished.

I was heartily vexed when I came home and found I had lost an opportunity of your company, but have since seen your observations on the
notes with great pleasure, only we beg of you to let us know (if you
recollect) some instances of an epithet that expresses any sort of smell for
the gourd or cucumis among the ancients, which may very well be, but
I can find none either in the gradus, or dictionaries, or indexes, and
because that would be a main proof for the present reading,[1] though
there are indeed some reasons for changing *smelling* to *swelling* (however scrupulous one should certainly be in such alterations), and however lawful and usual it is for a poet to derive epithets from any natural
quality; in the first place the word was used but two lines before, and
that in general, so that giving immediately after this particular instances,
seems a little remiss. But then what is abundantly more considerable is
that Milton has particularised all the productions that go in the same

[1] *PL* VII, 321.

period with this by circumstances that offer themselves to the *sight*. He has given the pictures of them, but specified no one natural quality. Forth flourished—clustering—crept—smelling—upstood—embattled, &c. *Humi repit—jacent crescunt* (Plin. xix. 45). My father gives his humble service to you, and I am your most obliged humble servant.

5. Meadowcourt on *Paradise Regain'd*

1732

Extract from [Richard Meadowcourt], *A Critique on Milton's Paradise Regain'd* (1732), 1-3, 15, 28-30.

Richard Meadowcourt (1695–1760), a minister and writer on a variety of subjects, produced the first full-length critical study devoted to one of Milton's works (aside from Addison's notes on *Paradise Lost*). The work appeared in 1732 and again, amplified, in 1748, under the title *A Critical Dissertation on Milton's Paradise Regain'd*. It employs much quotation from the poem, which it integrates usually through brief introductory comments. Some additional notes by Meadowcourt are incorporated into Newton's editions of the poetical works (1749–52).

The principal End of Poetry is Instruction. All the Powers and Charms which are given it to produce Delight, are given only as Means subservient to this End. Whatever is most pleasing is most instructive, as it's most effectual in engaging the Attention, and in stamping lively and lasting Impressions on the Mind. Hence, the secondary Aim of Poets has always been to please, in order to instruct with great Success: Hence have they invented Harmony in Sounds, and different Measures of Verse: From hence sprung Figures and Tropes, and all the Ornaments of Language: From hence the whole Art of Poetry derives its Birth.

The Poet who neglects the Instruction of his Readers; he whose Writings import only Pleasure, and not Profit to their Minds; he who warms the Imagination without enlightening the Understanding, is no more than an Under-Actor in his Profession; he performs but half a Poet's Part, and merits but half his Praise.

The Sister-Arts of Poetry and Painting agree in this, as in other respects, that their highest Excellence and Perfection are alike derived from their attaining the End which they alike pursue. The Picture that strikes the Fancy without touching the Heart, and excites Pleasure without raising any moral Sentiment, is far less valuable than the Piece that equally succeeds in both these Attainments. . . .

The foregoing Reflections were occasion'd by an *English* Poem, which tho' far from being generally read, deserves a general Reading, better than any Poem either antient or modern. A Performance that abounds with such instructive Doctrines, and with Sentiments of Morality so just, so useful, and so refined, the World has not yet receiv'd. And yet the World has receiv'd it with much Ingratitude, with much Neglect. The Reader will be supriz'd at hearing the Name of *Milton's Paradise Regain'd*. It labours under so much Discredit, that some Persons question whether it belongs to the Author whose Name it bears. It's a common Tradition, that *Milton* always spoke of it as his favourite Work, and preferr'd it to his *Paradise Lost*. Few Persons besides have judg'd so rightly of it. His other Poem perhaps exceeds it in Fruitfulness of Fancy, in Variety and Compass of Invention, and in Ornaments of Stile. The Verse of *Paradise Regain'd* is more artless, and is less embellish'd with Flights of Imagination, and with Figures of Speech. But it supplies a much richer Fund of intellectual Pleasure; it conveys the most important Truths to the Understanding; it inspires the most large and liberal Notions, and every where dissipates vulgar Prejudices and popular Mistakes.

Nor are fine Descriptions and beautiful Images wanting to entertain his Reader, and to add Life and Lustre to his Subject. But he is sparing of these, as being less conducive to his main Design, which was to give a right Direction to the Thoughts and Actions of Men.

The Subject of the Poem is the Temptation of the Son of God in the Wilderness, and his Victory over the Devil. The Characters both of the one and the other are as finely drawn, and are as suitable to the Persons as can possibly be conceiv'd. The one contrives the most artful Snares and most powerful Temptations, which the other eludes and defeats with consummate Prudence, with the greatest Strength of Reason, and with a Spirit that's truly heroical, and becoming a Person of Divine Extraction.

. . . *Milton* has been seen delivering his Thoughts on Wealth and Power [in Book II] in a perfectly right and true Way in the foregoing Chapter. He continues in the same way of thinking in the third Book, in which the Devil persists in tempting the Son of God to signalize himself in Arms for the sake of Glory and Fame. There are few Writers on these delicate Subjects who are not found to speak more conformably to vulgar Prejudices than to Reason and Truth. But every thing that *Milton* utters, is accompanied with strong Sense, with clear Light, with resistless Charms. His Doctrines in these Points, in which Mankind are generally deceiv'd, are more just, more rational, and more instructive, than those which any Philosopher before him has taught either in Prose or Verse. What Misery and Desolation! what Havock and Bloodshed! what Disorder and Confusion in human Affairs, have been owing to wrong Notions of Glory and Fame; to Notions which are quite the Reverse of what *Paradise Regain'd* conveys in these excellent Lines! [III, 47–59].

. . . That the Writer of the foregoing Observations may not seem partial to *Milton*, he thinks himself oblig'd, having recounted the Excellencies of *Paradise Regain'd*, to confess that this invaluable Poem is not without Defects, and that some slight Blemishes may be here and there discern'd, . . .

In the first Book the Poet detains his Reader with a long, and low, and unpleasing Soliloquy of *Jesus*, made up of several Circumstances which are before related, and are partly repeated over again in a Soliloquy of the Virgin *Mary* in the second Book. In other Parts of his Poem he affects to borrow his Similitudes and Allusions from Romance and Fable, thereby mixing up suppos'd Realities with acknowledg'd Fictions; disfiguring and deforming his Subject with unsuitable Images; sinking where he is to rise; lessening what he should augment; and overlaying thick Shade where he ought to throw on the strongest Light. There's an Instance of this in the third Book, where the Devil having given our Saviour a noble View of the *Parthian* Army marching out to Battel, the Poet adds, [III, 337–43].

The Reader has here the whole of the Remarks intended to be made on *Paradise Regain'd*. If the Remarker has open'd a new Field of Pleasure to his Countrymen, or discover'd hidden Stores of Instruction and Entertainment, he succeeds in his Aim of presenting the Fruits of a little Leisure to the Publick: He shall then think that he has not misemployed his Thoughts or his Time. Tho' he is not conceited of his own Judgment, yet he wishes, in respect to what he has said of this neglected Poem, with which he confesses himself delighted, that the Readers may concur with him in the same Opinion, as he wishes they may share with him in the same Delight.

6. Theobald on Bentley

1732

Extract from Lewis Theobald, *The Works of Shakespeare* (1732), 'The Preface', xxxix–xl.

Antagonist of Alexander Pope for his edition of Shakespeare, Lewis Theobald (1688–1744) restored many readings and supplied significant emendations. 'The Preface', in sections omitted here, also alleges Milton's debt to Shakespeare in 'L'Allegro' and 'Il Penseroso' and comments upon Milton's supposed Latinity.

For the late Edition of *Milton* by the Learned Dr. *Bentley* is, in the main, a Performance of another Species. It is plain, it is the Intention of that Great Man rather to correct and pare off the Excrescencies of the *Paradise Lost*, in the Manner that *Tucca* and *Varius* were employ'd to criticize the *Æneis* of *Virgil*, than to restore corrupted Passages. Hence, therefore, may be seen either the Iniquity or Ignorance of his Censurers, who, from some Expressions, would make us believe, the *Doctor* every where gives us his Corrections as the Original Text of the Author; whereas the chief Turn of his Criticism is plainly to shew the World, that if *Milton* did not write as He would have him, he ought to have wrote so.

7. Pearce on Bentley's emendations

1732–3

Extract from Zachary Pearce, *A Review of the Text of the Twelve Books of Milton's* Paradise Lost (1733), v–vi, 4–7, 27–8, 66–7, 81–2, 117–18, 128, 149, 180–2, 207–8, 211–12, 245–7, 252–4, 256–9, 298–9, 385–9.

As Bishop of Rochester, Zachary Pearce (1690–1774) appears in religious histories of the eighteenth century and its controversies. But though he contributed to various magazines and was a classical scholar, he is known by literary students today for his rebuttal of Bentley, here reprinted in excerpt.

He [Pearce] cannot agree with the Doctor [Bentley] that there was any such *Person of an Editor*, as made Alterations and added Verses at his Pleasure in the first Edition of this Poem: because the Account, which Mr. *Toland* gives us of *Milton's* Life, will not leave us room to suspect that he wanted One, or indeed many Learned Friends to have done him Justice on this occasion: most probably Several of his Acquaintance, we are sure that Some of them, had had the perusal of the Poem before it was publish'd; and would none of them have discover'd it to *Milton* if he had receiv'd such an Injury? Would none have warn'd him of the bold Alterations, time enough at least to have prevented their being continued in the second Edition, publish'd likewise in the Poet's Lifetime? Besides, the first Edition of *Paradise Regain'd* appear'd in 1671. and Dr. *B.* says that this Edition is *without Faults, because M. was then in high Credit, and had chang'd his old Printer and Supervisor.* How far this changing his Printer might contribute to make the first Edition of this Poem more correct than the first Edition of *Paradise Lost*, we cannot certainly say: but it may be ask'd of the Doctor, why *M*'s still higher Credit in 1674, (when the second Edition of *Paradise Lost* appear'd) could not have procur'd him the same Supervisor, or one at least as Good? . . .

[Book I]

Ver. 16.

while IT PURSUES
Things unattempted yet in Prose or RHIME.

Instead of this Dr. *B*. would have us read,

while I PURSUE
Things unattempted yet in Prose or SONG.

But the alteration of the first Verse is needless, since a *Song* may as well be said to *pursue things*, as it is said in *Parad. Reg*. I. 11. (before quoted) to *tell of Deeds*. But the Doctor's chief O[b]jection is to the Word *Rhime* which he changes to *Song* in this passage: he says, that it is odd, that *M*. should put *Rime* here as equivalent to *Verse*, who had just before (*i.e.* in the Preface) declar'd against *Rime*, as *no true Ornament to good Verse*, &c. But if the Doctor had consider'd the matter better, he might have observ'd that *M*. appears to have meant a different thing by *Rhime* here, from *Rime* in his Preface, where it is six times mention'd, and always spell'd without an *h*; whereas in all the Editions, till Dr. *B*'s appear'd, *Rhime* in this place of the Poem was spell'd with an *h*. *Milton* probably meant a difference in the Thing, by making so constant a difference in the spelling; and intended that we should here understand by *Rhime* not the *jingling sound of like Endings*, but Verse in general; the word being deriv'd from rythmus . . .: Thus *Spenser* uses the word *Rhime* for *Verse*, in his Verses to Lord *Buckhurst*, plac'd before his *Fairy Queen*; and in Book I. Cant. VI. 13. of that Poem. And so our Poet uses the word in his Verses upon 'Lycidas'.

he knew
Himself to sing, and build the lofty RHIME.

Where the Epithet *lofty* shews, that he could not mean *Rime*, or what Dr. *B*. understands by *Rhime*, for there cannot be any *loftiness* in That. Dr. *B*. is well aware that *Ariosto* had said,

Cosa, non detta in Prosa *mai, ne in* Rima,

which is word for word the same with what *Milton* says here; and therefore, lest this should be objected against the Dr's Alteration, he says that *Ariosto*'s Poem is in *Rime*: True, but could *Ariosto* mean that? if he had, how would *Rima* in this sense have been a full opposition to *Prosa*? for then (to argue as Dr. *B*. does) *Ariosto*'s Subject might have been *detta*, handled by any *Greek*, *Latin*, *Italian*, or other Poet, who had not us'd *Rime*.

Ver. 28.

Nor the deep TRACT *of Hell.*

Dr. *B.* would have it *Gulph*, because he says that *tract* is a plane expanded Surface, expos'd to view. But Servius on Virgil's *Georg.* II. 182. explains *tractus* by *plaga, regio*, a *climate* or *region*, both which names our Poet gives to Hell in *v.* 242. And therefore the sense seems to be; Nor can the Region or Climate of Hell, tho' it lies so *deep*, hide any thing from the Muse's Eyes. Equivalent to *deep tract*, is that expression in *v.* 177. *vast and boundless deep.*

Ver. 35.

deceiv'd
THE *Mother of Mankind.*

Dr. *B.* prefers THEE, *Mother*, &c. and says that This will raise the Sense. But neither *Homer* nor *Virgil*, nor *Tasso* nor *Ariosto* (our Author's chief Models) in the entrance of his Poem, addresses himself immediately to any of the Persons, who make a Part of the Poem: and therefore I cannot think that *M.* would attempt such a thing, which is without Precedent, and *raises the Sense* in a place where it ought not to be rais'd, if we may judge from the Practice of the best Poets. . . .

Ver. 306.

Hath vex'd the Red-Sea COAST

Dr. B reads, *the Red-Sea* GULPH, for (he says) it is commonly call'd, now and then too, the *Arabian Gulph*: but it is not call'd the *Arabian Sea Gulph*: either *Sea* or *Gulph* is superfluous in the Dr's reading, and the *Arabian Gulph* will only justify the calling it the *Red Gulph*, not the *Red-Sea Gulph*. Dr. *B.* takes *Coast* here to signify *litus*, and therefore asks how, if the *Coast* only were vex'd, Sedge could be set afloat in the Water? But by *Coast M.* may have meant that part of the *Red-Sea* which was nearest to the Coast; and where it is probable that the Sedge in a storm lay the thickest on the Water.

Ibid.

whose Waves o'erthrew
Busiris and his Memphian Chivalrie.

Dr. *B.* throws out 6 Lines here, as the Editor's, not *M*'s: His chief Reason is, That that single Event of Moses's passing the Red-Sea has no relation to a constant quality of it, that in stormy Weather it is strow'd with

Sedge. But it is very usual with Homer and Virgil (and therefore may be allow'd to *M.*) in a Comparison, after they have shew'd the Re-semblance, to go off from the main purpose and finish with some other Image, which was occasion'd by the Comparison, but is it self very different from it. *M.* has done thus in almost all his Similitudes, and therefore what He does so frequently, cannot be allow'd to be an Objection to the genuin[en]ess of This passage before us. See particularly III. 438, 439. and see more of this in my Note on II. 635. As to *M's* making *Pharaoh* to be *Busiris* (which is another of the Dr's Objections to the Passage), there is Authority enough for to justify a Poet in doing so, tho' not an Historian: It has been suppos'd by some, and therefore *M.* might follow that Opinion. *Chivalry* for *Cavalry*, and *Cavalry* (says Dr. *B.*) for *Chariotry*, is twice wrong. But it is rather, twice Right: for *Chivalry* (from the French *Chevalerie*) signifys not only *Knighthood*, but those who use Horses in Fight, both such as ride on Horses and such as ride in Chariots drawn by them: In the Sense of riding and fighting on Horseback this Word *Chivalry* is us'd v. 765. and in many places of Fairfax's Tasso, as in V. 9. VIII. 67. XX. 61. In the Sense of riding and fighting in Chariots drawn by Horses, *M.* uses the word *Chivalry* in *Parad. Reg.* III. v. 343. compar'd with v. 328. . . .

[Book II]
Ver. 635.

towering high,
As when far off at sea &c.

To This and several Verses which follow, Dr. *B.* has many Objections. Why a *Fleet* (says he) when a First-rate Man of War would do? Because a *Fleet* gives a nobler Image than a single ship. He asks, To whom does Satan appear *far off*, when none were in sight? But the words *far off* have no relation to Satan; it is only a *Fleet* seen *far off at sea*, which is compar'd to Satan seen, whether near or far off, it is no matter: the Comparison being founded only in Satan's and the Fleet's *towering high*, and *hanging in the Clouds*. He objects farther to *Bengala, Ternate* and *Tidore*; but these *exotic* names (as he calls them) give a less vulgar cast to the Similitude, than places *in our own Channel* would do: so does the *Æthiopic Sea* more than the Expression *Europæan Seas* would. As to what he adds, *Why is all this done nightly, to contradict the whole account, since at that time a sail cannot be descry'd?* It may be answer'd, that here is no Contradiction at all; for *Milton* in his Similitudes, (as is the practice of *Homer* and *Virgil* too), after he has shew'd the common resemblance, often takes the liberty of wandring into some unresembling Circumstances; which have no other relation to the Comparison, than that it gave him the Hint, and (as it were) set fire to the train of his Imagination: (see my Note on I. 306.) So here the common Resemblance ends at *Tidore*; what *M.* adds, *Whence Merchants bring* &c. is a new description, and in no part of it is bound to have any Resemblance or relation to what went before: See the same thing in III. 438. *Stemming nightly towards the Pole*, means that by Night they sail northward; and yet, for all that, by Day their *Fleet* may be *descry'd hanging in the Clouds.* . . .

Ver. 1051.

And fast by hanging in a Golden Chain
This pendant World, in bigness as a Star
Of smallest Magnitude close by the Moon.

Dr. *B.* by putting a Comma after *Magnitude,* (contrary to all the first Editions) has fallen into a strange mistake about the sense of these Verses, and has in consequence of it thrown away the last of the three, and chang'd *in bigness as a Star* into *this new-built Universe.* He supposes that *M.* by *pendant world*, means the Earth; that is one inadvertency which he charges *M.* with: and then he wonders that the *pendant World* or Earth should be pointed out from her Neighbourhood to the Moon, so much less than Her.

But if we take away the Dr's unhappy Comma after *Magnitude*, then these faults of the first Magnitude, as the Dr. seems to suppose them, will disappear at once: for the words *close by the Moon* are part of the Similitude, and don't relate to the *pendant World*: The sense is, This *pendant World* (seen far off *v.* 1047.) seem'd to be no bigger than a *Star of smallest magnitude*; nay not so large; it seem'd no bigger than such a *Star* appears to be, when it is *close by the Moon*; the superior Light of which makes any *Star* that happens to be very near her Disc, to seem exceedingly small and almost to disappear. *At the sight* of the Sun (says our Poet IV. 34.) *all the Stars hide their diminish'd heads*; just so the Stars are diminish'd by the Moon: but, because her Light is so much inferior to that of the Sun, the Stars which appear to be *diminish'd* by her, are those only which are *close by* her Orb, and so within the more immediate Verge of her Brightness. . . .

[Book IV]
Ver. 256.

Flours of all hue, and without Thorn the Rose.

Dr. *B.* rejects this Verse, because he thinks it a *jejune Identity* in the Poet to say, *The floury lap-spread Flours*: but tho' the expression be not very exact, it is not so bad as the Dr. represents it; for the Construction and Sense is, *The floury lap of some valley spread her store*; which store was what? why, *flours* of every colour or *hue.* But (says the Dr.) *of all hue* is not the Poet's stile, who in *v.* 698. has *Iris all hues*, without *of:* this is true; but the Poet's stile is not to be learn'd from one passage only, especially when he speaks otherwise in other places: as in the *Mask, Flours of more mingled hue*, and elsewhere he has *of various hue.* . . .

Ver. 499.

(as Jupiter
On Juno smiles, when he impregns the Clouds
That shed May Flours) and press'd her MATRON *Lip.*

Dr. *B.* throws out of the Poems, what is here in a Parenthesis, and to make the last words suit with the words that precede the Parenthesis, he rejects the Epithet *Matron* too. I think that the Similitude is a very Poetical one, approv'd of by other Poets, who have imitated it, or at least have fallen into the same thought. But as for the Dr's Objection to the Epithet *Matron*, I agree with him less still: I think it the very properest that *M.* could have pick'd out: It is the opposite to *Virgin* Lip, and means more than *womanly*: it implies that she was married to him, and that therefore the Kisses, which he gave her, were lawful, pure and innocent: we have in XI. 137. *first* MATRON *Eve.* . . .

Ver. 1002.

Battles and REALMS

Dr. *B.* objects to *Realms* here; because they are not Events (he says), nor do they any way concern the present Occasion: For *Realms* therefore he reads *Truce*; but I cannot approve of *Truce*: to answer Battles it should be *Truces*: Besides, *Battles* are no more Events than *Realms* are; so that if the Passage be wrong, it is but half emended: I believe that *M.* intended it as we now read it; and that the sentence is express'd in a brief, Poetical manner: probably *Milton* meant this, In these Golden Scales God *now* (since the Creation) *ponders all Events*, chiefly the Events of *Battles* and of *Realms*, i.e. Kingdoms, (VIII. 375.) He mentions *Battles*, because both *Homer* and *Virgil* represent *Jupiter* as using his Scales for weighing the *Events* of them; and he adds *Realms*, because in *Daniel* V. 26, 27. we find that *Belshazzar* was weigh'd *in the ballance*; and it is said, *God hath numbred thy Kingdom and finish'd it.* Instances of such abbreviated ways of speaking are frequent in *Milton.* . . .

[Book V]
Ver. 638.

Quaff Immortality and Joy (secure
Of Surfeit, where full measure only bounds
Excess) before th' all-bounteous King

Dr. *B.* finding that the two first of these Verses and the first word of the third are not in the first Edition, charges the Editor with inserting them in the second: he has great Objections to some expressions in them, but his Objections may be sufficiently answer'd. By *Immortality and Joy* may be meant, in the Scriptural Phrase, *Immortal Joy*: And to *drink* of any thing is in the same Stile to partake of it, as in *Rev.* 14. 10., in I *Cor.* 12. 13. and elsewhere: and agreeably to this way of speaking, to *quaff* or drink largely is to partake of it plentifully, to enjoy it in full measure. If these Verses were left out (as the Doctor would have them), the words in *v.* 641. which represent God as *rejoicing in their Joy*, wou'd refer to something that is no where to be found: and therefore *M.* (I suppose) inserted these Verses in the second Edition, that the *Joy* of the Angels might be express'd. *Secure of Surfeit* is another expression that the Doctor objects to: is it a *Surfeit* (he asks) of Immortality, or of eating and drinking? I think that *M.* meant a *Surfeit* both of eating and drinking, and of Immortal Joy: as I have plac'd the words *Secure of Surfeit,* &c. in a Parenthesis, the Construction will admit *Surfeit* to refer to both of those particulars. But can Angels be drunk with tippling too much Nectar? Can they by Intemperance get Fevers? These Questions the Doctor asks: but can he think them pertinent? If, according to *M*'s Theory, Angels eat and drink, no doubt but there is a possibility of their doing both to *Excess* and to *Surfeit,* and yet there is no occasion to suppose that Excess in Them would produce Drunkenness or Distempers. *Where full measure only bounds Excess,* i.e. (says the Doctor) only sets bounds to, disallows, forbids excess; and then how can they be *secure of surfeit*? but the meaning of this expression may be, Where full measure has no other effect than to set bounds to Excess; and not, as it happens often among Men, to tempt to it: Or rather the word *only* may belong to *full measure,* and the Sense may be this, Where excess is not restrain'd and prevented by Want, nor by any Quantity less than full measure: they have full enough and no more, and they can't be guilty of excess, because amidst all their Plenty, they have nothing beyond measure.

Ver. 648.

and wider far
Than all this Globous Earth in Plain out-spred
Such are the Courts of God.

These Verses Dr. *B.* by a savoury metaphor calls the Editor's *Ordure*, and calls upon him to *eat* it. But what is the quarrel with this Passage? Why, *Adam*, not being suppos'd to know the length of the Earth's Diameter, could have no notion, How wide the round Earth *out-spred in Plain* wou'd be. Be it so, yet why is the same Thought suffer'd to pass for *M*'s in VI. 77?

and many a Province wide
Tenfold the length of this Terrene.

If this was written by *M.* the other might deserve better Language from the Doctor: and after all, the Reader will gather from the beginning of the VIII Book, that *M.* has made *Adam* acquainted enough with Astronomy, to conceive that the Earth's Diameter was of a very considerable Extent. . . .

[Book VI]
Ver. 236.

The RIDGES *of grim War.*

Dr. *B.* thinks that *M.* gave it *Bridges* from *Homer*'s *gephirai polemoio*, which in common ac[c]eptation (he says) are *bridges*, but in *Homer* are the open Intervals between Rank and File. If so, and if *M.* copy'd from *Homer*, he would not methinks call them *Bridges*. The word *Ridge* signifies the Space between two Furrows; and this acceptation of the word *M.* has transferr'd to the Spaces between Rank and File, when an Army is set in array. . . .

Ver. 332.

A Stream of NECTAROUS *humor issuing flow'd*
Sanguin.

Dr. *B.* calls this an odious Blunder, because *Nectar* was the drink of the Gods, and *Satan*'s *Humor* or Blood was not a proper drink. I should have thought that an attentive Reader could not have miss'd observing that the *Stream*, which *M.* speaks of, was not of *Nectarous humor* only, but of *Nectarous humor sanguin*, i.e. converted into what *celestial Spirits bleed*: and what is that but the same which *Homer* expresses by one word

Ichor? If this was the Poet's meaning, the Doctor's Objection is wide of the mark. Besides, if *Nectarous* was wrong, yet *Ichorous* (which the Doctor would give us in the room of it) would not seem to be right, because the middle syllable of it should be long, according to the Prosody of the word from which it is deriv'd.

Ver. 356.

And with fierce ENSIGNS *pierc'd the deep array*

A Blunder again (says Dr. *B.*) Why are *Ensigns*, the Colours, called *fierce*, the tamest things in the whole Battle? But all this Blunder is gone, if we will allow a Poet the liberty of giving that Epithet to the *Ensigns* which belongs more properly to the Bearers of them. *M.* has taken this sort of liberty in some hundreds of places; and generally the Doctor has allow'd it him. . . . And besides, by *fierce Ensigns* are not only meant the Standard-bearers, but the whole Legion which belong'd to those Ensigns or Standards: 'Tis a Figure call'd Metonymy of the Part for the Whole, well known among Poets and Orators. Thus the Sense will be, where *Gabriel* and his followers pierc'd the deep array, *i.e.* broke in upon the many Lines of *Moloc's* Troops. . . .

[Book VIII]

Ver. 239.

THEN FOUNDED, THEN CONGLOB'D
Like things to like, THE REST TO SEVERAL *place*
Disparted, and between spun out the Air,
And Earth SELF-BALANC'D *on her Center hung.*

Dr. *B.* pronounces this Paragraph to be drawn with Inaccurateness and Indistinction, and therefore he changes several parts of it. But let us see whether he is right or no. *M.* had said that Messiah first purg'd downward the Infernal Dregs, which were adverse to Life; and that then of things friendly to Life he *founded and conglob'd* like to like, *i. e.* he caus'd them to assemble and associate together: the *rest*, i. e. such things as were not of the same nature and fit for composing the Earth, went off to other places, perhaps to form the Planets and fix'd Stars. This seems to be *M's* meaning. What is it now that Dr. *B.* would give us? why, he proposes as follows,

FOUR ELEMENTS THEN ROSE
Like things to like, FIRE TO THE HIGHEST *place*
Disparted, and between spun out the Air,
And Earth TERRAQUEOUS *on her Center hung.*

75

Terraqueous (says he) makes up the four Elements, Fire, Air, Land, and Waters. But *M.* did not intend here to mention all the four Elements; he is describing at present only the formation of the Earth, and does not mean (I suppose) to speak of *Fire* here, because he describes the Generation of *Light* afterwards in *v.* 243. The Epithet *Terraqueous* can never be join'd with *Earth*; then it would be Earth consisting of Earth and Water: but if it could, it would be needless in this place, because it was said in *v.* 237. to be a *Fluid Mass.* After all, why does the Doctor dislike the Epithet *self-balanc'd*? To hang on its Center (says he) supposes it *self-balanc'd*, without naming the word. But that so extraordinary a Phænomenon should be express'd more strongly than ordinary, is at lowest Allowable in a Poet. If not, I should rather have wish'd the expression *on her Center* alter'd; for *M.* has plainly drawn here his word *self-balanc'd* from what *Ovid* says *Met. l.* I. 8.

> *circumfuso* PENDEBAT *in aëre tellus*
> *Ponderibus* LIBRATA SUIS . . .

Ver. 321.

The SMELLING *Gourd;*

Dr. *B.* very justly reads here *The* SWELLING *Gourd*: and to the reasons which he gives, may be added that *M.* here assigns to each of the other Tribes or Species, an Epithet which he suits with all of the same Species: but *smelling*, tho' it suits with some kinds of the *Gourd*, does not suit with all the particulars of that Tribe, as *swelling* does. . . .

Ver. 387.

Let the Waters generate
REPTIL with Spawn abundant, living Soul;

By *Reptil* is meant *creeping thing*; and according to the Marginal reading of our English Version, *Gen.* i. 20 (which follows the LXX Version here) *creeping things* are said to have been created on this fifth day. *Le Clerc* too with the generality of Interpreters renders the Hebrew Word by *reptile*. To this Dr. *B.* objects that *creeping things* were created on the sixth day, according to the account given us both by *Moses* and by *Milton* himself. But by *reptil* or *creeping thing* here *M.* means all such Creatures as move in the Waters, (See *Le Clerc*'s Note on *Gen.* i. 20.) and by *creeping thing* mention'd in the sixth day's Creation he means *creeping things of the Earth*; for so both in *M*'s account *v.* 452. and in *Gen.* i. 24. the words *of the Earth* are to be join'd in Construction to *creeping thing*. Hence the Doctor's Objection is answer'd by saying that they were not the same *creeping things* which *M.* mentions in the two places. But let us hear how the Doctor proposes to mend the Passage,

Let the *Waters generate*
REPLETE *with Spawn abundant, living Soul;*

This reading cannot possibly be admitted, without making *M*'s words imply (contrary to the Fact) that the *Spawn* was preexistent to this fifth day's Creation, and the Waters were *replete* with it before God said, *Let the waters generate* &c.

Ver. 391.

And God created the great Whales; and each
Soul living, each that crept, &c.

Here Dr. *B.* would send eight Verses packing, as the Editor's Manufacture. He acknowledges that the sense of them is in *Genesis*, but (says he) they ought not to be in this Poem. I differ from the Doctor in this; let us examine the matter therefore farther. The Doctor asks, Whether *M.* could say *God created great Whales*, and himself create them afterwards again. But by *great Whales M.* means all the larger kinds of Fishes: and tho' he speaks afterwards of *Leviathan*, yet he does not mean a Whale by it. . . .

It is observable that *M.* in his account of the fourth, fifth and sixth day's Creation, takes a different method from what he does in his account of the divine work on the other days. In the Story of the fourth day, he first gives a short and general account of what was then created *v.* 346, &c. and then he begins in *v.* 354. to branch that account out into its several Particulars. So likewise in the Story of the sixth day's Work he gives a general account in *v.* 454, 455. and then proceeds to enter into the particulars of that day's Creation. The same *M.* has done here in the fifth day's Story. The Verses which the Doctor would throw out contain the short and general account, which is afterwards spread into its several Particulars and beautifully enlarg'd upon. From hence I would infer, that if Dr. *B.* will charge these eight Verses upon the Editor for that reason which he gives, he must by the same rule charge upon him three Verses in the sixth day's account, and eight Verses in the fourth day's account beginning at *v.* 346. and the Doctor's Objection against *Whales* being mention'd here will be equally strong against *Lights* being mention'd there. But in none of the three Places can we spare one Verse of them. . . .

Ver. 451.

Let th' Earth bring forth FOWLE *living in her kind*

Dr. *B.* very justly calls this reading a faulty one: it should be (as he observes) SOUL *living in her kind*, as in *v.* 388, we had *living* SOUL, and *v.* 392, SOUL *living*, in both which places the Expression is put for *living Creature*, which is in our English Version; and *living Creature* being the expression in *Gen.* i. 24. which *M.* here copies from, he must have given it here too *Soul living.* . . .

Ver. 463.

The grassy Clods now calv'd now half appear'd &c.,

Dr. *B.* says that this Verse and eleven which follow it are demonstrably an Insertion of the Editor's. To prove this he begins with joining *v.* 462. and *v.* 475. together, when the twelve Verses are thrown out; and finding *at once* mention'd in each of those two Verses, he thinks it plain that they must have followed close, without any thing intervening. But it was observ'd in my forgoing Note, that the words *at once* in *v.* 462. ought to be join'd to *pasturing*, not to the Participle *upsprung*; and then they will have no relation or connexion at all to the words *at once* in *v.* 475. *M.* (says the Doctor) had spoken before of the Generation of Beasts both wild and tame: True, but in general only; here he comes to speak of them particularly. This is no more than what our Poet did in his accounts of the Creation on the fourth and fifth days. . . . Thus much for the Doctor's general Objections. He comes next to examine the Expressions and Circumstances of these twelve Verses. First he quarrels with the *Clods calving*, and calls *calving* a Metaphor very Heroical, especially for wild beasts: But to *calve* (from the *Belgic* word *Kalven*) signifies to bring forth: it is a general word and does not relate to Cows only; for *Hinds* are said so *calve* in *Job* xxxix, 1. and *Psalm* xxix. 9. Next, the Doctor objects to the particular manners of rising ascrib'd here to the *Lion*, the *Ounce*, the *Stag*, the *Elephant*, &c. Mr. *Addison* thought that there was an *exquisite Spirit of Poetry* in the Description of the *Lion*'s rising, and I will venture to say that in the account of the rest *M*'s Genius plainly appears. The Doctor should have observ'd that *M.* is here describing only what happen'd to these several Animals, or what posture they were in at one single point of Time. This Observation answers what the Doctor objects to the account of the *Stag*'s only *bearing up his head from under ground*, &c. For the *Tygers* to throw the Earth above them in Hillocks, as the *Mole* does when it rises, does not shew *Weakness* in their birth (as the Doctor supposes): if they were stronger than they are, it could not have happen'd otherwise. It is only said of the *Stag*, that he bore up his branching head from underground. If *Behemoth* or the Elephant *scarce upheav'd his vastness*, this is properly said, for tho' he is the strongest creature, he is the clumsiest, and most *unwieldy* as *M*. calls him in IV. 345. How comes *M*. (adds the Doctor) to say that *fleec'd* THE *flocks and bleating rose, as Plants*? when he had before told us that the *Flocks at once upsprung in perfect forms*. But this is the Doctor's mistake, for tho' the *Earth teem'd* them perfect forms *v*. 455. yet they did not *upspring at once*, as I shew'd in my former Note. The Doctor asks farther, whether the Sheep rose as slowly *as Plants* grow, or bleating *as Plants* do. One would think it not very easy to mistake *M's* meaning here, which is that they rose as thick and as numerous *as Plants*. And in the last Sentence, tho' the Doctor thinks that there is no Verb put to it, yet we are to understand, the River-Horse and Crocodile *rose* ambiguous, *i. e.* of an amphibious and doubtful nature, whether to be reckon'd of the terrestial or the aquatic kind.

From what has been said in defence of these twelve Verses, I hope that they may be allow'd to pass for *M's*, and to be worthy of his Genius. . . .

[Book IX]

Ver. 163.

> *O foul descent! that I who erst contended*
> *With Gods to sit the highest, am now constrain'd*
> INTO *A Beast, and mix'd with bestial Slime*
> *This Essence to* INCARNATE *and imbrute,*
> *That to the highth of Deity aspir'd .*

Dr. *B*. has three several Objections to this Passage, as it now stands, in three several Notes: but I shall examine all in one. First he says, that *constrain'd into a Beast* is a vitious Expression, and not the Author's own. But yet the Author has us'd much the same Phrase again in his Treatise upon *Education* (to Mr. *Hartlib*) where he speaks of being CONSTRAIN'D INTO a *Persuasion*. We may reject then the Doctor's reading,

> *am now constrain'd,*
> INCLOS'D IN *Beast, and mix'd* &c.

To justify which he says, that the Construction is not, *Constrain'd into a Beast*; but *Constrain'd to incarnate*. But why may not the Construction be this? *Am now constrain'd into a Beast, and* (am) *mix'd with bestial Slime to incarnate and imbrute this Essence.* Thus the Sense and the Syntax too will stand good. The Doctor objects still farther, and dislikes the word *incarnate*, as if appropriated to our Saviour: but this Word is not at all apply'd to Him in the Scriptures, and in other Writings it is sometimes apply'd to the Devil, as when *Shakespeare* and others say, *Devil incarnate.* Lastly he would throw away a whole Verse, *That to the highth*, &c. as a spurious one: for this he gives his Reasons. He says, that this Verse is the same with, if not worse than, what went before, *contended with Gods to sit the highest*: but surely *Satan's* Ambition is more fully and strongly express'd ,when he says that he *aspir'd to the highth of Deity*, than when he only says, that he *contended with Gods*, that he might *sit the Highest*; since highth of Place was not all the highth of the Deity. He says again, that Satan's *Essence* did not aspire, it was his *Mind*, his *Person*. Aspiring is proper to the Mind, and that only; but by a figurative Way of speaking, the Doctor here applies it to Satan's *Person*: why then by the same Figure may it not be apply'd to his *Essence*? What the Doctor means by this Line's abscinding what follows, I don't understand; for the *Ambition* mention'd in the next Line, has an immediate relation with the *aspiring to the highth of Deity*, mention'd in this Verse.

[Book XII]
Ver. 648.

THEY *hand in hand with* WANDRING *Steps* AND SLOW
Through Eden took their SOLITARY *way.*

As the Poem closes with these two Verses, so Dr. *B.* finishes his Labour with Remarks upon them. He observes that Mr. *Addison* declar'd for ejecting them both out of the Poem; and supposes him to have been induc'd to this by a mistake of the Printer, THEY *hand in hand*: which reading (the Doctor thinks) makes the last Distich seem loose, unconnected and abscinded from the rest. But Mr. *Addison* was too good a Judge of *M*'s way of writing, to eject them upon that account only. He gave us another reason for his readiness to part with them, and said that they renew in the mind of the Reader that Anguish, which was pretty well laid by the Consideration of the two foregoing Verses. But it has been said more justly by another Gentleman (who seems well qualified to give a Judgment in the Case) that *considering the Moral and chief Design of this Poem, Terror is the last Passion to be left upon the Mind of the Reader.* Essay on *Pope's* Odyssey, *part* II. *p.* 89.

However this be, the Doctor's reason for keeping these two Verses is extraordinary: he says, that unless they are kept, *Adam* and *Eve* would be left in the Territory and Suburbane of Paradise, in the very view of the *dreadful faces*: and he adds, that they must therefore be dismiss'd *out of Eden*, to live thenceforward in some other part of the World. And yet both in the common reading and in the Doctor's too they are left *in Eden*, only taking their way *through* it. But this by the by.

Let us see how the Doctor would mend the matter; and then I will give my Objections to his Reading, and afterwards answer his Objections to *M*'s.

He proposes to read thus,

> THEN *hand in hand with* SOCIAL *steps their way*
> *Through Eden took* WITH HEAVENLY COMFORT CHEAR'D.

To this reading we may object that the Verb wants the word *they* before it; for it is too far to fetch it from *v*. 645. when two Verses, of a quite different Construction, are inserted between. Again, *chear'd with comfort* seems tautologous, for *comfort* is imply'd in *chear'd*, without its being mention'd. Lastly, if they went *hand in hand*, there is no need to tell us that their Steps were *social*; they could not be otherwise.

So much for the Doctor's reading. We are now to consider the Objections which the Doctor makes to the present reading. It contradicts (says he) the Poet's own Scheme, and the Diction is not unexceptionable. With regard to the Diction, he asks, Why were the Steps *wandring* ones, when *Providence was their Guide*? But it might be their *Guide*, without pointing out to them which way they should take at every Step: The words *Providence their Guide* signify that now since *Michael*, who had hitherto conducted them by the hand, was departed from them, they had no Guide to their Steps, only the general Guidance of Providence to keep them safe and unhurt. *Eve* (it is plain) expected that her Steps would be *wandring* ones, when upon being told that she was to leave Paradise, she breaks out into these words XI. 282.

> *How shall I part? and whither* WANDER *down*
> *Into a lower World?*

Again the Doctor asks, Why *slow* steps; when *Eve* profess'd her Readiness and Alacrity for the Journey, *v*. 614? But that Readiness was not an absolute one, it was a choosing rather to go than to stay behind there without *Adam v*. 615, &c. In that view she was ready to go: but in the view of leaving the Delights of Paradise, they were both backward and even *linger'd v*. 638. Their Steps therefore were *slow*.

And why (says the Doctor) is their way call'd *solitary*, when their

Walks in Paradise were as solitary as their Way now, there being no body besides them Two both here or there? It may be answer'd, that their Way was *solitary*, not in regard to any Companions whom they had met elsewhere; but because they were here to meet with no Objects of any kind that they were acquainted with: Nothing here was *familiar to their Eyes*, and (as *Adam*, then in Paradise, well expresses it in XI. 305.)

all places else
Inhospitable' appear and DESOLATE,
Not knowing Us, nor known.

The last, but the main, Objection which the Doctor makes, is that this Distich contradicts the Poet's own Scheme. To support this charge, he has refer'd us to half a dozen places of his Twelfth Book, where *Adam* or *Eve* are spoken of as having *Joy, Peace,* and *Consolation* &c. and from thence he concludes that this Distich ought not to dismiss our first Parents in Anguish, and the Reader in Melancholy. But the *Joy, Peace,* and *Consolation* spoken of in those Passages are represented always as arising in our first Parents from a view of some future Good, chiefly of the *Messiah*. The Thought of leaving Paradise (notwithstanding any other Comfort that they had) was all along a *sorrowful* one to them. Upon this account *Eve fell asleep wearied with sorrow and distress of heart v.* 613. Both *Adam* and *Eve linger'd* at their quitting Paradise *v.* 638. and they *drop'd some natural Tears* on that occasion *v.* 645. In this view the Archangel *v.* 603. recommends to our first Parents that they should live *unanimous, tho'* SAD *with cause for Evils past*. And, for a plainer proof that the Scheme of the Poem was to dismiss Them not without *Sorrow*, the Poet in XI. 117. puts these words into God's mouth, as his Instruction to *Michael*,

So send them forth, though SORROWING, *yet in Peace*.

8. Richardson on Milton's religious beliefs and *Paradise Lost*

1734

Extract from Jonathan Richardson, *Explanatory Notes and Remarks on Milton's Paradise Lost. By J. Richardson, Father and Son. With the Life of the Author, and a Discourse on the Poem. By J. R. Sen.* (1734), xlvi–l, cvi–cvii, cxiv–cxv, cxvii–cxix, cxxi–cxxii, cxxix–cxxxii.

An important portrait painter, Jonathan Richardson (1665–1745) wrote frequently on art theory and in 1734 produced a life of Milton, based on reminiscences of association with people who knew Milton directly or indirectly, plus the usual sources, and an extensive discussion and commentary on *Paradise Lost*. The work is advertised on its cover as written by J. Richardson, father and son, although the son seems to have assisted mainly in putting down the material and helping to see it through the press.

For Himself, he seems to have had little Regard to the Exteriour of Religion; We hear of Nothing of That even in his Last hours; and whatever he did in the Former Parts of his Life, he frequented no Publick Worship in his Latter years, nor used any Religious Rite in his Own Little Family. it seems very Probable that as he was Always very Anti-Episcopal, and no Lover of Our Establish'd Church, neither would he bear with the Tolerated Preachers after the Restoration; Those of whom he speaks, when he says, that they were seen *under Subtle Hypocrisy to have Preached their Own Follies, most of them not the Gospel, Time-servers, Covetous, Illiterate Persecutors, not Lovers of the Truth, Like in all things whereof they accused their Predecessors:* This Passage I have from a Fragment that was not Printed till several Years after *Milton*'s Death, Anno 1681. 'twas a Part of his History of England, and Expung'd, it being but a Sort of Digression, and to avoid giving Offence to a Party quite Subdu'd, and whose Faults the Government was then Willing to Have Forgotten. there is a great deal more to This Purpose, as also on the Villanous Abuse of Power in Mony-Matters of These People, and of That Party which Himself notwithstanding his great Merits with them had Tasted of Severely. . . .

the Sincerity I have Profest in Drawing This Picture, and which as I resolve to Practice, will not permit me to Pass over in Silence Another Conjecture which Some have made; I mean that *Milton* was an *Arian*; and This is built on Certain Passages in *Par. Lost*. Some of Those I am pretty Well Assur'd are very Capable of an Orthodox Construction, as All of them are for Ought I know. But as I neither Care to Meddle with a Dispute which I am not acquainted with; and as 'tis no Other than a Conjecture, which lies against him, and seems to be Over-rul'd by So many Pious and Learned Divines (Sound in This Fundamental Article) having Approv'd and Encourag'd the Book; and as Two have very Lately Expressly Acquitted him of That Charge; and as Moreover 'tis Certain, that in his Middle-Age he has shown he was Right as to This Point, I wave it, and claim in his Behalf that he be Esteem'd as Continuing So to the Last. the Passage I mention'd is in his Discourse of *Reformation*, just at the Close of it. . . .

Milton had Always a Firm Belief of the Being of a God, and a Mind which could not fail from his Existence to Infer his Government of the Universe, and all This in such a One must Produce True Piety, Veneration, Submission, Dependance, Love mix'd with Filial Awe, Joy, &c. This Appears Perpetually to every Observing Reader of His Works, Verse or Prose. His Other Speculative Religious Opinions whereby he is Distinguish'd, are rather Political than Religious, Such as relate to the Circumstantials rather than to the Essentials or Substance of Religion; Church-Government, Church-Communion, Ceremonies, the Millennium, &c. on which 'tis not necessary to Enlarge, and I am Glad it is not. . . .

My Other Delightful Task remains; 'tis to give the History of *Paradise Lost*, and Some Idea of it.

As *Milton* intended Some Such Work, tho' the Subject was not Resolv'd on, We must Date its Original from That Intention, Especially as it Answers to the Main Scope of what was Then invelop'd in a General Idea. This was So Early as his Acquaintance and Friendship with *Giov. Batta. Manso*, Marquiss of *Villa* at *Naples*; as appears by that admirable Latin Poem address'd to that Nobleman, and which must have been Written about the Year 1639. the Subject first thought on, was the Story of King *Arthur*. This is seen by his Latin Elegy on *Damon*, written upon his Return from *Italy* a little after the Other. . . .

After all Difficulties [of having the epic published] were Overcome, and Advantages Employ'd, the Book was in Danger of lying Buried in Manuscript, by the Impertinence, Folly, Malice, or whatever Else, of the Licencer, who besides Other Objections fancy'd there was Treason in that Noble Double Simile. *As when the Sun new ris'n* &c. I.594.

the Price for which *Milton* sold his Copy is Astonishing. and Here we were in Another Danger of Losing This Poem. Happy was it for the World that *Milton* was Poor and Depress'd, Certainly he must be so at This time. the Price this Great Man Condescended to take for Such a Work; Such a Work! was Ten Pounds, and if a Certain Number went off, then it was to be made up Fifteen. . . .

It has been a Current Opinion that the late Lord *Sommers* first gave this Poem a Reputation. is it not a sufficient Reproach to our Country that *Paradise Lost* lay Neglected for Two or Three Years? though even for Those it may be Pleaded that Party-Partiality, and the Then Gay Taste of Wit are answerable for a great Share of the Guilt. . . . Such a Work could not fail of reaching Better Eyes; as it did Soon, for whatever Cause it First Rose *Shorn of its Beams*. Sir *George Hungerford*, an Ancient Member of Parliament, told me, many Years ago, that Sir *John Denham* came into the House one Morning with a Sheet, Wet from the Press, in his Hand. What have you there, Sir *John*? Part of the Noblest Poem that ever was Wrote in Any Language, or in any Age. This was *Paradise Lost*. However 'tis Certain the Book was Unknown 'till about two Years after, when the Earl of *Dorset* produc'd it. . . .

Thus, what by One means, what by Another, and Those Complicated and Manag'd as Providence well Can, This Poem, this *Waste Paper*, (like an Acorn Hid and Lost) has, by its Inherent Life, and a Little Cultivation, Sprung Out of the Earth, Lifted up its Head and Spread its Branches, a Noble Oak; has become a Richer Treasure to the World than it has receiv'd from Most of Those Names which Glitter in the Records of Time.

Who would have Imagin'd Now that *Milton*'s *Paradise Lost* was not Yet Safe! 'tis in our Possession indeed in Many Editions, but *Milton*'s Blindness and Other Disadvantages has Occasion'd Suggestions and Assertions that we have it not as the Author *gave* it, but as Corrupted by Presumption, Folly, Carelessness, and I know not What. Presumption, Folly, or Something Worse, has been at Work, in Suggesting, or Believing Such things, which is the more Dangerous because founded on a Specious Probability, which Commonly Cheats Us, Few having the Opportunity, or the Skill to Distinguish between Probability and Truth; and Fewer yet that are not too Lazy to Examine with that Degree of Care and Pains which Truth will Demand. Persuasion is Cheaper come at by Probability. . . .

What has been alledg'd as Probabilities, appears in Fact to be Certain. That the Original MS. was of the Hand-writing of Several is Agreed, but does That appear by the Printed Book? Nothing Less; 'tis Uniform Throughout: it must have Then been Revis'd and Corrected by Some One, Directed at least. and that This was *Milton* himself is Evident by its Exact Conformity with his Spelling and Pointing in What he Publish'd when he had his Sight; as also with his Other Works after That was gone. for full Satisfaction, Those that please may have recourse to Those Works, the Original Editions, for They are to be had. in the Mean time if they will give Me Credit, they will be Assured, that not only the Printing is Equally Accurate with what is to be found in Any of them, but 'tis rather More So than in most of the rest. as indeed 'tis of more Importance, that it should be Just Here than in Any of his Other Works, as 'tis his Principal One, and That in which even the Points Direct and Determine the Sense most Often and most Remarkably. We have found, in Several Instances, that what seem'd at first Sight to be the True One, was far Inferior to what was indeed So, but would not have been Discover'd, unless by following Those Guides, Almost Universally Faithful.

There are Some Peculiarities in the Spelling of certain Words in *Paradise Lost*, not by Accident, but from One End to the Other; the Same is in what he Wrote with his Own Hand Years before. to go into a Detail of These would be Dry to the Reader, nor is it Agreeable to Me; but One remarkable Instance I will give: the Word *Their* in This Poem, as in Many of his Writings, is *Thir*. What led him to This way of Spelling this Word I know not, but he began it long After he was a Publisher, though long Before *Paradise Lost*. 'tis not an Ancient Way of Writing, it was Always *Their* or *Theyr*.

Several Other Particularities of This Kind are to be found in *Milton*'s Works, Which let any One peruse, they will be Convinc'd that there is Such a Similitude of Spelling between Those Published when he was Blind, and Those Before, that shows they *were All under the same Direction*. Had we not known it Otherwise the Author would not have been suspected to be Blind by Any want of Exactness in This. . . .

in *Paradise Lost* there is a Remarkable Proof of Care which we have

not Observ'd in any of our Author's Other Works, or Those of any
Other Writer; and that is, the Words *He, we, me, ye*, are with a Double
or a Single *e*, as the Emphasis lies upon them, or does not. We could
produce a great Number of Instances of This. Take only Two, II.1021–
2–3. VI.286, 288. Nay, a Neglect of This kind is put into the Errata
of the First Edition, the Fault is in II.414. but the Second Edition has
happen'd to Overlook it, though Otherwise Exceedingly Correct.

9. Jortin on *Paradise Regain'd*

1734

Extract from John Jortin, appendix on Milton, *Remarks on Spenser's Poems* (1734), 171–5.

John Jortin (1698–1770) was a clergyman and ecclesiastical
historian, who frequently contributed to periodicals on a variety
of subjects and who often delved into literary topics. His discussions of Milton are scattered or, like the present item, attached to
other, fuller studies.

MILTON

That I may not pass abruptly from *Spenser* to *Milton*, I say, purely for
the sake of introduction and connection, that *Milton*, the favourite poet
of this nation, has been, and I suppose will be, the subject of essays,
dissertations, notes, &c. that I have a mind to thrust my self in amongst
those who have labour'd on this celebrated author, . . . that I shall
offer a few remarks upon him, and so take a final leave of the *English*
poets.

Milton's Paradise Regain'd has not met with the approbation that it
deserves. It has not the harmony of numbers, the sublimity of thought,
and the beauties of diction, which are in *Paradise Lost*. It is composed in
a lower and less striking style, a style suited to the subject. Artful
sophistry, false reasoning set off in the most specious manner, and

refuted by the Son of God with strong unaffected eloquence, is the peculiar excellence of this Poem. *Satan* there defends a bad cause with great skill and subtilty, as one thoroughly versed in that craft. . . .

His character is well drawn. In his speeches we may observe his pretended frankness and ingenuity in confessing who he was, when he found he was discovered: [PR I, 358–60].

His plea for himself, that he was not a creature quite lost to all good: [PR I, 377–82].

His ingenious, moving, and humble apology for lying shuffling: [PR I, 468–80].

His strong and lively description of his own wretched state. *Christ* says to him: [PR III, 198–211].

His artful flattery to *Christ*. I shall, says he, be punish'd, . . . [PR III, 214–22].

His submissive and cunning reply taught him by his fear, after he had endeavoured to perswade *Christ* to worship him, and had received a severe reprimand: [PR IV, 196–208].

PARADISE REGAIN'D

Satan says to *Christ*: [PR I, 387–8, 397–402]. I think it will not be cavilling to say, that *each* man's *peculiar load* should not be put in the mouth of *Satan*, who was to man, who had confessed to *Christ* that he was the unfortunate Arch-Fiend, and who speaks of himself. If *Milton* had been aware of it, he would have corrected it thus:

> Nor lightens ought each *ones* peculiar load.

or in some other manner. Besides: the word *man* is repeated here too often.

> Nor lightens ought each *man's* peculiar load.
> Small consolation then, were *man* adjoin'd.
> This wounds me most (what can it less) that *man*,
> *Man* fall'n shall be restor'd, I never more. [PR I, 402–5]

10. Warburton on Milton and Toland's 'Life'

November 1737

William Warburton, letter iv to Thomas Birch (24 November 1737). John Nichols, ed., *Illustrations of the Literary History of the Eighteenth Century* (1817), II, 77–82.

Theological controversialist William Warburton (1698–1779) found in Milton much to criticize and to commend, as the next excerpt and Nos 15 and 17 show. The following discussion indicates the continued antagonism which Toland's view of religion raised and which was usually transferred uncritically to Milton. Bishop Warburton's separation of Toland from Milton allows him to consider the poetry and the prose more objectively and personally.

Dear Sir,

In compliance to your request, I shall throw together a few scattered remarks, as they come into my head, without any manner of order, concerning Milton's Character, and his Writings.

Toland was a poor creature in all respects, and never manifested his malignity and folly more than in the 'Life of Milton'.

There is one egregious instance of it you will do well to avoid. He represents Milton's moral character, as a member of society, to be excellent, which was certainly the most corrupt of any man's of that age. I do not say so on account of his either being a Presbyterian, an Independent, a Republican, for the Government of One 'for many honest men were in every one of these ways), but because he was all these in their turn, as they came uppermost, without (by any thing that appears to the contrary) a struggle or a blush. Imagine to yourself a thorough time-server, and you could not put him upon any task more completely conformable to that character than what Milton voluntarily underwent. For a Life-writer then to disguise this, is, in my opinion, a horrid violation of truth. It is true, he was steady in one thing, namely, in his aversion to the Court and Royal Family; but I suspect it was because he was not received amongst the Wits there favourably: he who was so far superior to them all. I take this to have been owing to the stiffness of his style and manner, so contrary to that of the Court-Wits, who were enervating themselves on the model of France very fast; for, you know, softness, easiness, and disengagedness, was the character of the Court Writers of that time.

The virulency of his pen against his adversaries is certainly another blemish to that great man; which, in *An Apology for the People of England*, was abominable, as violating and degrading the character he sustained.

His English prose style has in it something very singular and original. It has grandeur, and force, and fire; but is quite unnatural, the idiom and turn of the period being Latin. It is best suited to his 'English History;' his air of antique giving a good grace to it. It is wrote with great simplicity, contrary to his custom in his prose works, and is the better for it. But he sometimes rises to a surprising grandeur in the sentiment and expression, as at the conclusion of the Second Book: 'Henceforth we are to steer', &c. I never saw any thing equal to this, but the conclusion of Sir Walter Raleigh's *History of the World*.

He is the Author of three perfect pieces of Poetry. His *Paradise Lost*, *Samson Agonistes*, and 'Masque at Ludlow Castle'. The two dramatic pieces separately possess the united excellencies of this famous Epic Poem; there being in the last all the majesty of sentiment that ennobles the Tragedy, and all the sweetness of description that charms in the Masque. Indeed the Tragedy (as in imitation of the Antients) has, as it were, a gloominess intermixed with the sublime (the subject not very different, the fall of two Heroes by a Woman), which shines more serenely in his *Paradise Lost* as there is in the 'Masque' (in which he only copied Shakespeare) a brighter vein of Poetry, intermixed with a softness of description, than is to be found in the charming scenes of Eden.

The *Paradise Regained* is a charming Poem; surely nothing inferior in the poetry and sentiment to the *Paradise Lost*; but, considered as a just composition in the Epic way, infinitely inferior; and indeed no more an Epic Poem than his 'Mansus'.

It is said that it appeared by a Manuscript in Trinity College, Cambridge, now lost or mislaid, that he intended an Opera of the *Paradise Lost*. Voltaire, on the credit of this circumstance, amongst a heap of impertinences [in the *Essay on Epic Poetry*, p. 102], pretends boldly that he took the hint from a Comedy he saw at Florence, called *Adamo*; and others imagine too he conceived the idea in Italy. Now I will give you good proof that all this is a vision. In one of his political pamphlets, wrote early by him, I forget which, he tells the world he had conceived a notion of an Epic poem on the story of Adam or Arthur. What then, you will say, must we do with the circumstance of the Trinity College MS.? I believe I can explain that matter. When the Parliament got uppermost, they suppressed all playhouses; on which Sir John Denham (I think) and others contrived to get *Operas* performed. This took with the people, and was much in their taste; and religious ones being the favourites of that sanctified people, was, I believe, what inclined Milton, at that time (and neither before nor after) to make an Opera of it. This, I fancy, being the case, I would have you consider whether the plan of the Tragedy which you talk of in the MS. was not indeed the plan of an Opera.

Toland ['Life', p. 10] makes Milton contract an intimacy with his Excellency Spanheim in the year 1640, Spanheim being then but 11 years old; and for proof refers to a letter wrote to him in 1654. If, therefore, Toland had any authority for a friendship contracted with a Spanheim at that time, it must have been Frederick Ezechiel, pastor of Geneva; and by the letter wrote to the son it appears he had some knowledge of the father. Hear how this wretch talks of Usher and Salmasius ['Life', p. 12]. Of the former: 'Now Usher's *chief talent* lying in much reading, and being a great Editor and admirer of old writings'. His chief talent was the truest judgment and most profound knowledge of Antiquity. Of the latter:—'this man had got a great name', &c. p. 30, as if he was not in reality the greatest critic of his time, and as much superior to Milton in that way, as Milton was to him in the subject they engaged in.

I once saw the first edition of the Masque at Ludlow Castle, without Milton's name to it, and found that it was dedicated by Lawes the great Musician who made the music for it: from whence I concluded that Lawes only employed Milton, and paid him for it, and took the benefit of the Dedication. This shews his small acquaintance, or ill reception at Court. What is very odd is, the silence of his contemporary Poets on his character. I mean before the Restoration. I observed Anthony à Wood knew of Milton's and Denham's reciprocal services, which that silly creature *the compound R* [Jonathan Richardson, father and son, authors of *Explanatory Notes and Remarks*] makes such a bustle about as a discovery of his own.

The 'L'Allegro' and 'Il Penseroso' are certainly master-pieces in their kind. You will see in *Theobald's* heap of disjointed stuff, which he calls a 'Preface to Shakespeare,' an observation upon those Poems, which I made to him, and which he did not understand, and so has made it a good deal obscure by contracting my note; for you must understand, that almost all the Preface (except what relates to Shakespeare's Life, and the foolish Greek conjectures at the end) was made up of notes I sent him on particular passages, and which he has there stitched together without head or tail.

Of all his English Prose Tracts, those on *Divorce* are the best reasoned. In his controversy on *the Times* he is a horrid sophister; but what was fanaticism and cant in the rest of his party shews itself in him in a prodigious spirit of poetical enthusiasm; and he frequently breaks out into strains as sublime, or if possible more so, than any in his higher Poetry.

His *Apology for the Liberty of the Press* is in all respects a master-piece. The *Plan of Education, to Hartlib*, is a very noble one.

You see how willing I am to serve you, while I can prevail with myself to write this loose disjointed stuff to you. I would have you consider it only as hints, that are entirely at your service to make what use you please of.

I shall endeavour to give you what satisfaction I can, in any thing you want to be satisfied in, on the subject of Milton; and am extremely glad you intend to write his Life. Almost all the Life-writers we have had, before Toland and Des Maizeaux, are indeed strange insipid creatures; and yet I had rather read the worst of them, than be obliged to go through with this of Milton's or the other's *Life of Boileau*, where there is such a dull heavy succession of long quotations of uninteresting passages, that it makes their method quite nauseous. But the verbose, tasteless Frenchman seems to lay it down as a principle, that every Life must be a Book; and, what is worse, it proves a Book without a Life; for what do we know of Boileau after all his tedious stuff? You are the only one (and I speak it without a compliment) that, by the vigour of your style and sentiments, and the real importance of your materials, have the art (which one would imagine no one could have missed) of adding *agrémens* to the most agreeable subject in the world, which is, Literary History. . . .

11. Anonymous charge of Arianism

March 1738

'Theophilus', letter, *Gentleman's Magazine*, viii (March 1738), 124–5.

Tho' I look upon *Milton* as the chief of Poets, whether ancient or modern, and have as great an Opinion of his Genius as, perhaps, any Man in England, yet I could never think so well of his Religion; to which I believe he has done Dishonour by a Poem, which, tho' universally admir'd, tends greatly to corrupt our Notions of the most sacred Things, and to sensualize our Ideas of God, of Heaven and another World, by Glosses often profane, and sometimes ridiculous. Whether he was a Christian or no, could scarce be determined (I believe) by any thing that occurs in his Poem; much less could one determine, that Way, what Sect he was of; for he seems to shape his Religion so, as to give the most Scope for the Exercise of his own fine Imagination, and to leave the greatest Room for Scenery, and varied Amusement; but, whether for that Reason or no, I will not say, he has certainly adopted the *Arian* Principle into his *Paradise Lost*. This suiting his Religion to the Occasion of Entertainment, has made me often think, that he as little believed the Religion of his Country, as *Homer* or *Virgil* did that of theirs; notwithstanding they treat it with a great deal of Gravity, and affected Solemnity. But herein is the Difference between yᵉ Christian and Heathen Poets; these could be at no great Pains to represent their Religion ridiculous and sensual; for they found it so, and they left it no otherwise: But he has taken the Liberty (as to imitate them in his Composition, so) to bring his Religion to a Resemblance with theirs, as far as his fruitful Imagination could turn it. The Christian's Heaven is almost as sensual as the Heathen's: If in the one there were Feastings, and Junkettings, and Merriments; so in the other too: Nay, he has improv'd upon them, and introduced Dancing into the Entertainments on grand Holydays; and, if one may judge from the Description, it was Country Dancing too. (See B. 5. v. 618, &c.)—If they had a clownish, stupid, unmannerly God among their celestial Orders, so has he his *Mammon*,

The least erected Spirit that fell
From Heav'n; for even from Heav'n his *Looks* and Thoughts
Were always *downward* bent, admiring more
The *Riches* of Heaven's *Pavement*, trodden Gold,
Than ought divine. B. I. v. 679.

If theirs was a Goldsmith by Trade, his was a Mason, *that built in Heaven high Towers.* v. 749. ibid.

Tho' we are taught by an inspired Apostle, that there was War in Heaven (if that Passage in the *Apocalypse* is to be understood according to the Letter); yet to me it seems, at least, unbecoming the Reverence due to Religion, if it be not very prophane, professedly to take the Advantage of Fiction in order to embellish a Poem, pretended to be built upon religious Truth, and to make so free with the Scriptures of God's Word, as to introduce so many Circumstances purely invented. But neither is this all; for had this been done any Way analogously with what is revealed, it had been pardonable; but being quite otherwise, it must argue yᵉ Poet to have had but little Respect for those Holy Books. How much beyond even poetic Licence is it, to feign Beings of such an exalted Nature as Angels, and Angels too of a superior Order, so ignorant of God's Attributes, as to imagine they could either deceive his All-seeing Eye, or overcome his Almighty Power! Yet thus they are represented by *Milton*, Book 6. v. 86.

> For they ween'd
> That self-same Day by *Fight* or by *Surprize*
> To win the Mount of God, and on his Throne
> To set the Envier of his State. . . .

And thus again *Satan* addresses *Michael*:

> Thy utmost Force,
> And join him *nam'd Almighty* to thy Aid,
> I flie not. v. 293. ibid.

In this Mistake, indeed, he was after his Fall corrected; and gives the Reason of it, *viz.* that the Almighty had *concealed his Strength* (B. I. v. 641.) But *Satan* was never such an *Atheist*, and could never possibly entertain so low an Opinion of God's infinite Knowledge and Power, as is suggested in either of the former Instances; or in that towards the End of the 5th B. v. 860, where he so confidently urges his own, and the rest of his Crew's Self-Existence and Independence.—And what more ridiculous Scene could have been brought into a Religious Poem, than that foolish Apparatus of the apostate Spirits, their Cannon and Balls, and Powder and Matches, all described in such a Manner, and with such a Train of ludicrous Circumstances, as would make one believe he intended a Joke by it? I omit the String of Puns that follows, because, tho' the lowest Part of this Passage, it is yet, perhaps, the least offensive. Again, how nearly does the following Description resemble what the Heathen Poets have fabled of *Jupiter*! B. 6. 711.

> Ascend my Chariot, guide the rapid Wheels
> That *shake Heaven's Basis*, bring forth all my War,
> My Bow and Thunder, &c.

It is not much unlike that of *Horace*, Lib. 1. Ode 34. . . .

When the *Messiah* is gone out in Procession to the Work of Creation, what an Image does it present to the Mind, to see him standing with his Compasses (maugre they are golden ones) in Act to lay out and cast the Figure and Circumference of the World. (B. 7. v. 224.) Tho' some of the Antients have very elegantly stiled the Deity *the divine Geometrician*; yet this is making him so in a shamefully narrow Sense; and, but for the Importance of the Subject, the Fancy would be apt to make one laugh. Nor are the Images more proper, or natural, that are applied to the *Messiah* returning from Creation. (v. 574. *ibid*.)

> He, thro' Heav'n,
> That open'd wide her blazing Portals, led
> To God's eternal *House* direct the Way,
> A broad and ample Road, whose Dust is Gold, &c.

Does not this very much resemble the Heaven which Nurses pourtray to their Children, when, in the Simplicity of their Hearts, they would nurture them in what they think Piety? Not to mention that the Hint is plainly taken from *Ovid's Met.* Lib. 1. v. 168. . . .

And what may we think of that Passage, where he represents the Creator as sending a full Legion of Angels to watch the Gates of Hell, that no Spy nor Enemy should come forth while he was in his Work? And for this wond'rous Reason too, very injurious to the Honour and Wisdom of God, *viz.*

> Lest he, incens'd at such Eruption bold,
> Destruction with Creation might have mix'd. B. 8. v. 235.

To conclude, whatever Merit *Milton* may have as a Poet, I'm afraid he will have but little to plead in his Religious Character. Tho' it is likely the Poet had not shone so much if he had denied himself these

Liberties; yet I am certain the Christian had appeared to much greater Advantage: For it must be a great Impiety so deliberately and wantonly to corrupt our Notions of spiritual Things, by gross and sensual Representations; and to blend Heathenism and Christianity together in such an unnatural Medley. After the great Reputation that *Milton* has acquir'd, and after the many excellent Persons that have espoused his Fame, what I have at present undertook must needs appear rash; but since in that Light wherein I have consider'd him, I don't oppose any that I know of, I hope what I have advanced will not be imputed to any thing less justifiable than a Zeal for Truth.

12. Anonymous comment on charge of Arianism

April 1738

'Philo-Spec.', letter, *Gentleman's Magazine*, viii (April 1738), 201–2.

The Letter from *Theophilus*, in your last *Magazine*, occasions the Trouble of this, which I hope will not be unacceptable to the generality of your Readers, as I shall consider his Charge against *Milton* by the Opinion and Sentiments of a Writer, to whose Judgment, I am persuaded, *Theophilus* himself will pay no small deference, and whose Criticisms on that Poet are admirable. I am surprized that *Theophilus* in the conclusion of his Letter should say, 'I don't oppose any that I know of in that Light (meaning as a Christian) I have considered him (*Milton*).' This must be owing to forgetfulness, or he could never have asserted, as in the beginning of his Letter, That 'whether he (*Milton*) was a Christian or no, could scarce be determined by any Thing that occurs in his Poem.' This is the Plaintiff *Theophilus*'s Charge, and I hope you, Mr *Urban*, will hear what can be said on behalf of the Defendant, and direct the Town to find accordingly.—It is possible, that the Traditions on which the *Iliad* and *Æneid* were built, had more Circumstances in them than the History of *the Fall of Man*, as it is related in Scripture. Besides, it was easier for *Homer* and *Virgil* to dash the Truth with Fiction, as they were in no danger of offending the Religion of their Country by it. But as for *Milton*, he had not only a very few Circumstances upon which to raise his Poem, but was also obliged to proceed with the greatest Caution in every thing that he added out of his own Invention. And indeed notwithstanding all the Restraints he was under, he has filled his Story with so many surprizing Incidents, which bear so close an Analogy with what is delivered in holy Writ; that it is capable of pleasing the most delicate Reader, without giving offence to the most scrupulous. (*Spec*. No. 267.) If *Milton*'s Majesty forsakes him any where, it is in those parts of his Poem, where the Divine Persons are introduced as Speakers. One may, I think, observe that the Author proceeds with a kind of fear and trembling, whilst he describes the Sentiments of the Almighty. He dares not give his Imagination full play, but chuses to confine himself to such Thoughts as are drawn from the Books of the most Orthodox Divines, and to such Expressions as may be met with in Scripture, (same Vol. No. 315.) And a little lower. The Particular Beauties of the Speeches in the third Book consist in that shortness and perspicuity of Style, in which the Poet has couched the greatest Mysteries of Christianity, and drawn together in a regular Scheme, the whole Dispensation of Providence, with respect to Man. He has represented all the abstruse Doctrines of Predestination, Free-will and Grace, as also the great Points of Incarnation and Redemption (which naturally grow up in a Poem, that treats of the Fall of Man) with great Energy of Expression, and in a clearer and stronger Light, than I ever met with in any other Writer.—Thus much to shew, that *Theophilus* does differ from some in his Opinion of *Milton*'s Religion; if I find this has a Place in your next *Magazine*, I may perhaps trouble you with another on the same Subject, I shall for the present leave the above to the Consideration of your Readers, and only beg leave to add,

Errors, like Straws, upon the Surface flow;
He who would search for Pearls must dive below.
Dryden.

13. Anonymous reaction to
charge of Arianism

August 1738

Item in *Gentleman's Magazine*, viii (August 1738), 417, referring
to a letter in *Daily Gazetteer*, 7 August 1738.

A Letter-writer, who signs *Urbanus Sylvan*, challenges *Theophilus*,
(whose Letter concerning *Milton* we inserted in our *Mag.* for *March*
last, See p. 124 G) to produce some Passages from *Paradise Lost*, to
prove his Assertion that MILTON had *adopted the* Arian *Principle* into
that Poem: If this is not done in three Months, *Theophilus* must pass
for some conceited *Popish* Tool, whose Aim was to deter well-meaning
People from reading a Poem wherein the Idolatry and Superstition of
the *Heathens* and *Papists* are exposed with all possible Strength and
Beauty, by branding the Author with the odious Mark of a *Heretic*.

14. Warburton on epic

1738

Extract from William Warburton, *The Divine Legation of Moses Demonstrated* (1738). Richard Hurd, ed., *The Divine Legation of Moses Demonstrated* (1837), I, 261.

Before I leave these previous circumstances, permit me only to take notice, that this was the *second species* of the EPIC POEM; our own countryman, Milton, having produced the *third*: for just as Virgil rivaled Homer, so Milton was the emulator of both. He found Homer possessed of the province of MORALITY; Virgil of POLITICS; and nothing left for him, but that of RELIGION. This he seized, as ambitious to share with them in the government of the poetic world: and by means of the superior dignity of his subject, hath gotten to the head of that triumvirate which took so many ages in forming. These are the *three species* of the epic poem; for its largest sphere is HUMAN ACTION; which can be only considered in a *moral*, a *political*, or *religious* view: and these are the three great MAKERS; for each of their poems was struck out at a heat, and came to perfection from its first essay. Here then the grand scene was closed: and all further improvements of the epic at an end.

15. Anonymous rebuttal restating Arian charges

January 1739

'Theophilus', letter, *Gentleman's Magazine*, ix (January 1739), 5–6.

Mr Urban,

The Thoughts which I communicated to you on the Religion of *Milton*'s Poem, were such as had often cast up to me in reading it; whether they were just or not, for any thing *Philo-Spec* has said, may deserve a further Hearing. He has brought a great many Quotations from the *Spectator* to shew, that I was out on't when I said, 'In the Light wherein I had considered him, I did not oppose any that I knew of'. Both his Letters are almost *only* a continued Confutation of this single Assertion, which, whether true or false, was not material. But tho' I pay a great deal of Regard to the Judgment of such a Person as Mr *Addison*, and think his Authority the only Objection this Gentleman has alledged of any Consequence; yet I don't think it ought to be intirely decisive, and the rather, because he was himself a Poet, and, at the Time he wrote those excellent Criticisms, might be so heated with the Beauties of the Poem as to overlook Faults in it, that did not belong to its Character *as such*; and to palliate others out of an Unwillingness to condemn, or leave without Excuse, a favourite Author in so material a Point. But to come to Particulars.

'*Milton* has rather chose to neglect the numerousness of his Verse, than to deviate from those Speeches that are recorded on this great Occasion', (says *Spectator* on the Dialogue in *Eden* after the Fall, and God's Judgment on our first Parents and the Serpent, B. 10.) 'which is (says *Philo-Spec*) a pretty strong Proof of his reverencing the H. Writings'. But if *Philo-Spec* will stand by such Proofs, he must needs think it a Proof equally strong, that, where he introduces Fable and Fiction for the Sake of Embellishment, it is for want of Reverence of the same H. Writings. But as he will not (I believe) allow this, he must quit that Sort of Proof of the Poet's Religion, and account for the

Unadornedness of his Verse some other Way, *viz.* either by supposing he apprehended, that changing the Terms of the Sacred History in a Point so universally known and familiar to every Reader, would give him a kind of Disappointment, and thereby Distaste, to whose Mind the same Terms would naturally be present: Or else by supposing, that it was not indeed Matter for his Invention to work upon, or his Fancy to wanton in: And this seems indeed the Truth of the Case; for in those very Speeches, where he can play the Poet with Delight and Entertainment, and where the Circumstance offers an Image that would be affecting, there he neither neglects the Numerousness of his Verse nor any other Art; tho' to give Scope to his Fancy, he should deviate ever so much from his Original. See, for Instance, *Adam*'s natural and moving Speech, v. 124, *&c. ibid.*

To the Charge of *Milton*'s representing 'the Christians Heaven almost as sensual as the Heathens', *Philo-Spec* replies, by alledging the Angel's preparatory Caution before he satisfied the Father of Mankind's Curiosity concerning what pass'd in Heaven before his Creation. But it must be observed (and *Milton*'s ingenious Advocate ought not to have suppress'd it) that tho' *Raphael* does tell *Adam*, that

> What surmounts the Reach
> Of human Sense, he would delineate so,
> By lik'ning spiritual to corporeal Forms,
> As may express them best. [V, 571–4]

Yet he immediately suggests, that there was greater Propriety in so doing, than his first Caution seem'd to imply;

> Tho' what if Earth
> Be but the Shadow of Heaven, and things therein
> Each to other like, more than on Earth is thought. [V, 574–6]

And this (I say) is corrupting our Notions of spiritual Things, and sensualizing our Ideas of Heaven to a Degree that may have ill Effects on Religion in general: It is letting Fancy obtrude its wild Luxuriance into the Place of Truth and Reason, and making room for the grossest and most absurd Kind of Enthusiasm; and if one is to interpret his other Descriptions of Heaven by this Hint, it is every whit as sensual as the Mahometan's.

I see no Justness in *Philo-Spec*'s Defence of the Angel's Countrey Dances, nor of any of their Dances, by the Example of *David*; and therefore I shall only say upon the Whole, that whoever reads the

Poet's Description of this celestial Jubilee, and thinks it not unworthy of those Beings, and that Place, is qualified to preach in Bedlam, and almost outdo Paganism for Purity.

'The Character of *Mammon*, and the Description of *Pandæmonium* may have their Beauties', as Mr *Addison* observes, so far as they are considered as Pieces of mere Fancy and Invention, to which a Latitude may be allow'd where Religion is not concerned; (and this was the Light in which that ingenious Critic considered them): But to make religious Truths give Way to these, rather than spoil a Scene in a Poem, is what I am not yet convinc'd can be consistent with the Regard that is due to Religion. But neither does Mr *Addison*'s Criticism absolutely infer the Justness of representing Mammon *admiring more the Riches of Heaven's Pavement than ought divine*; but only the just Relation and Agreement between his Speech in the *second Book*, and this—his Character in *the first*; and I must here beg Leave to ask *Philo-Spec*, whether he thinks it possible *indeed*, that such a Being, yet in the Condition of an Angel of Light, cou'd have such Sentiments, were the Pavement of Heaven really as fine as it is describ'd?

What I objected to the Poet's representing *Satan* as ignorant of God's natural and incommunicable Attributes, *Philo-Spec* has answered with no little Wit; but (I'm obliged to tell him) nothing to the Purpose: For the Question is not, how it suited best with the Design of the Poet to represent him; (and this is the Ground upon which *Philo-Spec*'s Defence turns) but whether it was not contrary to Truth and Reason to represent him as he does, *viz.* A Being of such an Order ignorant of those Attributes which are first in Conception?

Tho' Mr *Addison*'s Defence of *Satan*'s Artillery is very ingenious, and as much as could be said for it, yet still it is not sufficient to take off the Imputation of its being both a very violent and ridiculous Machine in such a Poem, and a very odd Sort of Engineer-Work for Spirits to have plann'd; it is indeed (as he says) *a bold Thought*. Tho' (by the bye) I think it may well be doubted whether *Satan* had ever yet heard that Thunder, which these Engines are said to have been made for Imitation of.

Philo-Spec has an elegant Joke, and a *curious* (as being very *far fetcht*) on the Remark of the Messiah's Chariot, which (he says) 'raised those Clouds of Dust that seem to have rendered *my Eyes blind* to the Poet's Care and Regard for Decency and Religion:' And this was so natural too, that (as he assures us) 'he could not help saying it'. But I must tell him, for all so confident as he seems, that Passage in the Psalms which he alludes to, is no more a Vindication of *Milton*'s Machine of the war-like Chariot and its Motion, than it would be a Vindication of the *Bow* in the same Description, to alledge the *Rainbow* in the 9th Chap. of *Genesis*, which the Almighty there calls *his* Bow.

The Golden Compasses he next undertakes to defend, by a Quotation from the *Spectator*; where the ingenious Critic produces several Forms of Speech out of the Prophets, which have something of like Analogy in them; *as meting out the Heavens with a Span*, &c. But how wide the Difference is between these short Allegories and the Poet's Compasses, every body must see; the Preciseness of the Description here, and the Manner of the Messiah's *Operation*, one Foot he center'd, and the other turn'd, &c. (B. vii. v. 228) may indeed be *in the Spirit of Homer*, when speaking of his *Jupiter*, or his chief Ambassador *Mercury*; but carries in it such a Narrowness of Idea as, when applied to the Almighty Architect, is utterly profane. Allegories from sensible Things, when applied to the supreme Understanding, ought to be short, and not spun out into Particulars and Circumstances; for since we are reduced to the Use of them, merely by the Imperfection of our Minds, we ought to recover our Thoughts from them as soon as possible; otherwise, we must become shocking and ridiculous.

The last Thing that *Philo-Spec* resents is, finding fault with the Guard set to watch the Gates of Hell: But that was not all the Ground of the Objection; it was the Reason of the Angels being appointed Centinels there, *viz.*

> Lest he (the Almighty) incens'd at such Eruption bold,
> Destruction with Creation might have mixt. [VIII, 235–6]

And this (I said) was very injurious to the Honour and Wisdom of God: And what has *Milton* said to the contrary in the Words quoted by *Philo-Spec*? Or what has *Philo-Spec* himself said? It is not injurious to the Character of the Supream Being to suppose him capable of being acted by a furious and blind Impulse? *Milton* could make the Devils themselves out-reason him in this;

> Will he, so wise, let loose at once his Ire,
> Belike through Impotence, or unaware,
> To give his Enemies their Wish, and end
> Them in his Anger, whom his Anger saves
> To punish endless? [II, 155–9]

I could instance in many more Particulars of this Poem, that bear no good Aspect towards Religion; but do not incline to enter the Lists with *Philo-Spec*, and therefore shall take my Leave of the Subject by observing, that if Monsieur *Huet*'s Definition of Romance be proper, *viz*. That it is a History which hath Truth for the main Ground of it, but yet is interwoven with the Embellishments of Fiction; then this Poem may not improperly be called the *Romance of the War in Heaven, and the Fall of Man*.

16. Benson on Milton's verse

1739

[William Benson], *Letters Concerning Poetical Translations, and Virgil's and Milton's Arts and Verse* (1739), from letter v, pp. 39–50, dated 11 October 1736. Most examples are omitted.

William Benson (1682–1754), sometime politician and literary critic, erected a monument to Milton in Westminster Abbey in 1737, engraved a medal of him, and became William Dobson's patron for a Latin version of *Paradise Lost* (1750–3). He was often ridiculed for his politics as well as for elevating himself through other's fame.

Sir,

I am now to consider *Milton*'s Versification under the same Heads as I have considered *Virgil*'s, so far as there is Opportunity of doing it.

I. To begin with *The Varying of the Pause*, which is the Soul of all Versification in all Languages. Verse is Musick, and Musick is more or less pleasing as the Notes are more or less varied, that is, raised or sunk, prolonged or shortned.

In order to judge of the varying of *English* Versification, I first endeavour'd (as I have already said, with respect to the *Latin*) to find out the common Pause in *English* Verse, that is, where the Voice naturally makes some sort of Stop when a Verse is read. To this purpose I look'd into Mr. *Cowley*'s *Davideis* (for it would be of no use to quote such

Authors as *Quarles* and *Ogilby,* who never had any Reputation for
Poetry; but this Gentleman has been stil'd, and is at present recorded in
Westminster-Abbey, as *Anglorum Pindarus, Maro, Flaccus*) and there I
soon found the common Pause to be upon the last Syllable of the second
Foot. . . .

Thus I discovered from *Cowley* in *English* what I perceived from
Ovid in *Latin.* I then turned to the *Paradise Lost,* and there I found
Milton even surpasses *Virgil* in this particular. *Virgil* uses the common
Pause at the fifth Line of the *Georgicks,* but *Milton* does not use it till
he comes to the sixth Line in his *Paradise Lost.* [I, 1–6]

It would be needless to produce more Examples to this purpose; and
I believe I may venture to affirm that the Verse is varied at least with
as much Skill in the *Paradise Lost,* as even in the *Georgick* itself: I am
inclinable to think with more, because in this respect the *English*
Language surpasses the *Latin,* by reason of its Monosyllables, of which
I have said enough for any body at all versed in these Matters, to be
able to make out what is here advanc'd. . . .

II. I come now to the second Particular: *The Inversion of the Phrase.*
Every Page affords Instances of this Nature.

> Him the Almighty Pow'r
> Hurl'd headlong flaming from the ethereal Sky. [I, 44–5]

And in one of *Milton's* juvenile Poems we have

> Trip the pert Fairies. ['Comus', 118]

And,

> Revels the spruce [and] jocund Spring. ['Comus', 985]

III. The third thing to be consider'd, is, *The adapting the Sound to the
Sense.*

Who does not hear the Warbling of a *Brook,* the Rustling of *Wings,*
the rough Sound of *Trumpets* and *Clarions,* and the soft one of *Flutes*
and *Recorders* in the following Lines?

> Fountains, and ye that warble as ye flow
> Melodious Murmur warbling, tune his Praise. [V, 195–6]

Who does not see Porpoises and Dolphins tumbling about in the
Ocean when he reads this Line? [VII, 409–12]

How variously the Rivers run in these Verses? [VII, 297–300]

How is the Verse extended where the Whale lies at length upon the
Ocean! [VII, 412–14]

How does the Line labour when the Elephant is working himself through the stiff Clay, whilst the lesser Animals sprout up as it were in an Instant! [VII, 470–2]

IV. The fourth thing to be enquir'd into is, *The mixing of singular and plural Numbers*, in which *Milton* excels. . . .

V. As to the fifth Remark upon *Virgil*, which relates to his using the Particles *Que* and *Et* in his Verse, there can be nothing of that nature in *Milton*. So that I proceed to

VI. The sixth thing to be observed, which is, *The Collocatio Verborum*. *Milton* often places the Adjective after the Substantive, which very much raises the Stile. . . .

But the utmost of his Art in this respect consists in his removing the Adjective, the Substantive, and even the Verb, from the Line or Verse in which the Sense is previously contained, and the grammatical Construction inverted, to the Beginning of the next Line. This has a wonderful Effect; especially when the Word is a Monosyllable. . . .

This artful Collocation commands the Attention, and makes the Reader feel and see what is offer'd to him.

That this Effect is owing to the Collocation will appear by considering any one of the Instances now produc'd. For Example:

> Over their Heads triumphant Death his Dart
> Shook. [XI, 491–2]

This Passage makes the Reader see Death with his Dart in his Hand, shaking it over the Heads of the unhappy Creatures describ'd in the *Lazar-house* as plainly as if the whole was painted upon Canvas. But let this Line be alter'd thus:

> Over their Heads Death shook his dreadful Dart.

How much of the Fire and Spirit of this Passage is lost, will be easily perceiv'd.

I was long of Opinion that *Milton* had invented this Art himself, for I knew he had it not from *Virgil*: The *Latin* Language is hardly capable of it. But by Accident I found *Milton* learn'd it from *Homer*, though it is plain what is *Art* in the former was *Chance* in the latter; which cannot be disputed when it is considered that in so many thousand Lines that we have of *Homer*'s, there is I believe but one single Instance of this Monosyllable Collocation; but in *Milton* there are many, both Substantives, Adjectives and Verbs. . . .

Milton likewise uses his Monosyllables very artfully in placing them at the Conclusion of a Line, so as to divide the last Foot of the Verse, which has a very extraordinary Effect. . . .

Again he divides the last Foot by making a Monosyllable the Beginning of a new Sentence, which is very pleasing. . . .

Milton also sometimes places two Monosyllables at the End of the Line, stopping at the 4th Foot, to adapt the Measure of the Verse to the Sense; and then begins the next Line in the same manner, which has a wonderful Effect. [IV, 720–2, misquoted]

This artful Manner of writing makes the Reader see them *Stop* and *Turn* to worship God before they went into their Bower. If this Manner was alter'd, much of the Effect of the Painting would be lost. . . .

VII. The seventh Particular in *Virgil* was his *Varying the Common Pronunciation,* in which *Milton* has imitated him in several Places. . . .

VIII. *His Verses contrary to the Common Measure.* The following is an Example of this kind.

> Drove headlong down to the Bottomless Pit.

[the line is not Milton's.]

Those who may be apt to find fault with such Arts as these (for Arts they are in *Virgil* and *Milton*) little think what it is to write 10 or 12 thousand Lines, and to vary the Sound of them in such manner as to entertain the Ear from the Beginning to the End of the Work.

IX. I come now to the *Alliteratio.*

And 1. To speak of the single *Alliteratio.* This is so common in *Milton*, that you need but begin the Poem, or open any Page of it, and you will meet with it. . . .

17. Warburton in refutation of Bentley

April 1740

[William Warburton], 'Remarks on Milton's *Paradise Lost*', *The History of the Works of the Learned* (April 1740), Article xviii, pp. 273–80.

BOOK I.

Satan persuading Belzebub to continue in Opposition to God, says,

[ll. 116–18].

Here Satan is absurdly made to contradict himself and the present Experience of all his Followers, in saying that the *Strength of Gods*, (that is, the Strength of the fallen Angels) could not fail, when it had so fatally failed. The Copulative should be thrown out, and the Lines read thus,

> Since by Fate (the Strength of Gods)
> This Empyreal Substance cannot fail.

i. e. Since by Fate, which is the Strength of Gods, or God, (he impiously ranking himself and his Crew in equality with God) our Being is immortal. And this is the Sense the Context requires.

The saying God was upheld by Fate was the repeated and constant Blasphemy that *Satan* and his Followers are all along made to vomit against Heaven.

[ll. 376–9]

Dr. *Bentley* says,—'Here, in imitation of *Homer* and *Virgil*, who give Catalogues of their Captains and Forces, our Author gives a List of the principal *Devils*, with their Characters; but it is not the finest Part of his Poem.' I think it is, in the Design and Drawing, if not in the Colouring; for the *Paradise Lost*, being a Religious Epic, as a late Writer has shewn, nothing could be more artful than thus deducing the Original of Superstition. This gives it a great Advantage over the Catalogues he has imitated, for *Milton*'s becomes thereby a necessary Part of the Work, as the Original of Superstition, an essential Part of a Religious Epic, could not have been shewn without it. Had *Virgil's* or *Homer's* been omitted, their Poems would not have suffered materially, because in their Relations of the following Actions we find the Soldiers, which were catalogued: but by no following History of Superstition that *Milton* could have brought in, could we find these *Devils* Agency, it was therefore necessary he should inform us of the Fact.

[ll. 645–7]

Dr. *Bentley* says there is no Difference between *Fraud* and *Guile*, and therefore alters it to

Fraud and WILE.

But there is a great deal of Difference. They bear indeed this Idea in common of *deceiving covertly*, and therefore the Poet says—*to work by close Design*—But then they have this Difference: *Guile* is a Deceit, where the Deceived is supposed to co-operate with the Deceiver, *Fraud* where he is not. This Difference is clearer seen in the Verbs to *defraud*, to *beguile*; and this is a Difference much to the Purpose of the Story. . . .

BOOK II.

[ll. 146–51]

Dr. *B.* says—'Who (says the Poet) would be annihilated, lose his intellectual Being and all his Thoughts? MOTION therefore is an improper Word here, that's no Part of Thought, nor abstracted, has any Excellence in it'—So far is right—He goes on—'I am persuaded he gave it, *Devoid of Sense and ACTION*, deprived of our two Faculties, *to perceive and to act.*' I am persuaded he gave it with a much less Change from the present Reading,

Devoid of Sense and NOTION.

These are properly the two Faculties of the *intellectual Being*—*Sensation* and *Reflection*. . . .

[ll. 1037–40]

Dr. *B.* says—'If HER Works, then *Nature* retires, contrary to the Poet's thought.' But *Nature* is meant for the new made World, and is of our side against *Chaos*. So that the Author must have given it that *Chaos* retired.

As from HIS outmost Works a broken Foe.

Strange! *Chaos* is here represented as assailing, and *Nature* as defending. Must not then, according to all military Conceptions, the *Outworks* be *Nature*'s. The Construction of the Words too is as easy as the thought. Chaos *begins to retire from the outmost Works of Nature, as a broken Foe with less horrid Din.*

BOOK III.

[ll. 160–2]

Dr. *B.* says,—*This is miserably flat and creeping with wretched Accent: Raise it a little thus,* &c.—But if I have any Conception of the Poet's Art of Harmony, to raise it would be to spoil it. In this Reluctancy of the Numbers to move forward lies a great Beauty, the labouring of the Verse shewing that the Devil would draw very unwilling Followers. And the Image is vastly heightened by the System of *original Sin*, which the Poet goes upon, and which teaches, that notwithstanding all the Endeavours of *Adam*'s Posterity to regain God's Favour, they were inevitably doomed to Hell for his Transgression.

[ll. 298–9]

Dr. *B.* says—'Every one that reads with any Attention, must needs stumble at this Verse, *Giving to Death*, an odd Signification of giving. Is it the same as *yielding*? Allow that—yet why does he add *and dying*? As if *dying* and *yielding to Death* were not the same again. Perhaps the Poet might give it thus,

LIVING to TEACH and dying to redeem.'

But let us consider *Milton*'s System of Divinity, which taught, not only that Man was redeemed, but likewise that a real Price was paid for his Redemption; *dying to redeem* therefore signifying only Redemption in a vague uncertain Sense, but imperfectly represents his System; so imperfectly that it may as well be called the *Socinian*; the *Price paid* (which implies a proper Redemption) is wanting. But to pay a Price implying a voluntary Act, the Poet therefore well expresses it by *giving to Death*, i. e. giving himself to Death, which shews *yielding* is not equivalent to *giving*, Freedom and Choice not being implied in the former Word. And yet 'tis on this Supposition that the Doctor makes out, that *dying* and *giving to Death are the same*; so that the Sense of the Line fully expresses *Milton*'s Notion, *Heavenly Love gave a Price for the Redemption of Mankind, and by Virtue of that Price really redeemed them.*

18. Peck on Milton's style

1740

Francis Peck, 'An Examination of *Milton's Stile*', *New Memoirs of the Life and Poetical Works of Mr. John Milton* (1740), 106–32.

Francis Peck (1692–1743) was an antiquary who accumulated abstruse materials, as his *Desiderata Curiosa* (1732) shows. His *Memoirs of the Life and Actions of Oliver Cromwell* (1740) contains some spurious and some authentic pieces by Milton. *New Memoirs of John Milton* includes the un-Miltonic English translation of George Buchanan's *Baptistes*, a comparison of Laud and Wolsey, supposedly a vision by Milton, some totally disrelated items, and interestingly enough, Milton's second prolusion. Besides his discussion of style, here given, Peck illustrates Milton's and Shakespeare's works by excerpts from contemporary authors.

There is often something in Milton's phrase and expression so very singular, that few of all those many persons who have endeavoured to imitate his *stile*, have been able to come up to it. This observation led me, in this last reading of his works, to rework what particulars that singularity consists of. And that singularity, if I err not, among divers other arts of the like sort, consists mostly of such practices as these.

I. He sometimes, tho' rarely, *lengthens* a word. As, *Beëlzebub* for *Beêlzebub* (*PL*, I, 81); *Eremit*, for *Hermit* (*PL*, III, 474; *PR*, I, 8); *Hesebon*, for *Heshbon* (*PL*, I, 408). To add another instance [*PL*, IV, 265] where *attune*, for *tune*, to make them russle, or speak as it were in soft music.

II. He very often *shortens* a word. As, *illumin*, for *illuminate* (*PL*, I, 23, 666); *supernal*, for *supernatural* (*PL*, I, 241; VII, 573; XI, 359) [twenty-one further examples].

III. He often *softens* a word. As, *traverse*, for *transverse* (*PL*, I, 568); *panim*, for *paynim* (*PL*, I, 765) [six further examples].

IV. He often makes use of *old* words . . . As, *nathless*, for *nevertheless* (*PL*, I, 299); *earst*, for *e'erwhile* (*PL*, I, 360) [thirty-two further examples]. 'These words make his poems appear more venerable, to give them a great air of antiquity★.'

V. When he wants a proper word to express his sense, he coins a *new* one. As, *the bee with* honied *thigh* ('Il Pens.', 142); Sericana, *where* Chineses *drive/With sails & wind Thir* canie *waggons light* (*PL*, III, 438–9) [six further examples]. 'If the reader is offended at this liberty in our *English* poet (saith Mr. *Addison*) I would recommend to him a discourse in *Plutarch*, which shews how frequently *Homer* hath made use of the same liberty.'

VI. He very often *drops* a word. And indeed one of the greatest arts in composition, I think, is easing the verse of all superfluous words, by dropping or letting any or all the words be understood, which can possibly be so. This is a secret which our author knew well, & practised so frequently that you can hardly read ten lines in him, without observing something of it. I will therefore instance only in a few passages. As, *And where thir weakness, how attempted best,/By force or suttlety* (*PL*, II, 357). Admit only the words *dropped*, & we must read: *And where thir weakness* lies, & *how* it may be *best attempted* [six further examples].

VII. He sometimes *repeats* a word. As, so *good,*/So *fit*, so *acceptable*, so *divine* (*PL*, X, 138) [two examples from Shakespeare, three more from Milton, and one from Pope].

VIII. He naturalizes many *Greek* words. As, Cynosure ('Comus', 344; 'L'Allegro', 80); *phalanx* (*PL*, I, 550) [six further examples].

IX. And almost innumerable *Latin* words. As, *translucent* ('Comus', 886); *humid* ('Comus', 1017; *PL*, IX, 193) [forty further examples].

X. He often introduces *technical* words, or terms of art, peculiar to the several sciences & occupations of life. 'Thus, when he is upon building (saith Mr. *Addison*) he mentions Doric *pillars, pilasters, cornice, freeze, architrave*. When he talks of heavenly bodies you meet with *eccliptic, eccentric*, the *trepidation*, stars dropping from the *Zenith*, rays *culminating* from the Equator†.' Also [further examples]. And an organ-builder on the land; understanding,/ How *in an organ, from one blast of wind,/To many a row of pipes the* sound-board *breathes* (*PL*, I, 709). From which two last lines only I am satisfied that, before his eyes failed him, our author could take an organ to pieces, & clean it, & put it together again, without any other person to help him.

But the use of all technical words is generally reckoned a fault. 'Yet, saith Mr. *Spence*‡ tho' the banishing of all technical words be laid down as a rule never to be transgressed, I should imagine they might be admit-

★ Mr. Addison, *Spect.* No. 285.   † *Spectator*, No. 297.   ‡ On the *Odyssey*, p. 170.

ted in some cases, even where there is not that absolute necessity either of using them, or of losing the sense of the original.' And herein he thought with our author.

XI. As to his elisions, melting of syllables, & using something like an *English* dactyl foot: he generally cuts off the letter y in the word *many*, when the next word begins with a vowel (which yet seems not to be cut off, but rather to remain) whereby he gives a particular softness to the foot, & makes it read like an *English* dactyl. As, *so, over* many *a tract* / *Of heav'n they march'd, &* many *a province wide* (*PL*, VII, 76).

Here is another verse where y final is cut off, & again not cut off, before two words beginning each with a vowel: *Where* glory *is false* glory *attributed* / *To things not glorious* (*PR*, III, 69). A third, which reads as if it had two *dactyl* feet: *which wrought them pain* / *Implacable,* & many *a* dolorous *groan* (*PL*, VI, 657). A fourth, as if it had *three: Embryo's,* & *idiots, eremits,* & *friars* (*PL*, III, 474). A fifth, as if it had an *anapaest* foot: *Least entring on the* Canaanite *allarm'd* (*PL*, XII, 217). In the same manner our author often *melts* the word spirit, when it stands before a word beginning with a vowel, into a monosyllable. As, *Long strugling underneath, ere they could wind* / *Out of such prison, though* spirits *of purest light* (*PL*, VI, 659). And here is another verse, where he partly *melts* & partly *cuts* off the latter syllable of the word *ruin*, by the first syllable of the word *indeed: Of* ruin *indeed methought I heard the noise* (*Samson*, 1515). [Quotation from *Spectator*, no. 285.]

XII. He often makes the substantive an *adjective*, or, if you will, puts it adjectively. As, *soothing the* raven *downe* / *Of darkness till it smil'd* ('Comus', 251) [seven further examples and one from Horace].

XIII. He often makes the substantive a *verb*. As, *ayrie toungs that* syllable *mens names* ('Comus', 208) [four further examples].

XIV. He sometimes makes the substantive a *participle*. As, *Half-spi'd, so thick the roses* bushing *round* / *About her glow'd* (*PL*, IX, 426).

XV. And sometimes an *adverb*. As, If chance *the radiant sun with farewell sweet* / *Extend his ev'ning beam* (*PL*, II, 492) [two further examples].

XVI. He often places the substantive between *two adjectives,* which is very classical. As, *Bitter constraint* & sad occasion deare ('Lycidas', 6) [five further examples].

XVII. He often makes the adjective a *substantive*; whereby the epithet itself expresses the substantive. As, *Such place eternal justice had prepar'd* / *For those* rebellious (*PL*, I, 70) [twenty-seven further examples].

XVIII. He sometimes makes the adjective a *verb*. As, *perhaps more valid armes,* / *Weapons more violent, when next we meet,* / *May serve to* better *us* & worse *our foes* (*PL*, VI, 438).

XIX. He sometimes makes the adjective an *adverb.* As, *And all amid them stood the tree of life* / High *eminent* (*PL*, IV, 218) [four further examples].

XX. He sometimes puts the adjective after the *substantive.* As, *What* thanks sufficient *or what* recompense / Equal, *have I to render thee, divine* Hystorian? (*PL*, VIII, 5) [two further examples].

XXI. And sometimes before the *infinitive* mood, where it always runs very smoothly. As, Outragious *to devour* (*PL*, II, 435).

XXII. He often makes the verb a *substantive.* As, *Thee I re-visit now with bolder wing,* / *Escapt the* Stygian *pool, though long detain'd* / *In that obscure* sojourn (*PL*, III, 13) [ten further examples].

XXIII. He sometimes makes the verb an *adjective,* As, *Made so adorn for thy delight the more* (*PL*, VIII, 576).

XXIV. Sometimes a *participle.* As, *Thoughts which how found they harbour in thy brest,* / Adam, misthought *of her to thee so dear?* (*PL*, IX, 288–289) [two further examples].

XXV. And sometimes puts it *between two accusatives.* As, *My almightie arms* / Gird on, *& sword upon thy puissant thigh* (*PL*, VI, 713–714).

XXVI. He sometimes makes the participle *an adjective.* As, *as late clouds* / *Justling or pusht with winds rude in thir shock* / *Tine the* slant lightning (*PL*, X, 1073–75).

XXVII. And sometimes an adverb. As [*PL* VI, 671–4].

XXVIII. He very often uses the *complex* epithet. As, smooth-enamel'd *green* ('Arcades', 84) [numerous examples].

XXIX. And as often the *continuative* epithet, substantive, or verb. As, Unrespited, unpiti'd, unrepriev'd (*PL*, II, 185) [eight further examples]. In which case he affects to make his verse to consist of three words only. (So *Shakespeare.* Unhousel'd, unanointed, unaneal'd . . .) Tho' he sometimes admits of four such words. . . . So much for the *continuative epithet.* In the next place observe how he heaps the *substantive* in the same manner [*PL* X, 111; *PR* III, 187; *Samson*, 1180]. And the *Verb* [*PR* I, 412].

XXX. The *transposition* of his words is an art of our author's, for which some *blame,* but others, I think, more justly *commend* him. Of those who *blame* him for his transpositions, one writes thus. 'What *transpositions* is Milton forced to, as an equivalent for want of rhime, in the poetry of a language which depends upon a natural order of words? And even this would not have done his business, had he not given the fullest scope to his genius, by chusing a subject upon which there could be no hyperboles. We see (however he be deservedly successful) that the ridicule of his manner succeeds better than the imitation of it. Because *transpositions*, which are unnatural to a language, are to be fairly derided, if they ruin it, by being frequently introduced; & because hyperboles, which outrage every lesser subject where they are seriously used, are often beautiful in Ridicule'.[1]

Of those who *commend* him for his transpositions, one writes thus. 'There is a good deal of stifness which yet attends our language, from the stated order of words in such a repeated succession; &, tho' we are much freer than our neighbors the *French* in this particular, I should be glad to see our poets, at least, go yet farther towards the liberties of the old *Greeks* & *Romans*. Mr. *Pope* hath some strokes towards this: he is sometimes bold in varying the expected range of words, to give his sentences a new agreeable air: he *transposes* their order, often by his own judgment, & often in imitation of some of our *best* poets, who have succeeded in it before'. . . .[2]

XXXI. His frequent & beautiful *return* of the same, or very near the same words, after the manner of *Homer*, is another. As, [*PL* X, 1086–1100].

XXXII. His *metaphors* are very *just*. '*Metaphor* or translation is a figure', saith Vossius, 'wherein a word is transferred from its proper signification into another through a certain similitude. And therefore three things are to be respected in a metaphor, & those are the *proper* & *foreign signification* of the word, & the *similitude.*'

Now consider any of our author's underwritten metaphors in these three points of view, & you will immediately see the boldness & the justness of them. [*PL* IV, 505–8, plus four other examples.]

XXXIII. His *simile's* are very *fine*. . . .

XXXIV. His *descriptions* are very *lively*. Instead of an index of our author's most admired *descriptions*, Mr. *Richardson* gives us an index of his *pictures*. The fancy is pretty enough. For the alteration of the term makes it look like the discovery of so many new beauties. This is a certain proof that his descriptions are very lively. But, for the rest, it is only a genteel compliment to Mr. *Richardson's* own profession. For what Mr. *Richardson*, or any other painter, would call a Table of *Milton's* pictures, a poet, or any other writer, would only entitle an index of his descriptions.

1 Thomas Parnell, *Life*, preface.
2 Spence, *On the Odyssey*, p. 170.

XXXV. His *poetic preventions* are *inimitably beautiful.* The '*poetic prevention* is, when we speak of things yet to come, as if they were already present' (Mr. *Spence,* p. 212). As, in that celebrated instance of the supposed shaking of the earth, before the earth was, in the fight between the good & evil angels. [*PL* VI, 216-18]

Such again is that simile, where the waters hasting to their places are compared to soldiers running to their standards. [*PL* VII, 293-7]

XXXVI. His other *figures* are exceeding *bold.* As first, the *Metonymie* . . .

XXXVII. Secondly, the *Irony* . . .

XXXVIII. Thirdly, the *Catachresis* . . .

XXXIX. Fourthly, the *Exclamation* . . .

XL. Fifthly, the *Correction* (retraction of previous resolution) . . .

XLI. Sixthly, the *Apostrophe* . . .

XLII. Seventhly, the *suspension* . . .

XLIII. Eighthly, the prosopopeoia (giving voice to inanimate things) . . .

XLIV. Ninthly, the *Transition* . . .

XLV. Tenthly, the *Sentence* (an instructive or lively remark) . . .

XLVI. Eleventhly, the *Epiphonema* (an acclamation at the end of a passage) . . .

XLVII. His *mixtures* of *opposite passions* are admirable. As, 1. *Joy* & *fear* [*PL* I, 780-8]. 2. *Horror* & *joy* [*PL* II, 845-8].

XLVIII. His *imitations* of the antients are *delightful.* For instance, [*PL* IV, 460-72]. Now what a beautiful copy is this of the *Narcissus* of *Ovid,* viewing & admiring of himself in the fountain? [*Metamorphoses* III]

XLIX. And his *imitations* of *scripture* are as *charming.* Under this head I will mention two or three remarkable instances, none of which, I think, have been hitherto taken notice of by any writer.

1. That beautiful line, wherein our author calls the light,

Bright effluence of bright essence increate! PL. III. 6.

seems to me, not a thought of his own, but an imitation of *Solomon. She* [wisdom] *is a pure influence flowing from the glory of the almighty.* Wisdom vii. 25.

2. There is scarce a more sublime thought in all Milton, than in those three admirable lines which make a part of the description of that grand incident of the Messiah's driving the rebellious angels out of heaven [*PL* VI, 853-5]. Yet this thought, if I err not, is also borrowed from scripture. I see it, I think, twice there. First, in the *Maschil* of *Asaph. Yea*

many a time turned he his wrath away, & would not suffer his whole *displeasure to arise.* Ps. lxxviii. 39. And then, in *Solomon. Thou,* mastering thy power, *judgest with equity.* Wisd. xii. 18.

3. Adam's account of his own dream, in which, as he tells Raphael, he beheld the formation of Eve [*PL* VIII, 470–5], is, the latter part of it, sure taken from that easie, natural relation of that strange impression which the first view of *Judith* made upon the heart of *Holofernes.—Her beauty took his mind prisoner.* Judith xvi. 9. Words so exceeding soft & tender, that all the amplification in the world can add nothing to their great elegance & expressiveness. *Shakespeare,* as I shall hereafter show, was as fond of that passage as Milton.

L. Upon the whole, whenever I take up Milton, & sit down to read any of his nine best *English* Poems, he delights me, so that I am almost ready to apply his own beautiful words (with which he makes *Adam* address *Raphael*) to himself [*PL* VIII, 210–16].

[Note: Slight alterations have been made in indentation and punctuation.]

19. Davies' 'Rhapsody to Milton'

February 1740

Sneyd Davies, 'Rhapsody to Milton' (February 1740). John Whalley, *A Collection of Original Poems and Translations* (1745), 182–6.

Sneyd Davies (1709–69), a very minor poet of the period, was generally a recluse, who produced Latin verses and imitations of Horace, Milton, and Swift.

Soul of the Muses! Thou supreme of Verse!
Unskill'd and Novice in the sacred Art
May I unblam'd approach thee? May I crave
Thy Blessing, Sire harmonious! amply pleas'd
Shou'd'st thou vouchsafe to own me for thy Son;
Thy Son, tho' dwindled from the mighty Size,
And Stature; much more from the Parent's Mind.
Content and blest enough, if but some Line,
If some distant Feature, half express'd,
Tell whence I spring.—This Privilege deny'd,
Grant me at least thy Converse now and oft
To ruminate the Beauties infinite,
To trace thy Heav'nly Notions, to enquire
When from above they came, and how convey'd:
If darted on thee by the Sun's bright Ray,
Meridian Fire! Or rather by the Muse
Nocturnal wafted to thy favour'd Ear,
How else, explain, cou'd human Mind exile
Grasp universal Nature, Treasure huge!
Or even say, where could'st thou Language find
Able to bear the Burden of thy Thought?
Such Thought, such Language, that all other Verse
Seems trifling (not excepting *Greece* and *Rome*)
So lofty and so sweet, beyond compare,
Is thine: Whether thy sounding Pinion match

The Clang of Eagle's Flight: Or thy pois'd Plume,
Dove-like cut silently th' unconscious Sky,
Calm as the Summer's Breath, softer than Down.
Witness the Scene of *Eden*, Bow'r of Love,
Of Innocence, of Happiness; o'erlaid
With Fancy's finest Treasure; strew'd with Flow'rs
Of *Amaranth*; her Rivers *Nectar*; Winds,
To which *Arabia*'s spicy Gales are poor.
Witness a bolder Page, where coping Gods
In Battle rend the steadfast Hills, and shake
Heav'n's Basis: lively flash the painted Fires,
And the imagin'd Thunder rolls methinks
More terribly, than tearing the vext Air
When troubled Nature speaks.—But why select
A Charm from thousand? And what need of Praise?
Who fondly seeks to praise thee, does thee wrong,
Impairs thee, greatest in thyself. Thy Hell,
Copied by other Hand whate'er, will lose
It's Terrors; and thy Paradise it's Sweets,
Soil'd by rude Touch.—Enough then to admire,
Silent admire: and be content to feel:
Or, if we follow thy bright Track, advance
With Reverence, and shew that not Desire
To Rival, but Resemble, is our Aim:
Resemble thee, tho' in inferior Strain.

For O! great Pattern to succeeding Times!
Dost thou not smile indignant, to behold
The tinkling modern fetter'd, yet well pleas'd,
Dance to the tiresome Musick of his Chains;
While all *Parnassus* rings the silly Chime:
And *Pegasus*, that once with spurning Heel
Kick'd the dull Ground, Ridiculous and Tame
Can amble with a Monk upon his Back?—
Cou'd *Milton* think, when his high Standard rear'd
Th' Emblazonry of Freedom, none shou'd throng
To gaze, and kiss the Manumizing Staff?
Dastards in Choice! what, Legislator, then
Avail thy Charter, thy Example bright?
As when some Hero, to redeem a state

Long harrow'd by Oppression; lifts his Arm,
To crush th' imperious Yoke: the many scar'd
Stand tremblingly aloof, and love the Mace
That bruises 'em: Or, if the Chief return,
From the red Hall with Liberty proclaim'd,
Know not to prize, or keep, the mighty Gem;
The *Romans* on a Time, a Madman kill'd,
Rather than not be lorded, chose a Fool,
When *Claudius* in a lurking Hole was found
By Band Praetorian. Abject thus our Age
And Slaves, because their Fathers were, to Rhime—

Is it then Custom, (Superstition's Plea)
Ears poorly tickled with returning Sounds,
Why Jingling Charms? Is it to speed our Course!
A Peal of Bells were right, if we were Mules:
The Courser asks no Spur.—Ah me! I fear,
And see, and feel the Reason; Faulters why
The Muse this Moment, wearied, flags and pants
Despairing? Such a Distance hast thou got
From thy first start, and left Pursuit behind:
On the Top Brow of Fame, in laurel'd Chair
Seated, and thence look down on Mortal Toil,
That climbing emulous would pace in vain
Thy Footsteps, trackless thro' Excess of Light.

PERIOD OF ALLEGED PLAGIARISM, SOME ANALYSIS, PRAISE, AND DISPRAISE

1741-51

---

20. Anonymous analysis of Milton's imitations of the classics

1741

Extract from *An Essay upon Milton's Imitations of the Ancients, in His Paradise Lost. With some Observations on the Paradise Regain'd* ([Edinburgh], 1741), 3-7, 45-9, 52-7.

Aristotle ascribes the Origin of POETRY to the Pleasure Mankind takes in IMITATIONS, which distinguishes us from all other Creatures, and makes us Lovers not only of this ART, but PAINTING and SCULPTURE. This Pleasure arises from the Comparison the Mind makes betwixt the Imitation and the Thing imitated: For Example, in a Picture or Statue, from comparing them with the Original; and, in Poetry, from comparing the Descriptions with the Objects themselves. Hence it is evident.

THAT, when one good Poet imitates another, we have a double Pleasure; the first proceeding from comparing the Description with its Object: and the second, from comparing the one Description with the other from which it was imitated.

THAT, in every Simile we have a double Pleasure; the first, in comparing the Image it conveys with its Objects; the other, in comparing it with the Subject it was designed to Illustrate. But, if the Simile be imitated from another Author, we have still one Pleasure more.

THAT, when a Poet imitates a Description from another Poet, which very Description had been imitated from a Third, our Pleasure is still the greater; therefore, in this Respect, the Imitations in MILTON are beyond those in VIRGIL; because he has imitated some Places of VIRGIL which are Imitations of HOMER.

We must observe, that, in poetical Descriptions, Paintings, &c. the greater Likeness they bear to what we consider as their Original, our Pleasure is the more; and our Distaste in Proportion to their Variation: But here, 'tis different with those secondary Imitations we treat of in this ESSAY: For, frequently, in this Case, a considerable Alteration from the Original has a very agreeable Effect: For we have, in our Nature, a Principle to be delighted with what is NEW, to which, 'tis plain, this latter Kind of Imitations is not very conformable; upon which Account they ought to have, as well as a Likeness, a due Variation, that, at one and the same Time, they may gratify our several Dispositions, of being pleased with what is imitated, and with what is new. And from this it appears, that, in these Imitations, there ought generally to be observed a Medium betwixt a literal Translation and a distant Allusion; as the first destroys the Pleasure we have from what is new, and the latter encroaches on that we receive from Imitations. . . .

The Passages a Poet is to imitate ought to be selected with great Care, and should ever be the best Parts of the best Authors, and always ought to be improved in the Imitation: So that vastly less Invention and Judgment is required to make a good Original than a fine Imitation. Accordingly, we are told by the old Writer of the Life of VIRGIL, it was a Saying of that Poet's, That it would be easier to take the Club from *Hercules*, than a Line from HOMER.

But, from MILTON's having refined exceedingly upon some Passages of HOMER and VIRGIL, I would not pretend to infer, that he was a greater Poet than either of them, tho' the Consideration of the whole Poem will justly intitle him to that Rank; but only, that these Imitations would cost the Author more Pains, and give the Reader greater Pleasure than an original Composition. And, indeed, several of those Passages he has imitate[d], were so extremely fine in the Original, that to improve them required a Care and Happiness superior to that which produced them.

HOMER has used the Simile of a Flight of Fowls twice in his ILIAD, to express the Number and the Motions, the Order and the Clamours of an Army: As VIRGIL has done the same Number of Times in his ÆNEID. We also find the same Simile in the 4th *Georgic*, only in more general Terms, to delineate the Multitude of Spirits in the *Elysium*; and, again, with some Alterations, in the 6th *Æneid*, for the same Purpose. Hence, MILTON has taken both a Simile and Description; the first, in

Book 6th, to represent the March of MICHAEL's against *Satan's* Army; and the other in *Book* 7th; and, notwithstanding they had so often gone thro' the Hands of HOMER and VIRGIL, yet has given them farther Embellishments. . . .

'Tis one Particular of the Character of our Nation, that we have been much less successful in inventing, than in improving the Inventions of others. But the Genius of MILTON was confined to neither of these Qualities, as he is equally remarkable for original Beauties, and those which are imitated.

MILTON could make no Improvements in those Places of Scripture he has imitate[d]; but he has given them sometimes peculiar Graces in the Application: For Instance, the following is almost literally from the Scripture [VI, 841–3].

There is a great Beauty here in the Allusion to the late Battle, when Rocks and Mountains were used as offensive Arms.

The Story, on which MILTON has founded his Poem, is related in Scripture, in a very compendious Manner, without the Mention of many Particulars, and even those somewhat intricate: So that it was like a *Sic vos non vobis* to a Poet, as he would be obliged to supply Circumstances, and fill up the Chasms by mere Invention. This MILTON has done to a Wonder, and all he has invented, or added, is entirely consonant to Probability, and what we have of it in sacred Writ. All the other Authors who have tried to fill up the Out-lines of this Story, have had a very different Success. . . .

CRITICISM serves as much to strengthen the Judgment, as Poetry does to raise the Imagination; even the poorest, and most disagreeable Part of it, the picking out the Faults of a good Author, is of some Use, as it teaches us this important Lesson, always to found our Opinions on Reason, and never on the Authority of a Person. There are several Puns in the *Paradise Lost*, which are the grossest Faults in that Poem. In all the Crimes against Religion or Morality, the best Vindication of the Accused is, to prove they acted conform to their Judgment, however erroneous; but, in Matters of Arts and Criticism, 'tis quite otherwise: And the best Apology for the Faults of an Author, is, that they were contrary to his own Judgment, and in the Compliance with the ill Taste of those he composed for. How much Puns were the Mode of these Times, 'tis well known. And the Definition of Rhime, in the Advertisment prefixt to his Poem, furnishes us with some Sort of an Argument, that MILTON beheld a Pun in its true Light. *The gingling Sound of like Endings* he there declares against, defines a Pun almost as well as it does

Rhime, which indeed are nearly allied; and those Sorts of Puns which he has mostly made Use of, are literally such a Gingle: As, for Example, *beseeching* or *besieging*, &c.

We may divide the Puns of the *Paradise Lost* into two Kinds; the first, to which belongs the above Example, consists in the Similitude of the Sound of the Words; of this Sort is Rhime, with this Aggravation, that 'tis a Pun in every two Lines: The other, which is yet less excuseable, in their double Meaning; which is only a greater Similitude, or Sameness of Sound. Of this there is a very remarkable Instance in the Speeches of *Satan* and *Belial* in the 6th Book.

> O Friends, why come not on these Victors proud? &c. [VI, 609]

Besides the Puning, there is another very considerable Fault in that Passage, and several other Places of the Poem. Any Thing of Burlesque, or Drollery, is, by all the Criticks, excluded from the Seriousness of an Epick Poem. HOMER, in this Particular, has failed as well as MILTON, and VIRGIL has been constantly preferred to them both for his Conduct, according to the Criticks, entirely blameless in this Respect. . . .

There are several Contradictions, and such like little Faults in the *Paradise Lost*, which are to be imputed to the Blindness and ill Memory of the Author; the common Observation in this Case holding, that Strength of Imagination is generally accompanied with shortness of Memory. I shall here instance a Fault of this Kind, and, I think, the most flagrant One in the Poem, tho' many as ill may be found in the ILIAD or ÆNEID. It is in the Speech of *Moloch* in the 2d Book [II, 70–81].

If the Poet had designed to inform us, that the natural Motion of Spirits was upwards, and just the contrary of what we call Gravity, he should have told it in his own Person, or made some of the Angels relate it to *Adam*. But it is certainly most absurd, to make a Spirit, in the Time of a deep and important Consultation, spend a Dozen of Lines, in telling what every one of his Auditors must have known, as well as himself, if it was really the Case. 'Tis exactly the same, as if a General Officer, in the solemn Debates of a Council of War, should rise up, and with a long grave Speech inform his Colleagues, that it was easier to go down than Up-hill.

Doctor *Bentley* very well remarks the Contradiction, in the Word *Flight*, being applied to Sinking, which he amends, by putting Strife in its Place, which leaves the Matter just as it was; for the Impropriety lay in the Word *Sunk*.

SOME OBSERVATIONS ON THE *PARADISE REGAIN'D.*

The Prejudice of the World, in contemning this Poem, is yet less excuseable, than the Partiality of the Author, in preferring it to the *Paradise Lost*. 'Tis indeed far inferior to that noble Poem; but yet as far beyond any other Composition since the Times of VIRGIL. The Moral of it is a fit Sequel to that of the *Paradise Lost*: In that we had an Example of Disobedience, and the ill Effects of it; and here an illustrious Pattern of the contrary. We see a successive Triumph over all the Temptations of Luxury, Wealth, Glory and Power, tho' enforced in the strongest Manner. If we were to compare it to the *Odyssey*, in the Respect of its being a second Production; we shall find it entirely free of those Kind of Faults, which *Longinus* lays to the Charge of that Poem. And if the Reader can be prevailed upon to go through this Piece, notwithstanding what has been said of it, we shall assure him, that he'll neither find barren Wilds, nor meet with Monsters or Giants: And that he may not have barely our Word to rely on, we shall lay before him, as a Specimen of the Soil, some of those fine rich Grapes and Fruits it produces.

The first Lines allude to those four Verses which should begin the *ÆNEID*, but have been rejected as spurious by the Generality [I, 1–7].

These give us MILTON's Opinion about the *Ille égo* of VIRGIL; for he would never have imitated them, if he had not thought them genuine. The above Quotation deserves a better Commendation, than that it far excels its Original. The last Line may very well describe this whole Poem, if we consider its noble Beauties, and what barren Subject, as to a Production of this Kind, the Poet had to work upon.

21. Manwaring on Milton's verse

1744

Extract from Edward Manwaring, *Of Harmony and Numbers, in Latin and English Prose, and in English Poetry* (1744), 43–51.

The Reverend Edward Manwaring was a classical scholar, as the following excerpt indicates. He also published *An Historical and Critical Account of Classic Authors* (1737) and *Stichology; or, A Discovery of the Latin, Greek, and Hebrew Numbers* (1737).

Milton wants this Division of the Verse into musical Concords, where his Verse is composed of Polysyllable Words, which are often an Obstruction to this Division; but then the Grandeur of his Diction and Thoughts, and his most beautiful Transpositions, supply this Harmony, or Want of the Numbers; and the Misfortune is, that whenever this Poet has these Numbers or musical Concords, they are generally confounded by prosaic Stops. The first Verse of this Poem is a seventh in Music, or is divided into seven and three half Feet, that is, into a fifth and a *Tierce Minor*; thus divided:

Of Man's first Disobedience, // and the Fruit!

This Verse is musically pointed at the End of the Word Disobedience, where the Concord ends, or the Cæsural Stop is to be; and consequently the Reader cannot be deceived in reading this Verse, if he begins and ends in half a Foot; and if he reads this Verse in the rythmical Proportion of the Feet: But the following Verse, which has the same Concords, has these Concords confounded from the prosaic Stop; for it is pointed thus:

Of that forbidden Tree, whose mortal Taste.

Whereas this Verse should be pointed according to the Concords.

Of that forbidden Tree whose, // mortal, Taste.

The Reader may observe that the last Concord mōrtāl Tāste is a

Molossus, which should be a *Cretic*; thus corrected for the sake of the Quantity.

Of the forbidden Tree tho' be͞autĭfŭl.

Some may think this Rhythm is too effeminate, and that *Milton's* Number is more masculine, as it really is; and that this Neglect of Number in the *Exordium* may not be amiss, I have only expressed the natural Number, and the Reader may judge as he thinks fit. These three long Syllables at the End of the Verse is common to *Milton*, B. iii. *v.* I.

> Hail holy Light, Offspring of Heav'n first born,
> Or of the eternal co eternal Beam,
> May I express thee unblam'd? Since God is Light,
> And never // but in unapproached Light
> Dwelt, from Eternity dwelt // then in thee,
> Bright Effluence of bright Essence, // ĭncre͞āte.

These, and the following Lines, are wonderfully beautiful, and flow in the Concords. . . .

I have now specified the Principles of Harmony in *English* Poetry, and the Division of our Verse into Members, from these Principles; and the constant Harmony in this Division demonstrates the Truth of these Principles. Dr. *Pepusch*, a Gentleman of singular Humanity, and greatly skilled in antient Harmony, was so kind as to let me see *Morsennus on Antient Poetry*, where I found these Principles in his Reduction of *Iambic* Metre and Verse: And as our Verse originally flows from the *Greek* and *Latin Iambics*, I have applied these Principles to our Poetry, and the Application appears to be just. Should any one suspect this Reduction let him read the following Verses, where the Concords are not to be had, and this, or nothing, will teach him the Truth. *B.* v. *v.* 840. *B.* ix. *v.* 249

> Thrones, Dominations, Princedoms, Virtues, Powers.
> For Solitude sometimes is best Society.

And if the Concords are right with respect to the Division of the Syllables, and the Quantities wrong, the Harmony of the Verses is utterly lost; as,

> Delectable both // to behold and taste,
> For he who tempts, tho' in vain, // asperses
> The Attempted with Dishonour foul, suppos'd
> Not incorruptible of Faith, not Proof,
> Against Temptation: Thou thy Self with Scorn
> And Anger wouldst resent that offer'd Wrong.
>
> B. ix. *v.* 296.

This Verse is defective both in Accent and Quantity. *B.* iii. *v.* 266.

His Words here ended; // but his meek Aspect.

Here the first Syllable in Aspect is acuted and long, whereas this Syllable should be short and grav'd.

Milton is then defective in his Accents and Quantities, when his Imagination is most cool, or when he writes upon simple Subjects. The following Lines, to me, are no Poetry [VIII, 540–59].

But whenever this most incomparable Poet has his Imagination inflamed by a divine Enthusiasm, he is all Harmony. As in the following Lines, [VI, 760–3, 801–3; VII, 557–64].

From this it appears that our *Pentametre*, or *English* Heroics, is a seventh in Music, which is made up of a *Tierce Minor* and a fifth: The *Tierce Minor* is a Tone and a half, and the fifth has three Tones and a half, equal in all to ten half Tones in the *Diatonic Scale*, or to ten half Feet in the *Pentametre*. Or this Verse may be divided into two fourths; and as the fourth has two Tones and a half, these two fourths are equal to ten half Tones in the *Diatonic Scale*, or to ten half Feet in the *Pentametre*: And this is all the Division this Verse can have according to the Ratios of the musical Concords; and, if there is not a Division in the Composition of this Verse, at the End of a Word, in the third, seventh, or fifth half Foot, this Composition will have no Modulation; for ten Syllables are no more Poetry, without these Syllables are artfully disposed, than any Section of ten Syllables in Prose Composition. . . .

22. Harris on Milton's versification

1744

Extract from James Harris, 'A Discourse on Music, Painting, and Poetry', *Three Treatises* (1744), no. 2, ch. v, pp. 92–3, note.

James Harris (1709–80), known for his philosophic discourse *Hermes* (1751), in which references to Milton occur, was a classical scholar whose favourite subjects were music and language. *Three Treatises* offer a number of analytic statements concerning Milton's poems.

(*e*) That there is a *Charm* in *Poetry*, arising from its *Numbers* only, may be made evident from the five or six first Lines of the *Paradise Lost*; where, without any Pomp of Phrase, Sublimity of Sentiment, or the *least Degree of Imitation*, every Reader must find himself to be sensibly delighted; and that, only from the graceful and simple *Cadence* of the *Numbers*, and that artful Variation of the *Caesura* or *Pause*, so essential to the Harmony of every good Poem.

An *English Heroic* Verse consists of ten *Semipeds*, or Half-feet. Now in the Lines above-mentioned the *Pauses* are varied upon *different* Semipeds in the Order, which follows; as may be seen by any, who will be at the Pains to examine

PARADISE LOST, B. I.

Verse 1	Semiped 7
——2	—— 6
——3 has its Pause	—— 6
——4 fall upon	—— 5
——5	—— 3
——6	—— 4

23. Paterson on *Paradise Lost*

1744

Extract from James Paterson, *A Complete Commentary, with Etymo-logical, Explanatory, Critical and Classical Notes on Milton's* Paradise Lost (1744), 'To the Reader', i–viii. Italics are reversed.

James Paterson was apparently a medical doctor who is mentioned in histories of literature because of the present work on *Paradise Lost*. His life dates are not recorded.

Milton's PARADISE LOST, being an *Original* in it's kind, an *Honour* to the *British Nation*, and the *prime Poem* in the World; is justly esteemed and admired by every *Englishman*, and also by the *Learned* Abroad.

The *Iliads* and *Odysses* of *Homer*, and the Works of *Virgil* have had the Honour of a thousand *Commentators*; therefore I thought it neces-sary to add such a *Commentary* to this as the *Great Work* required.

. . . The *Critical Notes* of the judicious Mr. *Addison*, the various but arbitrary *Readings* of the learned Dr. *Bentley*, and the *Confutation* of them (so far as he went) by another learned *Author*, are all of a quite different *Nature* from my *Design*.

Two *Authors* only have attempted something of this Kind. The first is a very learned and judicious Gentleman of *North-Britain*, signed *P. H.* for *Peter Home*, about 50 Years ago [that is, Patrick Hume in the 1695 edition of *PL*].

But his *Notes* are (in my Opinion) useless to the *Unlearned*: Because they are full of the *Original Words* in *Hebrew* and *Greek* Characters, they abound with long and tedious *Quotations* out of the *Greek, Latin,* and *Italian Authors*. . . .

The next is Mr. *Richardson*, but he is not to be mentioned with the former, being most defective, and of little Service to the *Curious Reader*: for one half of his Book is taken up in an *History* of the *Life* and *Circum-stances* of Mr. *Milton*; wherein he is rather a *Biographer* than an *An-notator*. . . .

But I had almost finished this *Commentary* before I had seen either of these; and their *Imperfections* encouraged me to prosecute this with the more *Courage* and *Accuracy*.

In this I have translated almost every *Foreign Word* into proper *English*, express'd them all in the same *Number, Time, Mood,* and *Person,* as they stand in the *Poem* itself; with two, three or four *Words* of the same *Signification,* but better known to the *Unlearned.* I have shewn the *Original Language,* their *Etymology, Derivation* and *Composition*; given a *Reason* for the *Appellation* of them, so far as was possible, for the *Satisfaction* of the *Unlearned,* that know not the *Use* of *Dictionaries*; and of *Foreigners,* who are Strangers to the *Original Language* of Milton. . . . I have explained all the abstruse *Terms* of *Arts* and *Sciences,* all the *Fables* of the *Antients*; shewed all the *Similies* or *Comparisons,* pointed out all *Figures* of *Grammar* and *Rhetoric,* with the *Digressions*; and taken *Notice* of every *New Person* or *Subject* of each *new Paragraph,* where it was not very obvious and plain; that the *Reader* may the more readily *understand* what he reads, and may retain the Thread of the *History* in his Memory, as he goes on; and also may read with both *Profit* and *Pleasure*: I have placed all the *transposed Sentences* into a natural or plain *English Prose-Order,* but generally by Way of a short *Paraphrase,* not in the same *Words* of the *Poem,* for a certain *Reason* known to myself. For the *Transposition* of Words is an *Ornament* in *Poetry* only, and our *Author* has frequently made Use of that *Liberty* to his *Advantage.*

. . . By perusing this *Commentary,* the *Curious* will observe and see,

I. What a vast *Master* MILTON has been in the Round of all the known Languages, useful *Arts* and *Sciences* among Men.

II. That the *English Tongue* is one of the most copious and beautiful . . .

III. That this *Commentary* will be an useful *Vocabulary* to those that would learn this *Language.* . . .

IV. That this *Work* will display fully the *Benefits* and the *Ornaments* of this incomparable *Poem,* to the Satisfaction, I hope, of every curious Admirer of *Paradise Lost.* . . .

24. Ramsay and Pope on *Paradise Lost*

1744

Extract from Joseph Spence, *Observations, Anecdotes, and Characters, of Books and Men* [c. 1744] (1820), 93–5.

The popular Scottish poet Allan Ramsay (1686–1758) and Alexander Pope (1688–1744) were both influenced strongly by Milton, as seen in allusions and imitative lines in their poetry. The remarks which Pope's friend Joseph Spence (1699–1768) reports cannot be specifically dated.

Milton begins to be greatly admired at Paris since the translation of his *Paradise Lost* into French.[1] Even Cardinal Polignac, who used to think that most of the high things we said of him were overstrained and out of partiality, was convinced at once on an English gentleman's sending him only the contents of each book translated into French. 'The man (said he) who could make such a plain must be one of the greatest poets that ever was born.'—*Ramsey*.

Milton's style in his *Paradise Lost* is not natural; it is an exotic style.[2] As his subject lies a good deal out of our world, it has a particular propriety in those parts of the poem; and when he is on earth, whenever he is describing our parents in Paradise, you see he uses a more easy and natural way of writing. Though his forced style may fit the higher parts of his own poem, it does very ill for others who write on natural and pastoral subjects. Philips, in his *Cyder*, has succeeded extremely well in imitation of it, but was quite wrong in endeavouring to imitate it on such a subject.—*Mr. Pope*.

Milton was a great master of the Italian poets; and I have been told that what he himself wrote in Italian is in exceeding good Italian. I can't think that he ever intended to have made a tragedy of his Fall of Man; at least I have Andreino's, and I don't find that he has taken any thing from him.—*The same*.

[1] This was in 1729.
[2] See (ante) p. 87, Milton's imitation of Spenser.

25. Le Blanc on the majesty of nature in *Paradise Lost*

1745

Abbé Le Blanc, *Letters on the English and French Nations . . . Translated from the original French* (Dublin, 1747), letter lii, i, 286–7.

The French clergyman and literary critic Jean-Bernard Le Blanc (1707?–81) was usually translated into English soon after the French publication of his work, since much of his criticism dealt with British literature. His work is primarily on the theatre and Shakespeare, although the following letter comes from a general collection of remarks on relations between France and England.

In general, wherever amiable nature appears in all her simplicity, she inspires people of taste, with a nobler sort of pleasure, if I may be allowed to express myself so; and with a more agreeable and charming sensation, than the master-pieces of art themselves. There is a majesty in nature, that art can't arrive at. Shall one ever see any thing upon the stage here, where they crowd in heaps to admire the richness and the splendor of the *Palace of the Sun*, that comes up to the magnificent sight, a fine day-break offers us; and which men who have eyes, have never once deigned to view? The rude and ill-shaped rocks, the venerable trees in the forest of Fontainbleau, present our sight with a more majestic and grander aspect, than the laboured neatness of the best kept gardens. MILTON had never painted it so nobly or so pleasantly, if he had not well considered it; his understanding had no difficulty to describe the sensations which had warmed his imagination. One can't read his *Paradise Lost*, without perceiving, that he had a hundred times in his life, taken pleasure in seeing the sun, sometimes gild the horison, and re-animate all nature; and at others, withdraw its rays, and leave her buried in the horrors of darkness. There are some men, who imagine themselves painters, because they can copy pictures; and others, who imagine themselves poets, because they can translate VIRGIL, into English or

French verse; but if they have not the talent, to paint nature from herself; they are really neither painters nor poets. Men of genius, only imitate the great masters of those two sciences, in their noble and simple manner of expressing her. Those who take attitudes from RAPHAEL, or descriptions from VIRGIL; are, properly speaking, only copiers. MILTON, does not only describe the coolness of the morning, and the beautiful enamel of a meadow, or the verdure of a hill; he expresses even the sentiments of joy and pleasure these objects excite in our soul: and gives us the satisfaction of thinking, that as we feel the same sensations he does, we have the happiness to see nature with the same eyes.

26. Lauder's first charges of plagiarism

1747

William Lauder, 'An Essay on Milton's Imitations of the Moderns', *Gentleman's Magazine*, xvii (1747), 24–6, 82–5, 189, 285–6.

William Lauder, although a competent classical scholar, is remembered today only as a literary forger because of his charges of plagiarism levelled at Milton. The controversy is discussed in the present Introduction. Lauder died in 1771. The title of this essay had the following footnote: 'As there is just reason to apprehend, that the following ESSAY will excite no little speculation, it will enable the *English* reader to judge of the case, if our learned poetical friends would be pleased to send us a close version of the lines which are said therein to have furnished sentiment to *Milton*'. Grotius' *Adam Exsul* is given on pp. 312–14, 365–6, though omitted here. An expanded revision of these letters, along with some extracts of correspondence to the *Gentleman's Magazine*, was published by Lauder in London in 1750, under this same title. It is reproduced in this volume for comparison.

An ingenious gentleman*having some years ago published a small treatise intitled *An Essay on Milton's imitation of the Antients*, which was very favourably received both here and at *Edinburgh*, where it was written: I have after his example, adventured to publish the few following observations by way of *Essay on Milton's Imitation of the Moderns*; having lately happen'd to cast my eye on four or five modern authors in *Latin* verse, whom I have reason to believe *Milton* has consulted in composing his glorious poem, *PARADISE LOST*, no less than the antients. And if my conjecture shall appear founded on reason, the novelty of the subject, I hope, will, instead of excluding me from, rather entitle me to the favour of the reader. But here I beg leave to premise, in order to prevent mistakes and misconstructions, that *by this Essay on Milton's Imitation of*

* We shall, in our next, give some account of this author and his work, which was printed in 1742 at *Edinburgh*.

the moderns, I no way intend to derogate from the glory or merit of that noble poet, who certainly is intitled to the highest praise, for raising so beautiful a structure, even granting all the materials were borrowed; which is an assertion I will by no means take upon me absolutely to affirm. His incomparable poem begins thus; [I, 1–6].

These lines (now quoted) very probably owe their rise to the following most beautiful *Latin* ones, written by J A C O B U S M A S E N I U S, professor of rhetorick and poetry in the *Jesuits* college at *Cologne,* in the year 1650, and afterwards. . . .

From these lines, to me it seems highly probable, that *Milton* had this learned writer in his eye; what others will think I cannot pretend to determine, since every one ought to judge for himself, and what may seem convincing to one person, may not appear so to another. The same author's description of *Paradise* is truly charming, and has been copied by *Milton,* if I am not greatly mistaken, in more places than one. I desire only the reader would carefully compare them with the following: . . .

What others may fancy I know not, but to me it appears vastly probable that *Milton* has transferred the sense of the foregoing lines into his *Paradise Lost.* And here, I am sorry to say it, I am obliged to stop short, not having it in my power at present to produce any further specimen from the performance of this learned *Jesuit,* having unfortunately lost his fine work: however, for the reader's further satisfaction, I shall here set down the marginal heads of his work, *viz.* 'Propositio. Invocatio divini numinis. Orbis & eorum, quae in orbe universim geruntur, descriptio. Paradisi descriptio. Hominis primi creatio, ejusque descriptio. Comparatio figuli cum creatore Deo [etc.] . . .'. Now, if any one can imagine, after such ample quotations, that *Milton* could possibly write as he has done, without ever seeing or hearing of this author's performance, he may with equal reason assert, at least in my judgment, that a limner may draw a man's picture exactly like the original, without ever seeing him, which to me appears both absurd and impossible.

In the magazine for *January* last, I took the liberty to offer some thoughts concerning *Milton*'s imitation of the *moderns*; and, in support of my opinion, produced some verses from *Masenius*; they were part of his work intitled, *SARCOTIDOS libri quinque*; containing about 2500 lines. The author, in his preface says, That he did not intend it so much for a compleat model of an epic poem, as for a rude draught or the great out-lines of one to be worked up to perfection by a person of greater genius, or more leisure, than himself. And it must be owned, it fell into excellent hands. Tho' the merit of the improvement made upon it, may, by the by, admit some diminution, if the proverb *facile est inventis addere*, holds good in the poetical as in other sciences. I think that *Milton* pursues his steps pretty close in his two first books, where both their subjects seem much the same. He begins to leave him towards the beginning of his 3rd book, where *Masenius*, so to speak, begins to forsake himself, I mean his first plan, and instead of pursuing the *fall of man*, which at first he propos'd, begins to institute a comparison betwixt the different vices and virtues of mankind, their opposition and conflicts one with another. In this way he proceeds till he concludes, treating, all along, his subjects with great dignity and elegance, and giving such long historical arguments to his five books, as alone are sufficient to serve as a plan, for composing a noble Epic poem, though the learned author had not proceeded to illustrate the excellent rules, given in the former part of his work, of which till I can recover the whole, so much may suffice of him.

I shall proceed, therefore, to another work of no less eminence, to which that *Milton* was also obliged, the reader will scarce doubt, since it is most certain that he had seen it. A paper of his own hand-writing found in *Trinity* college, *Cambridge*, contains a catalogue of above 60 subjects,* taken from the sacred scripture, on which he seems to have designed to found tragedies. But, the truth is, they were only titles of tragedies† already written in *Latin* verse, by men of the highest rank and genius in the commonwealth of learning. In the front of this catalogue stands,

ADAM *unparadised*, or ADAM *in Banishment*

* They may be seen in the life of *Milton*, prefixed to a new edition of his works, published some years ago, by the Rev. Mr *Birch*, in two volumes in folio. Printed for *A. Millar* in the *Strand*.

† Some of these subjects, for the satisfaction of the curious reader, I shall just mention: *Abrahamus Sacrificans*, by Theodorus Beza; *Dinae raptus*, & *Sodomae conflagratio*, by Horatius Tursellinus; who also writes several others in *Milton*'s list. *Thamarae raptus per fratrem*; by Rochus Honerdus: *Sedechias*; by Carolus Malapertius: *Solymae halosis*; by Nicolaus Caussinus: *Christus Patiens*; by Hugo Grotius: *Christus Moriens & Resurgens*; by Joannes Franciscus Quintianus: *Herodes Infanticida*; from Daniel Heinsius: *Samson Agonistes & Heliadae*; from Hieronymus Zieglerus: *Ruth*; a pastoral comedy; from Nicodemus Frischlinus; and to name no more, the *Baptistes*; from George Buchanan: which last *Milton* actually translated into *English* verse, and published by order of the house of commons, *Anno* 1641 in quarto, as a satyr against King *Charles* the first and his Queen; according to the conjecture of the Rev. Mr *Francis Peck*, lately deceased, who, in a book entituled, *New Memoirs of* Milton's *Life*, published *Anno* 1740 in quarto, has given the publick a new edition of that tragedy both in *Buchanan*'s *Latin* and *Milton*'s *English*, placed opposite to one another.

which I affirm is only a translation of *Adamus Exsul*, written by the celebrated *Hugo Grotius* when but 18. This poem is not printed in his works, and was become so very scarce, that I could not get a copy either in *Britain*, or *Holland*; but the learned Mr *Abraham Gronovius*, keeper of the public library at *Leyden*, after great enquiry, procured the sight of one, and, as I have, for some time, been honoured with his correspondence and friendship, sent me transcribed by his own son, the first act of it.

Now as Mr *Fenton*, in his life of *Milton*, informs us, that *Paradise Lost* was first written in the form of a tragedy, the judicious reader will, by considering the following tragedy, (with the heads in its argument, as well as those in *Masenius*, and the similar Greek and Latin appellations in *Milton*,) begin to relish the unexpected discovery, that this great poet had recourse to a vast treasure, which he industriously kept secret; but I shall endeavour to bring to open light, more at large than I can do here, in a pamphlet for that purpose, and afterwards exhibit a beautiful and correct edition of the original authors, pursuant to the advice of several persons of learning and distinction. . . .

This Tragedy of *Grotius* has passed through no less than four editions; and tho' it has been little known in *Britain*, yet has it had the good fortune, on first publication, to merit the commendations of *Vossius, Heinsius, Douza*, and other learned men, who addressed poems to the author; and tho' they are all well worth the perusing, yet I shall content myself at present with inserting that of *Janus Douza*, which so beautifully recommends the writing on sacred subjects, and which probably gave *Milton* the first hint of writing this divine poem.

Further CHARGE *against* MILTON.

We have received several extracts from the Rev. Dr *Andrew Ramsay's* POEMATA SACRA, printed at *Edinburgh*, 1633, and dedicated to king *Charles I.* sent us by Mr *W. L.* who supposes that *Milton*, among other things, has borrow'd, from this author, his encomium on marriage, beginning,

Hail, wedded love, &c.

These extracts being too long for our book, and Mr *L.* intending to give them at large in a separate work, we shall only insert some of the shortest, as a specimen.

MILTON represents *Satan's* malignity against man, and envy at his happiness, as partly arising from the meanness of his origin, calling him *a man of clay, son of despight*, &c.—*Ramsay* also expresses the same sentiments. . . .

MILTON also represents the Devil as flattering *Eve* with lofty appellations, such as *Sovereign of creatures! Universal dame! Goddess humane,* &c.—RAMSAY had done the same before: . . .

MILTON, after *Eve's* eating the forbidden fruit, represents Nature as conscious of her fault, and dreading its consequence, in these lines: [IX, 782–4]. Again, on *Adam's* repeating the crime: [XI, 1000–4].

RAMSAY says to the same effect: . . . .

And again, on a like occasion: . . . .

MILTON has also an uncommon and remarkable simile, of a ship's working into port against wind, to illustrate the serpent's method of addressing our first mother [IX, 510–8].

The same appears in the following lines of *Ramsay*, with this difference only, that *Ramsay* applies it to Satan tempting our Saviour. . . .

Mr URBAN,

Since the literati have been pleased to approve of my attempt, I send you, in further prosecution of my charge against *Milton* (*See p.* 82, 3, 4, 5.) a few more passages, amongst innumerable others, from *Grotius,* with parallel ones from *Milton,* which the learned and judicious reader is desired seriously to consider. Not to repeat the two passages in the first act, *orcus sub pedibus tremit* (*See p.* 83F) '*Hell trembled as he strode,*' and that entirely literal translation, '*Better to reign in hell,* &c.' I proceed . . .

From these parallel places, I hope, it is abundantly plain, that *Milton* in composing his *Paradise Lost* had more assistance than is generally imagined, and, consequently, is not so much an original author as he has been hitherto universally reputed; I shall endeavour, God willing, to shew this still more fully hereafter.

I shall only remark further, that as the great Mr *Addison,* and Doctor *Bentley,* blame *Milton* for concluding his poem in so mournful a strain, the like conclusion in *Grotius,* which is quite proper in a tragedy, tho' not in an Epic poem, will convince the reader, that the great *English* poet was led into that error by treading too close on the heels of our young Latin tragedian.

27. Richardson against Lauder's allegations

1747

R[ichard] R[ichardson], letter, *Gentleman's Magazine*, xvii (1747), 22–4.

Richard Richardson was attached to Clare Hall, Cambridge, according to the title page of his collected remarks on the Lauder controversy, *Zoilomastix: or, a Vindication of Milton, from all the Invidious Charges of Mr. William Lauder with several new remarks on Paradise Lost* (Cambridge, 1747). See also No. 63, an article from the *Mirror* credited to him.

Mr Urban,

Some time has elaps'd since your correspondent, Mr *W. L.* first published his wonderful *Essay on* Milton's *Imitation of the Moderns.* I deferr'd giving you my private thoughts on it, both in expectation of seeing his arguments *particularly* refuted by a more able hand, and in hopes of your correspondent's fulfilling his promise to justify his assertions more largely in a pamphlet . . . which he has declin'd, and for his own credit I would have him decline, unless he brings *better specimens,* than he has in the *Magazine* for *January, p.* 24, *Apr. p.* 189, or more *candid assertions* than in that of *February, p.* 82. I shall at present only consider the former; and if this meets with approbation, shall give you my thoughts on his further charges against *Milton.*

Before we examine the *particular* passages of the two poems of *Milton* and *Masenius,* I think it would not be improper to consider them in general. That of *Masenius* was publish'd (according to *January* magazine, *p.* 2.) in the year 1654, or 1661, and *Paradise Lost* in 1667, and shewn as actually done in 1665.* And 'tis agreed by all, that this divine poem was wrote between the year 1665, and the year of his blindness 1650; and that he had long before chose the *Fall of Man* for his subject,

* Richardson's *Life of Milton, p.* 111.

is plain from the plans of his hand-writing in *Trinity College* library, and
from his own words
>—This subject for heroic song
>Pleas'd me *long chusing*, and beginning *late*!
>*Par. Lost*, B. ix. v. 25.

From hence it clearly appears that *Milton*'s poem was at least *begun*,
before that of *Masenius* was publish'd; which is sufficient for our present
purpose, for the passages in question are in the *beginning* of the poems of
their respective authors. Nor, in my opinion, is *Milton* more indebted to
Masenius for his plan (which to me seem to be widely different, considering their subject was the same) than for the beginning of his poem.
—Besides, it seems wonderful to me that from the year in which
Paradise lost was publish'd to this time (which is 80 years) no *Bentley*, no
Hearne [Thomas Hearne, an antiquary], no penetrating genius but *W. L.*
should be so eagle-ey'd as to hit upon this *rare discovery*; and, especially
at the time when *Masenius* was extant, when *Milton* was expos'd to
darkness and evil tongues,* that no publick enemy would brand him
with plagiarism.

But before I come to particulars, I must observe, that *Virgil* himself
was not free from the like calumnies. Macrobius† positively taxes that
most noble poet with having translated, almost *word for word*, the whole
2d book of the *Aeneis* from *Pisander*, and the 4th from *Apollonius
Rhodius*; which invidious calumny Dr *Trapp* [Joseph Trapp, who translated *Paradise Lost* into Latin, 1741–4]‡ has proved to be absolutely
false. And, I think, we may justly apply Mr *Voltaire*'s words in the defence of *Virgil* to the vindication of our much injur'd poet *Milton*,
'That the only answer which is to be made to such discoveries, is, that
such works are too great master-pieces of art to be *but copies*.'§

Let us now consider the particular passages of the two poets, and
first the *Proposition*: What that is, will be best known by consulting the
following verses of *Vida*. . . .

If then the *Proposition* is a short sketch of the contents of the whole
poem, or the poem in miniature; and as *Milton* and *Masenius* wrote on
the *very same* subject, how is it possible, unless they deviated from the
true rules of poetry (and *Milton* was too great a judge to do so) that
there should not be *some similitude* in their thoughts? But if the impartial

---

* *Paradise Lost*, B. VII. *v*. 26.
† *Saturnal, Lib.* v. *cap.* 17.
‡ *In his Note to B.* 11. *and* XVI. *of the Æneis. See likewise his note to B.* 111 *v.* 719.
§ *Essay on the Epic poetry of the* European *nations*.

reader carefully compares the beginning of the two poems, he will find that nothing could be more wide and different than their manner of expression, considering the thought and subject were common to them both; and will agree with your judicious correspondent *p.* 68 B. 'That if *Milton* had ever seen *Masenius*, and in any sort attempted to borrow from him, his poem would neither have been *the same*, nor *so good* as it is.' *Masenius*, in his *Proposition*, neither mentions the *forbidden fruit*, nor the *loss of Paradise*, which (according to his marginal heads) he ought to have done, as they are constituent parts of his poem; these *Milton* judiciously inserts in his *Proposition*, and adds, *Till one greater man, &c.* of which there is not so much as a thought in *Masenius*. . . .

Either these passages are not parallel, or *that Shepherd*, i.e. *Moses*, must be *David*. Here is another instance of *Milton*'s judgment, (who intended to sing in the beginning

—How the heav'ns and earth
Rose out of *Chaos*.—)

to mention *Moses*, who relates how 'In the beginning God created the heaven and the earth,' and whose steps he intended to follow in his sublime description of the creation. Was I of *W. L.*'s clan, I should rather think that *Cowley*, in the beginning of his *Davideis*, has copied this last sentence of *Masenius*, rather than *Milton*. . . . Unfortunately for himself, unfortunately for his beloved author, does this gentleman quote this place; for there is not a syllable like it in *Milton*. And now *Masenius himself* must be taxed with *imitating the moderns*, for it very much resembles the following lines of *Caspar Barlæus*. . . . But here *Masenius* shall have a more candid treatment from me than *Milton* has met with lately; for I cannot persuade myself to hold this maxim, 'That no body must pretend to write anything of *his own*, because another has wrote *before him.*'

As *Masenius* and *Milton* were both christian poets, and their subject founded on the same parts of holy writ, 'twas necessary that they should invoke *that spirit* which directed the divine pen-men. *Milton*'s great judgment in this case has already been mentioned.

The foregoing arguments on the *Propositions* will serve in general for the *Invocations*. What now deserves our more particular consideration are these passages: . . . These I confess to be *parallel*, tho' not *imitated* from *Masenius*, who closely follow the steps of *Homer* [*Iliad* II, 485; *PL* I, 20–2].

I cannot pass over these beautiful lines (tho' somewhat foreign to our purpose) which may be overlook'd by an ordinary reader. The poet here alludes to the 3d chapter, verse 22, of St *Luke*, where the holy spirit is represented in a *bodily appearance*, annexing the idea of *brooding*, which is imply'd in that expressive word of *Moses* [Hebrew word from Gen. I. 2], which our translation renders *mov'd*. Is this too *imitated* from *Masenius*? Or rather, has that Jesuit three verses in his whole poem equal to these in *Milton*, so noble, yet clear, so simple, yet learned and elegant? . . .

This passage, says *W. L. Milton* has pass'd over; and I think 'twas necessary he shou'd; since *Masenius* is now got *above the clouds*, and consequently *out of sight*. . . .

If there is *any thing* parallel in these passages, it is so *very little*, that *the one* can no more be thought to be an imitation of *the other*, than *Virgil*'s description of a horse to be *copied* from *Job*. The similitude of thought arises from the imitation of nature, which is the same, and always will be so; and that from the identity of the subject, which was deriv'd from the same stream of the holy scriptures; as the candid reader will find, by impartially comparing the passages of either poet. This and the foregoing reasons may be apply'd to vindicate our author from the last charge of plagiarism, *in copying in more places than one* Masenius's description of *Paradise*. I wish your correspondent had pointed them out, and told us where they were copy'd in *Paradise Lost*, for there are many descriptions of *Paradise* dispers'd thro' the poem, some of which consist of more than 100 lines. But *Milton*, who had *Homer* almost by heart, and comes nearest to his style of any poet, if he chose to transplant any flowers into his Garden of *Eden*, would certainly gather them from the Gardens of *Alcinous*, which he almost confesses he has regarded. . . .

To crown the whole criticism, i.e. the whole invective against *Milton*, *W. L.* concludes, *That he that can imagine that* Milton *could have wrote as he had done, without ever seeing or hearing of* Masenius's *performance, may with equal reason assert that a limner may draw a man's picture exactly like the original without ever seeing him*: That is, in plain *English*, *Milton*'s poem is *exactly* like *Masenius*'s. But if I may be allow'd the presumption to oppose my judgment against so great a critic's authority, I would ask, Whether it is strange or absurd to suppose, that two pictures by two different hands should have a *general likeness*, which are drawn from the same original?

28. Lauder's rebuttal

1747

William Lauder, letter, *Gentleman's Magazine*, xvii (1747), 363–4.

In your last Mag. p. 322, a gentleman who signs *R. R.* has endeavoured to defend *Milton* from the imputation of having owed any part of his *Paradise Lost* to *Masenius*.

First, by shewing that *Masenius's* work was published after *Milton's* was begun.

Secondly, That, if *Milton* was so apparent an imitator, he would probably have been long since detected, by someone among his numerous enemies, many of whom had zeal and abilities equal to the work; and yet that no such attempt had been made till my remarks appear'd in last *January* Magazine.

Thirdly, That the passages selected to prove the charge are not parallel.

To the first objection, I answer, that Mr *Richardson,* in his Life of *Milton,* quoted by *R. R.* says expressly, that he did not assiduously apply himself to that work till 1660,* when his leisure for such an undertaking commenced, being then divested of his public employments; and that even the plan of it was not form'd sooner than 1654, the very year in which *Masenius's* work first appear'd, and which, together with two or three pieces more, much to the same purpose, seems to have determined him, long fluctuating, to the choice of *Paradise Lost* for the subject of his intended *English* Epic.

But granting that *Milton* began his poem in the year of his blindness 1650, as *Masenius's* work appear'd in 1654, and the *Paradise Lost* not in M. S. till 1665, *Milton* had eleven years to take advantage of the Jesuit's performance. And I cannot forbear to observe here, that it is much more probable that he did so in those places where the resemblance is in-

---

* By comparing this paragraph with R. R.'s quotation of *Jan.* Mag. *p.* 2, and *Richardson's* Life of *Milton,* it will appear that he has been twice guilty of willful prevarication, by which he has forfeited the regard due to a fair disputant, and taken the most effectual method to ruin the cause he pretends to maintain.

disputable and striking, than that the same thoughts and expressions were equally and necessarily suggested to both writers, by their common subject, when they occur in the machinery of the poem; because this, as it is wholly fictitious, could have no other origin than the luxuriance of a poet's imagination. The least degree of prepollent probability must therefore determine the judgment of an impartial mind; it must be admitted that as *Milton* was plainly an imitator of *Masenius*, in that part which is arbitrary and indeterminate, so likewise the passages which might possibly have been suggested to them both by their subject, were more probably copied by the latter writer.

To the second, I answer, that those authors to whom *Milton* is indebted, have ever been very scarce. *Masenius's* poem, and the *Adamus Exsul* of *Grotius*, particularly, seem to have been almost unknown in *England*; nor is it difficult to assign the reason: Modern *Latin* poetry on sacred subjects, was more especially at that period, less likely to be read than any other kind of literature: the best of it being incontestably of an inferior class, with respect to the purity and elegance of the language, and the harmony of the numbers; and, at the same time, the subject was less likely than any other to atone for the defects in language, when libertinism was patronized at court, and all the fashionable wit was of the dissolute kind. It is probable that even *Milton* himself would never have taken the trouble to procure or read these pieces, but with a view to find materials for his own undertaking. It must be remembered too, that, as he was *Latin* secretary for foreign affairs to *Cromwell*, when *Masenius's* work was publish'd, he was more likely, by reason of his extensive correspondence with men of letters abroad, to hear of this work, and could more easily procure it than any other man—The modern *Latin* poets did not engage the attention of either *Bentley* or *Hearne*, or any other critics, who probably, if they heard of those pieces, already fallen into oblivion, deemed them beneath their notice; whereas no small portion of my leisure hours have been employ'd in such researches for these 7 years past.

To the third,—As my opponent has, for good reason, passed over those passages in which the resemblance is strongest, I shall wave this part of the dispute 'till he has given his thoughts of the literal translation of *Nam me judice*, &c. and shewn how it should happen that *the infernal council or Pandaemonium, Lucifer's habit and chariot, the fight of the angels, the excursion of the fallen spirits from hell*, became common to both authors, without *Milton's* seeing *Masenius*: When he has proved, that these and other similar parts are naturally suggested by the subject, are hinted in the scripture original, or have any necessary foundation in truth and reason, and are not the arbitrary work of fancy, then I will admit that different masters, from the same figure, drew a general likeness: Till this be done, I must insist, that, as great part, even of the drapery and ornaments of the piece, which depend on the artist's imagination only, and yet are the same in both their productions, it cannot but be highly absurd to suppose them both originals; and that consequently the latter is in this respect but a copy of the former, tho' it may be more highly finish'd, and embellish'd with additional ornaments.

29. Anonymous poem on attempted depreciation of Milton

August 1747

Y, 'On some late Attempts to depreciate Milton', *Gentleman's Magazine*, xvii (August 1747), 395.

To toil for fame asks all the *poet's* pains:
And yet how barren is the wreath he gains!
Thus *Milton*, scarce distinguish'd, bow'd to fate,
And the dear-purchas'd lawrel came too late!
Yet in the grave that lawrel found its root,
And flourish'd high—and bore immortal fruit.
His Muse a thousand imitators fir'd,
His Muse by distant nations lov'd, admir'd,
In her all *Homer's*—*Virgil's* beauties shone,
And *Britain* call'd the masterpiece her own.
    With pedant zeal, a modern *Bavius*[1] cries,
'*Milton* a genius!—how encomium lyes!

[1] W. L., the reviewer of *Adamus Exsul*.

From foreign stores his boasted plan he drew,
With borrow'd wings, like *Icarus*, he flew!
Like sly *Prometheus* stole the heav'nly ray,
That made his man, and warm'd the living clay:
Too long the wretch has fill'd the throne of fame,
Unjust usurper! with a spurious claim!
Not his, the sacred page the boaster writ,
A *Jesuit*[1] taught him *art*, a *Dutchman*[2] wit;
My pen the shameful plagiary shall show,
And blast the bays that bind his guilty brow!'
    Enervate critic!—cease thy fruitless rage,
Nor touch with impious hands the hallow'd page!
Bury'd a-new in learning's rev'rend dust,
Let good *Masenius* unmolested rust;
Let *Grotius* the *Civilian*'s honour boast,
But as a poet—let his name be lost!
These were like swallows, when the skies are clear
Who skim the earth, and rise to disappear!
Like *Jove*'s own bird, our *Milton* took his flight
To worlds unknown, and pierc'd the realms of light;
Tho' heav'n, all-wise, corporeal sight deny'd;
Internal day the lesser loss supply'd;
Disdaining succour, and oblig'd to none
His genius beam'd expansive like the sun:
And till that glorious orb shall cease to shine,
Till sick'ning nature feel her last decline,
Truth shall preserve great *Milton*'s honour'd page
From Time's encroachment, and from Envy's rage;
Shall blast all vain attempts to wound his fame,
And with new glories grace his honour'd name.

[1] Masenius.
[2] Grotius.

30. Hurd on Milton's language

1749

Extract from Richard Hurd, 'Notes on the Art of Poetry' (1749), *Works of Richard Hurd* (1811), I, 73–4.

Richard Hurd (1720–1808) was an editor of classical texts and a writer on various arts and aesthetics. Milton is prominent in his works as subject for discussion and as example of his aesthetic principles.

Next, it is necessary to keep the tragic style, though condescending, in some sort, to the familiar cast of conversation, from sinking beneath the dignity of the personages, and the solemnity of the representation. Now no expedient can more happily effect this, than what the poet prescribes concerning the *position* and *derivation* of words. For thus, the language, without incurring the odium of absolutely *invented* terms, sustains itself in a becoming stateliness and reserve, and, whilst it seems to stoop to the level of conversation, artfully eludes the meanness of a trite, prosaic style.—There are wonderful instances of this management in the *Samson Agonistes* of Milton; the most artificial and highly finished, though for that reason, perhaps, the least popular and most neglected, of all the great poet's works.

31. John Mason on the verse of *Paradise Lost*

1749

Extract from John Mason, *An Essay on the Power and Harmony of Prosaic Numbers* (1749), 47.

John Mason (1706–63) was a nonconformist clergyman, though moderate, and an educator of youths for the ministry. Out of this latter interest came *An Essay on Elocution* (1748), *An Essay on the Power of Numbers, and the Principles of Harmony in Poetical Composition* (1749), and *An Essay on the Power and Harmony of Prosaic Numbers* (1749), all of which show his interest in Milton and his reading.

If the antient Poetry was too lax in its Numbers, the modern is certainly too strict. The just Medium between these two Extreams seems to be that which *Milton* hath chosen for his Poem, *viz.* the Penthameter Verse; with the mixt Iambic Measure, free from the Shackle of Rhime; in which the Numbers are neither too free nor too confined; but are musical enough to entertain the Ear, and at the same Time leave Room enough to express the strongest Thought in the best and boldest Languages.

32. John Mason on Milton's versification

1749

[John Mason], *An Essay on the Power of Numbers, and the Principles of Harmony in Poetical Composition* (1749), chap. xiv: 'An Examination of Milton's Numbers', 53–8.

Let us next examine the Numbers in the first sixteen Lines of *Milton's Paradise Lost*; which contain almost all the various Combinations of Feet that are introduced into English Iambics: as a Specimen of that Liberty which the Author intended to take in his Measures throughout the Poem [I, 1–16].

Here we observe,

(1.) That of these sixteen Lines only one is pure Iambic, *viz.* the *eleventh*, and in that there is a Contraction of two short Syllables into one in the Word *Sïlŏă's*.

(2.) That of these sixteen Lines only two Couplets have just the same Measure, *viz.* the *tenth* and *twelfth*. (Each of which consists orderly of a Trochee, Iambic, Pyrrhic and two Iambics; Which creating a rapid Movement, are succeeded the one by a solemn pure Iambic, and the other by one that is nearly so;) And Lines the *fifth* and *seventh*, which are Iambic, with a Pyrrhic in the second Place. But a Line of a very different Movement is interposed, which prevents a dull Uniformity. And this judicious Mixture of Numbers and Change of Measures is the true Sourse of that Pleasure which the Ear finds in the Flow of *Milton's* Verse; who varies his Feet and diversifys his Measures (either through Art or Nature) more than any one of all our English Poets; and makes it what he himself calls

> —*a various-measur'd Verse.*
> *Parad. Reg.* B. iv. 1. 256.

(3.) In the first Line two short Syllables are contracted into one, in the Word *Disobedïeñce*; and since the Syllable *ence* is not one of those very short ones which easily admit of such a Contraction (it being naturally long, and put for a short one only as unaccented) the Number is defective. But the same Apology may be allowed *Milton* which is generally made for *Homer*, who hath also a false Quantity in the very first Line of his *Iliad*, *viz*. that the Poet's Mind was so warmed and possessed with the Grandeur of his Subject, that he was unattentive to the Exactness of his Numbers.

(4.) In the second Line the last Foot but one is a *Spondee*, which is a slow Movement. See Remark III.

(5.) The third Line begins with a Spondee, Pyrrhic, and Iambic, in order, which is a very agreeable Measure. See Remark IV.

(6.) Line the fourth has a Pyrrhic in the third Place, whose Rapidity is very agreeably corrected by Iambic. See Remark II.

(7.) The same may be said of Line the fifth, where the Pyrrhic possesses the second Place.

(8.) The sixth Line concludes with a Pyrrhic and two Iambics; which is a sweet and flowing Measure. See Remark II.

(9.) The seventh Line hath precisely the same Kind and Arrangement of Feet as the fifth. But the intermediate Line being a very different Movement renders this Similarity almost imperceptible. See Remark VIII.

(10.) The eighth Line hath a slow Movement, the first and third Feet being Spondees, but is very agreeably succeeded by two Lines whose Numbers are brisk and flowing. But though the Movement in these two Lines have an equal Rapidity, yet by varying the Order of the Feet it hath no Uniformity And the rapid Flow of the Numbers is seasonably checked in the eleventh Line, by a series of Iambics.

I believe no one that hath a Taste for Musick can read these four Lines without finding his Ear pleased with the Harmony of the Numbers, though he understood not the Sense of the Words.

(11.) In the ninth Line the four first Feet are Pyrrhics and Iambics alternately, which is a very quick Measure. See Remark II.

(12.) Line the tenth begins with a Choriambic; which Measure, if not too often used, is very beautiful at the Beginning of a Line. See Remark I.

The eleventh Line is pure Iambic.

The twel[f]th the same as the tenth.

The thirteenth is Iambic with a Pyrrhic in the Middle.

The fourteenth begins with a Pyrrhic and Iambic. See Remark II.

In the fifteenth the last Foot but one is a Trochee, which makes the Verse conclude with a Choriambic: This is a peculiar Close, but not unfrequent in *Milton*. See Remark VII.

The sixteenth Line gracefully concludes the Period with an Iambic Verse, introduced with a Choriambic.

Thus various are *Milton*'s Numbers. And it is this just and judicious Mixture of the short Numbers with the long, and the quick with the slow, that composes the Harmony of his Verse; in which he is very happy at the same Time that he appears very negligent.

But this great Master of Poetick Numbers was not without his Faults, even in this very Point in which he so much excelled; nay, so negligent is he sometimes of his Measure, that he hath now and then so disposed of his Numbers as quite to destroy the Form and Structure of Iambic Verse. *e. g.*

$$\breve{\,}\;\breve{\,}\;\;\overline{\,}\,\breve{\,}\;\;\breve{\,}\;\overline{\,}\;\;\;\overline{\,}\,\breve{\,}\;\;\breve{\,}\;\overline{\,}$$

In their | *triple* | *Degrees;* | *Regions,* | *to which*

B. v. i. 750.

Every Ear will perceive this to be no Verse; much less Iambic. And if you observe the Order of the Feet, the Reason is very Obvious. The first is a Pyrrhic, the second a Trochee, the third Iambic[,] the fourth a Trochee, and the last Iambic. Now as the first three Feet are a Pyrrhic, Trochee and Iambic, in this Order they make two Anapæsts; and the Line concluding with a Trochee and Iambic, makes the last Foot also an Anapæst. And there are wanting only two short Syllables at the End of the third Foot to make the whole Line purely Anapæstic, thus

$$\breve{\,}\;\breve{\,}\;\overline{\,}\;\;\breve{\,}\;\breve{\,}\;\overline{\,}\;\;\;\breve{\,}\;\breve{\,}\;\;\overline{\,}\,\breve{\,}\;\;\breve{\,}\;\overline{\,}$$

In their triple Degrees; and the Regions, to which

And the rapid Flow of Anapæstics, is of all Things most contrary to the stately Movement of Iambics. And the Line being a Composition of these two contrary Measures, and neither the one nor the other, it is no Verse, but downright Prose.

As *Milton*'s Numbers are so various, and the Times of which they are composed so unequal, it is impossible to Measure or beat Time to them regularly *per Arsin et Thesin*, as we do those Numbers that are pure and unmixt; that is, such as compose the pure Iambic, Trochaic, or Anapæstic Measure. And for the same Reason, they cannot with Propriety be set to any one uniform Piece of Music; because the Air of the Music must alter with the Flow of the Numbers.

33. Newton's notes to *Paradise Lost*

1749

Extracts from Thomas Newton, ed., *Paradise Lost* (1749), two volumes. Author of note is Newton unless otherwise specified.

Thomas Newton (1704–82), bishop of Bristol, produced the most reprinted life of Milton and the text generally employed for editions of Milton's poems during the last half of the eighteenth century. The notes to the poems were culled from prior published discussions and from manuscript notes and the like of various commentators, as well as being expressly written by Newton for the editions of the poetical works in 1749–51.

Volume I

I, 1, pp. 3–5

Besides the plainness and simplicity of these lines, there is a farther beauty in the variety of the numbers, which of themselves charm every reader without any sublimity of thought or pomp of expression: and this variety of the numbers consists chiefly in the pause being so artfully varied, that it falls upon a different syllable in almost every line. . . . Mr. Pope, in a letter to Mr. Walsh containing some critical observations on English versification, remarks that in any smooth English verse of ten syllables, there is naturally a pause at the fourth, fifth, or sixth syllable, and upon the judicious change and management of these depends the variety of versification. But Milton varies the pause according to the sense, and varies it through all the ten syllables, by which means he is a master of greater harmony than any other English poet: and he is continually varying the pause, and scarce ever suffers it to rest upon the same syllable in more than two, and seldom in so many as two, verses together. . . . But besides this variety of the pauses, there are other excellencies in Milton's versification. The English heroic verse approaches nearest to the Iambic of the Ancients, of which it wants only a foot; but then it is to be measur'd by the tone and accent, as well as by the time and quantity. An Iambic foot is one short and one long syllable ‿‾|, and six such feet constitute an Iambic verse: but the Ancients seldom made use of the pure Iambic, especially in works of any considerable length, but oftner of the mix'd Iambic, that is with a proper inter-mixture of other measures; and of these perhaps Milton has express'd as happy a variety as any poet whatever, or indeed as the nature of a verse will admit, that consists only of five feet, and ten syllables for the most part. Sometimes he gives us almost pure Iambics . . . Sometimes the Pyrrhichius or foot of two short syllables . . . Sometimes the Dactyle or foot of one long and two short syllables . . . Sometimes the Anapæst or foot of two short and one long syllable . . . Sometimes the Tribrachus or foot of three short syllables . . . And sometimes there is variety of these measures in the same verse, and seldom or never the same measures in two verses together.

I, 38, p. 13

Besides the other methods which Milton has employ'd to diversify and improve his numbers, he takes the same liberties as Shakespear and others of our old poets, and in imitation of the Greeks and Latins often cuts off the vowel at the end of a word, when the next word begins with a vowel, but still retains it in writing like the Latins. Another liberty, that he takes likewise for the greater improvement and variety of his versification, is pronouncing the same word sometimes as two syllables, and sometimes as only one syllable or two short ones. We have frequent instances in *spirit, ruin, riot, reason, highest,* and several other words. But then these excellencies in Milton's verse are attended with this inconvenience, that his numbers seem embarass'd to such readers, as know not, or know not readily, where such elision or abbreviation of vowels is to take place. . . .

I, 376, p. 44 (Warburton)

Homer at the beginning of his catalogue invokes his Muse afresh in a very pompous manner. Virgil does the like, and Milton follows both so far as to make a fresh invocation, though short; because he had already made a large and solemn address in this very book, at the beginning of his poem.

I, 589, p. 65

What a noble description is here of Satan's person! and how different from the common and ridiculous representations of him, with horns and a tail and cloven feet! and yet Tasso hath so describ'd him, Cant. IV. The greatest masters in painting had not such sublime ideas as Milton, and among all their Devils have drawn no portrait comparable to this; as every body must allow who have seen the pictures or the prints of Michael and the Devil by Raphael, and of the same by Guido, and of the last judgment by Michael Angelo.

II, 758, pp. 150–1

Sin is rightly made to spring out of the head of Satan, as Wisdom or Minerva did out of Jupiter's: and Milton describes the birth of the one very much in the same manner, as the ancient poets have that of the other, and particularly the author of the hymn to Minerva vulgarly ascribed to Homer. And what follows seems to be an hint improv'd upon Minerva's being ravish'd soon after her birth by Vulcan, as we may learn from Lucian. *Dial. Vulcani & Jovis, & De Domo.*

II, 817, pp. 155–6

Satan had now learned *his lore* or lesson, and the reader will observe how artfully he changes his language; he had said before, ver. 745. that he had never seen *sight more detestable*; but now it is *dear daughter*, and *my fair son.*

II, 871, p. 158 (Thyer)

It is one great part of a poet's art to know when to describe things in general, and when to be very circumstantial and particular. Milton has in these lines show'd his judgment in this respect. The first opening of the gates of Hell by Sin is an incident of that importance, that, if I can guess by my own, every reader's attention must be greatly excited, and consequently as highly gratified by the minute detail of particulars our author has given us. It may with justice be farther observed, that in no part of the poem, the versification is better accommodated to the sense. *The drawing up of the portcullis, the turning of the key, the sudden shooting of the bolts,* and *the flying open of the doors* are in some sort described by the very break and sound of the verses.

III, 1, p. 183

Our author's address to Light, and lamentation of his own blindness may perhaps be censur'd as an excrescence or digression not agreeable to the rules of epic poetry; but yet this is so charming a part of the poem, that the most critical reader, I imagin, cannot wish it were omitted. One is even pleased with a fault, if it be a fault, that is the occasion of so many beauties, and acquaints us so much with the circumstances and character of the author.

III, 37, p. 189

And the reader will observe the flowing of the numbers here with all the ease and harmony of the finest voluntary. The words seem of themselves to have fall'n naturally into verse almost without the poet's thinking of it. And this harmony appears to greater advantage for the roughness of some of the preceding verses, which is an artifice frequently practic'd by Milton, to be careless of his numbers in some places, the better to set off the musical flow of those which immediately follow.

III, 266, pp. 205–6 (Thyer)

What a charming and lovely picture has Milton given us of God the Son consider'd as our Saviour and Redeemer? not in the least inferior in its way to that grander one in the 6th book, where he discribes him cloathed with majesty and terror, taking vengeance of his enemies. Before he represents him speaking, he makes *divine compassion, love without end, and grace without measure visibly to appear in his face:* ver. 140. and carrying on the same amiable picture, makes him end it with a countenance *breathing immortal love to mortal men.* Nothing could be better contriv'd to leave a deep impression upon the reader's mind, and I believe one may venture to assert, that no art or words could lift the imagination to a stronger idea of a good and benevolent being. The mute eloquence, which our author has so prettily express'd in his *silent yet spake,* is with no less beauty described by Tasso at the end of Armida's speech to Godfrey. Cant. 4. St. 65.

III, 344, p. 211

If the reader pleases to compare this divine dialogue with the speeches of the Gods in Homer and Virgil, he will find the Christian poet to transcend the Heathen, as much as the religion of the one surpasses that of the other. Their deities talk and act like men, but Milton's divine Persons are divine Persons indeed, and talk in the language of God, that is in the language of Scripture. He is so very scrupulous and exact in this particular, that perhaps there is not a single expression, which may not be justify'd by the authority of holy Writ. We have taken notice of several where he seems to have copied the letter of Scripture, and the spirit of Scripture breathes in all the rest.

III, 686, pp. 246–7 (Thyer)

He must be very critically splenetic indeed, who will not pardon this little digressional observation. There is not in my opinion a nobler sentiment, or one more poetically express'd, in the whole poem. What great art has the poet shown in taking off the dryness of a mere moral sentence by throwing it into the form of a short and beautiful allegory!

IV, 152, p. 264 (Thyer)

This description exceeds any thing I ever met with of the same kind, but the Italians, in my opinion, approach the nearest to our English poet; and if the reader will give himself the trouble to read over Ariosto's picture of the garden of Paradise, Tasso's garden of Armida, and Marino's garden of Venus, he will, I think, be persuaded that Milton imitates their manner, but yet that the copy greatly excels the originals.

IV, 297, pp. 279–80

The curious reader may please to observe upon these two charming Lines, how the numbers are varied, and how artfully *he* and *she* are placed in each verse, so as the tone may fall upon them, and yet fall upon them differently. The author might have given both exactly the same tone, but every ear must judge this alteration to be much for the worse.

IV, 304, p. 281 (Thyer)

The poet has, I think, showed great judgment and delicacy in avoiding in this place the entering into a circumstantial description of Eve's beauty. It was, no doubt, a very tempting occasion of giving an indulgent loose to his fancy; since the most lavish imagination could not possibly carry too high the charms of Woman, as she first came out of the hands of her heavenly Maker. But as a picture of this kind would have been too light and gay for the graver turn of Milton's plan, he has very artfully mentioned the charms of her person in general terms only, and directed the reader's attention more particularly to the beauty of her mind. Most great poets have labor'd in a particular manner the delineation of their beauties (Ariosto's Alcina, Tasso's Armida, and Spenser's Belphoebe) and 'tis very probable that the portrait of Eve would have rival'd them all, if the chaste correctness of our author's Muse had not restrain'd him.

IV, 761, p. 320

In allusion to Heb. XIII. 4. *Marriage is honorable in all, and the bed undefiled.* And Milton must have had a good opinion of marriage, or he would never have had three wives. And tho' this panegyric upon wedded love may be condemned as a digression, yet it can hardly be call'd a digression, when it grows so naturally out of the subject, and is introduced so properly, while the action of the poem is in a manner suspended, and while Adam and Eve are lying down to sleep; and if morality be one great end of poetry, that end cannot be better promoted than by such digressions as this and that upon hypocrisy at the latter part of the third book.

V, 325, p. 377 (Thyer)

This is rather too philosophical for the female character of Eve: and in my opinion one of Milton's greatest faults is his introducing inconsistencies in the characters both of Angels and Man by mixing too much with them his own philosophical notions.

V, 468, p. 390 (Greenwood)

I would have it observed in what a beautiful manner Milton brings on the execution of those orders, which Raphael had received from God. To avoid all appearance of harshness or abruptness, which might have seemed, if the Angel had immediately entered upon his errand, the poet makes use of Adam's curiosity to introduce the subject, and puts such wary and modest questions into his mouth, as naturally led to those high matters, upon which the other was commissioned to discourse to him.

VI, 251, p. 449 (Warburton)

It shows how entirely the ideas of chivalry and romance had possessed him, to make Michael fight with *a two-handed* sword. The same idea occasion'd his expressing himself very obscurely in the following lines of his 'Lycidas',

> But that two-handed engin at the door
> Stands ready to smite once, and smite no more.

These are the last words of Peter predicting God's vengeance on his church by his ministry. The making him the minister is in imitation of the Italian poets, who in their satiric pieces against the church always make Peter the minister of vengeance. The *two-handed engin* is the two-handed Gothic sword, with which the painters draw him. *Stands ready at the door* was then a common phrase to signify a thing imminent. *To smite once and smite no more* signifies a final destruction, but alludes to Peter's single use of his sword in the case of the High Priest's servant.

VI, 568, pp. 477–8

We cannot pretend entirely to justify this *punning* scene: but we should consider that there is very little of this kind of wit any where in the poem but in this place, and in this we may suppose Milton to have sacrific'd to the taste of his times, when *puns* were better relish'd than they are at present in the learned world; and I know not whether we are not grown too delicate and fastidious in this particular. It is certain the Ancients practic'd them more both in their conversation and in their writings; and Aristotle recommends them in his book of Rhetoric, and likewise Cicero in his treatise of Oratory; and if we should condemn them absolutely, we must condemn half of the good sayings of the greatest wits of Greece and Rome. They are less proper indeed in serious works, and not at all becoming the majesty of an epic poem; but our author seems to have been betray'd into this excess in great measure by his love and admiration of Homer. For this account of the Angels jesting and insulting one another is not unlike some passages in the 16th book of the *Iliad*. Aeneas throws a spear at Meriones; and he artfully avoiding it, Aeneas jests upon his *dancing*, the Cretans (the countrymen of Meriones) being famous dancers. A little afterwards in the same book, Patroclus kills Hector's charioteer, who falls headlong from the chariot, upon which Patroclus insults him for several lines together upon his skill in *diving*, and says that if he was at sea, he might catch excellent oisters. Milton's jests cannot be lower and more trivial than these; but if he is like Homer in his faults, let it be remember'd that he is like him in his beauties too. And Mr. Thyer farther observes, that Milton is the less to be blam'd for this punning scene, when one considers the characters of the speakers, such kind of insulting wit being most peculiar to proud contemptuous Spirits.

VI, 748, pp. 493–4 (Greenwood)

Milton by continuing the war for three days, and reserving the victory upon the third for the Messiah alone, plainly alludes to the circumstances of his death and resurrection. Our Savior's extreme sufferings on the one hand, and his heroic behavior on the other, made the contest seem to be more equal and doubtful upon the first day; and on the second Satan triumphed in the advantages he thought he had gained, when Christ lay buried in the earth, and was to outward appearance in an irrecoverable state of corruption: but as the poet represents the almighty Father speaking to his Son ver. 699.

Two days are therefore past, the third is thine;
For thee I have ordain'd it, and thus far
Have suffer'd, that the glory may be thine
Of ending this great war, since none but Thou
Can end it.

Which he most gloriously did, when *the third sacred morn began to shine,* by vanquishing with his own almighty arm the powers of Hell, and rising again from the grave: and thus as St. Paul says Rom. I. 4. *He was declared to be the Son of God with power, according to the Spirit of holiness, by the resurrection from the dead.*

Volume II

VII, 98, p. 14

Our author has improv'd upon Homer, *Odyss.* XI. 372. where Alcinous by the same sort of arguments endevors to persuade Ulysses to continue his narration; only there it was night, and here the scene is by day. . . . Mr. Thyer is of opinion, that there is not a greater instance of our author's exquisite skill in the art of poetry, than this and the following lines. There is nothing more, really to be express'd, than Adam's telling Raphael his desire to hear the continuance of his relation, and yet the poet by a series of strong and noble figures has work'd it up into half a score of as fine lines as any in the whole poem. Lord Shaftsbury has observed, that Milton's beauties generally depend upon solid thought, strong reasoning, noble passion, and a continued thread of moral doctrin; but in this place he has shown what an exalted fancy and mere force of poetry can do.

VII, 412, p. 44 (Thyer)

Milton has here with very great art and propriety adopted the Italian verb *tempestare.* He could not possibly have expressed this idea in mere English without some kind of circumlocution, which would have weaken'd and enervated that energy of expression which this part of his description requir'd. Besides no word could be more proper in the beginning of the verse to make it labour like the troubled ocean, which he is painting out.

(Newton) The best critics and commentators upon Job by the *leviathan* understand the *crocodile,* and Milton in several particulars describes the *leviathan* like the author of the book of Job, and yet by others it seems as if he meant the *whale.*

VIII, 316, p. 91 (Greenwood)

These words make very good sense here in the common acceptation of them: but by Milton's placing them in such an emphatical manner at the end of the verse, I am of opinion that he might possibly allude to the name, which God gave himself to Moses, when he appeared to him in the bush. . . .

VIII, 440, p. 100 (Thyer)

Milton is upon all occasions a strenuous advocate for the freedom of the human mind against the narrow and rigid notions of the Calvinists of that age, and here in the same spirit supposes the very image of God in which man was made to consist in this liberty. The sentiment is very grand, and this sense of the words is, in my opinion, full as probable as any of those many which the commentators have put upon them, in as much as no property of the soul of man distinguishes him better from the brutes, or assimilates him more to his Creator. This notion, tho' uncommon, is not peculiar to Milton; for I find Clarius, in his remark upon this passage of Scripture, referring to St. Basil the great for the same interpretation. . . .

IX, 1, p. 123

These prologues or prefaces of Milton to some of his books, speaking of his own person, lamenting his blindness, and preferring his subject to those of Homer and Virgil and the greatest poets before him, are condemn'd by some critics: and it must be allow'd that we find no such digression in the *Iliad* or *Aeneid*; it is a liberty that can be taken only by such a genius as Milton, and I question whether it would have succeeded in any hands but his. As Monsieur Voltaire says upon the occasion, I cannot but own that an author is generally guilty of an unpardonable self-love, when he lays aside his subject to descant upon his own person; but that human frailty is to be forgiven in Milton; nay I am pleased with it. He gratifies the curiosity he has raised in me about his person; when I admire the author, I desire to know something of the man; and he, whom all readers would be glad to know, is allow'd to speak of himself. But this however is a very dangerous example for a genius of an inferior order, and is only to be justified by success. . . . But as Mr. Thyer adds, however some critics and Monsieur Voltaire may condemn a poet's sometimes digressing from his subject to speak of himself, it is very certain that Milton was of a very different opinion long before he thought of writing this poem. . . .

IX, 5, p. 125

As the author is now changing his subject, he professes likewise to change his stile agreeably to it. The reader therefore must not expect such lofty images and descriptions, as before. What follows is more of the *tragic* strain than of the *epic*. Which may serve as an answer to those critics who censure the latter books of the *Paradise Lost* as falling below the former.

IX, 11, p. 125

The pun or what shall I call it in this line may be avoided, as a great man observed to me, by distinguishing thus,

> That brought into this world (a world of woe)
> Sin and her shadow death.

but I fancy the other will be found more agreeable to Milton's stile and manner. We have a similar instance in XI. 627. . . . But in these instances Milton was corrupted by the bad taste of the times, and by reading the Italian poets, who abound with such verbal quaintnesses.

IX, 28, p. 127

By the Moderns as well as by the Ancients; wars being the principal subject of all the heroic poems from Homer down to this time. But Milton's subject was different, and whatever others may call it, we see he reckons it himself *An heroic poem*, tho' he names it only *A poem* in his title page. It is indeed, as Mr. Warburton most excellently observes in his *Divine Legation of Moses*, Book 2. Sect. 4. the *third* species of epic poetry. For just as Virgil rivaled Homer, so Milton emulated both. He found Homer possessed of the province of *morality*, Virgil of *politics*, and nothing left for him but that of *religion*. This he seised, as aspiring to share with them in the government of the poetic world; and by means of the superior dignity of his subject, got to the head of that triumvirate which took so many ages in forming. These are the three species of the epic poem; for its largest province is human action, which can be considered but in a moral, a political, or religious view; and these the three great creators of them; for each of these poems was struck out at an heat, and came to perfection from its first essay. Here then the grand scene is closed, and all farther improvements of the epic at an end.

IX, 176, p. 141 (Thyer)

I have often wonder'd that this speech of Satan's escaped the particular observation of the ingenious Mr. Addison. There is not in my opinion any one in the whole book that is worked up with greater judgment, or better suited to the character of the speaker. There is all the horror and malignity of a fiend-like Spirit express'd, and yet this is so artfully temper'd with Satan's sudden starts of recollection upon the meanness and folly of what he was going to undertake, as plainly show the remains of the Arch-Angel, and the ruins of a superior nature.

IX, 613, p. 177 (Warburton)

Milton has shown more art and ability in taking off the common objections to the Mosaic history of the temptation by the addition of some circumstances of his own invention, than in any other theologic part of his poem.

IX, 794, pp. 189–90 (Thyer)

As our author had in the preceding conference betwixt our first parents described with the greatest art and decency the subordination and inferiority of the female character in strength of reason and under-standing; so in this soliloquy of Eve's after tasting the forbidden fruit, one may observe the same judgment, in his varying and adapting it to the condition of her fall'n nature. Instead of those little defects in her intellectual faculties before the fall, which were sufficiently compensated by her outward charms, and were rather softenings than blemishes in her character, we see her now running into the greatest absurdities, and indulging the wildest imaginations. It has been remark'd that our poet in this work seems to court the favor of his female readers very much, yet I cannot help thinking, but that in this place he intended a satirical as well as a moral hint to the ladies, in making one of Eve's first thoughts after her fatal lapse to be, how to get the superiority and mast'ry over her husband. There is, however, I think, a defect in this speech of Eve's, that there is no notice taken of the Serpent in it. Our author very naturally represents her in the first transports of delight expressing her gratitude to the fruit, which she fancied had wrought such a happy change in her, and next to *experience her best guide*: but how is it possible that she should in these rapturous acknowledgments forget her guide and instructor the Serpent, to whom in her then notion of things she must think herself the most indebted? I don't doubt but Milton was sensible of this, but had he made Eve mention the Serpent, he could not have avoided too making her observe that he slunk away, which might have given her some suspicions, and would consequently have much alter'd the scene which follows betwixt Adam and her.

IX, 928, pp. 200–1 (Thyer)

How just a picture does Milton here give us of the natural imbecillity of the human mind, and its aptness to be warp'd into false judgments and reasonings by passion and inclination? Adam had but just condemn'd the action of Eve in eating the forbidden fruit, and yet drawn by his fondness for her immediately summons all the force of his reason to prove what she had done to be right. This may probably appear a fault to superficial readers, but all intelligent ones will, I dare say, look upon it as a proof of our author's exquisite knowledge of human nature. Reason is but too often little better than a slave ready at the beck of the will to dress up in plausible colors any opinions that our interest or resentment have made agreeable to us.

X, 169, p. 232 (Warburton)

This is badly express'd. The meaning is, As Man was not to be let into the mystery of the redomption at this time, it did not concern him to know that the serpent was but the instrument of the Devil. When Milton wrote this, I fancy he had it not then in his thoughts to make Michael reveal to Adam in the last book the doctrin of redomption; or if he did intend it, he forgot that a theological comment on those words in Genesis would ill agree with what was to follow.

X, 312, p. 247 (Warburton)

Art pontifical, this is a very bad expression to signify the art of building bridges, and yet to suppose a pun would be worse, as if the Roman priesthood were as ready to make the way easy to Hell, as Sin and Death did.

X, 513, pp. 260–1

We may observe here a singular beauty and elegance in Milton's language, and that is his using words in their strict and litteral sense, which are commonly applied to a metaphorical meaning, whereby he gives peculiar force to his expressions, and the litteral meaning appears more new and striking than the metaphor itself. We have an instance of this in the word *supplanted*, which is deriv'd from the Latin *supplanto*, to trip up one's heels or overthrow, a planta pedis subtus emota: and there are abundance of other examples in several parts of this work, but let it suffice to have taken notice of it here once for all.

X, 940, p. 300

This seems to have been drawn from a domestic scene. Milton's wife soon after marriage went to visit her friends in Oxfordshire, and refused to return at the time appointed: He often solicited her, but in vain; she declar'd her resolution not to cohabit with him any more. Upon this he wrote his *Doctrin and Disciplin of Divorce*, and to show that he was in earnest was actually treating about a second marriage, when the wife contrived to meet him at a friend's whom he often visited, and there fell prostrate before him, imploring forgiveness and reconciliation. It is not to be doubted (says Mr. Fenton) but an interview of that nature, so little expected, must wonderfully affect him: and perhaps the impressions it made on his imagination contributed much to the painting of that pathetic scene in *Paradise Lost*, in which Eve addresseth herself to Adam for pardon and peace. . . . Mr. Thyer thus farther inlarges upon the same subject.

This picture of Eve's distress, her submissive tender address to her husband, and his generous reconcilement to her are extremely beautiful, I had almost said beyond any thing in the whole poem; and that reader must have a very sour and unfriendly turn of mind, whose heart does not *relent* with Adam's, and melt into a sympathizing commiseration towards the mother of mankind; so well has our author here follow'd Horace's advice. . . . Milton with great depth of judgment observes in his *Apology for Smectymnuus*, that *he who would not be frustrate of his hope to write well in laudable things, ought himself to be a true poem, that is, a composition of the best and honorablest things,—and have in himself the experience and practice of all that which is praise-worthy:* of the truth of which observation he himself is, I think, a shining instance in this charming scene now before us, since there is little room to doubt but that the particular beauties of it are owing to an interview of the same nature which he had with his own wife, and that he is only here describing those tender and generous sentiments, which he then felt and *experienc'd.*

XI, 263, p. 338 (Thyer)

How naturally and justly does Milton here describe the different effects of grief upon our first parents! Mr. Addison has already remark'd upon the beauty and propriety of Eve's complaint, but I think there is an additional beauty to be observ'd when one considers the fine contrast which there is betwixt that and Adam's sorrow, which was silent and thoughtful, as Eve's was loud and hasty, both consistent with the different characters of the sexes, which Milton has indeed kept up with great exactness through the whole poem.

XI, 843, pp. 384–5 (Thyer)

This allusive comparison of the surface of the decreasing waters, wrinkled by the wind, to the wrinkles of a decaying old age is very far fetch'd and extremely boyish; but the author makes us ample amends in the remaining part of this description of the abating of the flood. The circumstances of it are few, but selected with great judgment, and express'd with no less spirit and beauty. In this respect, it must be own'd, Milton greatly excels the Italians, who are generally too prolix in their descriptions, and think they have never said enough whilst any thing remains unsaid. When once enough is said to excite in the reader's mind a proper idea of what the poet is representing, whatever is added, however beautiful, serves only to teize the fancy instead of pleasing it, and rather cools than improves that glow of pleasure, which arises in the mind upon its first contemplation of any surprising scene of nature well painted out. Of this Milton was very sensible, and throughout his whole poem has scarcely ever been hurried by his imagination into any thing inconsistent with it.

XII, 11, pp. 394–5 (Thyer)

Mr. Addison observes, that *if Milton's poem flags any where, it is in this narration*; and to be sure, if we have an eye only to poetic decoration, his remark is just: but if we view it in another light, and consider in how short a compass he has compris'd, and with what strenth and clearness he has express'd the various actings of God towards mankind, and the most sublime and deep truths both of the Jewish and Christian theology, it must excite no less admiration in the mind of an attentive reader, than the more spritely scenes of love and innocence in Eden, or the more turbulent ones of angelic war in Heaven. This contrivance of Milton's to introduce into his poem so many things posterior to the time of action fix'd in his first plan, by a visionary prophetic relation of them, is, it must be allow'd, common with our author to Virgil and most epic poets since his time; but there is one thing to be observ'd singular in our English poet, which is, that whereas they have all done it principally, if not wholly, to have an opportunity of complimenting their own country and friends, he has not the least mention of, or friendly allusion to his. The Reformation of our church from the errors and tyranny of popery, which corruptions he so well describes and pathetically laments, afforded him occasion fair enough, and no doubt his not doing it must be imputed to his mind's being so unhappily imbitter'd, at the time of his writing, against our government both in church and state; so that to the many other mischiefs flowing from the grand rebellion we may add this of its depriving Britain of the best panegyric it is ever likely to have.

XII, 128, p. 404 (Thyer)

Our poet, sensible that this long historical description might grow irksome, has varied the manner of representing it as much as possible, beginning first with supposing Adam to have a prospect of it before his eyes, next by making the Angel the relator of it, and lastly by uniting the two former methods, and making Michael see it as in a vision, and give a rapturous inliven'd account of it to Adam. This gives great ease to the languishing attention of the reader.

XII, 648, pp. 444-5

These two last verses have occasion'd much trouble to the critics, some being for rejecting, others for altering, and others again for transposing them: but the propriety of the two lines, and the design of the author are fully explained and vindicated in the excellent note of Dr. Pearce. And certainly there is no more necessity that an epic poem should conclude happily, than there is that a tragedy should conclude unhappily. There are instances of several tragedies ending happily; and with as good reason an epic poem may terminate fortunately or unfortunately, as the nature of the subject requires: and the subject of *Paradise Lost* plainly requires something of a sorrowful parting, and was intended no doubt for terror as well as pity, to inspire us to fear of God as well as with commiseration of Man. All therefore that we shall add is to desire the reader to observe the beauty of the numbers, the heavy dragging of the first line, which cannot be pronounced but slowly, and with several pauses . . . and then the quicker flow of the last verse with only the usual pause in the middle . . . as if our parents had moved heavily at first, being loath to leave their delightful Paradise, and afterwards mended their pace, when they were at a little distance. At least this is the idea that the numbers convey: and as many volumes might be compos'd upon the structure of Milton's verses, and the collocation of his words, as Erythraeus and other critics have written upon Virgil. We have taken notice of several beauties of this kind in the course of these remarks, and particularly of the varying of the pauses, which is the life and soul of all versification in all languages. It is this chiefly which makes Virgil's verse better than Ovid's, and Milton's superior to any other English poet's: and it is for want of this chiefly that the French heroic verse has never, and can never come up to the English. There is no variety of numbers, but the same pause is preserved exactly in the same place in every line for ten or ten thousand lines together: and such a perpetual repetition of the same pause, such an eternal sameness of verse must make any poetry tedious, and either offend the ear of the reader, or lull him asleep: and this in the opinion of several French writers themselves. There can be no good poetry without music, and there can be no music without variety.

Note, pp. 446–7.

And thus have we finish'd our collections and remarks on this divine poem. The reader probably may have observed that these two last books fall short of the sublimity and majesty of the rest: and so likewise do the two last books of the *Iliad*, and for the same reason, because the subject is of a different kind from that of the foregoing ones. The subject of these two last books of the *Paradise Lost* is history rather than poetry. However we may still discover the same great genius, and there are intermix'd as many ornaments and graces of poetry, as the nature of the subject, and the author's fidelity and strict attachment to the truth of Scripture history, and the reduction of so many and such various events into so narrow a compass, would admit. It is the same ocean, but not at its highest tide; it is now ebbing and retreating. It is the same sun, but not in its full blaze of meridian glory; it now shines with a gentler ray as it is setting. Throughout the whole the author appears to have been a most critical reader and a most passionate admirer of holy Scripture. He is indebted to Scripture infinitely more than to Homer and Virgil and all other books whatever. Not only his principal fable, but all his episodes are founded upon Scripture. The Scripture hath not only furnish'd him with the noblest hints, rais'd his thoughts and fir'd his imagination; but hath also very much enrich'd his language, given a certain solemnity and majesty to his diction, and supplied him with many of his choicest happiest expressions. Let men therefore learn from this instance to reverence those sacred Writings. If any man can pretend to deride or despise them, it must be said of him at least, that he has a taste and genius the most different from Milton's that can be imagin'd. Whoever has any true taste and genius, we are confident, will esteem this poem the best of modern productions, and the Scriptures the best of all ancient ones.

34. Johnson on 'Comus'

1750

Samuel Johnson, 'Prologue to *Comus*' (1750). *Prologue Written by Samuel Johnson And spoken by David Garrick at a Benefit-Performance of Comus April 1750*, Oxford Univ. Press, 1925.

Samuel Johnson (1709–84), the major literary critic of the eighteenth century, is represented here frequently; see Nos 35, 38, 42, 43, 64, 65, 66. On the one hand his criticism of Milton and his works has been coloured by his attitude toward Milton's anti-monarchism and religious persuasions; on the other by neoclassic concepts of form, subject, treatment, etc. Yet his major statements on Milton in the *Rambler* papers and in the 'Life' manifest a deep appreciation of Milton and an incisive eye for Milton's departures from standard form, prosody, etc. Modern criticism has used Johnson's comments often out of full context to present adverse criticism or to be the springboard into a defence against the strictures supposedly levelled by Johnson. A closer examination of Johnson's criticism will reveal a prejudice against Milton the man and some disagreement with Milton's breaking of rules, but it will also show that much of the allegedly negative comment is an attempt to present a balanced view of the works for a contemporary reader, comment which is variously nullified by further remarks.

Ye patriot Crouds, who burn for *England*'s Fame,
Ye Nymphs, whose Bosoms beat at MILTON's Name,
Whose gen'rous Zeal, unbought by flatt'ring Rhimes,
Shames the mean Pensions of *Augustan* Times;
Immortal Patrons of succeeding Days,
Attend this Prelude of perpetual Praise!
Let Wit, condemn'd the feeble War to wage
With close Malevolence, or public Rage;
Let Study, worn with Virtue's fruitless Lore,

Behold this Theatre, and grieve no more.
This Night, distinguish'd by your Smile, shall tell,
That never BRITON can in vain excel;
The slighted Arts Futurity shall trust,
And rising Ages hasten to be just.

At length our mighty Bard's victorious Lays
Fill the loud Voice of universal Praise,
And baffled Spite, with hopeless Anguish dumb,
Yields to Renown the Centuries to come.
With ardent Haste, each Candidate of Fame
Ambitious catches at his tow'ring Name:
He sees, and pitying sees, vain Wealth bestow
Those pageant Honours which he scorn'd below:
While Crowds aloft the laureat Bust behold,
Or trace his Form on circulating Gold,
Unknown, unheeded, long his Offspring lay,
And Want hung threat'ning o'er her slow Decay.
What tho' she shine with no MILTONIAN Fire,
No fav'ring Muse her morning Dreams inspire;
Yet softer Claims the melting Heart engage,
Her Youth laborious, and her blameless Age:
Hers the mild Merits of domestic Life,
The patient Suff'rer, and the faithful Wife.
Thus grac'd with humble Virtue's native Charms
Her Grandsire leaves her in *Britannia*'s Arms,
Secure with Peace, with Competence, to dwell,
While tutelary Nations guard her Cell.
Yours is the Charge, ye Fair, ye Wise, ye Brave!
Tis yours to crown Desert—beyond the Grave!

35. Johnson's preface to the revision of Lauder's charges

1750

Samuel Johnson, 'Preface' to William Lauder's *An Essay on Milton's Use and Imitation of the Moderns in His Paradise Lost* (1750). The preface was made to appear the product of Lauder's pen.

It is now more than half a century since the *Paradise Lost*, having broke through the clouds with which the unpopularity of the author, for a time, obscured it, has attracted the general admiration of mankind; who have endeavoured to compensate the error of their first neglect, by lavish praises and boundless veneration. There seems to have arisen a contest, among men of genius and literature, who should most advance its honour, or best distinguish its beauties. Some have revised editions, others have published commentaries, and all have endeavoured to make their particular studies, in some degree, subservient to this general emulation.

Among the inquiries to which this ardour of criticism has naturally given occasion, none is more obscure in itself, or more worthy of rational curiosity, than a retrospection of the progress of this mighty genius, in the construction of his work; a view of the fabrick gradually rising, perhaps from small beginnings, till its foundation rests in the centre, and its turrets sparkle in the skies; to trace back the structure, through all its varieties, to the simplicity of its first plan; to find what was first projected, whence the scheme was taken, how it was improved, by what assistance it was executed, and from what stores the materials were collected, whether its founder dug them from the quarries of nature, or demolished other buildings to embellish his own.

This inquiry has been, indeed, not wholly neglected, nor, perhaps, prosecuted with the care and diligence that it deserves. Several criticks have offered their conjectures; but none have much endeavoured to enforce or ascertain them. Mr. Voltaire tell[s] us, without proof, that the first hint of *Paradise Lost* was taken from a farce called Adamo, written by a player;[1] Dr. Pearce, that it was derived from an Italian tragedy, called *Il Paradiso Perso*;[2] and Mr. Peck,[3] that it was borrowed from a wild romance. Any of these conjectures may possibly be true, but, as they stand without sufficient proof, it must be granted, likewise, that they may all possibly be false; at least they cannot preclude any other opinion, which without argument has the same claim to credit, and may perhaps be shown, by resistless evidence, to be better founded.

It is related, by steady and uncontroverted tradition, that the *Paradise Lost* was at first a tragedy, and, therefore, amongst tragedies, the first hint is properly to be sought. In a manuscript, published from Milton's own hand, among a great number of subjects for tragedy, is *Adam Unparadised*, or *Adam in Exile*; and this, therefore, may be justly supposed the embryo of this great poem. As it is observable, that all these subjects had been treated by others, the manuscript can be supposed nothing more, than a memorial or catalogue of plays, which, for some reason, the writer thought worthy of his attention. When, therefore, I had observed, that *Adam in Exile* was named amongst them, I doubted not but, in finding the original of that tragedy, I should disclose the genuine source of *Paradise Lost*. Nor was my expectation disappointed; for, having procured the *Adamus Exsul* of Grotius, I found, or imagined myself to find, the first draught, the *prima stamina* of this wonderful poem.

Having thus traced the original of this work, I was naturally induced to continue my search to the collateral relations, which it might be supposed to have contracted, in its progress to maturity: and having, at least, persuaded my own judgment that the search has not been entirely ineffectual, I now lay the result of my labours before the publick; with full conviction, that in questions of this kind, the world cannot be *mistaken*, at least cannot long continue in error.

I cannot avoid acknowledgeing the candour of the author of that excellent monthly book, the *Gentleman's Magazine* [Johnson was one of the editors], in giving admission to the specimens in favour of this argument; and his impartiality in as freely inserting the several answers. I shall here subjoin some extracts from the xviith volume of this work,

---

[1] *Essay upon the Civil Wars of France, and also upon the Epick Poetry of the European Nations, from Homer down to Milton*, 8vo. 1727. p. 10.

[2] Preface to a review of the text of the twelve books of Milton's *Paradise Lost*, in which the chief of Dr Bentley's emendations are considered, 8vo. 1733.

[3] *New Memoirs of Mr. John Milton*, by Francis Peck, 4to. 1740, p. 52.

which I think suitable to my purpose. To which I have added, in order to obviate every pretence for cavil, a list of the authors quoted in the following essay, with their respective dates, in comparison with the date of *Paradise Lost*.

36. Lauder's revised charges of plagiarism

1750

Extract from William Lauder, *An Essay on Milton's Use and Imitation of the Moderns in His Paradise Lost* (1750), 2–3, 22–3, 47–54, 74–5, 77–8, 154–7, 160–4. See also the first version reproduced here as No. 26.

The first author I shall produce, as one of *Milton's* assistants, is *Jacobus Masenius*, professor of rhetoric and poetry, in the Jesuits college at *Cologne*, about the year 1650, who wrote a poem, entitled *Sarcotidos libri quinque*, consisting of about 2500 lines. The author, in his preface, observes that he did not intend it so much for a compleat model of an epic poem, as for a rude draught, or the great outlines of one to be worked up to perfection by a person of superior genius, or more leisure than himself. And it must be owned it fell into excellent hands: tho' the merit of the improvement made upon it, may admit of some diminution from the proverb, *facile est inventis addere*. *Milton* follows his steps pretty close in his two first books, in which both their subjects seem much the same. He begins to lose sight of him towards the opening of his third book, where *Masenius*, to speak truth, begins to lose himself, I mean his original plan, and instead of pursuing the fall of man, which at first he proposed, enters upon a comparison betwixt the different vices and virtues of mankind, their opposition to, and conflicts one with another. In this way he proceeds to his conclusion, treating all along his subject with great dignity and elegance, and prefixing such long historical arguments to his five books, as alone are sufficient to serve as a plan for composing a noble epic poem, tho' he had not proceeded to illustrate the excellent rules, given in the former part of his work, which exhibits directions for writing all kinds of *Latin* poetry; and is very justly entitled, *Palaestra ligatae eloquentiae.* . . .

The reader, I make no doubt, has already anticipated most of the observations I could possibly make, on the strong resemblance there is, betwixt the *plan* of *Paradise Lost*, and the *substance* of these arguments and marginal notes to *Masenius*'s poem. Therefore, not to insist on those things, which, it may be alledged, are either hinted at in the scriptures, or which the subject, common to both poets, might naturally suggest; I shall only remark, that the infernal council, or PANDÆ-MONIUM of *Masenius*, Lucifer's habit and chariot, the fight of the angels, especially as so circumstantiated, with the excursion of the fallen spirits from hell, and other particulars too obvious not to have been noticed undoubtedly gave birth to the similar constituent parts of *Milton*'s poem; in which, tho' they are more highly finished, and ampli-fied with additional ornaments, there are such strong traces of resem-blance left, as to make the assistance he derived from *Masenius* indisputably clear and obvious. I now proceed to the consideration of the poems themselves. *Milton*'s exordium is as follows, [I, 1–6].

These lines very probably owe their rise to the following most beautiful ones of *Masenius* and *Ramsay*, an author I shall have occasion to mention more particularly hereafter. . . .

But to come to a conclusion of this head. If any one can imagine, after such ample proofs produced from the poem itself, but especially from the arguments and marginal heads, where the constituent parts of *Paradise Lost* are plainly visible, and the whole poem, as it were, drawn out in miniature; whoever, I say, can imagine, that *Milton* could pos-sibly write as he has done, without seeing this author's performance, may, with equal reason, suppose, that a limner can draw a man's picture, exactly like the original, without ever viewing his person.

Having done with *Masenius*, I shall next proceed to a writer of no less eminence; to whom that *Milton* was also obliged, the reader will scarce doubt, since it is incontestable, that he had actually seen his performance. A paper of his own hand writing, found in Trinity College, *Cambridge*, contains a catalogue of above sixty subjects, taken from the sacred scripture, on which, it is conjectured, he designed to found tragedies. But, the truth is, they were only titles of tragedies, already written in Latin verse.

In the front of this catalogue stands,

ADAM UNPARADISED; or, *ADAM IN BANISHMENT*:

Which title is only a translation of *Adamus Exsul*, a tragedy written by the celebrated *Hugo Grotius*, when but 18 years old. This tragedy, tho' it has passed through no less than four editions, was yet never printed amongst the rest of that great author's works; and was become so very scarce, that I could not procure a copy either in *Britain* or *Holland*; till the learned Mr. *Abraham Gronovius*, keeper of the public library at *Leyden*, after great inquiry, obtained the sight of one; and, as I have, for some time, been honoured with his correspondence and friendship, sent me (transcribed by his own son) the first act of it, and afterwards the rest, together with the dedication, addressed to the Duke of *Bourbon*.

Now, as Mr. *Fenton*, as well as Mr. *Phillips*, *Milton*'s nephew, informs us, that *Paradise Lost* was first written (or intended to be written) in the form of a tragedy, where *Satan* was to pronounce the prologue; the judicious reader will, by considering this tragedy, (with the heads in its argument, and the similar Greek and Latin appellations in that and *Milton*) begin to be sensible, that this great poet, in composing his poem, had recourse to a vast treasure which he industriously kept secret. But I shall here endeavour to bring it to open light, tho' hitherto never so much as suspected; and, at some future time, take an opportunity to exhibit a beautiful and correct edition of the original authors, pursuant to the advice of several persons of learning and distinction, in case the design prove agreeable to the public.

The abovementioned noble tragedy is, perhaps, the incomparable author's master-piece in the poetical way; at least if we may judge of its excellence, from the encomiums conferred upon it by those eminent critics and poets, *Vossius, Heinsius, Douza, Potteius, Meursius*, and others; but, particularly, by the evident use *Milton* made of it, who has artfully transferred the substance of it into his *Paradise Lost*. The truth of this assertion will readily appear to any one, who will take the trouble to compare the one with the other. It contains 2000 lines and upwards; and, according to the best models of antiquity, consists of five acts, and a chorus subjoined to each, except the last. The first introduces *Satan* deliberating, in a long soliloquy, on the most likely means to operate man's destruction, declaring his resolution to effect it, by transforming himself into the shape of a serpent. The second exhibits a long conference betwixt *Adam* and an Angel, concerning the creation of the world: This part, *Milton* has thoroughly copied in his seventh book of

Paradise Lost; where, by way of episode, he gives an account how the world was created, and in what space of time; only, now and then, he enlarges beyond *Grotius*, with the addition of hints and allusions taken from *Ramsay*, *Du Bartas*, and Dr. *Ross's Virgilius Evangelizans*, as we shall have occasion to shew more fully afterwards. The third act contains an interview betwixt *Satan* and *Adam*, wherein the devil endeavours, under the guise of friendship, to seduce the father of mankind to disobedience; but, being overpowered by strength of argument, retires vanquished. This circumstance, the young poet has introduced, without the warrant of scripture, or rather in opposition to it. Perhaps he thought poetical licence would bear him out. In this *Milton* has not imitated him, and so far he was in the right: his extravagant admirers may wish he had always been as cautious. The fourth introduces the *Serpent* and *Eve* engaged in dispute; *Eve* defeated, *Adam* seduced, *Satan* triumphant, and the fall of man compleated. The last exhibits the catastrophe of the whole, the curse pronounced on *Adam* and *Eve* for their offence, with their final expulsion out of *Paradise*. This whole œconomy precisely answers to the plan of *Adam unparadised*; or, *Adam in Banishment*, in the paper of *Milton's* hand-writing. However, I shall here subjoin as much of *Grotius's* tragedy, as may sufficiently shew the truth of my assertion; namely, that *Milton*, besides other considerable helps, in composing his *Paradise Lost*, had also this performance of *Grotius* before him, of which he has made a very liberal use. . . .

Have not mankind, by giving too implicit a faith to this bold assertion, been deluded into a false opinion of *Milton's* being more an original author, than any poet ever was before him? And what but this opinion, and this only, has been the cause of that infinite tribute of veneration, that has been paid him these sixty years past? Hence so many editions, translations, commentaries, lives, encomiums, marble busts, pictures, gold and silver medals. The vindicator would not only have me excuse his author, but even commend him, for the freedom he has used with his friend *Grotius's* performance. But I must take the liberty to inform him, that my notions of morality taught me quite another lesson, than to bestow the praise due to ingenuity and integrity, on persons of a different character.

I shall now, in further support of my charge, produce a few passages from a work, nothing inferior to the two already cited: It was printed at *Edinburgh*, anno 1633, and addressed to King *Charles* the first, by the author, the Reverend Mr. *Andrew Ramsay*, at that time professor of divinity in the university of *Edinburgh*, as he had been of philosophy, for several years before, at *Saumur* in *France*. He was not only eminent in both these professions, but was also a most excellent poet, in the opinion of *Olaus Borrichius*, a very competent judge, who only blames him for his mixture of heathen mythology: but if that be a fault in a sacred poem (as it seems now universally agreed upon) *Milton* stands infinitely more obnoxious to the censure than he, who comparatively may plead not guilty; though, doubtless, his great authority and example have contributed not a little to mislead *Milton*. . . .

That *Milton* also has thought it a most noble performance, I shall shew from the extraordinary use he has made of it. 'Tis true, *Ramsay*'s poem has been lately called a cento from *Virgil*: but I hope to shew, (and I think I have partly done it already) that *Milton*'s stands infinitely more exposed to that censure, being compiled out of all authors, antient or modern, sacred or profane, who had any thing in their works, suitable to his purpose; nor do I blame him for this unlimited freedom, but for his industriously concealing it. But to proceed, *Ramsay*'s work is divided into four books, and consists of about fifteen or sixteen hundred lines. The first book contains a poetical paraphrase on the creation of the world, the substance of which, as I observed before, together with a few strictures from *Grotius*, *Du Bartas*, and *Ross*, *Milton* has thrown, by way of Episode, into his seventh book. The second exhibits a description of man's happiness in a state of innocence, together with a most exalted and sublime encomium on marriage, as the only lawful means appointed by God, for the propagation of the human species, to which *Milton* often alludes. The third represents the fall of man; and the fourth, man's redemption by *Christ*. As this excellent author's work (which may properly be called *Paradise Lost* in embrio, since it was wrote before *Milton*; as, on the other hand, it might justly have been named *Paradise Lost* abridged, had it been written after *Milton*) was inserted in the second volume of the *Deliciæ poetarum Scotorum*, printed at *Amsterdam*, anno 1637, and consequently is not so scarce as the other two pieces of *Grotius* and *Masenius*: As this is the case, I say, I shall content myself with presenting a few passages, only, from it, though *Milton* has transfused almost the whole substance of it into his poem, but with so much art, that it requires no small degree of attention to trace him out minutely. . . .

Dr. *Zachary Pearce*, now bishop of Bangor, is of opinion, that *Milton* took the first hint of his design of writing a tragedy, upon the subject of his poem, from an *Italian* tragedy, called, *Il Paradiso Perso*, still extant, and printed many years before he entered upon this work. And, indeed, I have been informed by several persons of unquestionable judgment and veracity, that almost all that is admir'd as lofty and sublime, in *Milton*'s description of the battle of the angels, in his sixth book, is wholly transcribed from this tragedy; where are to be seen the picture of the battle, and the final defeat of *Lucifer*, with his expulsion out of heaven, as described and delineated in *Paradise Lost*. Mr. *Addison* also makes no scruple to acknowledge, that *Milton* frequently borrows hints from *Tasso*, as others affirm he has done from *Dante*. So that, considering the evidences of this doctrine, it perhaps may be asserted, without a falsehood, or any injustice to *Milton*, that he is not the original author of any one single thought in *Paradise Lost*; but has only digested into order the thoughts of others, and cloathed them in an elegant *English* dress: though one might wish he had often been more cautious, what authors he made choice of, since it is certain, amongst many fine sentiments, he has given admission to low images, according to the nature and subject of the writer whom he copied. Now if *Milton* was so industrious (as we see he has been) to select an elegant thought, here and there, from writers of the lowest class, as it is reported of *Virgil*, that he collected gold from the dung of *Ennius*; how much more careful would he be, to convert to his use works wholly sterling, so far as they were subservient to his purpose? *Masenius, Grotius, Ramsay, Ross, Barlæus, Du Bartas, Taubmannus*, and others, have given irrefragable testimony against him.

I think it is now abundantly plain, from proofs and citations, that *Milton* has had all the abovementioned authors in his view, in composing his *Paradise Lost*. But to set this matter beyond all contradiction, it may be proper to inform my reader, that the very year after *Milton*'s death, namely, 1675, a book was published by *Edward Phillips, Milton*'s maternal nephew, entitled, *Theatrum poetarum*, or a compleat collection of the poets, both ancient and modern; which performance is, very probably, nothing else, but a short account of all the poetical authors in his uncle's library; of which he had the perfect use and knowledge, by his having been employed by him, as an *Amanuensis*, in writing out his *Paradise Lost*. In the exercise of this office he must have been privy to the secret practice of his uncle in rifling the treasures of others: and that he was privy to it, I think, is manifest, from his passing over in silence, in the abovementioned piece, such authors as *Milton* was most obliged to; or, if he chanced to mention them, doing it in the most slight and superficial manner imaginable; *Du Bartas* alone excepted. Of this I shall produce a few instances.

Mr. *Phillips*, in the supplement to this work, where he gives us an account of the matrimonial pieces of *Jacobus Catzius* (which have been formerly mentioned, as translated into *Latin* verse by *Cornelius Boius*, and *Caspar Barlæus*) exhibits a particular detail of all of them, except that entitled, *Paradisus*, or a poem on the marriage of *Adam* and *Eve*. Now, why he should expresly enumerate all the rest, and leave that alone unmentioned, though deserving the first place on more accounts than one, would, I believe, puzzle the wit of man to account for any other way, than by supposing that he was afraid, lest by making mention of a poem, entitled *Paradisus*, translated by so celebrated a poet as *Barlæus*, he should excite the jealousy, and awake the curiosity of scholars to peep into it, and consequently lay a fair foundation for discovering his uncle's resources. And for the same reason, doubtless, he omits the tragedy abovementioned, *Il Paradiso Perso*, or *Paradise Lost*. . . .

I must, after all, do Mr. *Phillips* the justice to own, that for once he has dealt ingenuously, where he informs us, that *Hieronymus Zieglerus* was the author of a tragedy, called *Samson*, as well as some others in *Milton's* list; namely, *Protoplastes*, or the *Fall of Man*, the *Immolation of Isaac*, and the *Eliadæ*. Whether this tragedy of *Samson*, by *Ziegler*, is the same with *Milton's*, I am not able to determine; as I have not yet procured a copy of it: but there is the strongest reason to suppose, that he is no more the original author of *Samson*, than he is of *Paradise Lost*, and *The life and death of* John *the* Baptist; which last, as Mr. *Peck* has demonstrated, is a literal translation of the *Baptistes* of *Buchanan*.

I cannot omit observing here, that *Milton's* contrivance, of teaching his daughters to read, but to read only, several learned languages, plainly points the same way, as Mr. *Phillips's* secreting and suppressing the books to which his uncles was most obliged. *Milton* well knew the loquacious and incontinent spirit of the sex, and the danger, on that account, of intrusting them with so important a secret as his unbounded plagiarism: he, therefore, wisely confined them to the knowledge of the words and pronunciation only, but kept the sense and meaning to himself.

From this point, so clearly stated and supported, it is no difficult task to reply to *Andrew Marvell's judicious query*, addressed to the author of *Paradise Lost*, in his commendatory verses prefixed to that poem;

> *Where* could'st thou words of such a compass find?
> *Whence* furnish such a vast expence of mind?

The answer is obvious, namely, *from every author who wrote any thing before him, suitable to his purpose, either in prose or verse, sacred or profane*: which is a much more proper solution, than that assigned by *Marvell* himself, who, immediately after, adds,

> Just heav'n thee, like *Tiresias*, to requite,
> Rewards with *prophecy* thy loss of sight.

But this was natural enough, where a knowledge of his resources was wholly wanting.

Mr. *Peck* assures us, that he has in his possession a picture of *Milton* when but 25 years old, with a book before him, having this inscription, *Paradise Lost*; which makes it evident, that he had formed a design to write upon this subject, at that early part of life. We may, therefore, certainly infer, that our author, like a wise master-builder collected all the necessary materials for such a structure, and, particularly, made his travelling into foreign countries subservient to this great purpose; and in this he was greatly commendable: but then, his industrious conceal-ment of his helps, his peremptory disclaiming all manner of assistance, is highly ungenerous, nay, criminal to the last degree, and absolutely un-worthy of any man of common probity and honour. By this mean practice, indeed, he has acquired the title of the BRITISH HOMER; nay, has been preferred to *Homer* and *Virgil* both, and, consequently, to every other poet of every age and nation. *Cowley, Waller, Denham, Dryden, Prior, Pope*, in comparison with *Milton*, have bore no greater proportion than that of dwarfs to a giant; who, now he is reduced to his true standard, appears mortal and uninspired, and in ability little superior to the poets abovementioned; but in honesty and open dealing, the best quality of the human mind, not inferior, perhaps, to the most unlicensed plagiary that ever wrote.

As I am sensible, this will be deemed most outrageous usage of the divine, the immortal *Milton*, the prince of *English* poets, and the incom-parable author of *Paradise Lost*; I take this opportunity to declare, in the most solemn manner, that a strict regard to TRUTH alone, and to do justice to those authors whom *Milton* has so liberally gleaned, without making the least distant acknowledgment to whom he stood indebted: I declare, I say, that these motives, and these only, have induced me to make this attack upon the reputation and memory of a person, hitherto universally applauded and admired for his uncommon poetical genius; and not any difference of country, or of sentiments in political or religious matters, as some weak and ignorant minds may imagine, or some malicious persons be disposed to suggest. And if, in the course of this essay, I may be thought not to have sufficiently confined myself within the bounds of decency and moderation, I must intreat the zealous abettors of *Milton* to consider, how very liberally he himself dealt his thunder on all with whom he happened to be engaged. . . .

37. Douglas's vindication of plagiarism

1750

Extract from John Douglas, *Milton Vindicated From the Charge of Plagiarism, Brought against him by Mr. Lauder* (1751), 7–10, 14–17, 23–6, 34–40, 62–3. The pamphlet actually appeared in November 1750.

John Douglas (1721–1807) was bishop of Salisbury and author of various political pamphlets, but he is most remembered for his exposure of Lauder's forgeries in 1750. The second edition, entitled *Milton no Plagiary*, appeared in 1756 and contained a postscript on the controversy.

Our Critic charges *Milton* with having borrowed both the *Plan of his Poem*, and also *particular Sentiments*: Suppose the Charge made good— yet, will it follow that his Pretensions to Genius are disproved? The same Charge may be brought against *Virgil*, and it may be objected to his Claim to a distinguished Seat on *Parnassus*, that scarce a Page of his *Æneid* can be instanced, where we do not meet with some Imitation of the *Iliad* or *Odyssey*. Do the Admirers of *Virgil* deny the Charge?—No: but think that their high Regard for his Poem, is perfectly consistent with their admitting that its Author borrowed Hints from *Homer*. And shall the Character of the *Englishman* be depreciated for doing what is thought no just Cause to detract from the Fame of the *Roman*?—Scarce an eminent Writer can be instanced who has not been indebted to the

Labors of former Authors; but how absurd would it be to urge this as an Argument that there is no Merit in their Productions? For as *one* may be what is called an *original Writer*, and yet have no Pretensions to *Genius*, so another may make use of the Labors of others in such a Manner as to satisfy the World of his own Abilities. There may be such a thing as an *original Work* without *Invention*, and a Writer may be an Imitator of others without *Plagiarism*. But as Authority will always weigh more than Assertion, and often more than Argument, I think I cannot take a more effectual Way to confirm and establish what I advance, than to bring up as an Evidence the great *Longinus*. What then is *his* Opinion? So far is he from thinking that Imitations of old Authors detract any thing from the Merit and Genius of those who have recourse to them, that, on the contrary, he expressly lays down the Imitation and Emulation of the former great Writers, and Poets, as one of the Ways that leads to the Sublime. This he particularly illustrates by the Example of *Plato*, who, he says, imitated *Homer* more closely than *Herodotus, Stesichorus*, and *Archilochus* had done before, and drew from the copious Stream of that Poet, ten Thousand Rivulets to enrich his own Works. And this, adds he, *is not to be looked upon as a Theft, but* (as I find the Passage translated by Mr. Dryden) *a beautiful Idea of him who undertakes to imitate, by forming himself on the Work and Invention of another Man*. And if *Longinus* be so far from looking upon *Imitation* to be *Plagiarism*, as to recommend it as one of the Sources of the Sublime, and to Praise *Plato* for his Observation of this Rule, who will venture to assert that *Milton*'s Imitations in his *Paradise Lost* detract anything from the Merit of the Poem? A *great Genius* looks upon himself as having a Right to convert to his own Use, and in order to furnish out a more perfect Entertainment, whatever has been already prepared and made ready. But he exercises this Right in such a Manner as to convince every one, that his having Recourse to it is not the Effect of the Sterility of his *Fancy*, but of the *Solidity of his Judgement*. He borrows only to shew his own Talents in heightening, refining and polishing all that is furnished him by others, and thereby secures his Character as a *fine Writer*, from being confounded with that of the *dull Copyer*. If his Touch convert base Metal into *Sterling Coin*; if from amidst indigested Heaps of Dulness he can extract the only shining Thought, the only striking Image; if he can so change and new-model what he borrows, as to add a Dignity of *Language* and Propriety of *Epithet* to Sentiments cloathed by their *Original Author* in the meanest Garb;—if an Author borrows in such a Manner (and that *Milton* has done so I need not illustrate by particular Instances as it is not controverted) the Skill shewn in making so judicious a Use of the Labors of others leaves the Reader no Time to give them any Share of the Praise, and leads him to this Conclusion, that to make a prudent and skilful Imitation, to accommodate it so as to make it correspond exactly to the present Occasion—and to drop it when the Prosecution of it would commence improper, are Marks of Genius and Capacity, far from being contemptible. . . .

But if *Milton* has been so much indebted to Mr. *Lauder's* Moderns, why does he so industriously conceal it? This is a Charge of some Consequence: But then, though it should prove true, it affects only his moral Character, it may bring him in guilty of *Disingenuity*, but ought not to brand him with *Plagiarism*; it may lessen our Regard to the *Man*, but does not destroy his Reputation as a *Poet*.—But what Foundation is there for this Charge, that *Milton* has industriously concealed his being assisted by others? Because, says our Critic (p. 74), *he has in the most express Terms, in the beginning of his Work, disclaimed all Manner of Assistance and Help in composing his Poem, by asserting that his Muse pursues*

Things unattempted yet in Prose or Rhime.

Now I shou'd be extremely glad if Mr. *Lauder* wou'd take the Trouble to prove that this Line of *Milton* implies, what he wou'd have us believe, a disclaiming of all Manner of Help and Assistance in composing his Poem.—Let us keep to the strict, grammatical Sense of the Line, and it will appear that *Milton* might make this Boast without any Disingenuity, and without any intention of deluding the World into a Belief that he was more of an *Original Writer* than he really is. For if there be so much as one Part of the Plan of *Paradise Lost*, if there be but one *Episode*, or even one Sentiment in that Poem, the Work of *Milton's* own Fancy (and even *Lauder* himself will not, I believe, deny that there are some Things *new* in the *Paradise Lost*) this intitled him to say that he sung *Things unattempted yet*.—Had *Milton* asserted that his Subject was unattempted yet in Prose or Rhime, then indeed the Charge of Disingenuity might have had a Foundation. But there is a wide Difference between saying that he sings *Things unattempted yet in Prose or Rhime*, and saying that the Subject of his Poem is entirely new and had never been thought of before. The Subject of the *Paradise Lost* is as Old as the sacred Volumes; and therefore, if the Line in Question is to be understood as our Critic interprets it, *Milton*, by it, disclaims the Assistance of the Scriptures as much as he disclaims the Assistance of *Lauder's* obscure

Moderns. But surely this cou'd never enter into his Head, because who-ever took the *Paradise Lost* into his Hands cou'd not but immediately perceive that it owed its Original to the Scriptures and to the *Fall of Man* as there related.

Or were we even to allow that all the constituent Parts of *Milton*'s Plan are borrowed (though this is far from being the Case) yet, even on the Supposition, his using of the Line objected to cou'd be defended; he might, even then, have said, without any Impeachment of Truth, that he sung *Things unattempted yet in Prose or Rhime*, because, as I have al-ready observed, the Composition of the Plan of his Poem is all his own, and makes it really an *Original Work*. A Physician who by the judicious Junction and Mixture of several Drugs composes a *Pill* or an *Electuary* of a sovereign Efficacy in certain Cases, wou'd have Reason to complain of hard Treatment, if the World refused to look upon him as the *Original Inventor* of this Medicine, merely because the Ingredients that compose it were already of Use in Physic. The Composition of these Drugs, which separately taken, cou'd have been of no Use, into one, well-proportioned Mass that has a sanative Virtue.—justly intitles the Con-triver of it to the Honor of being an Inventor—and it wou'd be ridicul-ous to accuse him of Disingenuity for calling his Medicine entirely new. In the same Manner it is equally ridiculous to refuse to look upon the *Paradise Lost* as an *Original Poem*, merely because the unshapen Materials out of which it was composed lay ready for *Milton* to make use of. . . .

Now, with what Shadow of Truth can the Critic of *Milton* assert, that the infinite Tribute of Veneration paid to him has arisen from Men's Ignorance of his having been indebted to the Assistance of other Authors in the composing of his Poem, when 'tis an indisputable Fact, that those very Persons who have done more than any body else to raise and ex-tend his Reputation, have been the principal Discoverers of his Imita-tions?—Long before Mr. *Lauder* ever was heard of, the World knew that *Milton* had been indebted for the Ground-work of his Plan, and the principal of Episodes of his Poem, to the Bible. And by turning to the late useful Edition of our Poet, where we have all the Notes of his different Commentators, we shall see that it has been, all along, their great Aim to trace their Author thro' the vast Compass of ancient and modern Learning, and to mark the Use he has made not only of the sacred but the profane Writers—not only of the *Greek* and *Latin*, but also of the *Italian* and *English* Poets. Their Veneration for the *Paradise Lost* cou'd not arise from the Source *Lauder* pretends, because the Helps and Assist-ance which, according to his own Account, *Milton* has got from the obscure Moderns he quotes, are a mere Trifle in Comparison of those which he has drawn from more eminent Authors, and which had been before taken Notice of by *Hume, Addison, Bentley, Pearce, Newton, Thyer,* and others.—How weak, therefore, must not our Critic's Judgment be, who can imagine that it will sink the Merit of *Milton*'s Poem, to acquaint the World that he copied his *Pandæmonium,* and two or three more Parts of his Plan from *Masenius,* when it did *not* sink the Merit of his Poem to know, as we did before, that far more important Parts of his Plan, nay indeed the principal Parts of it, were copied from the Scriptures? Or if we consider *Milton* as having imitated only the Sentiments, Similies and Descriptions of other Authors—have not his greatest Admirers pointed out vastly more of these Imitations than our Critic himself? By casting an Eye on the Notes in Dr. *Newton*'s '*Milton*', besides the frequent and close Imitations of Scripture, we shall find our Poet borrowing from *Homer, Sophocles, Euripides, Æschylus,* among the *Greeks,* from *Virgil, Horace, Lucan, Statius, Claudian* among the *Romans,* from *Tasso, Ariosto, Boiardo, Marino,* among the *Italians,* and from his own Countrymen *Fairfax, Spenser,* and *Shakespear.*—And will our Critic after this, have the Confidence to assert, that *Milton*'s having concealed that he was indebted to *Masenius* for his Comparison of *Satan* to a Tower, to *Ramsay* for his Simile of the Serpent compared to a Ship, to *Taubmannus* for his Thought of ascribing the Invention of Fire-arms to the Devil, to *Grotius* for his comparing the Serpent's Eyes to Carbuncles, will he, I say, assert, that the World's being ignorant of this, till he brought it to Light, has been the Cause that the *Paradise Lost* has gained so much Veneration? And can he be so foolish as to flatter himself that these important Discoveries will make the World change it's Opinion? . . .

In order, then, to open the Sources from which our Critic has derived many of his Quotations which bear so striking a Resemblance to Passages in the *Paradise Lost,* I must take Notice that so long ago as the Year 1690, there was printed at *London* a *Latin* Translation of the *Paradise Lost and Regained,* and of the *Samson Agonistes,* by one *Hogæus,* as he calls himself in the Title Page,—*Hog,* I suppose, if we strip the Name of the *Latin* Termination. This book seems to have been of mighty Use to our honest Critic. Being in Possession of a Copy of it, he has begun, in Time, to imagine that *his* was the only Copy; and, therefore, being resolved to do what was in his Power to lessen that *Tribute of Veneration* paid to *Milton,* he thought he cou'd not take a more effectual Way to fix the odious Character of an *unlicensed Plagiary* upon him, than by inserting into the Authors from whom he pretends *Milton* has borrowed, Lines from *Hogæus*, and which cou'd not but bear a striking Resemblance to Lines in the *Paradise Lost*, being indeed nothing more nor less than Translations of them.

That I have sufficient Grounds for asserting what appears so extraordinary, *your Lordship* will readily admit when I inform you, that I have actually in my Possession at present this very Translation of the *Paradise Lost* by *Hogæus*; and upon turning to the fourth Book, where he translates the famous Panegyric on Marriage, *I find, without the Variation of a Single Word, the eight Lines inserted by* L A U D E R *into the Text of* Staphoıstius. Had I not seen this, were it not in every Body's Power to see it, by turning to *Hogæus*, I shou'd not have ventured to assert a Fact so extremely improbable.—I shou'd have thought it impossible that the vilifying of a Person's Character now so long dead, cou'd be a Matter of such Moment, as that all the Rules of *common Probity and Honor* are to be trampled under Foot, rather than not have wherewithal to support an Accusation. It must certainly be thought extremely hard that *Milton* shou'd be run down as a Plagiary for having stolen from himself. And yet this is exactly the Case: *Hog* translates the *Paradise Lost* into *Latin*; *Lauder* inserts some of *Hog*'s Lines into *Staphorstius*, and urges these very Lines as a Demonstration that *Milton* copied him.

And now, *my Lord*, is not this single Instance of Forgery, so extraordinary in all its Circumstances, and so unexceptionably proved, enough to blast our Critic's Credit in all his other Quotations?—It certainly is. However let us follow him in one or two more, and we shall have accumulated Proofs of his *impudent Forgeries*.

In the fifth Book of the *Paradise Lost* we have the Morning Hymn, sung by *Adam* and *Eve*, and which begins thus,

These are thy glorious Works, Parent of Good!

This Hymn, one of the greatest Ornaments of the Poem, is, as Dr. *Newton* justly observes, 'an Imitation, or rather a Sort of Paraphrase, of the 148th Psalm, and (of what is a Paraphrase upon that) the Canticle placed after *Te Deum* in the Liturgy, *O all ye Works of the Lord, bless ye the Lord*, &c. which is the Song of the three Children in the Apocrypha'. *Lauder*, however, imagining perhaps, it wou'd be a greater Reflection on *Milton*'s Character as a Poet to convict him of imitating *Staphorstius*, than it wou'd be to convict him of imitating the *Psalmist*, tells us—'that he cannot help thinking but that *Milton* has borrowed from this Author

(*Staphorstius*) a great Part of the noble Hymn sung by *Adam* and *Eve*'
(p. 108).

In support of this Charge he quotes Thirty-three Lines from his
Dutchman. But as it wou'd swell this Letter to an immoderate Length,
were I to insert Quotations unnecessarily, I shall, therefore, refer to Mr.
Lauder's Book for the Quotation in question which begins thus,

> Cœlestes animæ! sublimia templa tenentes,

And Ends thus

> Collustrat terras dum lumine Titan Eoo.

Now tho' our Critic cannot help thinking *Milton*'s Morning Hymn
copied from the Lines of *Staphorstius*, last referred to, yet am I persuaded
that, upon comparing them, every impartial Person will think he has
Reason to conclude, that tho' there be some Resemblance of Sentiment,
yet this is no Proof that *Milton* ever saw *Staphorstius*; because this
Resemblance has arisen from their both having had before them the
Psalm and *Church Hymn* already mentioned.

But there are two Lines in the Quotation *Lauder* gives us from
Staphorstius, which he perhaps thinks are a Proof that *Milton* imitated in
this Place the *Dutch* Poet and not the inspired *Psalmist*. And indeed there
is a very striking Resemblance between them, and two Lines in the
Morning Hymn of the *Paradise Lost.—Milton*, having called upon every
Part of inanimate Nature to praise the Lord, adds

> Witness, if I be silent Even or Morn.

Now there is a Line in our Critic's Quotation from *Staphorstius* very
like this, 'tis as follows,

> Aurorâ, redeunte novâ, redeuntibus umbris.

Again, *Milton* has the following Line

> Him first, him last, him midst and without End;

And 'tis scarce possible to translate this Line more literally than in the
following Words which are also quoted as *Staphorstius*'s,

> Te primum, & medium, & summum, sed fine carentem.

Here, then, again our Critic thinks he has Reason to triumph over
Milton, as *pluming himself with the Feathers of* Staphorstius; and every one
who takes it for granted that these two Lines, especially the last, are in

the *Dutchman*'s Works, will very readily admit the Truth of the Charge. But, indeed, they are no more in *Staphorstius* than are the Eight Lines already taken Notice of. For upon collating *Lauder*'s Quotation with the *Dort* Edition, I found that they were both wanting, as is also another Line quoted by him as in his Author,

O miris mirande modis, ter maxime rerum;

They are wanting in the very Edition which, as I observed before, he tells us he used, and, therefore, that he has interpolated them to create a Resemblance between *Milton* and *Staphorstius* which had no Existence before, is evident beyond all Dispute. And certainly he cou'd not take a more effectual Way to prove this Resemblance, than by inserting into *Staphorstius*, as he had done in another Place, *Hog*'s Translation of those very Lines, which he pretends *Milton* has stolen. Upon examining *Hog*'s Translation of the *Morning Hymn*, I found the Lines in question, to have a Place there.—It seems so extremely improbable, that any one shou'd ever venture to put so gross an Imposition on the World, that, as I observed before, I almost despair of being believed, altho' *I know* the certainty of the Fact. . . .

From the Instances I have assigned, from the Facts I have appealed to, I think, my Lord, there results this Conclusion, That the Critic of *Milton* having been detected of *forgery* in several of the Authors he quotes, Copies of which we have been so lucky as to meet with, we may, without doing him any Injustice suspect that he has used the same Freedoms with regard to *Masenius* and the *Adamus Exsul of Grotius*, the two main Champions of his Cause, but *invisible* to all the World but himself. It rests upon him to shew that this suspicion is groundless, and that the old printed Copies of these two Pieces correspond exactly with the Account he gives of them, and contain all those Lines which he quotes as from them. And how can he do this in a satisfactory Manner? A new Edition of these Authors printed under his own Inspection will not do. He who cou'd quote *old Editions* of Books, for Lines which have been proved to have no Existence there, will make no Scruple to interpolate Lines into his *new Editions*, in order to put the Charge of Plagiarism he brings against *Milton* upon Record. We do not in the least doubt of Mr. *Lauder*'s being able to accommodate *Masenius*, or the *Adamus Exsul* to the Text of the *Paradise Lost* (for his Skill this way has been observed in repeated Instances) and, therefore, he must not only publish new Editions, but also produce the old ones from which they were taken. These he must deposit with his Bookseller, or in some public

Library: If this be not done he does nothing, and this I am satisfied he dares not do, without putting it in our Power to detect him in *Forgeries* as gross as those he already stands convicted of. That it may not be thought I assert without proving, or suspect without just Foundation of Suspicion, permit me now, *my Lord,* to give my Reasons for being of Opinion that *Lauder* cannot produce a *Masenius,* without satisfying the World, at the same Time, that he has basely *interpolated,* and changed the Text of this Author.

38. Johnson's rebuttal against Douglas

1751

Samuel Johnson, *A Letter to the Rev. Mr. Douglas, Occasioned by his Vindication of Milton* (1751). William Lauder was passed off as the author of this letter.

Sir,

Candour and tenderness are in any relation, and on all occasions, eminently amiable; but when they are found in an adversary, and found so prevalent as to overpower that zeal which his cause excites, and that heat which naturally increases in the prosecution of argument, and which may be in a great measure justified by the love of truth, they certainly appear with particular advantages; and it is impossible not to envy those who possess the friendship of him, whom it is even some degree of good fortune to have known as an enemy.

I will not so far dissemble my weakness, or my fault, as not to confess that my wish was to have passed undetected; but since it has been my fortune to fail in my original design, to have the supposititious passages which I have inserted in my quotations made known to the world, and the shade which began to gather on the splendour of Milton totally dispersed, I cannot but count it an elevation of my pain, that I have been defeated by a man who knows how to use advantages with so much moderation, and can enjoy the honour of conquest without the insolence of triumph.

It was one of the maxims of the Spartans, not to press upon a flying army, and therefore their enemies were always ready to quit the field, because they knew the danger was only in opposing. The civility with which you have thought proper to treat me when you had incontestable superiority, has inclined me to make your victory complete, without any further struggle, and not only publickly to acknowledge the truth of the charge which you have hitherto advanced, but to confess, without the least dissimulation, subterfuge, or concealment, every other interpolation I have made in those authors, which you have not yet had opportunity to examine.

On the sincerity and punctuality of this confession, I am willing to depend for all the future regard of mankind, and cannot but indulge some hopes, that they whom my offence has alienated from me, may by this instance of ingenuity and repentance, be propitiated and reconciled. Whatever be the event, I shall at least have done all that can be done in reparation for my former injuries to Milton, to truth, and to mankind, and entreat that those who shall continue implacable, will examine their own hearts, whether they have not committed equal crimes without equal proofs of sorrow, or equal acts of atonement. . . .

These are my interpolations, minutely traced without any arts of evasion. Whether from the passages that yet remain, any reader will be convinced of my general assertion, and allow, that Milton had recourse for assistance to any of the authors whose names I have mentioned, I shall not now be very diligent to inquire, for I had no particular pleasure in subverting the reputation of Milton, which I had myself once endeavoured to exalt [*Poetarum Scotorum Musae Sacrae in praefatione*, 1739]; and of which, the foundation had always remained untouched by me, had not my credit and my interest been blasted, or thought to be blasted, by the shade which it cast from its boundless elevation.

About ten years ago, I published an edition of Dr. Johnston's translation of the Psalms, and having procured from the general assembly of the church of Scotland a recommendation of its use to the lower classes of grammar-schools, into which I had begun to introduce it, though not without much controversy and opposition; I thought it likely that I should, by annual publications, improve my little fortune, and be enabled to support myself in freedom from the miseries of indigence. But Mr. Pope, in his malevolence to Mr. Benson, who had distinguished himself by his fondness for the same version, destroyed all my hopes by a distich, in which he places Johnston in a contemptuous comparison with the author of *Paradise Lost*.

From this time, all my praises of Johnston became ridiculous, and I was censured with great freedom for forcing upon the schools an author whom Mr. Pope had mentioned only as a foil to a better poet. On this occasion, it was natural not to be pleased, and my resentment seeking to discharge itself some where, was unhappily directed against Milton. I resolved to attack his fame, and found some passages in cursory reading, which gave me hopes of stigmatising him as a plagiary. The farther I carried my search, the more eager I grew for the discovery, and the more my hypothesis was opposed, the more I was heated with rage. The consequence of my blind passion, I need not relate; it has, by your detection, become apparent to mankind. Nor do I mention this provocation as adequate to the fury which I have shown, but as a cause of anger, less shameful and reproachful than fractious malice, personal envy, or national jealousy.

But for the violation of truth, I offer no excuse, because I well know, that nothing can excuse it. Nor will I aggravate my crime, by disingenuous palliations. I confess it, I repent it, and resolve, that my first offence shall be my last. More I cannot perform, and more therefore cannot be required. I intreat the pardon of all men, whom I have by any means induced to support, to countenance, or patronise my frauds, of which I think myself obliged to declare, that not one of my friends was conscious. I hope to deserve, by better conduct and more useful undertakings, that patronage which I have obtained from the most illustrious and venerable names by misrepresentation and delusion, and to appear hereafter in such a character, as shall give you no reason to regret that your name is frequently mentioned with that of,

Reverend Sir,
Your most humble servant,
William Lauder.

39. Lauder's remarks on Douglas's vindication

1751

Extract from William Lauder, *An Apology for Mr. Lauder* (1751), 6–24.

Being charged by the Reverend Mr. *Douglas* with interpolating a few Verses into some Authors quoted by me in my Essay on *Milton*'s Use and Imitation of the Moderns, I own the Charge to be just; for which I heartily profess my Sorrow, and most humbly ask Pardon, which (as it is my first Offence, as I am resolved it shall be my last) I hope may be indulged me; and the rather, because, when I might have availed myself of the Defence suggested and allowed by my Opponent, of having received the interpolated Verses in writing from abroad, I chose rather to admit the Charge, and thereby expose myself to the Reproach and Censure attending such Conduct, than at the Expence of Truth to blame my innocent Correspondents; which ingenuous Confession also will, I hope, plead in my Favour, and make some Atonement for my Fault.

But, at the same time, in Justice to myself, I cannot forbear to take notice, that my interpolating these Authors proceeded rather from my being hurried away by violent Passion (to which I am naturally too subject) and a rash Imprudence, not duly weighing the Consequences, nor considering the Malignity of the Crime, but chiefly from a fatal Anxiety not to fall short of my Proof in that arduous Undertaking, with the most partial Admirers of the great *English* Poet, than from a Design of imposing on the Public in general. As I humbly conceive my Argument was strong enough of itself to convince Persons of Candour, that *Milton* at least saw these Authors, and made some use of them, and consequently stood in no need of any such supposititious Assistance: Though I scruple not to own, that *Milton*'s Use of these Authors was such, that I was by no means authorised from thence to deduce Inferences in Impeachment either of his moral or poetical Character: But this, when blinded with Passion, I either would not or could not perceive. So much for the culpable Part, the Interpolations, which I am far from offering to defend, having only related the Motives that induced me to have recourse to make use of their Assistance.

As for the Attempt to stigmatize *Milton* as a Plagiary, for borrowing several of his Images, Comparisons and Descriptions from Poets who wrote before him, while under the Influence of Passion, I thought myself sufficiently justified by the Principle of Self-Defence, and the Law of Retaliation: And these indeed, when justly founded, are always allowed to be a strong Plea, according to the known Adage of the Poet,

Pellere vim vi jura finunt, & vulnere vulnus.
[Natural rights permit the power to strike with force, and the blow to wound]

On this therefore I solely rest my Defence, that my Attack on the Character of *Milton* was by no means ultroneous or unprovoked, as Mr. *Pope*, in Comparison with *Milton*, had egregiously abused an excellent Poet and fine Writer, Dr. *Arthur Johnston*, the Author of a very elegant Paraphrase of the Psalms in *Latin* Verse, an Edition of which I had published at *Edinburgh*: This Paraphrase, notwithstanding its extraordinary Merit, suffered very much in the Estimation of the Public, from the implicit and submissive Regard paid to Mr. *Pope*'s Authority, who, in this Instance especially, made a very ill Use of his Influence, as a Critic, with the learned World.

In Proof whereof I affirm for a Truth, that after I had obtained a Recommendation from the General Assembly of the Church of Scotland, (the Province of whose Ministers it is to inspect or superintend the Education of Youth) to have *Johnston*'s excellent Version of the Psalms introduced into all the Grammar Schools of that Kingdom, as a mighty proper Book both for paving a Way for a full Understanding of *Buchanan*'s more sublime, but difficult Performance on that Subject, and chiefly for seasoning the tender Minds of Christian Youth with Precepts of true Piety and Virtue; yet such was the blind Deference paid to Mr. *Pope*, that few School-masters in *Scotland* would receive *Johnston*'s Paraphrase into their Schools, after that capricious Critic testified his Dislike of that Performance by the slighting Manner in which he treated its Author in Comparison of *Milton*, whom he treated as a Giant in Poetry, and the other as a Dwarf or Pigmy only; notwithstanding, one would think the Recommendation of the whole Church, in a Body assembled, might easily have overbalanced any single Person's Authority, how great soever.

Nor was that all; but the ill Effects of Mr. *Pope*'s Influence appear'd still more conspicuous, after Mr. *Auditor Benson* had prepared several beautiful Editions of *Johnston*'s Paraphrase; no fewer than six in Number, two in Quarto, two in Octavo, and two in a lesser Form; all which now lie like Lumber in the Hand of Mr. *Vaillant*, Bookseller, occasioned by Mr. *Pope*'s ill-natur'd Criticism; tho' it is certainly a Performance, in its Kind, inferior to none that ever appeared in the World: One of these Editions in Quarto, illustrated with an Interpretation and Notes, after the Manner of the Classic Authors *in Usum Delphini*, was inscrib'd to his Royal Highness Prince *George*, as a fit Book for his Instruction in Principles of Piety, as well as Knowledge of the *Latin* Tongue, when he should arrive at due Maturity of Age.

As the worthy Editor proposed to have *Johnston*'s Version of the Psalms introduced into Schools in place of *Ovid*'s Epistles, tho', in the Judgment of many, a very unfit Book, taught in some; or his *Libri de Tristibus*, a mean, trifling Performance, taught in others; he had the Satisfaction accordingly to see his laudable Design in part crown'd with Success, as several learned Teachers were pleased to honour the Doctor's Paraphrase with Admission into their Schools, and still more were like to follow their Example: And when now there was a great Likelihood of that valuable and useful Book becoming daily more and more general, behold all that worthy Gentleman's Endeavours, attended also with very great Expence, in preparing so many beautiful Editions of that Work, as has been remarked already, quite defeated in *England*, as mine had been in *Scotland*, by one Dash of Mr. *Pope*'s pen in his *Dunciad*;

> On two unequal Crutches propped he * came,
> *Milton*'s on this, on that One *Johnston*'s Name.

Such remarkable Feats may a Man perform, who has once got an established Reputation! And such considerable Damage may Criticism occasion, when its Sting is unjustly levell'd, or improperly directed by Partiality, Prejudice, or Caprice!

When, therefore, I perceived all my Endeavours to revive Dr. *Johnston*'s excellent Version of the Psalms in *Scotland*, and Mr. *Benson*'s in *England*, quite frustrated by the immoderate Regard paid to Mr. *Pope*'s dogmatical Assertion without Proof, I began seriously to consider with

---

* *Benson*] This Man endeavoured to raise himself to Fame by erecting Monuments, striking Coins, and procuring Translations of *Milton*; and afterwards, by a great Passion for *Arthur Johnston*, a *Scots* Physician's Version of the Psalms, of which he printed many fine Editions.

Notes on the Dunciad

myself (especially as I had been often upbraided to my Face, as guilty of a false Taste, in shewing so great Respect for an Author whom Mr. *Pope*, the great Oracle of Learning and Criticism, had been pleased to honour with a Place in his *Dunciad*) if there was no effectual Way to enter the Lists with that formidable Antagonist, in order to disprove his unjust Assertion, and expose the Malice and Impropriety of his Contrast betwixt the *English* Poet and Dr. *Johnston*, whereby I might at once repel the Injustice of Mr. *Pope*'s Comparison, and restore *Johnston* to his primitive Reputation and the Possession of his just Glory: And as I fancied it impossible to make the Doctor greater than he was by any studied Panegyric of mine in his Praise, so I bethought me of this only Way left, of enhancing his Merit by lessening *Milton*'s, even as Mr. *Pope* had endeavoured to raise *Milton* by lessening *Johnston*. And as *Milton*'s chief Merit was thought to consist in the Fertility and Sublimity of his Invention in *Paradise Lost*, I thought if I could possibly strip him of any great Share of that, I should at once retrieve *Johnston*'s Honour, and convict Mr. *Pope* of pronouncing an erroneous Judgment, in giving so vast a Preference to *Milton* above *Johnston*: For *Milton*, thought I, being stripped of the principal Jewel in his poetical Crown, Invention, wherein does his extraordinary Merit above other Poets consist?

In order the better to accomplish my Design, I began diligently to turn over several modern Poets in *Latin* Verse, on similar Subjects with *Milton*'s, and as the Search has been of long Continuance and great Labour, so I flatter myself it has not been wholly in vain. Thus, if *Milton* had chanced to suffer any Diminution in his poetical Character, his Friends and Admirers might thank Mr. *Pope*'s officious Zeal for it, (tho' to speak the Truth, his Design, I believe, was more to wound Mr. *Benson*, than to aggrandize his poetical Predecessor) in unjustly preferring him to others, who deserved no such Usage at his Hand. For *Milton*'s Reputation stood on a firm enough Foundation before, and needed not to be confronted with *Johnston*, as a Foil, to make it appear with a more conspicuous Lustre.

Besides, this unhandsome Usage of *Johnston* by Mr. *Pope* was the more inexcusable, as I addressed him in behalf of *Johnston*, a little before he wrote his last *Dunciad*, in which he ridicules him, by a very courteous and obliging Letter, begging he would honour me with his Opinion relating to a Controversy then subsisting betwixt me and another person in *Scotland*, about *Johnston*'s and *Buchanan*'s Paraphrase of the Psalms, namely, which of the two were easiest and fittest for the Use of Schoolboys of ten or twelve Years of Age: At the same time I sent him a

Present of an handsome Edition of *Johnston's* Paraphrase, with some other *Latin* Poems on sacred Subjects, which a little before that I had published. I have been informed he received my Present by the Hands of Mr. *Mallet*; but the only Return I had to my Letter, by way of Thanks, was the civil Usage of my favourite Author we have seen recorded in his *Dunciad*.

I had other kind of Usage shewn me by the learned Mr. *Abraham Gronovius*, Dr. *Trapp*, the Authors of the *Universal History*, and Mr. *Ainsworth*, Author of the *Latin* and *English* Dictionary.

Thus have I shown, as briefly and impartially as I could, the Cause and Origin of my Attack on the poetical Character of the great *Milton*; and if I shall be thought to have levelled my Resentment against the wrong Mark, *Milton* instead of *Pope*, or to have pushed it *ultra Limites inculpatæ Tutelæ*, now Passion is subsided, I frankly own it, I am heartily sorry for it, and most humbly ask Pardon, and earnestly intreat that your Grace's Candour would impute it rather to an Error in my Judgment, than to any Perverseness or Malignity of Will.

I desire also that it may be remembred, in Extenuation of my Offence, that if I have endeavoured to lessen *Milton's* Reputation below its just Merit, in my late Essay, I had in a former Work of mine raised it as far perhaps, if possible, above it, where I pronounced him the greatest of Men—the most celebrated of Poets—an Ornament not to *England* only, his native country, but to Mankind in general—that his incomparable Poem, the noble Monument of an immortal Genius, stood fair to vie with Eternity itself in Duration—and even lamented, as a Crime of the deepest Dye, that no one before the Honourable Mr. Auditor *Benson* (whose elegant Taste, at the same time, I took occasion to applaud, for doing equal Honour to *Johnston* and *Milton*, as he was equally fond of both) had done Justice to his Merit by erecting a Monument to his Honour, among other illustrious poetical Heroes in *Westminster-Abbey*, to transmit his Memory to Posterity. All which Expressions are far enough from arguing Hatred or Contempt, but are, in Truth, indubitable Marks of the highest Value and Esteem.

And, lastly, may I beg leave to remark, that *Milton's* only surviving Posterity, Mrs. *Elizabeth Foster*, reaped more real Advantage from a Proposal of mine, addressed to the Public in her Favour, in a Postscript subjoined to my Dissertation, than from the Writers of the highest Encomiums and formal Panegyrics on the great Author, or his Works, put all together. And may the Public repeat the Benefaction once more, every Year of her Life, which now probably cannot be many! This, in my Opinion, would be one effectual Way to testify their Gratitude and Respect to the Memory of that great Writer.

These Observations laid together, and duly adverted to, make it plain to a Demonstration, that my Quarrel was not with *Milton*, nor the high Reputation he justly enjoys with all true Judges of noble Sentiment and exalted Poetry, but with the unfair Preference given him by Mr. *Pope*, in a malicious and improper Contrast over Dr. *Johnston*, the Injustice whereof I resolved to expose, and to supply by Proof wherein I fell short of him in Authority; and this not so much with a View to debase *Milton*, (against whom I had no Umbrage) as to restore *Johnston*'s admirable Version of the Book of Psalms (the Original whereof is certainly the most sublime and exalted Piece of Poetry in the World) to the Possession of its just Praise, of which Mr. *Pope*'s Authority, or rather Caprice in his *Dunciad*, had unjustly deprived it.

All this would have appeared in a very clear Light, had not my Bookseller (for Reasons which probably he thought best) suppressed the Preface I put into his Hands to be prefixed to my *Essay*, in which I gave a full Detail (as I have done above) of the Motives that induced me to engage in a Province every way so disagreeable, arduous, and unpopular; that had not Necessity, in a manner, compelled me, as the Author, whom I highly value, and on whose Reputation my Subsistence in Life, in a great measure, depended, was totally discredited by Mr. *Pope*, in *North* as well as *South Britain*, I should have been the last of all Men to have engaged in such an Undertaking as tended to lessen or detract from the Reputation of one of the greatest Writers that any Age or Nation ever produced, whose Verses I had so often read with equal Delight and Admiration, and on whom I had once conferred a Character as high and honourable, as the most sanguine of his Admirers had ever done; and as that was my cool and sincere Opinion of that wonderful Man several Years ago, I declare it is so still, and ever will be, notwithstanding all Appearances to the contrary, occasioned merely by Passion and Resentment, as I have expressed myself already, both in my Proposals, and in my letter to the Reverend Mr. *Douglas*.

To conclude this Subject, I wish *Milton* as well as *Johnston* (for in despite of Mr. *Pope*'s malicious Contrast I'll join them both together in Honour now, as well as formerly) the same good Fortune that was wished to, and obtained by the most celebrated Poet of ancient *Rome*, the immortal *Maro*. . . .

I shall conclude this Apology with a Couplet from the Writings of that excellent Author (an immoderate Zeal to vindicate whose Character, when unjustly attacked, rather than any invidious Design to depreciate the just Reputation of *Milton*) has brought me almost to the Brink of Ruin, if I am not restored to Favour upon my Submission and Repentance, that the same Hand which inflicted the Wound, may contribute to work the Cure. . . .

40. Anonymous comment on Bentley

1751

Anonymous, 'Upon Bentley's Emendations of Milton', *Student, or, The Oxford and Cambridge Monthly Miscellany* (1751), ii, 58.

When MILTON's forfeit life was in debate,
Some urg'd his crimes, and some th' unsettled state;
Hyde[1] paus'd:—now keen resentment filled his breast,
Now softness sooth'd, while genius shone confess'd:—
At length the ling'ring statesman thus his thoughts express'd.
    When I consider, with impartial view,
The crimes he wrought, the good he yet may do;
His violated faith and fictions dire,
His tow'ring genius and poetic fire;
I blame the rebel, but the bard admire.
Mercy unmerited his muse may raise,
To sound his monarch's, or his maker's praise.
    Yet come it will, the day decreed by fate;—
By BENTLEY's pen reduc'd to woful state,
Far more thou'lt dread his friendship than our hate.
PROCRUSTES like, he'll ever find pretence
To strain, or pare thee to this wretched sense.
Back'd, skrew'd, enerv'd by emendation sad,
The hangman had not us'd thee half so bad.

[1] Lord Clarendon.

41. Hurd on Milton's invention

1751

Extract from Richard Hurd, ed., Q. Horatii Flacci, *Epistola ad Augustum . . . To which is added, A Discourse Concerning Poetical Imitation* (1751), 180–1.

Our *Milton*, who was most ambitious of this fame of *invention*, and whose vast and universal genius could not have missed of new *analogies*, had nature's self been able to furnish them, is a glaring instance to our purpose. He was so averse from resting in the old imagery of Homer, and the other epic poets, that he appears to have taken infinite pains in the investigation of new *allusions*, which he picked up out of the rubbish of every silly legend or romance, that had come to his knowledge, or extracted from the dry and rugged materials of the sciences, and even the mechanic arts. Yet, in comparison of the genuine treasures of nature, which he found himself obliged to make use of, in common with other writers, his own proper stock of *images*, imported from the regions of *art*, is very poor and scanty; and, as might be expected, makes the least agreeable part of his divine work.

42. Johnson on Milton's versification

1751

Samuel Johnson, *Rambler*, no. 86 (12 January 1751); no. 88 (19 January 1751); no. 90 (26 January 1751); no. 94 (9 February 1751).

No. 86

One of the ancients has observed, that the burthen of Government is increased upon princes by the virtues of their immediate predecessors. It is indeed, always dangerous to be placed in a state of unavoidable comparison with excellence, and the danger is still greater when that excellence is consecrated by death; when envy and interest cease to act against it, and those passions, by which it was at first vilified and opposed, now stand in its defense, and turn their vehemence against honest emulation.

He that succeeds a celebrated writer, has the same difficulties to encounter; he stands under the shade of exalted merit, and is hindered from rising to his natural height, by the interception of those beams which should invigorate and quicken him. He applies to that attention which is already engaged, and unwilling to be drawn off from certain satisfaction; or perhaps to an attention already wearied, and not to be recalled to the same object.

One of the old poets congratulates himself, that he has the untrodden regions of *Parnassus* before him, and that his garland will be gathered from plantations which no writer had yet culled. But the imitator treads a beaten walk, and with all his diligence can only hope to find a few flowers or branches untouched by his predecessor; the refuse of contempt, or the omissions of negligence. The *Macedonian* conqueror, when he was once invited to hear a man that sung like a nightingale, replied with contempt, 'that he had heard the nightingale herself;' and the same treatment must every man expect, whose praise is that he imitates another.

Yet, in the midst of these discouraging reflections, I am about to offer to my reader some observations upon *Paradise Lost*, and hope, that however I may fall below the illustrious writer who has so long dictated to the commonwealth of learning, my attempt may not be wholly useless. There are, in every age, new errors to be rectified, and new prejudices to be opposed. False taste is always busy to mislead those that are entering upon the regions of learning; and the traveller, uncertain of his way, and forsaken by the sun, will be pleased to see a fainter orb arise on the horizon, that may rescue him from total darkness, though with weak and borrowed lustre.

Addison, though he has considered this poem under most of the general topics of criticism, has barely touched upon the versification, not probably because he thought the art of numbers unworthy of his notice, for he knew with how minute attention the ancient critics considered the disposition of syllables, and had himself given hopes of some metrical observations upon the great *Roman* poet; but being the first who undertook to display the beauties, and point out the defects of *Milton*, he had many objects at once before him, and passed willingly over those which were most barren of ideas, and required labour rather than genius.

Yet versification, or the art of modulating his numbers, is indispensably necessary to a poet. Every other power by which the understanding is enlightened, or the imagination enchanted, may be exercised in prose. But the poet has this peculiar superiority, that, to all the powers which the perfection of every other composition can require, he adds the faculty of joining music with reason, and of acting at once upon the senses and the passions. I suppose there are few who do not feel themselves touched by poetical melody, and who will not confess that they are more or less moved by the same thoughts, as they are conveyed by different sounds, and more affected by the same words in one order than in another. The perception of harmony is indeed conferred upon men in degrees very unequal, but there are none who do not perceive it, or to whom a regular series of proportionate sounds cannot give delight.

In treating on the versification of *Milton*, I am desirous to be generally understood, and shall therefore studiously decline the dialect of grammarians; though, indeed, it is always difficult, and sometimes scarcely possible, to deliver the precepts of an art, without the terms by which the peculiar ideas of that art are expressed, and which had not been invented but because the language already in use was insufficient. If, therefore, I shall sometimes seem obscure, it may be imputed to this voluntary interdiction, and to a desire of avoiding that offence which is always given by unusual words.

The heroic measure of the *English* language may be properly considered as pure or mixed. It is pure when the accent rests upon every second syllable through the whole line.

> Courage uncertain dangers may abate,
> But whó can béar th' appróach of cértain fáte. Dryden.

> Here love his golden shafts employs, here lights
> His cónstant lámp, and wáves his púrple wíngs,
> Reigns here, and revels: not in the bought smile
> Of hárlots, lóveless, jóyless, únendéar'd. [*PL* IV, 763–6]

The accent may be observed, in the second line of *Dryden*, and the second and fourth of *Milton*, to repose upon every second syllable.

The repetition of this sound or percussion at equal times, is the most complete harmony of which a single verse is capable, and should therefore be exactly kept in distichs, and generally in the last line of the paragraph, that the ear may rest without any sense of imperfection.

But, to preserve the series of sounds untransposed in a long composition, is not only very difficult, but tiresome and disgusting; for we are soon wearied with the perpetual recurrence of the same cadence. Necessity has therefore enforced the mixed measure, in which some variation of the accents is allowed; this, though it always injures the harmony of the line considered by itself, yet compensates the loss by relieving us from the continual tyranny of the same sound, and makes us more sensible of the harmony of the pure measure.

Of these mixed numbers every poet affords us innumerable instances, and Milton seldom has two pure lines together, as will appear if any of his paragraphs be read with attention merely to the music [*PL* IV, 720–35].

In this passage it will be at first observed, that all the lines are not equally harmonious, and upon a nearer examination it will be found that only the fifth and ninth lines are regular, and the rest are more or less licentious with respect to the accent. In some the accent is equally upon two syllables together, and in both strong. As,

> Thus at their shady lodge arriv'd, *both stood*,
> *Both turn'd*, and under open sky ador'd
> The God that made both sky, *air*, *earth*, and heaven.
> [720–2]

In others the accent is equally upon two syllables, but upon both weak.

—a race
To fill the earth, who shall with us extol
Thy goodness *infinite*, both when we wake,
And when we seek, as now, thy gift of sleep.
[732–5]

In the first pair of syllables the accent may deviate from the rigour of exactness, without any unpleasing diminution of harmony, as may be observed in the lines already cited, and more remarkably in this,

—Thou also mad'st the night.
Maker omnipotent! and thou the day.
[724–5]

But, excepting in the first pair of syllables, which may be considered as arbitrary, a poet who, not having the invention or knowledge of *Milton*, has more need to allure his audience by musical cadences, should seldom suffer more than one aberration from the rule in any single verse.

There are two lines in this passage more remarkably unharmonious:

—This delicious place,
For us too large; *where thy* abundance wants
Partakers, and uncrop'd *falls* to the ground.
[729–31]

Here the third pair of syllables in the first, and fourth pair in the second verse, have their accents retrograde or inverted; the first syllable being strong or acute, and the second weak. The detriment which the measure suffers by this inversion of the accents is sometimes less perceptible, when the verses are carried one into another, but is remarkably striking in this place, where the vicious verse concludes a period; and is yet more offensive in rhyme, when we regularly attend to the flow of every single line. This will appear by reading a couplet in which *Cowley*, an author not sufficiently studious of harmony, has committed the same fault:

—his harmless life
Does with substantial blessedness abound,
And the soft wings of peace *cover* him round.

In these the law of metre is very grossly violated by mingling combinations of sound directly opposite to each other, as *Milton* expresses in his sonnet, by *committing short and long*, and setting one part of the measure at variance with the rest. The ancients, who had a language more capable of variety than ours, had two kinds of verse, the *iambick*, consisting of short and long syllables alternately, from which our heroick measure is derived, and the *Trochaick*, consisting in a like alternation of long and short. These were considered as opposites, and conveyed the contrary images of speed and slowness; to confound them, therefore, as in these lines, is to deviate from the established practice. But where the senses are to judge, authority is not necessary, the ear is sufficient to detect dissonance, nor should I have sought auxiliaries on such an occasion any name but that of *Milton*.

No. 88

'There is no reputation for genius (says *Quintilian*) to be gained by writing on things, which, however necessary, have little splendor or shew. The height of a building attracts the eye, but the foundations lie without regard. Yet since there is not any way to the top of science, but from the lowest parts, I shall think nothing unconnected with the art of oratory, which he that wants cannot be an orator.'

Confirmed and animated by this illustrious precedent, I shall continue my inquiries into Milton's art of versification. Since, however minute the employment may appear, of analysing lines into syllables, and whatever ridicule may be incurred by a solemn deliberation upon accents and pauses, it is certain, that without this petty knowledge no man can be a poet; and that from the proper disposition of single sounds results that harmony that adds force to reason, and gives grace to sublimity; that shackles attention, and governs passions.

That verse may be melodious and pleasing, it is necessary, not only that the words be so ranged as that the accent may fall on its proper place, but that the syllables themselves be so chosen as to flow smoothly into one another. This is to be effected by a proportionate mixture of vowels and consonants, and by tempering the mute consonants with liquids and semivowels. (The Hebrew grammarians have observed, that it is impossible to pronounce two consonants without the intervention of a vowel, or without some emission of the breath between one and the other; this is longer and more perceptible, as the sounds of the consonants are less harmonically conjoined, and, by consequence, the flow of the verse is longer interrupted.)

It is pronounced by *Dryden*, that a line of monosyllables is almost always harsh. This, with regard to our language, is evidently true, not because monosyllables cannot compose harmony, but because our monosyllables being of *Teutonic* original, or formed by contraction, commonly begin and end with consonants, as,

> —Every lower faculty
> *Of sense, whereby they hear, see, smell, touch, taste.*
> [V, 410–11]

The difference of harmony arising principally from the collocation of vowels and consonants, will be sufficiently conceived by attending to the following passages:

> Immortal *Amarant*—there grows
> And flow'rs aloft, shading the fount of life,
> And where the river of bliss thro' midst of heav'n
> *Rolls o'er Elysian flow'rs her amber stream;*
> With these that never fade, the spirits elect
> *Bind their resplendent locks inwreath'd with beams.*
> [III, 352–7]

The same comparison that I propose to be made between the fourth and sixth verses of this passage, may be repeated between the last lines of the following quotations:

> Under foot the violet,
> Crocus, and hyacinth, with rich in-lay
> *Broider'd the ground, more colour'd than with stone*
> Of costliest emblem. [IV, 700–3]

> Here in close recess,
> With flowers, garlands, and sweet-smelling herbs,
> Espoused *Eve* first deck'd her nuptial bed;
> *And heav'nly choirs the hymenean sung.* [IV, 708–11]

Milton, whose ear had been accustomed, not only to the music of the ancient tongues, which, however vitiated by our pronunciation, excel all that are now in use, but to the softness of the *Italian*, the most mellifluous of all modern poetry, seems fully convinced of the unfitness of our language for smooth versification, and is therefore pleased with an opportunity of calling in a softer word to his assistance; for this reason, and I believe for this only, he sometimes indulges himself in a long series of proper names, and introduces them where they add little but music to his poem.

> —The richer feat
> Of *Atabalipa*, and yet unspoil'd
> *Guiana*, whose great city *Gerion's* sons
> Call *El Dorado*.— [XI, 408–11]

The moon—The *Tuscan* artist views
At evening, from the top of *Fesole*
Or in *Valdarno*, to descry new lands.—
[I, 288–90]

He has indeed been more attentive to his syllables than to his accents, and does not often offend by collisions of consonants, or openings of vowels upon each other, at least not more often than other writers who have had less important or complicated subjects to take off their care from the cadence of their lines.

The great peculiarity of *Milton*'s versification, compared with that of later poets, is the elision of one vowel before another, or the supression of the last syllable of a word ending with a vowel, when a vowel begins the following words; as,

Knowledge—
Oppresses else with surfeit, and soon turns
Wisdom to *folly*, as nourishment, to wind.
[VII, 129–30]

This licence, though now disused in *English* poetry, was practiced by our old writers, and is allowed in many other languages ancient and modern, and therefore the critics on *Paradise Lost* have, without much deliberation, commended *Milton* for continuing it. But one language cannot communicate its rules to another. We have already tried and rejected the hexameter of the ancients, the double close of the *Italians*, and the alexandrine of the *French*; and the elision of vowels, however graceful it may seem to other nations, may be very unsuitable to the genius of the *English* tongue.

There is reason to believe that we have negligently lost part of our vowels, and that the silent *e* which our ancestors added to most of our monosyllables, was once vocal. By this detruncation of our syllables, our language is overstocked with consonants, and it is more necessary to add vowels to the beginning of words, than to cut them off from the end.

Milton therefore seems to have somewhat mistaken the nature of our language, of which the chief defect is ruggedness and asperity, and has left our harsh cadences yet harsher. But his elisions are not all equally to be censured; in some syllables they may be allowed, and perhaps in a few may be safely imitated. The abscission of a vowel is undoubtedly vicious when it is strongly sounded, and makes, with its associate consonant, a full and audible syllable.

—What he gives,
Spiritual, may to purest spirits be found
No ingrateful food, and food alike these pure
Intelligential substances require. [V, 405–8]

Fruits,—*Hesperian* fables true,
If true, here *only*, and of delicious taste.
[IV, 250–1]

—Evening now approach'd.
For we have *also* our evening and our morn. [V, 627–8]

Of guests he makes them slaves,
Inhospita*bly*, and kills their infant males. [XII, 167–8]

And vital Vir*tue* infus'd, and vital warmth
Throughout the fluid mass.— [VII, 236–7]

God made *thee* of choice his own, and of his own
To serve him. [X, 766–7]

I believe every reader will agree, that in all those passages, though not equally in all, the music is injured, and in some the meaning obscured. There are other lines in which the vowel is cut off, but it is so faintly pronounced in common speech, that the loss of it in poetry is scarcely perceived; and therefore such compliance with the measure may be allowed.

Nature breeds
Perverse, all monstrous, all prodigious things,
Abomina*ble*, inuttera*ble*; and worse
Than fables yet have feign'd— [II, 624–7]

—From the shore
They view'd the vast immeasura*ble* abyss. [VII, 210–11]

Impenetra*ble*, impal'd with circling fire. [II, 647]

To none communica*ble* in earth or heav'n. [VII, 72]

Yet even these contractions increase the roughness of a language too rough already; and though in long poems they may be sometimes suffered, it never can be faulty to forbear them.

Milton frequently uses in his poems the hypermetrical or redundant line of eleven syllables.

—Thus it shall befal
Him who to worth in woman over-trust*ing*,
Lets her will rule— [IX, 1182–4]

I also err'd in over-much admir*ing*. [IX, 1178]

Verses of this kind occur almost in every page; but though they are not unpleasing or dissonant, they ought not to be admitted into heroic poetry, since the narrow limits of our language allow us no other distinction of epic and tragic measures, than is afforded by the liberty of changing at will the terminations of the dramatic lines, and bringing them by that relaxation of metrical rigour nearer to prose.

No. 90

It is very difficult to write on the minuter parts of literature without failing either to please or instruct. Too much nicety of detail disgusts the greatest part of readers, and to throw a multitude of particulars under general heads, and lay down rules of extensive comprehension, is to common understandings of little use. They who undertake these subjects are therefore always in danger, as one or other inconvenience arises to their imagination, of frighting us with rugged science, or amusing us with empty sound.

In criticising the work of *Milton*, there is, indeed, opportunity to intersperse passages that can hardly fail to relieve the languors of attention; and since, in examining the variety and choice of the pauses, with which he has diversified his numbers, it will be necessary to exhibit the lines in which they are to be found, perhaps the remarks may be well compensated by the examples, and the irksomeness of grammatical disquisitions somewhat alleviated.

Milton formed his scheme of versification by the poets of *Greece* and *Rome*, whom he proposed to himself for his models, so far as the difference of his language from theirs would permit the imitation. There are indeed many inconveniencies inseparable from our heroic measure compared with that of *Homer* and *Virgil*; inconveniencies, which it is no reproach to *Milton* not to have overcome, because they are in their own nature insuperable; but against which he has struggled with so much art and diligence, that he may at least be said to have deserved success.

The hexameter of the ancients may be considered as consisting of fifteen syllables, so melodiously disposed, that, as every one knows who has examined the poetical authors, very pleasing and sonorous lyric measures are formed from the fragments of the heroic. It is, indeed, scarce possible to break them in such a manner, but that *invenias etiam disjecti membra poetæ* some harmony will still remain, and the due proportions of sound will always be discovered. This measure therefore allowed great variety of pauses, and great liberties of connecting one verse with another because where-ever the line was interrupted, either part singly was musical. But the ancients seem to have confined this privilege to hexameters; for in their other measures, though longer than the *English* heroic, those who wrote after the refinements of versification, venture so seldom to change their pauses, that every variation may be supposed rather a compliance with necessity than the choice of judgment.

Milton was constrained within the narrow limits of a measure not very harmonious in the utmost perfection; the single parts, therefore, into which it was to be sometimes broken by pauses, were in danger of losing the very form of verse. This has, perhaps, notwithstanding all his care, sometimes happened.

As harmony is the end of poetical measures, no part of a verse ought to be so separated from the rest as not to remain still more harmonious than prose, or to shew, by the disposition of the tones, that it is part of a verse. This rule in the old hexameter might be easily observed, but in *English* will very frequently be in danger of violation; for the order and regularity of accents cannot well be perceived in a succession of fewer than three syllables, which will confine the *English* poet to only five pauses; it being supposed, that, when he connects one line with another, he should never make a full pause at less distance than that of three syllables from the beginning or end of a verse.

That this rule should be universally and indispensably established, perhaps cannot be granted; something may be allowed to variety, and something to the adaptation of the numbers to the subject; but it will be found generally necessary, and the ear will seldom fail to suffer by its neglect.

Thus when a single syllable is cut off from the rest, it must either be united to the line with which the sense connects it, or be sounded alone. If it be united to the other line, it corrupts its harmony; if disjoined, it must stand alone, and with regard to music be superfluous; for there is no harmony in a single sound, because it has no proportion to another.

> Hypocrites austerely talk,
> Defaming as impure what God declares
> *Pure*; and commands to some, leaves free to all. [IV, 744–6]

When two syllables likewise are abscinded from the rest, they evidently want some associate sounds to make them harmonious.

> —Eyes—
> —more wakeful than to drouze,
> Charm'd with Arcadian pipe, the past'ral reed
> Of *Hermes*, or his opiate rod. *Meanwhile*
> To re-salute the world with sacred light
> *Leucothea* wak'd. [XI, 131–5]

> He ended, and the sun gave signal high
> To the bright minister that watch'd: *he blew*
> His trumpet. [XI, 72–4]

> First in the east his glorious lamp was seen,
> Regent of day; and all th' horizon round
> Invested with bright rays, jocund to run
> His longitude through heav'n's high road; *the gray*
> Dawn, and the Pleiades, before him danc'd,
> Shedding sweet influence. [VII, 370–5]

The same defect is perceived in the following line, where the pause is at the second syllable from the beginning.

> The race
> Of that wild route that tore the *Thracian* bard
> In *Rhodope*, where woods and rocks had ears
> To rapture, 'till the savage clamour drown'd
> Both harp and voice; nor could the muse defend
> *Her son.* So fail not thou, who thee implores. [VII, 33–8]

When the pause falls upon the third syllable or the seventh, the harmony is better preserved; but as the third and seventh are weak syllables, the period leaves the ear unsatisfied, and in expectation of the remaining part of the verse.

> He, with his horrid crew,
> Lay vanquish'd, rolling in the fiery gulph,
> Confounded though immor*tal*. But his doom
> Reserv'd him to more wrath; for now the thought
> Both of lost happiness and lasting pain
> Torments *him*. [I, 51–6]

> God,—with frequent intercourse,
> Thither will send his winged messengers
> On errands of supernal grace. So sung
> The glorious train ascending. [VI, 571–4]

It may be, I think, established as a rule, that a pause which concludes a period should be made for the most part upon a strong syllable, as the fourth and sixth; but those pauses which only suspend the sense may be placed upon the weaker. Thus the rest in the third line of the first passage satisfies the ear better than in the fourth, and the close of the second quotation better than of the third.

> The evil soon
> Drawn back, redounded (as a flood) on those
> From whom it *sprung*; impossible to mix
> With *blessedness*. [VII, 56–9]

> —What we by day
> Lop overgrown, or prune, or prop, or bind,
> One night or two with wanton growth derides,
> Tending to *wild*. [IX, 209–12]

> The paths and bow'rs doubt not but our joint hands
> Will keep from wilderness with ease as wide
> As we need walk, till younger hands ere long
> Assist *us*. [IX, 244–7]

The rest in the fifth place has the same inconvenience as in the seventh and third, that the syllable is weak.

> Beast now with beast 'gan war, and fowl with fowl,
> And fish with fish, to graze the herb all leaving,
> Devour'd each *other*: Nor stood much in awe
> Of man, but fled *him*, or with countenance grim,
> Glar'd on him pass*ing*. [X, 710–14]

The noblest and most majestic pauses which our versification admits, are upon the fourth and sixth syllables, which are both strongly founded in a pure and regular verse, and at either of which the line is so divided, that both members participate of harmony.

> But now at last the sacred influence
> Of light *appears*, and from the walls of heav'n
> Shoots far into the bosom of dim night
> A glimmering *dawn*: here nature first begins
> Her farthest verge, and chaos to retire. [II, 1034–8]

But far above all others, if I can give any credit to my own ear, is the rest upon the sixth syllable, which taking in a complete compass of sound, such as is sufficient to constitute one of our lyric measures, makes a full and solemn close. Some passages which conclude at this stop, I could never read without some strong emotions of delight or admiration.

> Before the hills appear'd, or fountain flow'd,
> Thou with the eternal wisdom didst converse,
> Wisdom thy sister; and with her didst play
> In presence of the almighty Father, pleas'd
> With thy celestial *song*. [VII, 8–12]

> Or other worlds they seem'd, or happy isles,
> Like those *Hesperian* gardens fam'd of old,
> Fortunate fields, and groves, and flow'ry vales,
> Thrice happy isles! But who dwelt happy there,
> He staid not to in*quire*. [III, 567–71]

> He blew
> His trumpet, heard in *Oreb* since, perhaps
> When God descended; and, perhaps, once more
> To sound at general *doom*. [XI, 72–5]

If the poetry of *Milton* be examined, with regard to the pauses and flow of his verses into each other, it will appear, that he has performed all that our language would admit; and the comparison of his numbers with those who have cultivated the same manner of writing, will show that he excelled as much in the lower as the higher parts of his art, and that his skill in harmony was not less than his invention or his learning.

No. 94

The resemblance of poetic numbers, to the subject which they mention or describe, may be considered as general or particular; as consisting in the flow and structure of a whole passage taken together, or as comprised in the sound of some emphatical and descriptive words, or in the cadence and harmony of single verses.

The general resemblance of the sound to the sense is to be found in every language which admits of poetry, in every author whose force of fancy enables him to impress images strongly on his own mind, and whose choice and variety of language readily supplies him with just representations. To such a writer it is natural to change his measure with his subject, even without any effort of the understanding, or intervention of the judgment. To revolve jollity and mirth necessarily tunes the voice of a poet to gay and sprightly notes, as it fires his eye with vivacity; and reflection on gloomy situations and disastrous events, will sadden his numbers, as it will cloud his countenance. But in such passages there is only the similitude of pleasure to pleasure, and of grief to grief, without any immediate application to particular images. The same flow of joyous versification will celebrate the jollity of marriage, and the exultation of triumph; and the same languor of melody will suit the complaints of an absent lover, as of a conquered king.

It is scarcely to be doubted, that on many occasions we make the music which we imagine ourselves to hear; that we modulate the poem by our own disposition, and ascribe to the numbers the effects of the sense. We may observe in life, that it is not easy to deliver a pleasant message in an unpleasing manner, and that we readily associate beauty and deformity with those whom for any reason we love or hate. Yet it would be too daring to declare that all the celebrated adaptations of harmony are chimerical; that *Homer* had no extraordinary attention to the melody of his verse when he described a nuptial festivity; . . . that *Vida* was merely fanciful, when he supposed *Virgil* endeavouring to represent by uncommon sweetness of numbers the adventitious beauty of *Æneas*; . . . or that *Milton* did not intend to exemplify the harmony which he mentions:

> Fountains! and ye that warble as ye flow,
> Melodious murmurs! warbling tune his praise. [V, 195–6]

That *Milton* understood the force of sounds well adjusted, and knew the compass and variety of the ancient measures, cannot be doubted, since he was both a musician and a critic; but he seems to have considered these conformities of cadence, as either not often attainable in our language, or as petty excellencies unworthy of his ambition; for it will not be found that he has always assigned the same cast of numbers to the same objects. He has given in two passages very minute descriptions of angelic beauty; but though the images are nearly the same, the numbers will be found upon comparison very different [III, 636–42]. Some of the lines of this description are remarkably defective in harmony, and therefore by no means correspondent with that symmetrical elegance and easy grace which they are intended to exhibit. The failure, however, is fully compensated by the representation of Raphael, which equally delights the ear and imagination [V, 277–87].

The adumbration of particular and distinct images by an exact and perceptible resemblance of sound, is sometimes studied, and sometimes casual. Every language has many words formed in imitation of the noises which they signify. Such are *Stridor, Balo,* and *Beatus,* in *Latin*;

and in *English* to *growl*, to *buzz*, to *hiss*, and to *jarr*. Words of this kind give to a verse the proper similitude of sound, without much labour of the writer, and such happiness is therefore rather to be attributed to fortune than skill; yet they are sometimes combined with great propriety, and undeniably contribute to enforce the impression of the idea. We hear the passing arrow in this line of *Virgil*; . . . and the creaking of hell-gates, in the description by *Milton*;

> Open fly
> With impetuous recoil and jarring sound
> Th' infernal doors; and on their hinges grate
> Harsh thunder. [II, 879–82]

But many beauties of this kind, which the moderns, and perhaps the ancients, have observed, seem to be the product of blind reverence acting upon fancy. *Dionysius* himself tells us, that the sound of *Homer's* verses sometimes exhibits the idea of corporeal bulk: is not this a discovery nearly approaching to that of the blind man, who, after long inquiry into the nature of the scarlet colour, found that it represented nothing so much as the clangour of a trumpet? The representative power of poetic harmony consists of sound and measure; of the force of the syllable singly considered, and of the time in which they are pronounced. Sound can resemble nothing but sound, and time can measure nothing but motion and duration.

The critics, however, have struck out other similitudes; nor is there any irregularity of numbers which credulous admiration cannot discover to be eminently beautiful. Thus the propriety of each of these lines has been celebrated by writers whose opinion the world has reason to regard: . . . If all these observations are just, there must be some remarkable conformity between the sudden succession of night to day; the fall of an ox under a blow, and the birth of a mouse from a mountain; since we are told of all these images, that they are very strongly impressed by the same form and termination of the verse.

We may, however, without giving way to enthusiasm, admit that some beauties of this kind may be produced. A sudden stop at an unusual syllable may image the cessation action, or the pause of discourse; and *Milton* has very happily imitated the repetitions of an echo:

> I fled, and cried out *death*:
> Hell trembled at the hideous name, and sigh'd
> From all her caves, and back resounded *death*. [II, 787–9]

The measure or time in pronouncing may be varied so as very strongly to represent, not only the modes of external motion, but the quick or slow succession of ideas, and consequently the passions of the mind. This at least was the power of the spondaick and dactylick harmony, but our language can reach no eminent diversities of sound. We can indeed sometimes, by incumbering and retarding the line, shew the difficulty of a progress made by strong efforts and with frequent interruptions, or mark a slow and heavy motion. Thus *Milton* has imaged the toil of *Satan* struggling through chaos:

> So he with difficulty and labour hard
> Mov'd on: with difficulty and labour he— [II, 1021–2]

thus he has described the leviathans or whales;

> Wallowing unwieldy, enormous in their gait. [VII, 411]

But he has at other times neglected such representations, as may be observed in the volubility and levity of these lines, which express an action tardy and reluctant [II, 76–81].

In another place, he describes the gentle glide of ebbing waters in a line remarkably rough and halting;

> Tripping ebb; that stole
> With soft foot tow'rds the deep, who now had stopp'd
> His sluices. [XI, 847–9]

It is not indeed to be expected, that the sound should always assist the meaning, but it ought never to counteract it; and therefore *Milton* has here certainly committed a fault like that of the player, who looked on the earth when he implored the heavens, and to the heavens when he addressed the earth.

Those who are determined to find in *Milton* an assemblage of all the excellencies which have ennobled all other poets, will perhaps be offended that I do not celebrate his versification in higher terms; for there are readers who discover that in his passage,

> So stretch'd out huge in length the arch fiend lay, [I, 209]

a *long* form is described in a *long* line; but the truth is, that length of body is only mentioned in a *slow* line, to which it has only the resemblance of time to space, of an hour to a maypole.

The same turn of ingenuity might perform wonders upon the description of the ark:

> Then from the mountains hewing timber tall,
> Began to build a vessel of huge bulk;
> Measur'd by cubit, length, and breadth, and height. [XI, 728-30]

In these lines the poet apparently designs to fix the attention upon the bulk; but this is effected by the enumeration, not by the measure; for what analogy can there be between modulations of sound, and corporeal dimensions?

Milton, indeed, seems only to have regarded this species of embellishment so far as not to reject it when it came unsought; which would often happen to a mind so vigorous, employed upon a subject so various and extensive. He had, indeed, a greater and nobler work to perform; a single sentiment of moral or religious truth, a single image of life or nature, would have been cheaply lost for the thousand echoes of the cadence to the sense; and he who had undertaken to *vindicate the ways of God to man*, might have been accused of neglecting his cause, had he lavished much of his attention upon syllables and sounds.

43. Johnson on *Samson Agonistes*

July 1751

Samuel Johnson, *Rambler*, nos 139 (16 July 1751) and 140 (20 July 1751).

No. 139

It is required by *Aristotle* to the perfection of a tragedy, and is equally necessary to every other species of regular composition, that it should have a beginning, a middle, and an end. 'The beginning,' says he, 'is that which has nothing necessarily previous, but to which that which follows is naturally consequent; the end, on the contrary, is that which by necessity, or at least according to the common course of things, succeeds something else, but which implies nothing consequent to itself; the middle is connected on one side to something that naturally goes before, and on the other to something that naturally follows it.'

Such is the rule laid down by this great critic, for the disposition of the different parts of a well-constituted fable. It must begin, where it may be made intelligible without introduction; and end, where the mind is left in repose, without expectation of any farther event. The intermediate passages must join the last effect to the first cause, by a regular and unbroken concatenation; nothing must be therefore inserted which does not apparently arise from something foregoing, and properly make way for something that succeeds it.

This precept is to be understood in its rigour only with respect to great and essential events, and cannot be extended in the same force to minuter circumstances and arbitrary decorations, which yet are more happy as they contribute more to the main design; for it is always a proof of extensive thought and accurate circumspection, to promote various purposes by the same act; and the idea of an ornament admits use, though it seems to exclude necessity.

Whoever purposes, as it is expressed by *Milton, to build the lofty rhyme*, must acquaint himself with this law of poetical architecture, and take care that his edifice be solid as well as beautiful; that nothing stand single or independent, so as that it may be taken away without injuring the rest; but that from the foundation to the pinnacles one part rest firm upon another.

This regular and consequential distribution, is among common authors frequently neglected; but the failures of those, whose example can have no influence, may be safely overlooked, nor is it of much use to recall obscure and unregarded names to memory for the sake of sporting with their infamy. But if there is any writer whose genius can embellish impropriety, and whose authority can make error venerable, his works are the proper objects of critical inquisition. To expunge faults where there are no excellencies, is a task equally useless with that of the chemist who employs the arts of separation and refinement upon ore, in which no precious moral is contained to reward his operations.

The tragedy of *Samson Agonistes* has been celebrated as the second work of the great author of *Paradise Lost*, and opposed with all the confidence of triumph to the dramatic performances of other nations. It contains indeed just sentiments, maxims of wisdom, and oracles of piety, and many passages written with the ancient spirit of choral poetry, in which there is a just and pleasing mixture of *Seneca's* moral declamation, with the wild enthusiasm of the *Greek* writers. It is therefore worthy of examination, whether a performance thus illuminated with genius, and enriched with learning, is composed according to the indispensible laws of *Aristotelian* criticism: and, omitting at present all other considerations, whether it exhibits a beginning, a middle, and an end.

The beginning is undoubtedly beautiful and proper, opening with a graceful abruptness, and proceeding naturally to a mournful recital of facts necessary to be known [*SA*, 1–17]. His soliloquy is interrupted by a chorus or company of men of his own tribe, who condole his miseries, extenuate his fault, and conclude with a solemn vindication of divine justice. So that at the conclusion of the first act there is no design laid, no discovery made, nor any disposition formed towards the subsequent event.

In the second act, *Manoah*, the father of *Samson*, comes to seek his son, and being shewn him by the chorus, breaks out into lamentations of his misery, and comparisons of his present with his former state, representing to him the ignominy which his religion suffers, by the festival this day celebrated in honour of *Dagon*, to whom the idolaters ascribed his overthrow [ll. 430–9].

Samson, touched with this reproach, makes a reply equally penitential and pious, which his father considers as the effusion of prophetic confidence [ll. 465–75].

This part of the dialogue, as it might tend to animate or exasperate *Samson*, cannot, I think, be censured as wholly superfluous; but the succeeding dispute, in which *Samson* contends to die, and which his father breaks off, that he may go to solicit his release, is only valuable for its own beauties, and has no tendency to introduce any thing that follows it.

The next event of the drama is the arrival of *Delilah*, with all her graces, artifices, and allurements. This produces a dialogue, in a very high degree elegant and instructive, from which she retires, after she has exhausted her persuasions, and is no more seen nor heard of; nor has her visit any effect but that of missing the character of *Samson*.

In the fourth act enters *Harapha*, the giant of *Gath*, whose name had never been mentioned before, and who has now no other motive of coming, than to see the man whose strength and actions are so loudly celebrated [ll. 1082–90].

Samson challenges him to the combat; and after an interchange of reproaches, elevated by repeated defiance on one side, and imbittered by contemptuous insults on the other, *Harapha* retires; we then hear it determined, by *Samson* and the chorus, that no consequence good or bad will proceed from their interview [ll. 1250–6].

At last, in the fifth act, appears a messenger from the lords assembled at the festival of *Dagon*, with a summons, by which *Samson* is required to come and entertain them with some proof of his strength. *Samson*, after a short expostulation, dismisses him with a firm and resolute refusal; but during the absence of the messenger, having a while defended the propriety of his conduct, he at last declares himself moved by a secret impulse to comply, and utters some dark presages of a great event to be brought to pass by his agency, under the direction of Providence [ll. 1381–9].

While *Samson* is conducted off by the messenger, his father returns with hopes of success in his solicitation, upon which he confers with the chorus till their dialogue is interrupted, first by a shout of triumph, and afterwards by screams of horror and agony. As they stand deliberating where they shall be secure, a man who had been present at the show enters, and relates how *Samson*, having prevailed on his guide to suffer him to lean against the main pillars of the theatrical edifice, tore down the roof upon the spectators and himself [ll. 1648–58].

This is undoubtedly a just and regular catastrophe, and the poem, therefore, has a beginning and an end which *Aristotle* himself could not have disapproved; but it must be allowed to want a middle, since nothing passes between the first act and the last, that either hastens or delays the death of *Samson*. The whole drama, if its superfluities were cut off, would scarcely fill a single act; yet this is the tragedy which ignorance has admired, and bigotry applauded.

No. 140

It is common, says *Bacon*, to desire the end without enduring the means. Every member of society feels and acknowledges the necessity of detecting crimes, yet scarce any degree of virtue or reputation is able to secure an informer from public hatred. The learned world has always admitted the usefulness of critical disquisitions, yet he that attempts to shew, however modestly, the failures of a celebrated writer, shall surely irritate his admirers, and incur the imputation of envy, captiousness, and malignity.

With this danger full in my view, I shall proceed to examine the sentiments of *Milton*'s tragedy which, though much less liable to censure than the disposition of his plan, are, like those of other writers, sometimes exposed to just exception for want of care, or want of discernment.

Sentiments are proper and improper as they consist more or less with the character and circumstances of the person to whom they are attributed, with the rules of the composition in which they are found, or with the settled and unalterable nature of things.

It is common among the tragic poets to introduce their persons alluding to events or opinions, of which they could not possibly have any knowledge. The barbarians of remote or newly-discovered regions often display their skill in *European* learning. The god of love is mentioned in *Tamerlane* with all the familiarity of a *Roman* epigrammatist; and a late writer has put *Harvey*'s doctrine of the circulation of the blood into the mouth of a *Turkish* statesman, who lived near two centuries before it was known even to philosophers or anatomists.

Milton's learning, which acquainted him with the manners of the ancient eastern nations, and his invention, which required no assistance from the common cant of poetry, have preserved him from frequent outrages of local or chronological propriety. Yet he has mentioned *Chalybean Steel*, of which it is not very likely that his chorus should have heard, and has made *Alp* the general name of a mountain, in a region where the *Alps* could scarcely be known [ll. 627–8].

He has taught *Samson* the tales of *Circe* and the *Syrens*, at which he apparently hints in his colloquy with *Delilah* [ll. 932–5].

But the grossest error of this kind is the solemn introduction of the Phœnix in the last scene: which is faulty, not only as it is incongruous to the personage to whom it is ascribed, but as it is so evidently contrary to reason and nature, that it ought never to be mentioned but as a fable in any serious poem [ll. 1697–1707].

Another species of impropriety, is the unsuitableness of thoughts to the general character of the poem. The seriousness and solemnity of tragedy necessarily rejects all pointed or epigrammatical expressions, all remote conceits and opposition of ideas. *Samson's* complaint is therefore too elaborate to be natural [ll. 99–105].

All allusions to low and trivial objects, with which contempt is usually associated, are doubtless unsuitable to a species of composition which ought to be always awful, though not always magnificent. The remark therefore of the chorus on good and bad news, seems to want elevation [ll. 1536–8].

But of all meanness, that has least to plead which is produced by mere verbal conceits, which depending only upon sounds, lose their existence by the change of syllable. Of this kind is the following dialogue [ll. 1061–8].

And yet more despicable are the lines in which *Manoah's* paternal kindness is commended by the chorus [ll. 1485–6].

Samson's complaint of the inconveniences of imprisonment is not wholly without verbal quaintness [ll. 7–8].

From the sentiments we may properly descend to the consideration of the language, which, in imitation of the ancients, is through the whole dialogue remarkably simple and unadorned, seldom heightened by epithets, or varied by figures; yet sometimes metaphors find admission, even where their consistency is not accurately preserved. Thus *Samson* confounds loquacity with a shipwreck [ll. 197–202]. And the chorus talks of adding fuel to flame in a report [ll. 1350–1].

The versification is in the dialogue much more smooth and harmonious than in the parts allotted to the chorus, which are often so harsh and dissonant, as scarce to preserve whether the lines end with or without rhymes, any appearance of metrical regularity [ll. 124–8].

Since I have thus pointed out the faults of *Milton*, critical integrity requires that I should endeavour to display his excellencies, though they will not easily be discovered in short quotations, because they consist in the justness of diffuse reasonings, or in the contexture and method of continued dialogues; this play having none of those descriptions, similes, or splendid sentences, with which other tragedies are so lavishly adorned.

Yet some passages may be selected which seem to deserve particular notice, either as containing sentiments of passion, representations of life, precepts of conduct, or sallies of imagination. It is not easy to give a stronger representation of the weariness of despondency than in the words of *Samson* to his father [ll. 594–8].

The reply of *Samson* to the flattering *Delilah* affords a just and striking description of the stratagems and allurements of feminine hypocrisy [ll. 748–58].

When *Samson* has refused to make himself a spectacle at the feast of *Dagon*, he first justifies his behaviour to the chorus, who charge him with having served the *Philistines*, by a very just distinction; and then destroys the common excuse of cowardice and servility, which always confound temptation with compulsion [ll. 1363–75].

The complaint of blindness which *Samson* pours out at the beginning of the tragedy is equally addressed to the passions and the fancy. The enumeration of his miseries is succeeded by a very pleasing train of poetical images, and concluded by such expostulations and wishes, as reason too often submits, to learn from despair [ll. 83–97].

Such are the faults and such the beauties of *Samson Agonistes*, which I have shewn with no other purpose than to promote the knowledge of true criticism. The everlasting verdure of *Milton's* laurels has nothing to fear from the blasts of malignity; nor can my attempt produce any other effect, than to strengthen their shoots by lopping their luxuriance.

44. Baretti on Voltaire's 'Essay'

1753

Extract from Giuseppi Baretti, *A Dissertation upon the Italian Poetry in which are interspersed some remarks on Mr. Voltaire's 'Essay on Epic Poets'* (1753). Giuseppi Baretti, *Prefazioni e Polemiche*, ed. Luigi Piccioni (Bari, 1911), 109–11.

Giuseppi Marc'Antonio Baretti (1719–89) came to London in 1751. His best-known and most frequently reprinted work was an Italian and English dictionary. A friend of Johnson, he nevertheless defended Milton against the detraction of Voltaire, who had argued that Milton based *Paradise Lost* on a lost play by Andreini. That this was Milton's 'source' was ignorantly to be repeated in later years, e.g., by William Cowper.

Voltaire, in his *Essay*, speaking of the *Paradise lost*, says that Milton, as he was travelling through Italy in his youth, saw at Florence a comedy called *Adamo*, writ by one Andreino, . . . The subject of the play was the fall of man; the actors God, the devils, the angels, Adam, Eve, the serpent, death, and the seven mortal sins. That topic so improper for a drama (continues Voltaire) but so suitable to the absurd genius of the Italian stage, as it was at that time, was handled in a manner entirely conformable to the extravagance of the design. . . . Milton pierced through the absurdity of that performance to the hidden majesty of the subject, which being altogether unfit for the stage, yet might be for the genius of Milton, and for his only, the foundation of an epic poem. He took from that ridiculous trifle the first hint of the noblest work which human imagination hath ever attempted, and which he executed more than twenty years after.

I know not upon what foundation it is, that Voltaire assures us that the taste of the Italian stage in the time of Milton was so bad as to relish the comedy he mentions. If he had read the life, or even the writings of Milton himself, he would have perceived by them that Florence, when that poet travelled through Italy, was full of learned men; and if he had the least notion of the Florentine people, he would have spoken with less contempt of them. But setting this aside, how can he so positively affirm that Milton took the first hint of *Paradise lost* from the above-mentioned absurd comedy of Andreino? I have some doubts of his veracity and really suspect the existence of the play and its author. Yet to drop this extravagant anecdote, suffer me to say that to me it seems ridiculous that such a man as Milton could have raked among the rubbish of Andreino (if such a man ever existed) so bright a jewel as the *Paradise lost*. Milton understood the Italian authors so well and was so fond of Dante in particular, that he wrote some Italian verses, yet extant, in the style of that epic poet: a thing not only extremely difficult for a foreigner, but also for an Italian, since to understand Dante perfectly we are obliged to study him in the schools and Universities with almost as much labour as we do Virgil. If then Milton was so much master of Dante's style that he could write verses in his manner, and if the thoughts and images of both the poems have a great resemblance to each other, as the reader may see by the quotations I have given; if the very subjects and titles are alike, is it not more reasonable and probable to say that Milton took the first hint of his *Paradise lost* from a noble and famous epic poet, than from a mean ridiculous comedian?

45. William Mason on *Samson Agonistes*

1753

Extract from William Mason, *Elfrida* (1753), Prefatory Letter ii, pp. v–vii.

William Mason (1724–97), the poet, wrote a monody on Pope in 1744 in imitation of 'Lycidas'; it was published in 1747 with a title page illustration showing Pope dying in his chair and joining the triumvirate of Chaucer, Shakespeare, and Milton. Many of Mason's poems allude to Milton or quote from him or show direct influence in language and prosody. He edited Thomas Gray's poems and letters, and frequently called attention to Milton's influence in them. He also used the pseudonym Malcolm Macgreggor, whose poems are also replete with Miltonic allusion.

Milton, you will tell me, is a noble exception to this observation. He is so, and would have been a nobler, had he not run into the contrary extreme. The contempt, in which perhaps with Justice, he held the age he liv'd in, prevented him from condescending either to amuse or to instruct it. He had, before, given to his unworthy Countrymen the noblest Poem that genius, conducted by antient art could produce; and he had seen them receive it with disregard, if not with dislike. Conscious therefore of his own dignity, and of their demerit, he look'd to posterity only for his reward, and to posterity only directed his future labours. Hence it was perhaps, that he form'd his *SAMPSON AGONISTES* on a model more simple and severe than Athens herself would have demanded; and took Æschylus for his master, rather than Sophocles or Euripides: intending by this conduct to put as great a distance as possible between himself and his contemporary writers; and to make his work (as he himself said) *much different from what amongst them passed for the best.*

The success of the Poem was, accordingly, what one would have expected. The age, it appeared in, treated it with total neglect; neither hath that posterity, to which he appealed, and which has done justice to most of his other writings, as yet given to this excellent piece its full measure of popular and universal fame. Perhaps in your closet, and that of a few more, who unaffectedly admire genuine nature and ancient simplicity, the *Agonistes* may hold a distinguished rank. Yet, surely, we cannot say (in Hamlet's phrase) *'that it pleases the Million; it is still Caviar to the general.'*

Hence, I think, I may conclude, that unless one would be content with a very late and very learned posterity, Milton's conduct in this point should not be followed. A Writer of Tragedy must certainly adapt himself more to the general taste; because the Dramatic, of all kinds of Poetry, ought to be most universally relish'd and understood. The Lyric Muse addresses herself to the imagination of a reader; the Didactic to his judgment; but the Tragic strikes directly on his passions.

46. Joseph Warton on Milton's defects

October 1753

Joseph Warton, letter, *Adventurer*, no. 101 (23 October 1753).

A most important literary critic of the eighteenth century, Joseph Warton (1722–1800) was frequently a champion of Milton. His contention in *An Essay on the Genius and Writings of Pope* (1756), from which an excerpt is here included as No. 48, that a 'correct' poetry does not exist goes a long way in nullifying the remarks of adverse critics of Milton earlier (and at times later) in the century.

Sir,

If we consider the high rank which Milton has deservedly obtained among our few English classics, we cannot wonder at the multitude of commentaries and criticisms of which he has been the subject. To these I have added some miscellaneous remarks; and if you should at first be inclined to reject them as trifling, you may, perhaps, determine to admit them, when you reflect that they are new.

The description of Eden in the fourth book of the *Paradise Lost*, and the battle of the angels in the sixth, are usually selected as the most striking examples of a florid and vigorous imagination: but it requires much greater strength of mind to form an assemblage of natural objects, and range them with propriety and beauty, than to bring together the greatest variety of the most splendid images, without any regard to their use or congruity; as in painting, he who, by the force of his imagination, can delineate a landscape, is deemed a greater master, than he who, by heaping rocks of coral upon tesselated pavements, can only make absurdity splendid, and dispose gaudy colours so as best to set off each other.

'Sapphire fountains that rolling over orient pearl run nectar, roses without thorns, trees that bear fruit of vegetable gold, and that weep odorous gums and balms,' are easily feigned; but having no relative beauty as pictures of nature, nor any absolute excellence as derived from truth, they can only please those who, when they read, exercise no faculty but fancy, and admire because they do not think.

If I shall not be thought to digress wholly from my subject, I would illustrate this remark, by comparing two passages, written by Milton and Fletcher, on nearly the same subject. The spirit in 'Comus' thus pays his address of thanks to the water-nymph Sabrina:

> May thy brimmed waves for this,
> Their full tribute never miss,
> From a thousand petty rills,
> That tumble down the snowy hills:
> Summer drought, or singed air,
> Never scorch thy tresses fair;
> Nor wet October's torrent flood
> Thy molten crystal fill with mud. [924–31]

Thus far the wishes are most proper for the welfare of a river goddess: the circumstance of summer not scorching her tresses, is highly poetical and elegant; but what follows, though it is pompous and majestic, is unnatural and far fetched:

> May thy billows roll ashore
> The beryl and the golden ore;
> May thy lofty head be crown'd
> With many a tow'r and terras round;
> And here and there thy banks upon,
> With groves of myrrh and cinnamon! [932–7]

The circumstance in the third and fourth lines is happily fancied; but what idea can the reader have of an English river rolling gold and the beryl ashore, or of groves of cinnamon growing on its banks? The images in the following passage of Fletcher are all simple and real, all appropriate and strictly natural:

> For thy kindness to me shewn,
> Never from thy banks be blown
> Any tree, with windy force,
> Cross thy stream to stop thy course;
> May no beast that comes to drink,
> With his horns cast down thy brink;
> May none that for thy fish do look,
> Cut thy banks to dam thy brook;
> Barefoot may no neighbour wade
> In thy cool streams, wife or maid,
> When the spawn on stones do lie,
> To wash their hemp, and spoil the fry.

The glaring picture of Paradise is not, in my opinion, so strong an evidence of Milton's force of imagination, as his representation of Adam and Eve when they left it, and of the passions with which they were agitated on that event.

Against his battle of the angels I have the same objections as against his garden of Eden. He has endeavoured to elevate his combatants by giving them the enormous stature of giants in romances, books of which he was known to be fond; and the prowess and behaviour of Michael as much resemble the feats of Ariosto's knight, as his two-handed sword does the weapons of chivalry: I think the sublimity of his genius much more visible in the first appearance of the fallen angels; the debates of the infernal peers; the passage of Satan through the dominions of Chaos, and his adventure with Sin and Death; the mission of Raphael to Adam; the conversations between Adam and his wife; the creation; the account which Adam gives of his first sensations, and of the approach of Eve from the hand of her Creator; the whole behaviour of Adam and Eve after the first transgression; and the prospect of the various states of the world, and history of man, exhibited in a vision to Adam.

In this vision, Milton judiciously represents Adam as ignorant of what disaster had befallen Abel, when he was murdered by his brother; but, during his conversation with Raphael, the poet seems to have forgotten this necessary and natural ignorance of the first man. How was it possible for Adam to discern what the angel meant by 'cubic phalanxes, by planets of aspect malign, by encamping on the foughten field, by van and rear, by standards and gonfalons and glittering tissues, by the griding sword, by embattled squadrons, chariots, and flaming arms, and fiery steeds?' And although Adam possessed a superior degree of knowledge, yet doubtless he had not skill enough in chymistry to understand Raphael, who informed him, that

> —Sulphurous and nitrous foam
> They found, they mingled, and with subtle art,
> Concocted and adusted, they reduc'd
> To blackest grain, and into store convey'd. [VI, 512–15]

And, surely, the nature of cannon was not much explained to Adam, who neither knew nor wanted the use of iron tools, by telling him that they resemble the hollow bodies of oak or fir,

> With branches lopt, in wood or mountain fell'd. [VI, 575]

He that never beheld the brute creation but in its pastimes and sports, must have greatly wondered, when the angel expressed the flight of the Satanic host, by saying, that they fled

> —As a herd
> Of goats or timorous flock, together throng'd. [VI, 856–7]

But as there are many exuberances in this poem, there appears to be also some defects. As the serpent was the instrument of the temptation, Milton minutely describes its beauty and allurements: and I have frequently wondered that he did not, for the same reason, give a more elaborate description of the tree of life; especially as he was remarkable for his knowledge and imitation of the sacred writings, and as the following passage in the Revelations afforded him a hint, from which his creative fancy might have worked up a striking picture: 'In the midst of the street of it, and of either side the river, was there the tree of life; which bare twelve manner of fruits, and yielded her fruit every month, and the leaves of the tree were for the healing of the nations.'

At the end of the fourth book, suspense and attention are excited to the utmost; a combat between Satan and the guardians of Eden is eagerly expected, and curiosity is impatient for the action and the catastrophe: but this horrid fray is prevented, expectation is cut off, and curiosity disappointed, by an expedient which, though applauded by Addison and Pope, and imitated from Homer and Virgil, will be deemed frigid and inartificial, by all who judge from their own sensations, and are not content to echo the decisions of others. The golden balances are held forth, 'which,' says the poet, 'are yet seen between Astrea and the Scorpion', Satan looks up, and perceiving that his scale mounted aloft, departs with the shades of night. To make such a use, at so critical a time, of Libra, a mere imaginary sign of the Zodiac, is scarcely justifiable in a poem founded on religious truth.

Among innumerable beauties in the *Paradise Lost*, I think the most transcendent is the speech of Satan at the beginning of the ninth book; in which his unextinguishable pride and fierce indignation against God, and his envy towards man, are so blended with an involuntary approbation of goodness, and disdain of the meanness and baseness of his present undertaking, as to render it, on account of the propriety of its sentiments and its turns of passion, the most natural, most spirited, and truly dramatic speech, that is, perhaps, to be found in any writer, whether ancient or modern; and yet Mr. Addison has passed it over, unpraised and unnoticed.

If an apology should be deemed necessary for the freedom here used with our inimitable bard, let me conclude in the words of Longinus: 'Whoever was carefully to collect the blemishes of Homer, Demosthenes, Plato, and of other celebrated writers, of the same rank, would find they bore not the least proportion to the sublimities and excellences with which their works abound.'

I am, Sir, your humble servant,

PALÆOPHIUS.

47. Shenstone on 'Lycidas'

1754

Extract from William Shenstone, 'A Prefatory Essay on Elegy' (c. 1754). William Shenstone, *Works* (1773), I, 21-2.

William Shenstone (1714–63) was a well-known but minor poet of the mid-eighteenth century. His poetry frequently reflects a study and love of Milton's works.

It is not impossible that some may think this metre too lax and prosaic: others, that even a more dissolute variety of numbers may have superior advantages. And, in favour of these last, might be produced the example of MILTON in his 'Lycidas', together with one or two recent and beautiful imitations of his versification in that monody. But this kind of argument, I am apt to think, must prove *too much*; since the writers I have in view seem capable enough of recommending any metre they shall chuse; though it must be owned also, that the choice *they* make of any, is at the same time the strongest presumption in its favour. . . .

The *previous* rhime in MILTON's 'Lycidas' is very frequently placed at such a distance from the following, that it is often dropt by the memory (much better employed in attending to the sentiment) before it be brought to join its partner: and this seems to be the greatest objection to *that* kind of versification. But then the peculiar *ease* and *variety* it admits of, are no doubt sufficient to overbalance the objection, and to give it the preference to any other, in an elegy of *length*.

48. Joseph Warton on the 'Nativity Ode'

1756

Extract from Joseph Warton, *An Essay on the Genius and Writings of Pope* (1806), I, 35–9; II, 178.

It may be observed in general, that description of the external beauties of nature, is usually the first effort of a young genius, before he hath studied manners and passions. Some of Milton's most early, as well as most exquisite pieces, are his 'Lycidas', 'L'Allegro', and 'Il Penseroso'; if we may except his 'Ode on the Nativity of Christ', which is, indeed, prior in the order of time, and in which a penetrating critic might have discovered the seeds of that boundless imagination, which afterwards was to produce the *Paradise Lost*. This ode, which, by the way, is not sufficiently read nor admired, is also of the descriptive kind; but the objects of its description are great, and striking to the imagination; the false deities of the Heathen forsaking their temples on the birth of our Saviour; divination and oracles at an end; which facts, though, perhaps, not historically true, are poetically beautiful ['Nativity Ode', ll. 181–8]. The lovers of poetry (and to such only I write) will not be displeased at my presenting them also with the following image, which is so strongly conceived, that, methinks, I see at this instant the daemon it represents: [ll. 205–10]. Attention is irresistibly awakened and engaged by that air of solemnity and enthusiasm that reigns in the following stanzas: [ll. 173–80]. Such is the power of true poetry, that one is almost inclined to believe the superstitions here alluded to, to be real; and the succeeding circumstances make one start, and look around: [ll. 189–94]. Methinks we behold the priests interrupted in the middle of the secret ceremonies they were performing, 'in their temples dim,' gazing with ghastly eyes on each other, and terrified, and wondering from whence these aërial voices should proceed! I have dwelt chiefly on this ode as much less celebrated than 'L'Allegro' and 'Il Penseroso', which are now universally known; but which, by a strange fatality, lay in a sort of obscurity, the private enjoyment of a few curious readers, till they were set to admirable music by Mr. Handel. And, indeed, this volume of Milton's Miscellaneous Poems has not till very lately met with suitable regard. Shall I offend any rational admirer of POPE, by remarking, that these juvenile descriptive poems of Milton, as well as his Latin Elegies, are of a strain far more exalted than any the former author can boast? Let me add, at the same time, what justice obliges me to add, that they are far more incorrect. For in the very ode before us, occur one or two passages, that are puerile and affected to a degree not to be paralleled in the purer, but less elevated, compositions of POPE. The season being winter when Jesus was born, Milton says,

> Nature, in awe to HIM,*
> Had dofft her gawdy trim. [ll. 32–3]

And afterwards observes, in a very epigrammatic and forced thought, unsuitable to the dignity of the subject, and of the rest of the ode, that 'she wooed the air, to hide her guilty front with innocent snow,' [ll. 40–4].

But it was the vigorous and creative imagination of MILTON, superior to the prejudices of his time,† that exhibited in his EDEN, the first hints and outlines of what a beautiful garden should be; for even his beloved ARIOSTO and TASSO, in their luxuriant pictures of the gardens of ALCINA and ARMIDA, shewed they were not free from the unnatural and *narrow* taste of their countrymen; and even his master, SPENSER, has an *artificial fountain* in the midst of his *bowre of bliss*.

---

* This conceit, with the rest, however, is more excusable, if we recollect how great a reader, especially at this time, Milton was of the Italian Poets. It is certain that Milton, in the beginning of the ode, had the third sonnet of Petrarch strong in his fancy.

† How astonishing, that his spirit could not be diminished or crushed by poverty, danger, blindness, disgrace, solitude, and old age!

49. William Mason on Milton's achievement

1756

Extract from William Mason, 'Ode I: To Memory' (1756), stanza
iii. William Mason, *Poems* (1764), 25–6.

Rise, hallow'd MILTON! rise, and say,
  How, at thy gloomy close of day;
How, when 'deprest by Age, beset with wrongs;'
When 'fall'n on evil days and evil tongues;'
    When Darkness, brooding on thy sight,
    Exil'd the sov'reign lamp of light;
Say, what could then one chearing hope diffuse?
What friends were thine, save Mem'ry and the Muse?
    Hence the rich spoils, thy studious youth
    Caught from the stores of antient Truth:
Hence all thy classic wandrings could explore,
When Rapture led thee to the Latian shore;
    Each Scene, that Tiber's bank supply'd;
    Each Grace, that play'd on Arno's side;
The tepid Gales, thro' Tuscan glades that fly;
The blue Serene, that spreads Hesperia's sky;
    Were still thine own: thy ample Mind
    Each charm receiv'd, retain'd, combin'd,
And thence 'the nightly Visitant,' that came
To touch thy bosom with her sacred flame,
    Recall'd the long-lost beams of grace,
    That whilom shot from Nature's face,
When GOD, in Eden, o'er her youthful breast
Spread with his own right hand Perfection's gorgeous vest.

50. Burke on Milton's sublimity

1756

Extract from Edmund Burke, *A Philosophical Enquiry into the Origin of Our Ideas of the Sublime and Beautiful* (1757), 48–9, 182–3.

Best known for his political achievement as Member of Parliament, Edmund Burke (1729–97) championed the emancipation of the American colonies (but not the French revolution), the Irish, India, and the House of Commons from various governmental controls. *A Philosophical Enquiry into the Origin of Our Ideas of the Sublime and Beautiful* first appeared in 1756. Its thrust is that the source of the sublime lies in that which excites pain and danger and that beauty, while creating love, is brief, smooth, and bright.

The ideas of eternity, and infinity, are among the most affecting we have, and yet perhaps there is nothing of which we really understand so little, as of infinity and eternity. We don't any where meet a more sublime description than this justly celebrated one of Milton, wherein he gives the portrait of Satan with a dignity so suitable to the subject [I, 589–99]. Here is a very noble picture; and in what does this poetical picture consist? in images of a tower, an archangel, the sun rising through mists, or in an eclipse, the ruin of monarchs, and the revolutions of kingdoms. The mind is hurried out of itself, by a croud of great and confused images; which affect because they are crouded and confused. For separate them, and you lose much of the greatness, and join them, and you infallibly lose the clearness. The images raised by poetry are always of this obscure kind; though in general the effects of poetry, are by no means to be attributed to the images it raises; which point we shall examine more at large hereafter. But painting, with only the superadded pleasure of imitation, can only affect simply by the images it presents; but even in painting a judicious obscurity in some things contributes to the effect of the picture; because the images in painting are exactly similar to those in nature; and in nature dark, confused, uncertain images have a greater power on the fancy to form the grander passions than those which are more clear and determinate. But where and when this observation may be applied to practice, and how far it shall be extended, will be better deduced from the nature of the subject, and from the occasion, than from any rules that can be given. . . . As a further instance, let us consider those lines of Milton, where he describes the travels of the fallen angels through their dismal habitation, [II, 618–22]. Here is displayed the force of union in

Rocks, caves, lakes, dens, bogs, fens and shades;

which yet would lose the greatest part of their effect, if they were not the

Rocks, caves, lakes, dens, bogs, fens and shades—of death. [II, 621]

This idea or affection caused by a word, which nothing but a word could annex to the others, raises a very great degree of the sublime; and it is raised yet higher by what follows, a *'universe of death.'* Here are again two ideas not presentible but by language; and an union of them great and amazing beyond conception. Whoever attentively considers this passage of Milton, and indeed all of the best and most affecting descriptions of poetry, will find, that it does not in general produce its end by raising the images of things, but by exciting a passion similar to that which real objects excite by other instruments.

51. Hume on Milton

1757

Extract from David Hume, *The History of England, from The Invasion of Julius Caesar, to the Abdication of James the Second* (1762), V, 529–30.

David Hume (1711–76) was a major philosopher, most frequently known today for his *Enquiry Concerning Human Understanding* (1748). He concluded that knowledge results from causation; it is the linkage of 'rational' judgments which are but impressions arising from custom or expectations arising from experience. His *History of Great Britain*, which appeared in 1754–7, proposed to examine the path by which inroads on the monarchic prerogative came about. With such a Tory position, his attitude toward Milton is evident.

It is, however, remarkable that the greatest genius by far that shone out in England during this period, was deeply engaged with those fanatics, and even prostituted his pen in theological controversy, in factious disputes, and in justifying the most violent measures of the party. This was John Milton, whose poems are admirable, though liable to some objections; his prose writings disagreeable, though not altogether defective in genius. Nor are all his poems equal: his *Paradise Lost*, his 'Comus', and a few others, shine out amidst some flat and insipid compositions. Even in the *Paradise Lost*, his capital performance, there are very long passages, amounting to near a third of the work, almost wholly destitute of harmony and elegance, nay, of all vigor of imagination. This natural inequality in Milton's genius was much increased by the inequalities in his subject; of which some parts are of themselves the most lofty that can enter into human conception; others would have required the most labored elegance of composition to support them. It is certain that this author, when in a happy mood, and employed on a noble subject, is the most wonderfully sublime of any poet in any language, Homer, and Lucretius, and Tasso not excepted. More concise

237

than Homer, more simple than Tasso, more nervous than Lucretius, had he lived in a later age, and learned to polish some rudeness in his verses; he had enjoyed better fortune, and possessed leisure to watch the returns of genius in himself; he had attained the pinnacle of perfection, and borne away the palm of epic poetry.

It is well known that Milton never enjoyed in his lifetime the reputation which he deserved. His *Paradise Lost* was long neglected: prejudices against an apologist for the regicides, and against a work not wholly purged from the cant of former times, kept the ignorant world from perceiving the prodigious merit of that performance. Lord Somers, by encouraging a good edition of it, about twenty years after the author's death, first brought it into request; and Tonson, in his dedication of a smaller edition, speaks of it as a work just beginning to be known. Even during the prevalence of Milton's party, he seems never to have been much regarded; and Whitlocke talks of one Milton, as he calls him, a blind man, who was employed in translating a treaty with Sweden into Latin. These forms of expression are amusing to posterity, who consider how obscure Whitlocke himself, though lord-keeper and ambassador, and indeed a man of great ability and merit, has become in comparison of Milton![1]

It is not strange that Milton received no encouragement after the restoration: it is more to be admired that he escaped with his life. Many of the cavaliers blamed extremely that lenity towards him, which was so honorable in the king, and advantageous to posterity. It is said that he had saved Davenant's life during the protectorship; and Davenant in return afforded him like protection after the restoration; being sensible that men of letters ought always to regard their sympathy of taste as a more powerful band of union, than any difference of party or opinion as a source of animosity. It was during a state of poverty, blindness, disgrace, danger, and old age, that Milton composed his wonderful poem, which not only surpassed all the performances of his contemporaries, but all the compositions which had flowed from his pen during the vigor of his age and the height of his prosperity. This circumstance is not the least remarkable of all those which attend that great genius. He died in 1674, aged sixty-six.

[1] See Sir Bulstrode Whitelocke, *Memorials of the English Affairs* (1682), p. 633, under May 1656.

52. Wilkie on epic poetry

1757

Extract from William Wilkie, *The Epigoniad* (Edinburgh, 1757), preface.

Known as the Scottish Homer, William Wilkie (1721–72) was a professor of natural philosophy and author of *The Epigoniad* (1757), in nine books, based on the fourth book of the *Iliad*. His use of heroic couplets indicates his displeasure with Milton's verse.

But, instead of a thousand arguments to this purpose, let us only consider the machinery which must be employed in an epic poem: how Heaven and Hell must both be put in motion, and brought into the action, how events altogether out of the common road of human affairs, and no ways countenanced either by reason or by experience, must be offered to men's imagination, so as to be admitted for true. Let us consider all this, and it will appear, that there is nothing which poets ought more carefully to avoid, than interfering with such regular and well vouched accounts of things as would effectually confute their fable, and make the meanest reader reject it with contempt. This is a point of prudence which no poet has yet neglected with impunity. Lucan, according to his usual rashness, has taken for the subject of an epic poem, one of the best known events which he could have pitched upon in the whole series of human affairs; and in order to distinguish himself from a mere historian, is often under a necessity of starting from his subject, and employing the whole force of a very lively and fruitful invention, in unnecessary descriptions and trifling digressions. This, besides other inconveniences of greater importance, gives such an appearance of labour and straining to his whole performance, as takes much from the merit of it, with all who have any notion of ease, majesty, and simplicity in writing. He, and all other poets who have fallen into the same errour, find always this disadvantage attending it, that the true and fictitious parts of their work refuse to unite, and standing as it were at a distance, upon terms of mutual aversion, reproach each other with their peculiar defects. Fiction accuses truth of narrowness and want of dignity; and this again represents the other as vain and extravagant. Spenser, who, in his *Fairy Queen*, not only treats of matters within the sphere of regular history, but describes even the transactions of his own time, in order to avoid the inconveniences which he knew to be almost inseparable from such an attempt, covers his story with a veil of allegory, that few of his readers are able to penetrate. This stratagem leaves him at full liberty in the exercise of his invention; but he pays, in my opinion, too dear for that privilege, by sacrificing to it all the weight and authority which a mixture of received tradition and real geography would have given to his fable. Milton takes the subjects of both his great poems from true history, yet does not succeed the worse upon that account. But it is to be remembered, that his chief actors are not men, but divine and angelical beings; and that it is the human nature only which suffers by a just representation, and loses in point of dignity, when truly known. Besides, the historical circumstances upon which he builds are so few, and of so extraordinary a nature, that they are easily accommodated to poetical fiction; and therefore, instead of limiting him, and setting bounds to his invention, they serve only to countenance and give a degree of credibility to whatever he pleases to feign. . . .

It must be acknowledged, that in Milton's *Paradise Lost*, the persons in machinery over-shadow the human characters, and that the heroes of the poem are all of them immortals: but then it is to be remembered, that *Paradise Lost* is a work altogether irregular; that the subject of it is not epic, but tragic; and that Adam and Eve are not designed to be objects of admiration, but of pity: it is tragic in its plot, and epic in its dress and machinery: as a tragedy, it does not fall under the present question; and as an epic poem, it evades it likewise, by a circumstance very uncommon, viz. that in the part of it which is properly epic, there are no human persons at all.

I have in this manner endeavoured to prove that mythology is necessary to an epic poem, and that the chief objections to the use of it are of little consequence. I proceed to establish the other proposition which I mentioned, and show, that the true God ought not to be brought into a work of that nature. And if this proposition can be made out, it will easily appear from it and the preceding one taken together, that poets are under a necessity of having recourse to a false theology, and that they are not to be blamed for doing what the nature of epic poetry on the one hand, and respect to the true religion on the other, render necessary and unavoidable. For proving the point in question, I need only observe, that no person can appear with advantage in poetry, who is not represented according to the form and condition of a man. This art addresses itself chiefly to the imagination, a faculty which apprehends nothing in the way of character that is not human, and according to the analogy of that nature of which we ourselves are conscious. But it would be equally impious and absurd to represent the deity in this manner, and to contrive for him a particular character, and method of acting, agreeable to the prejudices of weak and ignorant mortals. In the early ages of the church, he thought fit to accommodate himself, by such a piece of condescension, to the notions and apprehensions of his creatures: but it would be indecent in any man to use the same freedom, and do that for God, which he only has a right to do for himself. The author of *Paradise Lost* has offended notoriously in this respect; and, though no encomiums are too great for him as a poet, he is justly chargeable with impiety, for presuming to represent the Divine Nature, and the mysteries of religion, according to the narrowness of human prejudice: his dialogues between the Father and the Son; his employing a Being of infinite wisdom in discussing the subtleties of school divinity; the sensual views which he gives of the happiness of Heaven, admitting into it, as a part, not only real eating and drinking, but another kind of animal pleasure too by no means more refined: these, and such like circumstances, though perfectly poetical, and agreeable to the genius of an art which adapts every thing to the human mode, are, at the same time, so inconsistent with truth, and the exalted ideas which we ought to entertain of divine things, that they must be highly offensive to all such as have just impressions of religion, and would not choose to see a system of doctrine revealed from Heaven, reduced to a state of conformity with heathen superstition. True theology ought not to be used in an epic poem, for another reason, of no less weight than that which has been mentioned, *viz.* That the human characters which it represents should never be formed upon a perfect moral plan, but have their piety (for instance) tinctured with superstition, and their general behaviour influenced by affection, passion, and prejudice. This will be thought a violent paradox, by such as do not know that imperfect characters interest us more than perfect ones, and that we are doubly instructed when we see, in one and the same example, both what we ought to follow and what we ought to avoid. Accordingly Horace, in his Epistle to Lollius, where he bestows the highest encomiums upon the *Iliad*, as a work which delineated vice and virtue better than the writings of the most celebrated philosophers, says of it, notwithstanding, that it is taken up in describing the animosities of foolish kings and infatuated nations. To go to the bottom of this matter, it will be proper to observe, that men are capable of two sorts of character, which may be distinguished by the names of natural and artificial. The natural character implies all those feelings, passions, desires, and opinions, which men have from nature and common experience, independent of speculation and moral refinement. A person of this character looks upon outward prosperity as a real good, and considers the calamities of life as real evils; loves his friends, hates his enemies, admires his superiors, is assuming with respect to his inferiors, and stands upon terms of rivalship with his equals; in short, is governed by all those passions and opinions that possess the hearts and determine the actions of ordinary men. The force and magnitude of this character is in proportion to the strength of these natural dispositions; and its virtue consists in having the generous and beneficent ones predominant. As to that sort of character, again, which I distinguished by the name of artificial; it consists in a habit of mind formed by discipline, according to the cool and dispassionate dictates of reason. This character is highly moral, but, in my opinion, far less poetical than the other, by being less fit for interesting our affections, which are formed by the wise Author of our nature for embracing such beings as are of the same temper and complexion with ourselves, and are marked with the common infirmities of human nature. Persons of the high philosophic character, are too firm and unmoved, amidst the calamities they meet with, to excite much sympathy, and are too much superior to the sallies of passion and partial affection, the popular marks of generosity and greatness of mind, ever to be much admired by the bulk of mankind. If the most accomplished poet in the world should take a rigid philosopher for the chief character either of an epic poem or a tragedy, it is easy to conjecture what would be the success of such an attempt, the work would assume the character of its hero, and be cold, dispassionate, and uninteresting. There is, however, a species of panegyric proper for such sort of perfection, and it may be represented to advantage, either in history or prose dialogue, but it will never strike the bulk of mankind. Plato, in his apology of Socrates, deceives us; as Mr. Addison likewise does in his tragedy of Cato: for both of them attempt to persuade us, that we are affected with the contemplation of unshaken fortitude, while we are only sympathizing with suffering innocence. The tenderness of humanity appearing through the hardness of the philosophic character, is that which affects us in both instances, and not that unconquered greatness of mind, which occasions rather wonder and astonishment than genuine affection.

From what has been said, it is easy to infer, that the great characters, both in epic poetry and tragedy, ought not to be formed upon a perfect moral plan, and therefore heroes themselves must often be represented as acting from such motives, and governed by such affections, as impartial reason cannot approve of: but it would be highly indecent to make a being, whom religion teaches us to consider as perfect, enter into the views of such persons, and exert himself in order to promote their extravagant enterprizes. This would be to bring down the infinite wisdom of God to the level of human folly, and to make him altogether such an one as ourselves.

A false theology, therefore, ought rather to be employed in poetical compositions than the true; for, as the superior beings which are introduced must of necessity be represented as assuming the passions and opinions of those whom they favour, it is surely much safer to employ a set of imaginary beings for this purpose, than God himself, and the blessed angels, who ought always to be objects of our reverence.

The same reasoning which leads to this conclusion, will likewise make us sensible, that among false religions, those ought to be preferred which are least connected with the true; for the superstitions which priests and poets have built upon the Christian faith, dishonour it, and therefore should, if possible, be buried in oblivion. The ancient Greek theology seems upon all accounts the fittest. It has no connection with the true system, and therefore may be treated with the greatest freedom, without indecency or ground of offence. It consists of a number of beautiful fables, suited to the taste of the most lively and ingenious people that ever existed, and so much calculated to ravish and transport a warm imagination, that many poets in modern times, who proceeded upon a different theology, have notwithstanding been so bewitched with its charms, as to admit it into their works, though it clashed violently with the system which they had adopted. Milton is remarkable in this respect; and the more so, as his poem is altogether of a religious nature, and the subject of it taken from holy writ.

53. Blair on the sublime, the twin poems, and *Paradise Lost*

1759-60

Extract from Hugh Blair, *Lectures on Rhetoric and Belles Lettres* (1796). Lecture 4: i, 78–9; lecture 40: iii, 154–5; lecture 42: iii, 209; lecture 44: iii, 265–71.

A Scottish divine and professor of rhetoric, Hugh Blair (1718–1800), known also for his sermons, contributed the important *Lectures*, written and delivered *c.* 1759–60, to the wealth of eighteenth-century aesthetics and language-oriented literary criticism.

The boldness, freedom, and variety of our blank verse, is infinitely more favourable than rhyme, to all kinds of Sublime poetry. The fullest proof of this is afforded by Milton; an author whose genius led him eminently to the Sublime. The whole first and second books of *Paradise Lost*, are continued instances of it. Take only, for an example, the following noted description of Satan, after his fall, appearing at the head of the infernal hosts: [I, 589–600]. Here concur a variety of sources of the Sublime: the principal object eminently great; a high superior nature, fallen indeed, but erecting itself against distress; the grandeur of the principal object heightened, by associating it with so noble an idea as that of the sun suffering an eclipse; this picture shaded with all those images of change and trouble, of darkness and terror, which coincide so finely with the Sublime emotion; and the whole expressed in a style and versification, easy, natural, and simple, but magnificent. . . . But, of all the English Poems in the Descriptive Style, the richest and most remarkable are, Milton's 'Allegro' and 'Penseroso'. The collection of gay images on the one hand, and of melancholy ones on the other, exhibited in these two small, but inimitably fine Poems, are as exquisite as can be conceived. They are, indeed, the storehouse whence many succeeding Poets have enriched their descriptions of similar subjects; and they alone are sufficient for illustrating the observations which I made concerning the proper selection of circumstances in Descriptive Writing. Take, for instance, the following passage from the 'Penseroso': [ll. 65–94].

Here, there are no unmeaning general expressions; all is particular: all is picturesque; nothing forced or exaggerated; but a simple Style, and a collection of strong expressive images, which are all of one class, and recal a number of similar ideas of the melancholy kind: particularly, the walk by moon-light; the sound of the curfew bell heard distant; the dying embers in the chamber; the bellman's call; and the lamp seen at midnight, in the high lonely tower. We may observe, too, the conciseness of the Poet's manner. He does not rest long on one circumstance, or employ a great many words to describe it; which always makes the impression faint and languid; but placing it in one strong point of view, full and clear before the Reader, he there leaves it. . . .

It has been the practice of all Epic Poets, to select some one personage, whom they distinguish above all the rest, and make the hero of the tale. This is considered as essential to Epic Composition, and is attended with several advantages. It renders the unity of the subject more sensible, when there is one principal figure, to which, as to a centre, all the rest refer. It tends to interest us more in the enterprize which is carried on; and it gives the Poet an opportunity of exerting his talents for adorning and displaying one character, with peculiar splendour. It has been asked, who then is the hero of *Paradise Lost*? The Devil, it has been answered by some Critics; and, in consequence of this idea, much ridicule and censure has been thrown upon Milton. But they have mistaken that Author's intention, by proceeding upon a supposition, that, in the conclusion of the Poem, the hero must needs be triumphant. Whereas Milton followed a different plan, and has given a tragic conclusion to a Poem, otherwise Epic in its form. For Adam is undoubtedly his hero; that is, the capital and most interesting figure in his Poem. . . .

Milton, of whom it remains now to speak, has chalked out for himself a new, and very extraordinary road, in Poetry. As soon as we open his *Paradise Lost*, we find ourselves introduced all at once into an invisible world, and surrounded with celestial and infernal beings. Angels and Devils are not the machinery, but principal actors, in the Poem; and what, in any other composition, would be the marvellous, is here only the natural course of events. A subject so remote from the affairs of this world, may furnish ground to those who think such discussions material, to bring it into doubt, whether *Paradise Lost* can properly be classed among Epic Poems. By whatever name it is to be called, it is, undoubtedly, one of the highest efforts of poetical genius; and in one great characteristic of the Epic Poem, Majesty and Sublimity, it is fully equal to any that bear that name.

How far the Author was altogether happy in the choice of his subject, may be questioned. It has led him into very difficult ground. Had he taken a subject that was more human, and less theological; that was more connected with the occurrences of life, and afforded a greater display of the characters and passions of men, his Poem would, perhaps, have, to the bulk of Readers, been more pleasing and attractive. But the subject which he has chosen, suited the daring sublimity of his genius. It is a subject for which Milton alone was fitted; and in the conduct of it, he has shewn a stretch both of imagination and invention, which is perfectly wonderful. It is astonishing how, from the few hints given us in the Sacred Scriptures, he was able to raise so complete and regular a structure; and to fill his Poem with such a variety of incidents. Dry and harsh passages sometimes occur. The Author appears, upon some occasions, a Metaphysician and a Divine, rather than a Poet. But the general tenor of his work is interesting; he seizes and fixes the imagination; engages, elevates, and affects us as we proceed; which is always a sure test of merit in an Epic Composition. The artful change of his objects; the scene laid now in Earth, now in Hell, and now in Heaven, affords a sufficient diversity; while unity of plan is, at the same time, perfectly supported. We have still life, and calm scenes, in the employments of Adam and Eve in Paradise; and we have busy scenes, and great actions, in the enterprize of Satan, and the wars of the Angels. The innocence, purity, and amiableness of our first parents, opposed to the pride and ambition of Satan, furnishes a happy contrast, that reigns throughout the whole Poem; only the Conclusion, as I before observed, is too tragic for Epic Poetry.

The nature of the subject did not admit any great display of characters; but such as could be introduced, are supported with much propriety. Satan, in particular, makes a striking figure, and is, indeed, the best drawn character in the Poem. Milton has not described him, such as we suppose an infernal spirit to be. He has, more suitably to his own purpose, given him a human, that is, a mixed character, not altogether void of some good qualities. He is brave and faithful to his troops. In the midst of his impiety, he is not without remorse. He is even touched with pity for our first parents; and justifies himself in his design against them, from the necessity of his situation. He is actuated by ambition and resentment, rather than by pure malice. In short,

Milton's Satan is no worse than many a conspirator or factious chief, that makes a figure in history. The different characters of Beelzebub, Moloch, Belial, are exceedingly well painted in those eloquent speeches which they make in the Second Book. The good Angels, though always described with dignity and propriety, have more uniformity than the Infernal Spirits in their appearance; though among them, too, the dignity of Michael, the mild condescension of Raphael, and the tried fidelity of Abdiel, form proper characteristical distinctions. The attempt to describe God Almighty himself, and to recount dialogues between the Father and the Son, was too bold and arduous, and is that wherein our Poet, as was to have been expected, has been most unsuccessful. With regard to his human characters; the innocence of our first parents, and their love, are finely and delicately painted. In some of his speeches to Raphael and to Eve, Adam is, perhaps, too knowing and refined for his situation. Eve is more distinctly characterised. Her gentleness, modesty, and frailty, mark very expressively a female character.

Milton's great and distinguishing excellence is, his sublimity. In this, perhaps, he excels Homer; as there is no doubt of his leaving Virgil, and every other Poet, far behind him. Almost the whole of the First and Second Books of *Paradise Lost* are continued instances of the sublime. The prospect of Hell and of the fallen Host, the appearance and behaviour of Satan, the consultation of the infernal chiefs, and Satan's flight through Chaos to the borders of this world, discover the most lofty ideas that ever entered into the conception of any Poet. In the Sixth Book also, there is much grandeur, particularly in the appearance of the Messiah; though some parts of that book are censurable; and the witticisms of the Devils upon the effect of their artillery, form an intolerable blemish. Milton's sublimity is of a different kind from that of Homer. Homer's is generally accompanied with fire and impetuosity; Milton's possesses more of a calm and amazing grandeur. Homer warms and hurries us along; Milton fixes us in a state of astonishment and elevation. Homer's sublimity appears most in the description of actions; Milton's, in that of wonderful and stupendous objects.

But though Milton is most distinguished for his sublimity, yet there is also much of the beautiful, the tender, and the pleasing, in many parts of his work. When the scene is laid in Paradise, the imagery is always of the most gay and smiling kind. His descriptions show an uncommonly fertile imagination; and in his similes, he is, for the most part, remarkably happy. They are seldom improperly introduced; seldom either low, or trite. They generally present to us images taken from the sublime or the beautiful class of objects; if they have any faults, it is their alluding too frequently to matters of learning, and to fables of antiquity. In the latter part of *Paradise Lost*, there must be confessed to be a falling off. With the fall of our first parents, Milton's genius seems to decline. Beauties, however, there are, in the concluding Books, of the tragic kind. The remorse and contrition of the guilty pair, and their lamentations over Paradise, when they are obliged to leave it, are very moving. The last Episode of the Angel's showing Adam the fate of his posterity, is happily imagined; but, in many places, the execution is languid.

Milton's language and versification have high merit. His Style is full of majesty, and wonderfully adapted to his subject. His blank verse is harmonious and diversified, and affords the most complete example of the elevation, which our language is capable of attaining by the force of numbers. It does not flow like the French verse, in tame, regular, uniform melody, which soon tires the ear; but is sometimes smooth and flowing, sometimes rough; varied in its cadence, and intermixed with discords, so as to suit the strength and freedom of Epic Composition. Neglected and prosaic lines, indeed, we sometimes meet with; but, in a work so long, and in the main so harmonious, these may be forgiven.

On the whole; *Paradise Lost* is a Poem that abounds with beauties of every kind, and that justly entitles its Author to a degree of fame not inferior to any Poet; though it must be also admitted to have many inequalities. It is the lot of almost every high and daring genius, not to be uniform and correct. Milton is too frequently theological and metaphysical; sometimes harsh in his language; often too technical in his words, and affectedly ostentatious of his learning. Many of his faults must be attributed to the pedantry of the age in which he lived. He discovers a vigour, a grasp of genius equal to every thing that is great; if at some times he falls much below himself, at other times he rises above every Poet, of the antient or modern world.

54. Lyttelton on Milton

1760

Extract from George, Lord Lyttelton, 'Dialogues of the Dead', no. xiv (1760). George E. Ayscough, ed., *The Works of George, Lord Lyttelton* (1776), ii, 196–7.

George, Lord Lyttelton (1709–73), an important political and literary figure of the mid-century, published his *Dialogues of the Dead* in 1760. These imaginary conversations offer comment on literature, philosophy, religion, politics, etc.

POPE. But let me now, in my turn, desire your opinion of our epick poet, Milton.

BOILEAU. Longinus perhaps would prefer him to all other writers: for he surpasses even Homer in the *sublime*. But other criticks, who require variety, and agreeableness, and a correct regularity of thought and judgement, in an epick poem, who can endure no absurdities, no extravagant fictions, would place him far below Virgil.

POPE. His genius was indeed so vast and sublime, that his poem seems beyond the limits of criticism: as his subject is beyond the limits of nature. The bright and excessive blaze of poetical fire, which shines in so many parts of the *Paradise Lost*, will hardly permit the dazzled eye to see its faults.

BOILEAU. The taste of your countrymen is much changed since the days of Charles II, when Dryden was thought a greater poet than Milton!

POPE. The politicks of Milton at that time brought his poetry into disgrace: for it is a rule with the English; they see no good in a man whose politicks they dislike. But, as their notions of government are apt to change, men of parts, whom they have slighted, become their favourite authors; and others, who have possest their warmest admiration, are in their turn under-valued.

55. Gray on Milton's prosody

1760

Extract from Thomas Gray, 'Observations on English Metre' (c. 1760). Edmund Gosse, ed., *The Works of Thomas Gray* (1884), I, 332–3.

The chief poet of the mid-century was Thomas Gray (1716–71). His poetry shows Milton's influence often through quotation, through allusion, and through general similarities of language.

Verses of *eight* syllables are so far from being obliged to have their cesura on the fourth, that Milton, the best example of an exquisite ear that I can produce, varies it continually, as,

To live with her, / and live with thee . . .	On the 4th
In unreproved / pleasure free	5th
To hear the lark / begin his flight	4th
And singing / startle the dull night . . .	3d
Where the great sun / begins his state . . .	4th
The clouds / in thousand liveries dight . .	2d
With masque / and antique pageantry . . .	2d

The more we attend to the composition of Milton's harmony, the more we shall be sensible how he loved to vary his pauses, his measures, and his feet, which gives that enchanting air of freedom and wildness to his versification, unconfined by any rules but those which his own feeling and the nature of his subject demanded. Thus he mixes the line of eight syllables with that of seven, the Trochee and the Spondee with the Iambic foot, and the single rhyme with the double. He changes the cesura as frequently in the heptasyllabic measure, as,

Oft on a plat / of rising ground . .	(Octosyll.)	
I hear / the far-off curfew sound . .	(Oct.)	On the 2d
Over some / wide-water'd shore . .		3d
Swinging slow / with sullen roar: .		3d
Or if the air / will not permit, &c .	(Oct.)	4th

Far from all resort / of mirth. . .		On the 5th
Save the cricket / on the hearth . .		4th
Or the bellman's / drowsy charm .		4th

56. Gibbon on the relationship of religion

1761

Extract from Edward Gibbon, *Essay on the Study of Literature* (1764), 23–4.

Edward Gibbon (1737–94), author of the major *History of the Decline and Fall of the Roman Empire*, first published the work excerpted here in French in 1761. The English version appeared in 1764.

XIII.* The ancient mythology, which attributed life and intelligence to all nature, extended its influence to the pen of the Poet. Inspired by the muse, he sung the attributes, the adventures and misfortunes of his fabulous deities. That Infinite Being, which religion, and philosophy have made known to us, is above such description: the sublimest flights become puerile on such a subject. The almighty *Fiat* of Moses strikes us with admiration; but reason cannot comprehend, nor imagination describe, the operations of a deity, at whose command alone millions of worlds are made to tremble: nor can we read with any satisfactory pleasure of the devil, in Milton, warring for two whole days in heaven against the armies of the Omnipotent.†

* The golden compasses, with which the Creator, in Milton, measures the universe, excite surprize. Perhaps, however, it is puerile in him; tho' such an image had been truly sublime in Homer. Our philosophical ideas of the Deity are injurious to the Poet. The same attributes debase our Divinity which would have extolled the Jupiter of the Greeks. The sublime genius of Milton was cramped by the system of our religion, and never appeared to so great an advantage as when he shook it a little off; while on the contrary, Propertius, a cold and insipid declaimer, owes all his reputation to the agreeable pictures of his Mythology.

† In religion [marginal note].

57. Kames on rhyme and blank verse

1762

Extract from Henry Home, Lord Kames, *Elements of Criticism* (Boston, 1796), ii, 128–30, 133, 156, 302–3.

Henry Home, Lord Kames (1696–1782), produced two works significant in our own times as well as his: a study of psychology, *Introduction to the Art of Thinking* (1761), and a major statement of aesthetic theory, *Elements of Criticism* (1762).

Our verse is extremely cramped by rhyme; and the peculiar advantage of blank verse is, that it is at liberty to attend the imagination in its boldest flights. Rhyme necessarily divides verse into couplets; each couplet makes a complete musical period, the parts of which are divided by pauses, and the whole summed up by a full close at the end: the melody begins anew with the next couplet: and in this manner a composition in rhyme proceeds couplet after couplet. I have often had occasion to mention the correspondence and concord that ought to subsist between sound and sense; from which it is a plain inference, that if a couplet be a complete period with regard to melody, it ought regularly to be the same with regard to sense. As it is extremely difficult to support such strictness of composition, licences are indulged, as explained above; which, however, must be used with discretion, so as to preserve some degree of concord between the sense and the music; there ought never to be a full close in the sense but at the end of a couplet; and there ought always to be some pause in the sense at the end of every couplet: the same period as to sense may be extended through several couplets; but each couplet ought to contain a distinct member distinguished by a pause in the sense as well as in the sound; and the whole ought to be closed with a complete cadence. Rules such as these, must confine rhyme within very narrow bounds: a thought of any extent, cannot be reduced within its compass: the sense must be curtailed and broken into parts, to make it square with the curtness of the melody; and beside, short periods afford no latitude for inversion.

I have examined this point with the stricter accuracy, in order to give a just notion of blank verse; and to show, that a slight difference in form may produce a great difference in substance. Blank verse has the same pauses and accents with rhyme, and a pause at the end of every line, like what concludes the first line of a couplet. In a word, the rules of melody in blank verse, are the same that obtain with respect to the first line of a couplet, but being disengaged from rhyme, or from couplets, there is access to make every line run into another, precisely as to make the first line of a couplet run into the second. There must be a musical pause at the end of every line; but this pause is so slight as not to require a pause in the sense: and accordingly the sense may be carried on with or without pauses, till a period of the utmost extent be completed by a full close both in the sense and the sound: there is no restraint, other than that this full close be at the end of a line; and this restraint is necessary, in order to preserve a coincidence between sense and sound, which ought to be aimed at in general, and is indispensable in the case of a full close, because it has a striking effect. Hence the fitness of blank verse for inversion: and consequently the lustre of its pauses and accents; for which, as observed above, there is greater scope in inversion, than when words run in their natural order.

In the second section of this chapter it is shown, that nothing contributes more than inversion to the force and elevation of language: the couplets of rhyme confine inversion within narrow limits; nor would the elevation of inversion, were there access for it in rhyme, readily accord with the humbler tone of that sort of verse. It is universally agreed, that the loftiness of Milton's style supports admirably the sublimity of his subject; and it is not less certain, that the loftiness of his style arises chiefly from inversion. Shakespear deals little in inversion; but his blank verse being a sort of measured prose, is perfectly well adapted to the stage, where laboured inversion is highly improper, because in dialogue it never can be natural. . . . I cannot set this matter in a better light, than by presenting to the reader a French translation of the following passage of Milton: [*PL* IV, 288–99]. Were the pauses of the sense and sound in this passage but a little better assorted, nothing in verse could be more melodious. In general, the great defect of Milton's versification, in other respects admirable, is the want of coincidence between the pauses of the sense and sound. . . .

Milton has a peculiar talent in embellishing the principal subject by associating it with others that are agreeable; which is the third end of a comparison. Similes of this kind have, beside, a separate effect: they diversify the narration by new images that are not strictly necessary to the comparison: they are short episodes, which, without drawing us from the principal subject, afford great delight by their beauty and variety. . . .

After a proper subject is chosen, the dividing it into parts requires some art. The conclusion of a book in an epic poem, or of an act in a play, cannot be altogether arbitrary; nor be intended for so slight a purpose as to make the parts of equal length. The supposed pause at the end of every book, and the real pause at the end of every act, ought always to coincide with some pause in the action. In this respect, a dramatic or epic poem ought to resemble a sentence or period in language divided into members that are distinguished from each other by proper pauses; or it ought to resemble a piece of music, having a full close at the end, preceded by imperfect closes that contribute to the melody. Every act in a dramatic poem ought therefore to close with some incident that makes a pause in the action; for otherwise there can be no pretext for interrupting the representation: it would be absurd to break off in the very heat of action; against which every one would exclaim: the absurdity still remains where the action relents, if it be not actually suspended for some time. This rule is also applicable to an epic poem: though in it a deviation from the rule is less remarkable; because it is in the reader's power to hide the absurdity, by proceeding instantly to another book. The first book of *Paradise Lost* ends without any close, perfect or imperfect: it breaks off abruptly, where Satan, seated on his throne, is prepared to harangue the convocated host of the fallen angels; and the second book begins with the speech. Milton seems to have copied the *Æneid*, of which the two first books are divided much in the same manner. Neither is there any proper pause at the end of the fifth book of the *Æneid*. There is no proper pause at the end of the seventh book of *Paradise Lost*, nor at the end of the eleventh. In the *Iliad* little attention is given to this rule.

58. Webb on imagery

1762

Extract from Daniel Webb, *Remarks on the Beauties of Poetry* (1762), 81–4.

Daniel Webb (1719?–98) wrote on the theory of art and aesthetics, including *Remarks on the Beauties of Poetry* (1762) and *Observations on the Correspondence Between Poetry and Music* (1768), both worthy of perusal by students of Milton.

Eug. The purpose of Imagery is either to illustrate, or aggrandize our ideas: of the former, enough has been said.

The greatness of an image is most obvious, when it strikes us by its immediate power, and with a sudden effect; as, in the description of Satan in *Paradise Lost*.

> He, above the rest
> In shape and gesture proudly eminent,
> Stood like a tow'r. [I, 589–91]

A second species of the sublime consists in giving a gradation to imagery. There is not, perhaps, in Poetry, a nobler instance of this, than in the description of Satan's return to hell—

> He through the midst, unmark'd,
> In show Plebeian Angel militant
> Of lowest order, pass'd; and from the door
> Of that Plutonian hall, invisible
> Ascended his high throne, which under state
> Of richest texture spread, at th' upper end
> Was placed in regal lustre. Down a while
> He sat, and round about him saw unseen:
> And last as from a cloud his fulgent head
> And shape Star-bright appear'd. [X, 441–50]

Hort. While you repeated these lines, Eugenio, I felt myself affected with the same kind of pleasure, as when we see a cloud rising slowly from the vale, becomes by degrees the ornament of the heavens. Might I, therefore, judge from my own feelings, I should conclude, that such images as are in motion, and which, by a gradual enlargement, keep our senses in suspense, are more interesting than those, which owe their power to a single impression, and are perfect at their first appearance. Where there can be no gradation in an object, its influence on the mind is immediately determined.

Eug. In this observation, we see the reason, why the principal beauties in *Paradise Lost*, have been naturally thrown on the person of Satan. To describe a permanent and unchangeable glory, is to paint without shades; the Sun is more delightful in its setting, than in its meridian. The divine Perfection, pure and Angelic natures, can have no clouds, no contrasts; they are all one blaze. But, it is not so, in the description of fallen Greatness; of diminished and interrupted splendor; of a superior nature sunk and disgraced, but emerging at intervals from its degradation. This is a subject so truly poetic; it gives rise to such a train of fluctuating images, that, let the object be ever so obnoxious, if the danger, as in the present case, be remote, it seizes on the imagination, all calmer considerations are thrown aside, and the senses are hurried away beyond the reach of reflection.

Asp. This is the best apology I ever heard for a diabolical greatness.

59. Hurd on romance in Milton's works

1762

Extract from Richard Hurd, *Letters on Chivalry and Romance* (1762), 57–8, 117–18.

Milton, it is true, preferred the classic model to the Gothic. But it was after long hesitation; and his favourite subject was *Arthur and his Knights of the round table*. On this he had fixed for the greater part of his life. What led him to change his mind was, partly, as I suppose, his growing fanaticism; partly, his ambition to take a different rout from Spenser; but chiefly perhaps, the discredit into which the stories of chivalry had now fallen by the immortal satire of Cervantes. Yet we see thro' all his poetry, where his enthusiasm flames out most, a certain predilection for the legends of chivalry before the fables of Greece.

This circumstance, you know, has given offence to the austerer and more mechanical critics. They are ready to censure his judgment, as juvenile and unformed, when they see him so delighted, on all occasions, with the Gothic romances. But do these censors imagine that Milton did not perceive the defects of these works, as well as they? No: it was not the *composition* of books of chivalry, but the *manners* described in them, that took his fancy; as appears from his 'Allegro' [ll. 117–24].

And when in the 'Penseroso' he draws, by a fine contrivance, the same kind of image to sooth melancholy which he had before given to excite mirth, he indeed extolls an *author* of one of these romances, as he had before, in general, extolled the *subject* of them; but it is an author worthy of his praise; not the writer of *Amadis*, or *Sir Launcelot of the Lake*, but Chaucer himself, who has left an unfinished story on the Gothic or feudal model [ll. 109–15]. . . .

With these helps the new Spirit of Chivalry made a shift to support itself for a time, when reason was but dawning, as we may say, and just about to gain the ascendent over the portentous spectres of the imagination. It's growing splendour, in the end, put them all to flight, and allowed them no quarter even amongst the poets. So that Milton, as fond as we have seen he was of the Gothic fictions, durst only admit them on the bye, and in the way of simile and illustration only.

And this, no doubt, was the main reason of his relinquishing his long-projected design of Prince Arthur, at last, for that of the *Paradise Lost*; where, instead of Giants and Magicians, he had Angels and Devils to supply him with the *marvellous*, with great probability. Yet, tho' he dropped the tales, he still kept to the allegories of Spenser. And even this liberty was thought too much, as appears from the censure passed on his *Sin and Death* by the severer critics.

60. Evans on Milton's literary use of the Psalms

1772

Extract from Nathaniel Evans, *Poems on Several Occasions, with Some Other Compositions* (Philadelphia, 1772). 'On the Psalm xcvii Paraphrased', 82–3.

I have thus far premised, to induce, if possible, those youths among us, who have enjoyed the advantage of a liberal education, and have leisure for literary pursuits and a taste and capacity for poetry, which some have lately evinced, to turn their talents towards such instructive per-formances.—The Holy Scriptures are the true fountain from which to extract the richest draughts of poesy, both as to dignity of matter and embellishment of figures; witness the noble use the great *Milton* made of them in his marvellous poems, and though few must expect to reach to such heights as did that prodigy of learning and genius, yet all, according to their ability, may follow his illustrious example; and if we would wish to excel and atchieve any thing great and laudable, we should always look to a mark superior to ourselves.

61. Monboddo on Milton's greatness of language

1774–89

Extracts from James Burnet, Lord Monboddo, *Of the Origin and Progress of Language* (Edinburgh, 1773–92), ii, 354–60, 388 note, 558–65; iii, 21–2, 25, 27–30, 52–3 note, 59, 68–72, 74–6, 94–6, 98–102, 112–13, 130–3, 138–40, 142–3; iv, 104 note, 129–32, 133–4, 268–9, 270–1; v, 235–6, 253–69, 468–9.

James Burnet, Lord Monboddo (1714–99), a Scotsman who furthered the cause of anthropology, is unfortunately little read today and almost totally unknown to students of Milton for his important statements on the poems and language in *Of the Origin and Progress of Language* (1773–92). *Antient Metaphysics* (1779–99) likewise contains brief comment.

Vol. II

The thing will be better understood by an example; and I will take one from the last stanza of an ode of Horace, which Milton has translated literally, and thereby indeed shewn very clearly, that the genius of the English language will not bear such an arrangement. But the question is, Whether the genius of the Latin be equally stinted? and whether there be any beauty or utility in ranging the words in so perverse an order, as those gentlemen would call it? The passage is as follows.

—Me tabulâ sacer
Votivâ paries indicat uvida
Suspendisse potenti
Vestimenta maris Deo.
Od. 5.

Now, according to those gentlemen, the natural and proper arrangement is that which a schoolboy learning Latin is ordered by his master to put the words in. As thus: *Sacer paries indicat tabulâ votivâ me suspendisse uvida vestimenta potenti deo maris.* If this be elegant and beautiful, then indeed the Greeks and Romans were in a great mistake when they studied a composition the very reverse of this. For we are not to imagine, that it was the necessity of the verse, and not choice, that made them use such a composition. For, as shall be shewn afterwards, it is as common in their prose writings as in their verse. And indeed it was one of the chief beauties of the Attic dialect, and which distinguished more perhaps than any thing else the Attic from the other Greek writers. This beauty the Romans, particularly in later times, imitated very much; for not only Horace is full of it, but even in Virgil's eclogues, where one should have expected more simplicity of style, there is a great deal of it to be found. I shall give but one instance out of many:

> Hinc tibi, quæ semper vicino ab limite sepes
> Hyblæis apibus florem depasta salicti,
> Sæpe levi somnum suadebit inire susurro.

Of this artificial composition in English I will give an example from Milton: it is from the speech of Satan in the beginning of the second book of *Paradise lost*: [II, 18-23]. Here many objections may be made by the advocates for the natural order. In the first place, Milton has taken advantage of the pronoun *I* having an accusative, and has placed it at the head of the sentence, at a great distance from its verb *established*; so that we do not know what he would be at, till welcome to the sixth line; and instead of saying plainly, and naturally, 'That the loss they had sustained had established him much more firmly than ever in his throne,' he has contrived to express it in the most perplexed way, throwing in betwixt the verb and the word it governs, which naturally ought to have followed it immediately, whole sentences concerning the laws of Heaven, the free choice of his subjects, the atchievements in battle and in council, and the recovery of their loss so far; and some of these are parentheses, such as, *with what besides, &c.* and, *thus far at least recovered,* which might be both left out in the reading, having no necessary connection with what goes before and follows, and serving only to make the connection more remote betwixt the verb and the pronoun which it governs, and by consequence the composition more intricate.

This, I think, is the opinion of those gentlemen fairly stated, and applied to one of the finest passages of our greatest poet, and which, according to my notions of style, is a perfect pattern of rhetorical composition, hardly to be equalled in English. The pronoun, that in the passage I quoted from Horace, and in this from Milton, is so far separated from its verb, and which is the great objection to the composition, is, I think, in both passages, most properly placed in the beginning, because it is of himself that the person is speaking; and therefore the pronoun is naturally made the leading word. And what is thrown in betwixt in both passages, particularly in the English poet, is not idle words, but such as fill up the sense most properly, and give a solidity and compactness to the sentence, which it otherwise would not have. And so to the parentheses in the passage from Milton, it is well known to those who understand any thing of speaking, that if parentheses be not too long, or too frequent, and be spoken with a proper variation of voice, they produce a wonderful effect, with respect both to the pleasure of the ear and to the sense, which is often thrown, or as it were darted in, with more force than it could be in any other way.

To be convinced of the truth of what I say, let this period be taken down in the manner that a schoolboy construes the passage of Horace above quoted. Suppose, for example, it were to be put into this form: 'This loss, which we have so far recovered, hath established me in my throne more firmly than the laws of Heaven, which ordained me your leader, or than even your own free choice, and all that I have atchieved in council or in battle.' Now, I ask any reader of taste or judgement, whether the period thus frittered down, does not lose one half of the strength and vigour of the expression, as well as of the beauty and pomp of sound? and whether there be not wanting in it, not only that roundness, which fills and pleases the ear so much of a popular assembly, but likewise that density of sense which makes such an impression, and which the critics praise so much in Demosthenes? In short, it appears to me, that by such a change, one of the most beautiful periods that ever was composed, by which Milton has deserved the praise which Cicero bestows upon poets, of studying the beauty of oratorial composition, though under the fetters of strict numbers is rendered flat and languid, losing not only its *oratorial numbers*, but enervated in its sense. . . .*

---

* One may say of Milton thus *travesti* what he makes Beelzebub say of Satan: 'If this be he—But, O ! how changed, how fallen !' from him who contends even with Demosthenes in strength, and beauty of composition; and, if the language could have supported him. . . . *Hom. Il.* 23, *v.* 382. Demosthenes excelled, among other things, in the vehemence of altercation. Let any man of taste read the altercation betwixt Satan and Death, in the second book of *Paradise lost*, and say, whether there be any thing of the kind better in Demosthenes. Demosthenes excells also in strength of reasoning, as well as in vehemence

It may be observed, that Milton uses a little freedom sometimes in the beginning of this verse, by making the first foot of it a Trochee instead of an Iambus: that is, beginning with an accented syllable; as in this verse:

> Daughter of God and man, accomplish'd Eve. [IV, 660]

And he has been followed in this by later poets; Mr. Pope particularly, as in this verse:

> Pleasures the sex, as children birds pursue.

It is an irregularity, if it may be called one, which gives a beautiful variety to the verse, by interrupting the monotony of the Iambics; and I wonder that it is not more used. But Milton, who has varied his versification, I think, more than any other of our poets, sometimes breaks the measure of the verse altogether; as in this line:

> Burnt after him to the bottomless pit. [VI, 866]

Nor are we to imagine, that Milton did this through negligence, or as not knowing the nature of the verse he used; but it was to give a variety to his verse, and some relief to the ear, which might otherwise be tired with the constant repetition of the same measure. It is for this reason that we have, both in Homer and Virgil, irregularities of a like kind; such as Anapæsts in place of Dactyls, and Iambics or Trochaics in place of Spondees, which have been noted by the critics; and the effect they had upon the verse observed, either in making it empty, and as it were hollow, or tumid and big-bellied. . . .

This kind of plain work is entirely out of fashion in our poetry, for the reason I have mentioned, and but little used even in our prose, and every thing in both is embroidery and ornament. But the taste of Milton, and I may add of the age in which he wrote, was very different; for in him we have many passages, not only beautiful, but even sublime, without metaphor or figure, or any thing of what is now called *fine language*. I will mention one or two of them. In the council of fallen angels, after

---

of contention. I will venture, in that respect too, to compare the dispute betwixt the Angel and Satan, when he was detected at the ear of Eve, in book 4. of *Paradise lost*, or betwixt Samson and Dalilah, in *Samson Agonistes*, with any thing of that kind in the Greek orator. But it was only by imitating Demosthenes that Milton could equal him. And accordingly it is evident, that among the Greek orators, he was his particular study: and as he had practised the rhetorical manner so much in his religious and political disputes, it is no won- der that the speeches in the *Paradise lost* are so admirable, and so much surpassing every thing of the kind we have in English.

Moloch had done speaking, he describes Belial rising up to speak in the following lines [II, 106–18]. No body of any taste or understanding will deny that this is a most beautiful passage; and yet in the whole of it there is not one metaphorical or figurative word. In what then does the beauty of it consist? I say, in the justness of the thought, and propriety of the expression; and no less in the art of composition. And, first, the versification is most beautifully varied by pauses and different feet; and to give still greater variety, there are two verses, viz.

> For dignity compos'd, and high exploit [II, 111]

and the last

> And in persuasive accents thus began. [II, 118]

where there is no pause from the sense, nor any stop at all, except a little *cæsura* towards the middle, which this English verse requires, as well as the Latin hexameter. Then from the words,—'On the other side up-rose,'—all is one period variously divided into members of different lengths, and in such a manner that though it be of extraordinary length, it is perfectly clear, to those at least who are accustomed to such artificial composition. There is in it a pretty long parenthesis, which I have marked, but is not marked, so far as I know, in any edition of Milton, and perhaps never was observed before. The parenthesis I mean is after the words,—'But all was false and hollow;'—and in it he translates the Greek, . . . the impudent profession of Gorgias the sophist, which after his time was charged against all the sophists, and even the philosophers. This parenthesis comes down to the words,—'for his thoughts were low,'—which can only connect with the words,—'But all was false and hollow;'—so that all betwixt is interjected, or what is called a parenthesis. This figure of composition, which is hardly ever used in common discourse, is much employed by the best writers of antiquity, in order to give a cast and colour to their style different from common idiom; and by Demosthenes particularly; and not only by the orators, but the poets. There is a remarkable instance of one in Virgil, longer than this of Milton, and which may serve as an apology for Milton to such readers as think he needs one. It is in the beginning of the Georgics, . . . speaking of the place that Augustus Cæsar was to have among the gods. . . .

I need not observe how beautifully Milton, in the speech of Belial, which follows the passage above quoted, changes the colour of the style, and gives it the rhetorical cast; preserving, however, still the simplicity of the diction, and making the rhetoric consist only in the figure of the composition. This will be obvious to every man who has formed his taste upon the study of the best authors. And I proceed to another example of the beauty of composition, without the least of what we call fine language, and with less still of art or variety than is to be observed in the preceding example. And I quote it the rather, that there is in it an allusion, which I think has not been observed, to a very fine passage of Plato. It is the beginning of book 8.

> The angel ended, and in Adam's ear
> So pleasing left his voice, that he a while
> Thought him still speaking, still stood fixt to hear;
> Then, as new-wak'd, thus gratefully replied. [51–4]

The composition here, as well as the diction, is sweetly simple; the versification sufficiently varied by the pauses, and concluding, like the last passage, with a flowing line, without any pause, which makes it go off with a roundness and smoothness that is very agreeable. The allusion I mean is to a passage in the *Protagoras* of Plato, where Socrates describes the effect that Protagoras's discourse had upon him, in much the same terms that Milton has used to describe the effect of the angel's speech upon Adam.

The passages I have quoted are beautiful and fine, but cannot be said to be great or sublime: but I will mention one or two, where there is the greatest sublimity, consisting altogether in the thought expressed in proper words. The first I shall mention is just in the beginning, where he opens the wonderful scene of his poem in the following lines.

> Nine times the space that measures day and night
> To mortal man, he with his horrid crew
> Lay vanquish'd, rolling in the fiery gulph,
> Confounded, though immortal, &c. [I, 50–3]

When Milton thus begins to sound his trumpet, almost every other poet in English, compared with him, may be said,

> Stridenti miserum stipulâ disperdere carmen.
> [to spoil his wretched song with his grating reed;
> Vergil, Eclogue iii, 27]

Of the same kind is what he says, after his catalogue and description of the host of fallen angels: [I, 587–600]. Where, among other things, the reader may observe the noble simplicity of that expression,—'Nor appear'd less than archangel ruin'd,'—much like that in the passage above quoted,—'Battle dangerous to less than gods:'—Expressions which the reader may be assured no man would have used who had not formed his taste upon the chastest and most correct models.

I should never have done, if I were to quote every passage of this kind in Milton; I will therefore have done with him, and return to the antient composition; from which, however, I hope the reader will not think that I have digressed far by what I have said of Milton's composition.

Vol. III

Milton, in his verse, has used a much more judicious elision when he has run together two vowels, one ending the preceding word, and another beginning the subsequent, as in the following fine verses, expressing so well by the sound the idea they mean to convey: [II, 1021–2]. In these, and many such to be met with in this poem, Dr. Bentley, in his edition, has marked the elision by an apostrophe, as I have done; and he has observed, that in this Milton has chosen to follow the Latins, who only absorbed the vowel in the pronunciation, rather than the Greeks, who strike it out in writing.

Milton has, in other respects, used as much freedom with single words as the genius of the language would permit, and perhaps more. Thus, instead [of] *disdain*, he has said, *'sdain*, cutting off the first syllable: [IV, 50–2]. By a like liberty, from the word *impregnate*, he has cut off the last syllable, and made it *impregn*: [IV, 500–2]. Whereas, according to the analogy of the language, it should have been *impregnates*, as it is commonly used, being derived from the barbarous Latin verb *impregno*; and sometimes, instead of eliding letters and syllables, he has enlarged words, by adding syllables; as, for example, the corrupted word *hermit*, he has restored to its proper etymological orthography, and called it *eremite*, as in this line,

Embryos and idiots, eremites and friars [III, 574]

It is, however, permitted to a poet to use a little freedom of this kind; and, accordingly, Milton has used many words in a sense different from that which they denoted, I believe, even in his time. Thus the word *buxom*, in English, did antiently signify yielding, or obedient; and therefore Milton has made it an epithet to the air, tho', I am persuaded, that in his days it had lost that original signification, and was used to signify much the same thing that it now signifies, in which sense it is used by Milton in other passages, as when he says of Euphrosyne, that she is

So *buxom*, blyth, and debonair . . . .

In English, we have a great many words borrowed from the Latin, but a Latin much corrupted, in which the words were changed from their proper and classical signification. To restore them to that signification makes the style both proper and learned. Of this I shall give an example or two from our learned poet Milton. He describes Eve as going forth with a *pomp* of winning graces attendant on her, *book* 8. v. 61. Here the word *pomp* is used, not as it is at present, to signify *show* or *ostentation*, but in its proper and etymological sense, which is to denote *attendance* upon any one, either for honour or defence; or, as it is expressed by a French word, now used in English, *escorte*. Another example is, his use of the word *intend*, in that passage of Satan's speech in the second book, where he desires the devils, while he was away on the adventure which he had undertaken, to *intend* at home, while that should be their home, what best might ease their present misery; where the word *intend* is used in its proper signification of bent or application to any thing; and in this sense the Latins say, *intendere animum*. Whereas, in corrupt Latinity, from which we have taken it, it signifies to design or project any thing; and in this sense we now use the word *intend*, our words of Latin extraction being formed, as I have observed, mostly from such Latinity.

I shall give another example from the same author. It is the use of the word *observe*, which, in our common language, is a word of no force and emphasis; but, in good Latinity, it is a word of great significance; and, in this classical sense, it is used by Milton in his first book, where, speaking of the host of fallen angels drawn up and reviewed by Satan, he says,

> —Thus far these beyond
> Compare of mortal prowess, yet *observed*
> Their dread commander. [V, 586–8]

where it denotes, as in Latin, *observed with particular attention*; or, as it is expressed by one native English word, *marked*.

The last example I shall give, is likewise from the same author, where, speaking of Helen, he calls her *Jove-born Helena*, in those beautiful lines in his 'Comus', where he makes the enchanter say to the lady, when he recommends his cup to her,

> Not that Nepenthe, which the wife of Thon,
> In Egypt gave to Jove-born Helena,
> Was of such power to stir up joy as this,
> To life so friendly, or so cool to thirst. [675–8]

Here the English word *born*, which answers to the Latin word *natus*, he has used in the classical sense of *natus*; for the Romans said, *natus ex patre*, as well as *ex matre*; whereas, in common English, we say only, *born of the mother*. . . .

This, I think, is a specimen of noble and manly eloquence. For, not to mention the weight of matter that it contains, and the high republican spirit which animates it, I ask those gentlemen, who despite the Greek and Roman learning, and admire only the French authors, or some later English writers, that they are pleased to set up as models (for Milton, I know, they think uncouth, harsh, and pedantic), whether they can produce any thing themselves, or find any thing in their favourite authors, which they can set against this passage in Milton, either for the choice of the words, or the beauty and variety of the composition? It may be considered as a *gauntlet* that Milton, for the honour of antient literature, has thrown down to those gentlemen, which he must be a bold man among them who will venture to take up. . . .

Or, if my reader is not learned, let him have recourse to Milton, and study the speeches in the *Paradise Lost*, particularly those in the second book; there he will find that fine period, in the beginning of Satan's first speech, which I have elsewhere quoted and commented upon. And there is another in the beginning of Belial's speech in the same book, also worthy of his attention. It runs thus:

> I should be much for open war, O peers!
> As not behind in hate, if what was urged,
> Main reason to persuade immediate war,
> Did not dissuade me most. [II, 119–22]

And, if he further wants an example of a good period in prose, I think the one I have given above, from Milton's *Eiconoclastes*, may suffice. And if he would desire to have here likewise a contrast, he may go to some of the fashionable productions of this age, where he will find a short, smart cut of style, imitated from Tacitus; or, if the imitator is not learned enough to understand him, from some late French writers, very different from the composition of Milton, and other good writers in English. . . .

But I will give one or two examples of it from our great Milton, who wrote at a time when there was no imitation of French authors among us, nor of any other, except the great antient authors, and of the Greek

more than the Roman, who were themselves considered only as imitators. The authors, therefore, of that age endeavoured to bring our
language as near to this classical standard as possible, and particularly
Milton, from whom I am to take my examples.* There is one passage
that furnishes two examples of the ellipsis. It is where Adam, taking
leave of the angel, says,

—Since to part,
Go heavenly guest, ætherial messenger,
Sent from whose sovereign goodness I adore.   book 8. v. 645.

* This author I have frequently mentioned before, and shall, in the sequel, quote him
oftener than any other English writer, because I consider him as the best standard for style,
and all the ornaments of speech, that we have in our language. He was a singular man in
this respect, that he had as much original genius as any man, and, at the same time, more
learning than perhaps any, even of that learned age in which he lived. For, it appears from
his writings, both in prose and verse, and particularly from his little tractate upon education, that his course of study had taken in the whole circle of human knowledge. His
poetic genius appeared very early, both in Latin and English; and there is an elegiac epistle
of his in Latin, written, as it is supposed, when he was about seventeen or eighteen years
old, to his companion Carolus Diodati, who, it seems, had pressed him much to leave
London, where he was then residing, and return to the university of Cambridge, where he
had been educated, which I will venture to set against any thing of the elegiac kind to be
found in Ovid, or even in Tibullus. I shall only quote four verses of it, which will give the
reader some taste of the whole. It is where he speaks of his residence in London, the place
of his birth: [Elegia I, 9–10, 21–2]. There can be nothing, I think, finer of the elegiac kind
than in these lines. In the first, London is most beautifully and poetically described, by the
circumstance of its being washed by the refluent water of the Thames. The second line has
the proper cadence, as well as turn of expression of this kind of verse; and the two last
lines, for the elegance of the composition, and the sweetness of the versification, are hardly
to be matched in Latin, or in any other language. It is pleasant, I think, to observe this
great genius 'teneris juvenescens versibus,' to use an expression of Horace, wantoning in
the soft elegiac, playing with fable and mythology, as he does in those Latin poems; and,
by this exercise of his young muse, preluding to his great work, which he executed in the
full maturity of his age,

Long chusing and beginning late; [IX, 26]

I mean his *Paradise Lost*. To his other accomplishments, he joined the advantage of travelling, and in a country which was then the seat of arts and sciences; I mean Italy, where it
appears that he applied himself much to the study of the Italian authors, particularly the
poets. And his muse exercised herself in that language, as well as in Greek, Latin, and
English. And though his genius was so early, and even what may be called premature; yet
it did not, like other things that grow hastily, decline soon. For, at the age of sixty-two,
when, besides his blindness, and the infirmities accompanying so advanced a period of life,
he was involved in the ruin of his party, and, as he himself has said,

Fallen on evil days, and evil tongues;
With dangers and with darkness compass'd round,
And solitude. [VII, 25–7]

He wrote the *Sampson Agonistes*, the last and the most faultless, in my judgment, of all his
poetical works. . . .

In the first we must supply, *it is necessary*; so that the full phrase is, *since to part is necessary*. This is an ellipsis common enough in Greek, where the word *dei*, signifying *it must be*, is understood. The other is the ellipsis of the pronoun *him*; so that the complete phrase is, *sent from him, whose goodness I adore*. There is another of the same kind, where he says, speaking to his muse,

> So fail not thou, who thee implores. B. 7. v. 38.

It is like that of the word *illa* in Virgil, where he says,

> Canto quæ solitus, si quando armenta vocaret. *Ecl.* 2.

Milton has sometimes left out the sign of the infinitive mood, viz. the particle *to*, where he thought it would occasion no ambiguity; as where he makes Beelzebub say, in the council of the devils, that, by getting possession of this earth, they would be lifted up nearer to their antient seat:

> —Perhaps in view
> Of those bright confines, whence, with neighbouring arms,
> In opportune excursion, we may chance
> Re-enter heaven. [II, 94–7]

unless we should chuse to understand *chance* there as an adverb, of the same signification with *perhaps*.

But there is another example where there can be no doubt of the ellipsis. It is where he says,

> —Champions bold
> Wont ride in armed . . . Book I. v. [763–]764.

in place of *wont to ride*.

Another ellipsis, in the same author, is to be found, book 10. v. 157.

> So having said, he thus to Eve in *few*—

where *words* are understood; an ellipsis very common both in Greek and Latin. . . .

Milton in this, as in other things, followed the taste and judgment of the antients, thinking that he could not vary his composition sufficiently, nor sometimes convey the sense so forcibly as he would wish, without the use of this figure. Accordingly, he has used it very much, more than, I believe, has been commonly observed, of which I have elsewhere*

---

* See *Dissert* . . . vol. 2. p. 561 [reprinted before].

given an instance, in that fine passage of the second book, where he describes Belial rising to speak. And, as Horace begins an ode with a parenthesis, so he begins Satan's speech, in the beginning of the second book, with one, and a very long one too, in this manner: [II, 11–18].

I will give one other instance from Milton of a parenthesis, which I think very beautiful. It is in the 'Comus', where the younger brother, speaking of the situation of his sister, says [366–72]. The whole passage is exceedingly beautiful; but what I praise in the parenthesis is, the pathos and concern for his sister that it expresses. . . .

It is no doubt a figure that varies the style, and throws it much out of common speech. But the use of it is dangerous; and, if it makes the style obscure or ambiguous, it ought to be condemned as a solecism, of which it has, no doubt, the appearance; and, accordingly, the Greek critics call it *soloichophanes*. Our English writers do not attempt it, unless *we* dignify with the name of this figure some such anomalous expressions as *methinks*, and *he would needs do it*. But we must except Milton, who was resolved to be an antient in this respect, as well as every other. There is one instance that I remember, among others that may be found. It is in the third book of *Paradise Lost*, beginning at verse 344[–9].

The lines are so wonderfully fine, that if it were a real solecism, not to be justified by any antient authority, I could excuse it. But it is to be justified in the same way as those passages I have quoted from Homer. And I have no doubt but that Milton, who had all Homer by heart, as Dr. Bentley somewhere says, had those passages in view, particularly the first, which very much resembles this of Milton. I would, therefore, make out the syntax by supplying the verb *shouted*, or *received*; so that the full construction will be, *The angels shouted with a shout*, or *received*, viz. what God Almighty had said *with a shout, loud as from numbers without number*, &c. But, whatever way we solve the difficulty of the syntax, there is nothing obscure in the sense; and therefore I cannot condemn the figure, though it be, no doubt, a very unusual one in English. . . .

But Milton drew the ornaments of his style from a better source, namely, the Greek and Latin, and chiefly the Greek. For it is evident, that not only his English, but his Latin, is cut upon Greek, as much, or perhaps more, than that written by any Roman. Of those Greek or Latin constructions his works are full. I shall give an instance of one or two of them. In the second book of *Paradise Lost*, he makes Beelzebub say,

Upborne with indefatigable wings,
Over the vast abrupt, ere he arrive
The happy isle. [II, 408–10]

The construction in English is, *arrive* at *the isle*. But, instead of that, he has chosen the Latin idiom of *accessit insulam*, or *ingressus est insulam*, or the Greek *eisylthe tyn nyson*.

There is another instance in the beginning of book 9. v. 42. where he says,

—Me, of these
Nor skill'd nor studious, higher argument
Awaits. [41–3]

The usual construction in English is, *skilled in a thing*; but the Latin construction is, *peritus alicujus rei*. Again, in book 9. v. 845. he says,

Yet oft his heart, divine of something ill,
Misgave him. [845–6]

which is just the Latin, *mens divina futuri*. Again, speaking of death, he says, that

—he upturned
His nostrils wide into the murky air,
Sagacious of his quarry; [X, 279–81]

which is likewise a Latin idiom.

There is a third passage that I remember, which may be referred to this head. It is in the 'Comus', where he makes that magician address the lady in a very high style of classical gallantry: [265–70]. As Cicero says of Plato's language, that, if Jupiter were to speak Greek, he would speak as Plato has written; so we may say of this language of Milton—that, if Jupiter were to speak English, he would express himself in this manner. The passage is exceeding beautiful in every respect; but all readers of taste will acknowledge, that the style of it is much raised by the expression—*unless the goddess*, an elliptical expression, unusual in our language, though common enough in Greek and Latin. But if we were to fill it up and say, *unless thou beest the goddess*; how flat and insipid would it make the composition, compared with what it is.

I will mention another idiom of construction in Milton, and which, as far as I know, is neither Greek nor Latin, but intirely Milton's own, and which, I think, does more violence to the language than any other that he has used. It is where he describes Eve just parting from her husband to go to work by herself in the garden, which exposed her to the temptation of the devil. As this is the last description of her in a state of innocence, Milton has bestrowed upon her the richest colours of his poetry, and has compared her to every thing most beautiful of the kind that is to be found in the antient fable, with which he found it necessary to adorn even his Christian poem [*PL* IX, 85–96]. This expression, *virgin of Proserpina*, is certainly not common English, and many will deny it to be English at all; but let any man try to express the same thought otherwise, and he will be convinced how much Milton has raised and ennobled his style by an idiom so uncommon, but which is, notwithstanding, sufficiently intelligible.

The last example I shall give from Milton of this kind of figure, is one by which the natural construction of the language is not altered, but interrupted and broken in a very unusual way. It is in the 'Comus', where the lady sitting inchanted, and endeavouring to rise, Comus says to her [659–62], where, instead of saying *root-bound, as Daphne was, that fled Apollo*, he throws in *root-bound* into the middle, betwixt the antecedent and the relative, a trajection altogether unusual in our language, but which must be allowed both to vary and raise the style; and as the connection is not so remote as to make the language obscure, I think it may not only be tolerated, but praised. . . .

In English, and more still in French, common conversation is most unnaturally swelled, and raised by the intemperate use of this figure, and from thence it has crept into our writings; so that a style, perfectly chaste and correct in this respect, is now very rarely to be found. But our great Milton has in this, as well as in other things, faithfully copied his masters, the antients. For, though his poetical style is, in many passages, by far the most sublime we have in English; yet it has less froth or bombast than any modern composition of the kind that I know. I have elsewhere instanced some expressions that shew the modesty of his style, such as,

> Battle dangerous to less than Gods; [II, 107–8]

and,

> Nor appeared less than arch-angel ruined. [I, 592–3]

And I will here give only one instance more: It is where he describes the rising of the council of the devils in Pondæmonium [sic], the noise of which a less correct and judicious author would have compared to loud thunder; but he compares it to thunder heard at a distance:

> Their rising all at once was as the sound
> Of thunder heard remote; Book 2. v. 476[–7]

which is a sound not loud or strong, but awful, and very like that produced by the movement of a great multitude. . . .

As poetry is an art imitative of characters, as well as of actions, the poets ought, above all others, to excell in this figure of style; and, accordingly, Homer, the father of poetry, is most eminent in it. All the characters he has imitated are of the heroic kind, excepting only one ridiculous personage, that he has but once exhibited, I mean *Thersites.* But he has contrived, notwithstanding, to give them a great variety; for Achilles, Ajax, Hector, Diomede, &c. are all heroes, but very different from one another. Virgil, it has been observed, has not such a variety; and indeed the truth is, that he has only three, Æneas, Turnus, and Dido; whereas we may reckon in Homer a dozen that are distinctly characterized. Milton's subject is particularly unfortunate in this respect; for it is such as affords him only one character fit for poetry. His divine personages are such as cannot have characters, like those of Homer's deities, who are as much characterized as his heroes: And Adam and Eve, while in their state of perfection, can hardly be considered as human characters; and, after their fall, the part they act is very short; so that there remains only Satan, of whom he indeed has made a very fine poetic personage, but not without doing some violence to his character as devil. For he has not made him perfectly bad, which would not have been a character so fit for poetry; but he has mixed with his devilish qualities some remorse and feeling of what goodness is; and, by doing so, he has brought the character nearer to human.

Milton appears to have been sensible of this defect of his subject; and, accordingly, he has been at great pains to supply it; for, in the council of the devils, in the second book, he has exhibited different characters of them in very fine speeches, the finest, in my opinion, that are to be found in English. But those devils appear only there, and are no more seen; so that Satan may be truly said to be his only character; for he is carried through the whole poem, and every where appears like himself, of which I shall give but one example out of many. It is the end of his speech, with which he concludes the debate in the council of Pandæ-monium; where, after setting forth the dangers that any one must run who should undertake the discovery of the new created world, he says [II, 445–66]. The whole passage is wonderfully beautiful in every respect. But the reason why I have quoted it is, to shew how he supports Satan's

Monarchial pride, conscious of highest worth, [II, 428–9]

as he expresses it. In the first of these lines I have no doubt but he had in view the speech of Sarpedon in Homer; but he only took the hint from that poet; and to shew the learned reader how far he is from a servile imitator, even of Homer, I have transcribed the passage below. . . .

In order to help him to conceive this variety, I will take a period of some length, and show him the different ways in which it may be composed. The example I shall use is a period that I have mentioned more than once before, viz. that of Milton in Satan's first speech in the council of devils, in the second book of *Paradise Lost*; and I will take in the whole passage, containing an argument which shews, as much as any thing in the whole work, Milton's rhetorical faculty; for by it he endeavours to prove, that hell is, at least in some respects, better than heaven: [II, 18–42].

As every composition is made up of certain materials, let us consider, *first* of what materials the composition here is made. And these are the following propositions (for there is no need to analyse it further): 1*st*, I was created your leader, by the fixed laws of Heaven: 2*dly*, I was likewise by you chosen for leader: 3*dly*, This choice was confirmed by my atchievements: 4*thly*, But I was liable to envy while in heaven: For, 5*thly*, there is envy in heaven, because there is in it good for which to contend: But, 6*thly*, There is no envy here in hell, because there is no good to contend for. From these premises, the conclusion is drawn, that he was more established in his throne, and they in a better condition, and surer to prosper than before their fall. These materials may be put together in the following plain manner, without any figure or other ornament of language. . . .

Other turns might be given to this sentence; but these will suffice to shew, *first*, how much more copious the language of Milton is, and how much more rounded, compact, and nervous his composition is, than any that I, at least, can give to this passage. 2*do*, If there be so much variety in turning one single argument, how much more must there be in the composition of a whole discourse or oration, though the substance of the matter, and the order of treating it, still continue the same? *Lastly*, And, what is more to our present purpose, it may be observed, that all the variety is here produced, without using any of the figures, of which I have treated in the two preceeding chapters; for there is here neither the pathetic nor the ethic, nor any thing but the argument variously turned and figured. This then shews, that there are ways of figuring the sense of composition otherwise than either by passion or by manners; and it is of such figures that I am now to treat. . . .

Vol. IV

[B]y not opening their mouth sufficiently, the English make their pronunciation of the Greek as faulty, as Milton observes the pronunciation of their own language is.—See Milton's *Tractate of Education*; He says, that the speech of the scholar 'should be fashioned to a distinct clear pronunciation, as near as may be to the Italian, especially in the vowels. For we Englishmen, being northerly, do not open our mouths in the cold air wide enough to grace a Southern tongue; but are observed by all other nations, to speak exceeding close and inward: So that to smatter Latin with an English mouth, is as ill a hearing, as Law French.' I would recommend the whole treatise to the Reader, as the best thing both for matter and stile, that has been written upon the subject of education, in modern times. . . .

Thus much of single words in English, considered both with regard to their sound and their sense.—I am now to consider the composition of them in sentences. In which, how defective a language must be, that wants genders, numbers, and cases, every scholar must know that understands Greek and Latin, and at the same time knows the science of language, which I doubt is not the case of every man who thinks himself a Greek and Latin scholar. Besides the tiresome repetition of those monosyllables, by which we form our cases, and of our auxiliary verbs, by which we form our tenses, such as, *have, shall, will,* and *can*—*had, should, would,* and *could,* occurring so frequently, the want of numbers, genders, and cases formed by flexion, forbids almost all variety of arrangement, the great beauty, as we have seen, of the antient composition, and obliges us to connect our words in syntax by juxta-position only. To be convinced how contemptible a composition this is, compared with the Greek and Latin, let him read Horace's ode to Pyrrha, and then Milton's translation of it, as near as possible, not only to the words, but to the arrangement of them, nearer indeed, than the stinted genius of our language will admit; and then he will clearly see how much more beautiful and elegant, as well as shorter, the Latin arrangement is. It is so various, that, in the first stanza, hardly two words that are construed together stand together.*

* The first stanza runs thus.

> Quis multa gracilis te puer in rosa
> Perfusus liquidis urget odoribus
> Grato, Pyrrha, sub antro?

where we may observe, that the only words construed together and placed together, are

As much, however, of variety of arrangement as the language will admit, so much I think we should use. And accordingly Milton has done so in his prose, as well as verse, which gives his prose a cast and colour very different from what is fashionable at present among us; for we arrange every thing as the French do, in what we call the Natural Order, but which is certainly most tiresomely uniform. And because Milton does not follow that order, we say his prose is harsh and un-couth, tho' we cannot say that it is obscure, nor consequently, that he has done any violence to the Language. . . .

In this way, Milton composes in Latin, particularly, in his *Defensio pro Populo Anglicano*, where there is a variety and beauty of Composition of the kind I have mentioned, not exceeded, hardly equalled, by any Latin author, with the variety, however, of short commatic sentences thrown in here and there; for the finest things must not be too often repeated. In English, the language not permitting, he has been more sparing in this highly varied composition, but enough of it to make his stile pass for very rough and unpleasant to those who are not classical scholars, and are accustomed to the stile now in fashion, of a colour and complexion perfectly different, where there is either that broken disjointed composition, hardly deserving the name of composition, and which is worse still in English than it is in the Latin of Sallust, Seneca, or Tacitus;—or, if it be composed in periods, it is in periods of two, or perhaps three members, of the same structure of words, inartificially tacked together by the copulative; and, in some late authors, who affect to distinguish themselves by the beauty of their stile, the period is tagged with two nouns, and each its attendant epithet. Such composi-tion, I think, is worse than no composition; and therefore I prefer the

---

the prepositions *in* and *sub*; which, being indeclinable words, cannot be otherwise con-nected with the words they govern, except by juxta-position. The translation, Milton has given us of this ode, was, I am persuaded, intended to show how inferior, in point of composition, the English was to the Latin; for, in the translation of the line,

Qui nunc te fruitur credulus aureâ,

into the English,

Who now enjoys thee, credulous, all gold,

he must have understood that the word *credulous*, must apply to *thee*, as well as the words *all gold*; whereas in the Latin it is clear, from the genders and cases, that *credulous* applies to the lover, and *aureâ* to the mistress. And, in the next verse of the translation,

Who always vacant, always amiable,
Hopes thee, of flattering gales unmindful,

it is evident, that according to our method of arrangement by juxta-position, *always vacant, always amiable*, and likewise the words, *of flattering gales unmindful*, must apply to the lover, and not to the mistress.

stile of the authors I have mentioned, and their modern imitators in French or English, who cut their stile into shreds and patches, to those who compose in so bad a taste.—I will only add, that, however rough and unpleasant Milton's stile may appear to the fashionable reader, I would nevertheless advise him to study his Polemical writings, both Political and Theological, if not for the stile, at least for the matter; for he will find there a variety of argument, with which his most extensive learning, antient and modern, sacred and prophane, furnished him, such as, I think, is not to be found in any other modern author. . . .

As to the making verse like prose, this is done by composing poetry, as we do prose, in periods, and making the periods and their several members cut the verse, and run into different verses. Of this he gives some beautiful examples from Homer, the greatest author, according to his judgment, that ever wrote, and the most perfect model of every beauty of stile, either in the words or composition. Of this Milton's blank verse in the *Paradise Lost* is as good an example as we could have; for we have there periods often of ten or twelve lines, and one I have observed in Satan's first speech to Beelzebub, in the first book, of no less than twenty-one lines, divided among the several verses; which has a fine effect, giving to verse all the beauty and variety of prose composition. How different, in this respect, the blank verse of Shakespeare is from Milton's, every reader of taste and judgment must observe. . . .

How much variety is wanted both in our verse and prose at present, we may judge by comparing them with those of Milton, who in this, as well as every thing else, has imitated the antient composition as far as the stinted genius of his language would permit him. How agreeably he has varied his verse by composition in periods of different lengths, consisting too of members different both in length and number, I have just now observed; and as to his prose, I have given, in the third Volume of this work, an example of his skill in composing rhetorical periods. As to his plain stile, didactic or narrative, he periodises it also, but in a manner very different. Of this plain stile you have a very good example in his preface to the *Paradise Lost*, which, tho' it be not so much varied in the composition as his rhetorical stile, (nor indeed ought it to be so), has nothing of that tedious uniformity, which is to be observed in our present writings. . . .

Vol. V

As I have mentioned modern historians, it would be improper to omit the greatest writer in English, both in verse and prose, and who has also merit as an historian; I mean Milton, who has given us a history of England from the earliest times down to the conquest. As to the matter of this history, it appears that he has collected it from a great many authors, very faithfully, I am persuaded, but not fully; for his history is to be considered as an abridgement, and therefore we have no speeches in it; so that if he had not written any thing more, we should have known nothing of his rhetorical talents, which in my opinion were very great. The stile of this history is altogether classical, such as might be expected from so great a scholar as Milton. But it is not so much composed in periods, as I am persuaded it would have been, if it been a formal history at full length; and I am persuaded that, if the abridgement, which the Halicarnassian made, of his history, had come down to us, it would have been found to have been composed in the same manner. There is nothing however in Milton like what I call the short cut of stile; and he has distinguished his language from common speech by all the variety of arrangement, and all the abbreviations, which the language could admit of: And, upon the whole, though I do not think it one of the best of Milton's writings, it is a work that does him no dishonour, and is such that the writers of history at present may profit by it. . . .

The stile in English likest to the Halicarnassian's, and liker still I think to that of Thucydides, is the stile of Milton, who in my opinion is the greatest writer both in verse and prose that we have in our language. As a poet his merit is generally acknowledged. His blank verse is so written as to be the finest composition that our language or, I believe, any modern language, is capable of; and his rhyming verse I think is also excellent. In his 'Comus', the best poem in my opinion he ever wrote, he has made a very agreeable variety, by mixing together the blank verse and the rhyme, after the manner of the Italian opera, which he has imitated throughout in that piece, and accordingly has, intermixed with the rest of the poetry, songs in it the finest in English. As to his prose, if it be true that the antient authors ought to be our standards for that composition, and that the nearer we can bring our language to the idiom of Greek and Latin, the more perfect our style is, it must be confessed, that Milton's prose, as well as his verse, is the best we have in English; for it certainly comes as near to the Greek and Latin composition as the imperfect grammar of our language will admit, so near that I know it is by many thought to be harsh, obscure, and perplexed; and so I know it must appear to those who are not learned.

But Milton wrote for a learned age; and I am persuaded his stile was not then obscure, otherwise he would not have been employed so much by the parliament and Oliver Cromwell to write on public business. At the same time, considering it as a classical stile, it must be allowed to be an artificial one, . . . or what may be called in English *a made stile*, that is, a stile very different from common speech. His history being, as I have observed, an abridgement, the stile of it is, as it ought to be, much simpler and plainer, and such as any man, who has learned the English grammar, may easily enough understand. But his controversial writings are in a stile very different; and they ought to be so, for they are of the rhetorical kind, and the stile of rhetoric should be very different from that of narrative; and it is a difference which Milton appears to me to have perfectly known, as well as the difference betwixt either of these stiles and the epistolary, of which we have evidence from the letters he wrote in name of the commonwealth and Oliver Cromwell to sundry kings and states, which we have both in Latin and English, and they are as good letters of business as ever were written.

That he excelled in this rhetorical stile is evident from the speeches of the *Paradise Lost*, which are out of all degree of comparison the best orations we have in English. And it appears to me to be a stile which he had practised more than any other, having been engaged in controversies civil or religious from his youth upwards down to the restoration. The variety of matter in these controversies is wonderful: They abound more with learning of all kinds, divine and human, and there is in them a greater copiousness of arguments, of facts from antient and modern, civil and ecclesiastical history, of authorities from scripture, from Fathers of the Church and modern divines, and lastly from heathen poets, philosophers, and historians, than is to be found in any one book I know; with all this, there is a keenness of satire, of wit too and ridicule, which is hardly to be paralleled. And he concludes his discourse upon the Reformation in England with an invective upon the Prelatical party, much more violent than any thing that Demosthenes has said against Philip.

The stile of these Philippics, as they may be called, has all that variety of composition, which I have praised in the Halicarnassian, and is brought as near to the Greek and Latin idiom, and as much figured as the poverty of our language will admit. In these works there is much more of composition in periods, as there ought to be, than there is in his history. I have given elsewhere an example of what I think a very fine period in the beginning of his *Eiconoclastes*, and I will here give an example of two in the beginning of another polemical work of his, entitled *The Reason of Church Government urged against Prelaty*. He begins his preface thus: 'In the publishing of human laws, which for the most part aim not beyond the good of civil society, to set them barely forth to the people without reason or preface, like a physical prescript, or only with threatnings, as it were a lordly command, in the judgment of Plato, was thought to be done neither generously nor wisely. His advice was, seeing that persuasion certainly is a more winning and manlike way to keep men in obedience than fear, that to such laws as were of principal moment, there should be used, as an induction, some well tempered discourse, showing how good, how gainful, how happy it must needs be to live according to honesty and justice; which being uttered with these natural colours and graces of speech, as true eloquence the daughter of virtue can best bestow upon her mother's praises, would so incite and in a manner charm the multitude into the love of that which is really good, as to embrace it ever after, not of custom and awe, which most men do, but of choice and purpose, with true and constant delight.' Here it may be observed the first period consists only of two members, the one much longer than the other, ending with the word *command*; the other short, and concluding the period with a very natural cadence. The second period I would divide into four members; the first a short member ending with the word *fear*; the other longer, concluding with the word *justice*; the other of much the same length ending with the word *praises*; and the fourth, longer than any of the former, concludes the period, and in the way in which Aristotle says it should be concluded, by the natural cadence of the words, and not by the sense only. And the reader will observe that the two periods are wholly different from one another, and the several members also different, both in the structure and composition of the words, and in their way of being joined together; so that we have here that variety without which there can be no beauty, as I have had frequently occasion to observe in the course of this work, in any of the works of art.

Besides this classical composition in those controversial works, there is a richness of words that I do not find in other English authors; and, though many of these words are now obsolete, they are such as, in my opinion, ought to be revived and brought again into fashion.

Such a stile therefore must have, as was said before, a great deal of the colour of Thucydides, whose stile was varied and distinguished from common speech by all the variety of figures, which even the Greek language will admit. And as Thucydides's stile is not to be understood except by a very good Greek scholar, so neither is Milton's (though not near so obscure in English as Thucydides is in Greek) to be perfectly understood, except by a scholar who has formed his taste of good writing upon the antient masters of the art.* It was no wonder, therefore, that such a critic as Dr. Johnson, who, in my opinion, was neither a scholar nor a man of taste, should pronounce, among the other oracles which he has uttered from his tripod, that Milton does not write English, (and I have heard some of the Doctor's admirers say the same), but a Babylonish dialect. And indeed an unlearned critic, who judges of the English language, by what is now written in it, will be disposed to censure those classical idioms of Milton above mentioned as harsh and uncouth; though, if he be more candid and good natured than the Doctor, he may not give so hard an epithet to Milton's stile, and which indeed is the worst thing that could be said of any stile, as to call it Babylonish. But the Doctor, who was not a Greek scholar, and could not read the Halicarnassian's critical works in the original, which cannot be understood in the translation, where the several ways of distinguishing stile from common speech by the grammatical figures of construction, are better explained than by any other author, knew of no other way of adorning his stile, and making what he thought fine writing, except by epithets, antitheses, and coining new words. Now, if he had been scholar enough to have read Thucydides, the great standard for what I call the *made* stile, he would have seen that it could be made without either epithet or antithesis: And as to new coined words, if Thucydides had attempted that, the people of Athens had such regard for the purity and chastity of their language, that they would not have born it, any more than I think the people of England should have born the words that Dr Johnson has made, and the reflections that he has thrown out upon an author, who does so much honour to modern times and to the English nation in particular. The commendation of the *Paradise Lost*, with which he concludes his life of Milton, is I think more absurd than his censures of him, and so ridiculous

* The edition of Milton's prose works, I use, is in 3 volumes in folio, printed in Amsterdam [actually London] in 1698. And, as it is printed in a foreign country, by a printer, who, it is likely, understood little or no English, and under the inspection of a corrector of the press, who, we may suppose, did not perfectly understand Milton's Attic English, it is not to be wondered that there are sundry errors of the press in it, (and indeed I wonder there are not more), which really make it obscure. There is no other edition that I have heard of; and the book is so rare, that I could not find it, when I wanted it, (such is the taste of the age), in the shop of any bookseller in London. In this manner, so great a treasure of learning, arguments, and words, may be said to be lost to the public.

that, if I had had a better opinion of the Doctor's critical talents, I should have imagined that he said it by way of irony and ridicule of Milton. He says that 'the *Paradise Lost* is not the greatest of heroic poems, only because it is not the first'. Now, as the chief merit of a poem, a picture, or indeed of every work of art, is the choice of the subject, if Dr Johnson had been but the twentieth part the tythe of a critic, (to use an expression of Shakespear), he would have known that, by the nature of things, it was impossible, of such a subject as that of the *Paradise Lost*, to make so fine a poem as the *Iliad* of Homer. For an epic poem as well as a tragedy is, as Aristotle tells us, the imitation of a human action. Now the subject of the *Paradise Lost*, as I have observed elsewhere,* is divine and supernatural; and there is hardly any thing human in it, except the speeches in the council of the Devils, which are the best of the rhetorical kind to be found in English, the seduction of Eve by the flattery of the Devil, and the quarrel betwixt the Man and Wife after the Fall: For, as to his battles of Angels fighting in *Cubic Phalanx*, they are altogether out of nature, at least human nature. The characters likewise are either too good or too bad, not mixed, as characters in poetry ought to be. The subject therefore of the *Paradise Lost* is much too high for poetical imitation; whereas the story of Homer's *Iliad* is the best subject for an epic poem that ever was invented, or to speak more properly, that ever was chosen; for though the genius of the poet might adorn and embellish such a subject, by adding or taking away circumstances, I hold it to be beyond the power of man to have invented altogether such a story. All therefore he could say, with any show of reason, in praise of Milton above Homer, is, that, if Homer had had the same subject, he could not have made so much of it as Milton has done.

The Doctor has been pleased not only to censure the English of Milton, in the strong terms above mentioned, but to attack his Latin in that noble work which gained him so much reputation all over Europe, I mean his *Defensio pro Populo Anglicano*, in which he encountered a man who was reputed the greatest scholar of the age, and with such success, that it is said to have proved the cause of his death. In this work Milton has endeavoured to show that Milton's Latin is as bad; but in this he has not suceeded.†

---

* Preface to Vol. 3 of *Ant. Metaph.* p. xliii.

† The Latin which the Doctor finds fault with, is in the beginning of his Preface to his *Defence*; where, after exposing a French Idiom which Salmasius has used, where he speaks of the *Persona Regis*, he adds, *Cæterum ob hujusmodi noxas Gallico-Latinas, quibus passim*

Before I read this criticism, though I knew the Doctor was no Greek scholar, I believed that he had understood Latin as much at least as any man can understand a learned language, who understood not the science of language nor any other science. But I am now in doubt, whether he was even a complete Latin scholar in the common sense of the word, though he had not only learned it as other men do, but taught it. . . .

---

scates, non tam mihi, reque enim est otium, quam ipsis tuis Grammatistis pœnas dabis; quibus ego te deridendum et vapulandum propino. Upon which the Doctor's Remark is, That 'Milton has inforced the charge of a Solecism against Salmasius, by an expression in itself *grossly solecistical*, when, for one of these supposed blunders, he says, as Ker, and, I think, some one before him, has remarked, *propino te tuis Grammatistis Vapulandum.* From *Vapulo*, which has a passive sense, *Vapulandus* can never be derived. No man forgets his original trade: the rights of nations and of Kings sink into questions of Grammar, if Grammarians discuss them.' Here the Doctor has used a liberty, not uncommon with him, to coin a new word *viz. Solecistical*, to express this gross blunder of Milton; but a word, formed not according to the analogy of the Language, and, what is worse, confounding a distinction which the Grammatical Art makes betwixt a Barbarism and a Solecism; the first relating to single words, the other to the composition and construction of them. This distinction is laid down in the Philosophical Greek Grammar of the learned Greek of modern times, Theodorus Gaza, but which I would have excused the Doctor for not knowing, as that Grammar is not translated. But the same distinction is laid down in the common Grammars and Dictionaries. Now Milton's error, if it be one, is a Barbarism and not a Solecism; and one should have thought that the real name for the thing would have pleased the Doctor more than the wrong name he has given it: so that here it appears that the Doctor has forgotten his original trade as, he says, Milton has done. The expression is such, that, as it stands in Milton, it is impossible to mistake the meaning of it; and it is only the *obscure diligence* (to use an expression of Terence) of a Pedantic Schoolmaster that would have observed it, tho' the Doctor has not even the glory of having first discovered it. This Blunder, so gross, that it could not be expressed in the common words of the Language, comes only to this, that Milton has used a Participle of the word *Vapulo*, derived from the passive voice of the Verb, which, the Doctor says, it has not: And he may be in the right, at least I do not remember to have read any Tense or Participle of the Verb derived from *Vapulor*. But so far Milton is in the right, that he uses the Verb only in a passive sense; for if he had given it an active signification in any of its Voices or Tenses, I should have thought it an error. But all he has done is to borrow from the passive voice a future Participle, and which I think was of necessity, if he was to use the word at all; for if he had used the future active Participle, I should not, for my part, have understood him; nor do I believe there is an example of *Vapulaturus* being used in that sense. Now he could have used no word so proper as *Vapulandus*; for *Verberandus* would not have been so proper, because Milton certainly did not mean that he was to be *whipt* by his Scholars, but only *derided* and *railed at*, as pretending to understand. Now in this sense of *being railed at*, the word is used by Cicero; for he says *sermone vapulo*, that is *I am abused and railed at*. Another thing to be observed is that the gerund *vapulandum* of this verb is in common use. Now the Gerund is nothing else but the neuter of the passive participle future. All therefore that Milton has done is to use the passive participle *Vapulandus*, not in the neuter Gender only and as a substantive, but as an adjective. But farther, if the transferring a Participle from one voice to another, was without example in the Latin Language, there might be some truth in the Doctor's Criticism; But there is a well known Example in the word *sequor* which is a verb in the passive voice with an active signification; and yet it has the present participle of the

It may be objected to Milton's versification, that, by his periods and members of periods, he has made his composition so perfectly prosaical, that the verse is lost. But to this I answer, that he has always contrived to terminate his verse with a word upon which the sense requires that some emphasis be laid, even if the composition were altogether prose. Now, where an emphasis is laid upon a word, there is always some stop of the voice more or less, and that stop will mark the verse: But, as I have elsewhere observed, it is a matter of delicacy just to mark this stop, but not to make it too long; for that would destroy the beauty of the composition in periods, and even make the sense obscure. I have observed that in Shakespeare's blank verse, when he runs the verses into one another, which happens but seldom, (for he does not compose verse in periods, as Milton does), and in other blank verse of that age, the poet is not sufficiently attentive to conclude the line with a word of emphasis; so that there can be no stop at all properly made at the end of the verse; and therefore either the verse must not be marked, or the sense must be injured.

---

active voice *viz. sequens*, as well as the future passive participle *sequendus*; and it likewise borrows from the active voice a future participle *secuturus*; and the same is the case of *loquor*, and several other *deponent verbs*. Now, if a verb of a passive form with an active signification can borrow two participles from the active form of the same verb, why may not a verb of an active form with a passive signification, such as *vapulo*, borrow one participle from the passive form of the same verb? I therefore say that the use of the passive participle *vapulandus* by Milton is according to the analogy of the Language. But further still I say that if the expression could not be justified by the common analogy of the Language, there are other Expressions in the best authors more contrary to that analogy; for in Virgil we read *Ventosa per æquora vectis*, where the defect of the Latin Language, in not having a present participle passive, is supplied by the use of the past participle passive: And by Cicero it is supplied in a more extraordinary manner by using the present participle active; for he has said *Marinis invehens belluis.* (See what further I have said upon this subject p. 85. of vol. 4th. of this work.) Now I think Milton in this instance has done no more than supply a defect in the Latin Language; for certainly the Language was defective, if it afforded no word to express the futurity of *Vapulo* in a passive sense.

62. Beattie on Milton's learning

1776

Extract from James Beattie, *Essays* (Edinburgh, 1776), 'On the Utility of Classical Learning', I, 738–40.

A Scottish professor of moral philosophy, James Beattie (1735–1803) was the author of the Spenserian *The Minstrel*. The *Essays*, however, contain much comment on Milton and reflect his philosophic and poetic study of *Paradise Lost*.

Milton was one of the most learned men this nation ever produced. But his great learning neither impaired his judgement, nor checked his imagination. A richer vein of invention, as well as a more correct taste, appears in the *Paradise Lost*, written when he was near sixty years of age, than in any of his earlier performances. *Paradise Regained*, and *Samson Agonistes*, which were his last works, are not so full of imagery, nor admit so much fancy, as many of his other pieces; but they discover a consummate judgement; and little is wanting to make each of them perfect in its kind.—I am not offended at that profusion of learning which here and there appears in the *Paradise Lost*. It gives a classical air to the poem: it refreshes the mind with new ideas; and there is something, in the very sound of the names of places and persons whom he celebrates, that is wonderfully pleasing to the ear. Admit all this to be no better than pedantic superfluity; yet will it not follow, that Milton's learning did him any harm upon the whole, provided it appear to have improved him in matters of higher importance. And that it did so, is undeniable. This poet is not more eminent for strength and sublimity of genius, than for the art of his composition; which he owed partly to a fine taste in harmony, and partly to his accurate knowledge of the ancients. The style of his numbers has not often been imitated with success. It is not merely the want of rhyme, nor the diversified position of pauses, nor the drawing out of the sense from one line to another; far less is it the mixture of antiquated words and strange idioms, that constitutes the charm of Milton's versification; though many of his imitators, when they copy him in these or in some of these respects, think they have acquitted themselves very well. But one must study the best Classic authors with as much critical skill as Milton did, before one can pretend to rival him in the art of harmonious writing. For, after all the rules that can be given, there is something in this art, which cannot be acquired but by a careful study of the ancient masters, particularly Homer, Demosthenes, Plato, Cicero, and Virgil; every one of whom, or at least the two first and the last, it would be easy to prove, that Milton has imitated, in the construction of his numbers.—In a word, we have good reason to conclude, that Milton's genius, instead of being overloaded or encumbered, was greatly improved, enriched, and refined, by his learning. At least we are sure this was his own opinion. Never was there a more indefatigable student. And from the superabundance of Classic allusions to be met with in every page of his poetry, we may guess how highly he valued the literature of Greece and Rome, and how frequently he meditated upon it.

63. Richardson on the companion poems

1779

Extract from [Richard Richardson], *Mirror*, no. 24 (17 April 1779). *Mirror* (Edinburgh, 1781), I, 187–90.

If the scene he describe be solemn, no lively nor fantastic image can have admission: but if, in a sprightly mood, he displays scenes of festivity, every pensive and gloomy thought is debarred. Thus the figures he delineates have one undivided direction; they make one great and entire impression.

To illustrate this remark, let us observe the conduct of Milton in his two celebrated poems, 'L'Allegro', and 'Il Penseroso'.

In the 'L'Allegro', meaning to excite a cheerful mood, he suggests a variety of objects; for variety, by giving considerable exercise to the mind, and by not suffering it to rest long on the same appearance, occasions brisk and exhilarating emotions. Accordingly, the poet shews us, at one glance, and, as it were, with a single dash of his pen, [ll. 71–6]. The objects themselves are cheerful; for, besides having brooks, meadows, and flowers, we have the whistling plowman, the singing milk-maid, the mower whetting his scythe, and the shepherd piping beneath a shade. These images, so numerous, so various, and so cheerful, are animated by lively contrasts: We have the mountains opposed to the meadows, 'Shallow brooks and rivers wide.' Add to this, that the charms of the landscape are heightened by the bloom of a smiling season; and that the light poured upon the whole is the delightful radiance of a summer morning [ll. 59–62]. Every image is lively; every thing different is with-held; all the emotions the poet excites are of one character and complexion.

Let us now observe the conduct of his 'Il Penseroso'. This poem is, in every respect, an exact counterpart to the former. And the intention of the poet being to promote a serious and solemn mood, he removes every thing lively: 'Hence vain deluding joys.' He quits society; he chuses silence, and opportunities for deep reflection; 'Some still removed place will fit.' The objects he presents are few. In the quotation, beginning with 'Russet lawns,' there are eight leading images; in the following, of equal length, there is only one: [ll. 67–72]. The sounds that can be, in any respect, agreeable to him, must correspond with his present humour: Not the song of the milkmaid, but that of the nightingale; not the whistling plowman, but the sound of the curfeu. His images succeed one another slowly, without any rapid or abrupt transitions, without any enlivening contrasts; and he will have no other light for his landscape than that of the moon: Or, if he cannot enjoy the scene without doors, he will have no other light within than that of dying embers, or of a solitary lamp at midnight. The time, and the place he chuses for his retreat, are perfectly suited to his employment; for he is engaged in deep meditation, and in considering

> What worlds or what vast regions hold
> Th' immortal mind. [ll. 90–1]

Every image is solemn; every thing different is with-held: Here, as before, all the emotions the poet excites are of one character and complexion. It is owing, in a great measure, to this attention in the writer, to preserve unity and consistency of sentiment, that, notwithstanding considerable imperfections in the language and versification, 'L'Allegro' and 'Il Penseroso' have so many admirers.

64. Johnson on Cowley and Milton

1779

Extract from Samuel Johnson, 'Life of Cowley', *Prefaces, Biographical and Critical to the Works of the English Poets* (1779), vol. 59 (of *Works*) and vol. 1 (of *Prefaces*), 25–6, 49.

At the same time were produced from the same university, the two great Poets, Cowley and Milton, of dissimilar genius, of opposite principles; but concurring in the cultivation of Latin poetry, in which the English, till their works and May's poem[1] appeared, seemed unable to contest the palm with any other of the lettered nations.

If the Latin performances of Cowley and Milton be compared, for May I hold to be superior to both, the advantage seems to lie on the side of Cowley. Milton is generally content to express the thoughts of the ancients in their language; Cowley, without much loss of purity or elegance, accommodates the diction of Rome to his own conceptions. . . . Milton tried the metaphysick stile only in his lines upon Hobson the Carrier.

[1] Thomas May's *Continuation of Lucan*.

65. Johnson on Philips and Milton

1779

Extract from Samuel Johnson, 'Life of John Philips', *Prefaces, Biographical and Critical to the Works of the English Poets* (1779), vol. 62 (of *Works*) and vol. 4 (of *Prefaces*), 11–12, 14–15.

The *Splendid Shilling* has the uncommon merit of an original design, unless it may be thought precluded by the ancient *Centos*. To degrade the sounding words and stately construction of Milton, by an application to the lowest and most trivial things, gratifies the mind with a momentary triumph over that grandeur which hitherto held its captives in admiration; the words and things are presented with a new appearance, and novelty is always grateful where it gives no pain.

But the merit of such performances begins and ends with the first author. He that should again adapt Milton's phrase to the gross incidents of common life, and even adapt it with more art, which would not be difficult, must yet expect but a small part of the praise which Philips has obtained; he can only hope to be considered as the repeater of a jest.

'The parody on Milton', says Gildon, 'is the only tolerable production of its author.' . . .

He imitates Milton's numbers indeed, but imitates them very injudiciously. Deformity is easily copied; and whatever there is in Milton which the reader wishes away, all that is obsolete, peculiar, or licentious, is accumulated with great care by Philips. Milton's verse was harmonious, in proportion to the general state of our metre in Milton's age; and, if he had written after the improvements made by Dryden, it is reasonable to believe that he would have admitted a more pleasing modulation of numbers into his work; but Philips sits down with a resolution to make no more musick than he found; to want all that his master wanted, though he is very far from having what his master had. Those asperities, therefore, that are venerable in the *Paradise Lost* are contemptible in the *Blenheim*.

66. Johnson on Milton's life and works

1779

Extract from Samuel Johnson, 'Life of Milton', *Prefaces, Biographical and Critical to the Works of the English Poets* (1779), vol. 60
(of *Works*) and vol. 2 (of *Prefaces*), 1, 112–20, 150 ff. Phrases in
round brackets were added, or replaced others, in the 1781 edition
of *The Lives of the Poets*.

The Life of Milton has been already written in so many forms, and
with such minute enquiry, that I might perhaps more properly have
contented myself with the addition of a few notes to Mr. Fenton's
elegant Abridgement, but that a new narrative was thought necessary
to the uniformity of this edition.

. . . Next year, when the danger of infection had ceased, he returned
to Bunhill-fields, and designed the publication of his poem [i.e.,
Paradise Lost]. A license was necessary, and he could expect no great
kindness from a chaplain of the archbishop of Canterbury. He seems,
however, to have been treated with tenderness; for though objections
were made to particular passages, and among them to the simile of the
sun eclipsed in the first book, yet the license was granted; and he sold
his copy, April 27, 1667, to Samuel Simmons for an immediate payment of five pounds, with a stipulation to receive five pounds more
when thirteen hundred should be sold of the first edition; and again,
five pounds after the sale of the same number of the second edition,
and another five pounds after the same sale of the third. None of the
three editions were to be extended beyond fifteen hundred copies.

The first edition was of ten books, in a small quarto. The titles were
varied from year to year; and an advertisement and the arguments of
the books were omitted in some copies, and inserted in others.

The sale gave him in two years a right to his second payment, for
which the receipt was signed April 26, 1669. The second edition was
not given till 1674; it was printed in small octavo; and the number of
books was encreased to twelve, by a division of the seventh and twelfth;

and some other small improvements were made. The third edition was published in 1678; and the widow, to whom the copy was then to devolve, sold all her claims to Simmons for eight pounds, according to her receipt given Dec. 21, 1680. Simmons had already agreed to transfer the whole right to Brabazon Aylmer for twenty-five pounds; and Aylmer sold to Jacob Tonson half, August 17, 1683, and half, March 24, 1690, at a price considerably enlarged. (In the history of *Paradise Lost* a deduction thus minute will rather gratify than fatigue.)

The slow sale and tardy reputation of this poem, have been always mentioned as evidences of neglected merit, and of the uncertainty of literary fame; and enquiries have been made, and conjectures offered, about the causes of its long obscurity and late reception. But has the case been truly stated? Have not lamentation and wonder been lavished on an evil that was never felt?

That in the reigns of Charles and James the *Paradise Lost* received no publick acclamations, is readily confessed. Wit and literature were on the side of the Court: and who that solicited favour or the fashion would venture to praise the defender of the regicides? All that he himself could think his due, from *evil tongues* in *evil days*, was that reverential silence which was generously preserved. But it cannot be inferred that his poem was not read, nor not, however unwillingly, admired.

The sale, if it be considered, will justify the publick. Those who have no power to judge of past times but by their own, should always doubt their conclusions. The sale (call) for books was not in Milton's age what it is in the present. To read was not then a general amusement; neither traders, nor often gentlemen, thought themselves disgraced by ignorance. The women had not then aspired to literature, nor was every house supplied with a closet of books (knowledge). Those, indeed, who professed learning were no less learned than at any other time; but of that middle race of students who read for pleasure or accomplishment, and who buy the numerous products of modern typography, the number was then comparatively small. To prove the paucity of readers, it may be sufficient to remark, that the nation had been satisfied, from 1623 to 1664, that is, forty-one years, with only two editions of the works of Shakespeare, which probably did not together make one thousand copies.

The sale of thirteen hundred copies in two years, in opposition to so much recent enmity, and to a style of versification new to all and disgusting to many, was an uncommon example of the prevalence of genius. The demand did not immediately encrease; for many more readers than were supplied at first the nation did not afford. Only three thousand were sold in eleven years; for it forced its way without assistance: its admirers did not dare to publish their opinion; and the opportunities now given of attracting notice by advertisement were then very few; for the means of proclaiming the publication of new books have been produced by that general literature which now pervades the nation through all its ranks.

But the reputation and price of the copy still advanced, till the Revolution put an end to the secrecy of love, and *Paradise Lost* broke into open view with sufficient security of kind reception.

Fancy can hardly forbear to conjecture with what temper Milton surveyed the silent progress of his work, and marked his reputation stealing its way in a kind of subterraneous current through fear and silence. I cannot but conceive him calm and confident, little disappointed, not at all dejected, relying on his own merit with steady consciousness, and waiting, without impatience, the vicissitudes of opinion, and the impartiality of a future generation.

. . . In the examination of Milton's poetical works, I shall pay so much regard to time as to begin with his juvenile productions. For his early pieces he seems to have had a degree of fondness not very laudable: what he has once written he resolves to preserve, and gives to the publick an unfinished poem, which he broke off because he was *nothing satisfied with what he had done*, supposing his readers less nice than himself. These preludes to his future labours are in Italian, Latin, and English. Of the Italian I cannot pretend to speak as a critick; but I have heard them commended by a man well qualified to decide their merit. The Latin pieces are lusciously elegant; but the delight which they afford is rather by the exquisite imitation of the ancient writers, by the purity of the diction, and the harmony of the numbers, than by any power of invention, or vigour of sentiment. They are not all of equal value; the elegies excell the odes; and some of the exercises on Gunpowder Treason might have been spared.

The English poems, though they make no promises of *Paradise Lost*, have this evidence of genius, that they have a cast original and unborrowed. But their peculiarity is not excellence: if they differ from verses of others, they differ for the worse; for they are too often distinguished by repulsive harshness; the combination of words are new, but they are not pleasing; the rhymes and epithets seem to be laboriously sought, and violently applied.

That in the early parts of his life he wrote with much care appears from his manuscripts, happily preserved at Cambridge, in which many of his smaller works are found as they were first written, with the subsequent corrections. Such reliques shew how excellence is acquired; what we hope ever to do with ease, we may learn first to do with diligence.

Those who admire the beauties of this great poet, sometimes force their own judgement into false approbation of his little pieces, and prevail upon themselves to think that admirable which is only singular. All that short compositions can commonly attain is neatness and elegance. Milton never learned the art of doing little things with grace; he overlooked the milder excellence of suavity and softness; he was a *Lion* that had no skill *in dandling the Kid*.

One of the poems on which much praise has been bestowed is 'Lycidas'; of which the diction is harsh, the rhymes uncertain, and the numbers unpleasing. What beauty there is, we must therefore seek in the sentiments and images.

It is not to be considered as the effusion of real passion; for passion runs not after remote allusions and obscure opinions. Passion plucks no berries from the myrtle and ivy, nor calls upon Arethuse and Mincius, nor tells of rough *satyrs* and *fauns with cloven heel*. Where there is leisure for fiction there is little grief.

In this poem there is no nature, for there is no truth; there is no art, for there is nothing new. Its form is that of pastoral, easy, vulgar, and therefore disgusting: whatever images it can supply, are long ago exhausted; and its inherent improbability always forces dissatisfaction on the mind. When Cowley tells of Hervey that they studied together, it is easy to suppose how much he must miss the companion of his labours, and the partner of his discoveries; but what image of tenderness can be excited by these lines? [27–9] We know that they never drove a field, and that they had no flock to batten; and though it be allowed that the representation may be allegorical, the true meaning is so uncertain and remote, that it is never sought, because it cannot be known when it is found.

Among the flocks, and copses, and flowers, appear the heathen deities; Jove and Phoebus, Neptune and Æolus, with a long train of mythological imagery, such as a College easily supplies. Nothing can less display knowledge, or less exercise invention, than to tell how a shepherd has lost his companion, and must now feed his flocks alone, without any judge of his skill in piping; and how one god asks another god what is become of Lycidas, and how neither god can tell. He who thus grieves will excite no sympathy; he who thus praises will confer no honour.

This poem has yet a grosser fault. With these trifling fictions are mingled the most awful and sacred truths, such as ought never to be polluted with such irreverend combinations. The shepherd likewise is now feeder of sheep, and afterwards an ecclesiastical pastor, a superintendent of a Christian flock. Such equivocations are always unskilful; but here they are indecent, and at least approach to impiety, of which, however, I believe the writer not to have been conscious.

Such is the power of reputation justly acquired, that its blaze drives away the eye from nice examination. Surely no man could have fancied that he read 'Lycidas' with pleasure, had he not known its author.

Of the two pieces, 'L'Allegro' and 'Il Penseroso', I believe opinion is uniform; every man that reads them, reads them with pleasure. The author's design is not, what Theobald has remarked, merely to shew how objects derive their colours from the mind, by representing the operation of the same things upon the gay and the melancholy temper, or upon the same man as he is differently disposed; but rather how, among the successive variety of appearances, every disposition of mind takes hold on those by which it may be gratified.

The *chearful* man hears the lark in the morning; the *pensive* man hears the nightingale in the evening. The *chearful* man sees the cock strut, and hears the horn and hounds echo in the wood; then walks *not unseen* to observe the glory of the rising sun, or listen to the singing milk-maid, and view the labours of the plowman and the mower; then casts his eyes about him over scenes of smiling plenty, and looks up to the distant tower, the residence of some fair inhabitant; thus he pursues rural gaiety through a day of labour or of play, and delights himself at night with the fanciful narratives of superstitious ignorance.

The *pensive* man, at one time, walks *unseen* to muse at midnight; and at another hears the sullen curfew. If the weather drives him home, he sits in a room lighted only by *glowing embers*; or by a lonely lamp outwatches the North Star, to discover the habitation of separate souls, and varies the shades of meditation, by contemplating the magnificent or pathetick scenes of tragick and epic poetry. When the morning comes, a morning gloomy with rain and wind, he walks into the dark trackless woods, falls asleep by some murmuring water, and with melancholy enthusiasm expects some dream of prognostication, or some musick plaid by aerial performers.

Both Mirth and Melancholy are solitary, silent inhabitants of the breast that neither receive nor transmit communication; no mention is therefore made of a philosophical friend, or a pleasant companion. Seriousness does not arise from any participation of calamity, nor the gaiety from the pleasures of the bottle.

The man of *chearfulness*, having exhausted the country, tries what *towered cities* will afford, and mingles with scenes of splendor, gay assemblies, and nuptial festivities; but he mingles a mere spectator, as when the learned comedies of Jonson, or the wild dramas of Shakespeare, are exhibited, he attends the theatre.

The *pensive* man never loses himself in crowds, but walks the cloister, or frequents the cathedral. Milton probably had not yet forsaken the Church.

Both his characters delight in musick; but he seems to think that chearful notes would have obtained from Pluto a compleat dismission of Eurydice, of whom solemn sounds only procured a conditional release.

For the old age of Chearfulness he makes no provision; but Melancholy he conducts with great dignity to the close of life.

Through these two poems the images are properly selected, and nicely distinguished; but the colours of the diction seem not sufficiently discriminated. (His Chearfulnes is without levity, and his Pensiveness without asperity.) I know not whether the characters are kept sufficiently apart. No mirth can, indeed, be found in his melancholy; but I am afraid that I always meet some melancholy in his mirth. They are two noble efforts of imagination.

The greatest of his juvenile performances is the 'Mask of Comus'; in which may very plainly be discovered the dawn or twilight of *Paradise Lost*. Milton appears to have formed very early that system of diction, and mode of verse, which his maturer judgement approved, and from which he never endeavoured nor desired to deviate.

Nor does 'Comus' afford only a specimen of his language; it exhibits likewise his power of description, and his vigour of sentiment, employed in the praise and defence of virtue. A work more truely poetical is rarely found; allusions, images, and descriptive epithets, embellish almost every period with lavish decoration. As a series of lines, therefore, it may be considered as worthy of all the admiration with which the votaries have received it.

As a drama it is deficient. The action is not probable. A Masque, in those parts where supernatural intervention is admitted, must indeed be given up to all the freaks of imagination: but, so far as the action is merely human, it ought to be reasonable, which can hardly be said of the conduct of the two brothers; who, when their sister sinks with fatigue in a pathless wilderness, wander both away together in search of berries too far to find their way back, and leave a helpless lady to all the sadness and danger of solitude. This however is a defect over-balanced by its convenience.

What deserves more reprehension is, that the prologue spoken in the wild wood by the attendant Spirit is addressed to the audience; a mode of communication so contrary to the nature of dramatick representation, that no precedents can support it.

The discourse of the Spirit is too long; an objection that may be made to almost all the following speeches: they have not the spriteliness of a dialogue animated by reciprocal contention, but seem rather declamations deliberately composed, and formally repeated, on a moral question. The auditor therefore listens as to a lecture, without passion, without anxiety.

The song of Comus has airiness and jollity; but, what may recommend Milton's morals as well as his poetry, the invitations to pleasure are so general, that they excite no distinct images of corrupt enjoyment, and take no dangerous hold on the fancy.

The following soliloquies of Comus and the Lady are elegant, but tedious. The song must owe much to the voice, if it ever can delight. At last the brothers enter, with too much tranquillity; and when they have feared lest their sister should be in danger, and hoped that she is not in danger, the Elder makes a speech in praise of chastity, and the Younger finds how fine it is to be a philosopher.

Then descends the Spirit in form of a shepherd; and the brother, instead of being in haste to ask his help, praises his singing, and enquires his business in that place. It is remarkable, that at this interview the brother is taken with a short fit of rhyming. The Spirit relates that the Lady is in the power of Comus; the brother moralises again; and the Spirit makes a long narration, of no use because it is false, and therefore unsuitable to a good Being.

In all these parts the language is poetical, and the sentiments are generous; but there is something wanting to allure attention.

The dispute between the Lady and Comus is the most animated and affecting scene of the drama, and wants nothing but a brisker reciprocation of objections and replies to invite attention, and detain it.

The songs are vigorous, and full of imagery; but they are harsh in their diction, and not very musical in their numbers.

Throughout the whole, the figures are too bold, and the language too luxuriant for dialogue. It is a drama in the epic style, inelegantly splendid, and tediously instructive.

The *Sonnets* were written in different parts of Milton's life, upon different occasions. They deserve not any particular criticism; for of the best it can only be said, that they are not bad; and perhaps only the eighth and the twenty-first are truly entitled to this slender commendation. The fabrick of a sonnet, however adapted to the Italian language, has never succeeded in ours, which, having greater variety of termination, requires the rhymes to be often changed.

Those little pieces may be dispatched without much anxiety; a greater work calls for greater care. I am now to examine *Paradise Lost*; a poem, which, considered with respect to design, may claim the first place, and with respect to performance the second among the productions of the human mind.

By the general consent of criticks, the first praise of genius is due to the writer of an epick poem, as it requires an assemblage of all the powers which are singly sufficient for other compositions. Poetry is the art of uniting pleasure with truth, by calling imagination to the help of reason. Epick poetry undertakes to teach the most important truths by the most pleasing precepts, and therefore relates some great event in the most affecting manner. History must supply the writer with the rudiments of narration, which he must improve and exalt by a nobler art, animate by dramatick energy, and diversify by retrospection and anticipation; morality must teach him the exact bounds, and different shades, of vice and virtue: from policy, and the practice of life, he has to learn the discriminations of character, and the tendency of the passions, either single or combined; and physiology must supply him with illustrations and images. To put these materials to poetical use, is required an imagination capable of painting nature, and realizing fiction. Nor is he yet a poet till he has attained the whole extension of his language, distinguished all the delicacies of phrase, and all the colours of words, and learned to adjust their different sounds to all the varieties of metrical modulation.

Bossu is of opinion that the poet's first work is to find a *moral*, which his fable is afterwards to illustrate and establish. This seems to have been the process only of Milton; the moral of other poems is incidental and consequent; in Milton's only it is essential and intrinsick. His purpose was the most useful and the most arduous; *to vindicate the ways of God to man*; to shew the reasonableness of religion, and the necessity of obedience to the Divine Law.

To convey this moral there must be a *fable*, a narration artfully constructed, so as to excite curiosity, and surprise expectation. In this part of his work, Milton must be confessed to have equalled every other poet. He has involved in his account of the Fall of Man the events which preceded, and those that were to follow it: he has interwoven the whole system of theology with such propriety, that every part appears to be necessary; and scarcely any recital is wished shorter for the sake of quickening the progress of the main action.

The subject of an epick poem is naturally an event of great importance. That of Milton is not the destruction of a city, the conduct of a colony, or the foundation of an empire. His subject is the fate of worlds, the revolutions of heaven and of earth; rebellion against the Supreme King, raised by the highest order of created beings; the overthrow of their host, and the punishment of their crime; the creation of a new race of reasonable creatures; their original happiness and innocence, their forfeiture of immortality, and their restoration to hope and peace.

Great events can be hastened or retarded only by persons of elevated dignity. Before the greatness displayed in Milton's poem, all other greatness shrinks away. The weakest of his agents are the highest and noblest of human beings, the original parents of mankind; with whose actions the elements consented; on whose rectitude, or deviation of will, depended the state of terrestrial nature, and the condition of all the future inhabitants of the globe.

Of the other agents in the poem, the chief are such as it is irreverence to name on slight occasions. The rest are lower powers;

> —of which the least could wield
> Those elements, and arm him with the force
> Of all their regions. [VI, 221–3]

powers, which only the controul of Omnipotence restrains from laying creation waste, and filling the vast expanse of space with ruin and confusion. To display the motives and actions of beings thus superiour, so far as human reason can examine them, or human imagination represent them, is the task which this mighty poet has undertaken and performed.

In the examination of epick poems much speculation is commonly employed upon the *characters*. The characters in the *Paradise Lost*, which admit of examination, are those of angels and of man; of angels good and evil; of man in his innocent and sinful state.

Among the angels, the virtue of Raphael is mild and placid, of easy condescension and free communication; that of Michael is regal and lofty, and, as may seem, attentive to the dignity of his own nature. Abdiel and Gabriel appear occasionally, and act as every incident requires; the solitary fidelity of Abdiel is very amiably painted.

Of the evil angels the characters are more diversified. To Satan, as Addison observes, such sentiments are given as suit *the most exalted and most depraved being*. Milton has been censured, by Clark, for the impiety which sometimes breaks from Satan's mouth. For there are thoughts, as he justly remarks, which no observation of character can justify, because no good man would willingly permit them to pass, however transient, through his own mind. To make Satan speak as a rebel, without any such expressions as might taint the reader's imagination, was indeed one of the great difficulties in Milton's undertaking, and I cannot but think that he has extricated himself with great happiness. There is in Satan's speeches little that can give pain to a pious ear. The language of rebellion cannot be the same with that of obedience. The malignity of Satan foams in haughtiness and obstinacy; but his expressions are commonly general, and no otherwise offensive than as they are wicked.

The other chiefs of the celestial rebellion are very judiciously discriminated in the first and second books; and the ferocious character of Moloch appears, both in the battle and the council, with exact consistency.

To Adam and to Eve are given, during their innocence, such sentiments as innocence can generate and utter. Their love is pure benevolence and mutual veneration; their repasts are without luxury, and their diligence without toil. Their addresses to their Maker have little more than the voice of admiration and gratitude. Fruition left them nothing to ask, and Innocence left them nothing to fear.

But with guilt enter distrust and discord, mutual accusation, and stubborn self-defence; they regard each other with alienated minds, and dread their Creator as the avenger of their transgression. At last they seek shelter in his mercy, soften to repentance, and melt in supplication. Both before and after the Fall, the superiority of Adam is diligently sustained.

Of the *probable* and the *marvellous*, two parts of a vulgar epick poem, which immerge the critick in deep consideration, the *Paradise Lost* requires little to be said. It contains the history of a miracle, of Creation and Redemption; it displays the power and the mercy of the Supreme Being; the probable therefore is marvellous, and the marvellous is probable. The substance of the narrative is truth; and as truth allows no choice, it is, like necessity, superior to rule. To the accidental and adventitious parts, as to every thing human, some slight exceptions may be made. But the main fabrick is immovably supported.

It is justly remarked by Addison, that this poem has, by the nature of its subject, the advantage above all others, that it is universally and perpetually interesting. All mankind will, through all ages, bear the same relation to Adam and to Eve, and must partake of that good and evil which extend to themselves.

Of the *machinery*, so called from *theos apo mechanis*, by which is meant the occasional interposition of supernatural power, another fertile topick of critical remarks, here is no room to speak, because every thing is done under the immediate and visible direction of Heaven; but the rule is so far observed, that no part of the action could have been accomplished by any other means.

Of *episodes*, I think there are only two, contained in Raphael's relation of the war in heaven, and Michael's prophetick account of the changes to happen in this world. Both are closely connected with the great action; one was necessary to Adam as a warning, the other as a consolation.

To the compleatness or *integrity* of the design nothing can be objected; it has distinctly and clearly what Aristotle requires, a beginning, a middle, and an end. There is perhaps no poem, of the same length, from which so little can be taken without apparent mutilation. Here are no funeral games, nor is there any long description of a shield. The short digressions at the beginning of the third, seventh, and ninth books, might doubtless be spared; but superfluities so beautiful, who would take away? or who does not wish that the author of the *Iliad* had gratified succeeding ages with a little knowledge of himself? Perhaps no passages are more frequently or more attentively read than those extrinsick paragraphs; and, since the end of poetry is pleasure, that cannot be unpoetical with which all are pleased.

The questions, whether the action of the poem be strictly *one*, whether the poem can be properly termed *heroick*, and who is the hero, are raised by such readers as draw their principle of judgement rather from books than from reason. Milton, though he intituled *Paradise Lost* only a *poem*, yet calls it himself *heroick song*. Dryden, petulantly and indecently, denies the heroism of Adam, because he was overcome;

but there is no reason why the hero should not be unfortunate, except established practice, since success and virtue do not go necessarily together. Cato is the hero of Lucan; but Lucan's authority will not be suffered by Quintilian to decide. However, if success be necessary, Adam's deceiver was at last crushed; Adam was restored to his Maker's favour, and therefore may securely resume his human rank.

After the scheme and fabrick of the poem, must be considered its component parts, the sentiments and the diction.

The *sentiments*, as expressive of manners, or appropriated to characters, are, for the great part, unexceptionably just.

Splendid passages, containing lessons of morality, or precepts of prudence, occur seldom. Such is the original formation of this poem, that, as it admits no human manners till the Fall, it can give little assistance to human conduct. Its end is to raise the thoughts above sublunary cares or pleasures. Yet the praise of that fortitude, with which Abdiel maintained his singularity of virtue against the scorn of multitudes, may be accommodated to all times; and Raphael's reproof of Adam's curiosity after the planetary motions, with the answer returned by Adam, may be confidently opposed to any rule of life which any poet has delivered.

The thoughts which are occasionally called forth in the progress, are such as could only be produced by an imagination in the highest degree fervid and active, to which materials were supplied by incessant study and unlimited curiosity. The heat of Milton's mind might be said to sublimate his learning, to throw off into his work the spirit of science, unmingled with its grosser parts.

He had considered creation in its whole extent, and his descriptions, are therefore learned. He had accustomed his imagination to unrestrained indulgence, and his conceptions therefore were extensive. The characteristick quality of his poem is sublimity. He sometimes descends to the elegant, but his element is the great. He can occasionally invest himself with grace; but his natural port is gigantick loftiness. He can please when pleasure is required; but it is his peculiar power to astonish.

He seems to have been well acquainted with his own genius, and to know what it was that Nature had bestowed upon him more bountifully than upon others; the power of displaying the vast, illuminating the splendid, enforcing the awful, darkening the gloomy, and aggravating the dreadful: he therefore chose a subject on which too much could not be said, on which he might tire his fancy without the censure of extravagance.

The appearance of nature, and the occurrences of life, did not satiate his appetite of greatness. To paint things as they are, requires a minute attention, and employs the memory rather than the fancy. Milton's delight was to sport in the wide regions of possibility; reality was a scene too narrow for his mind. He sent his faculties out upon discovery, into worlds where only imagination can travel, and delighted to form new modes of existence, and furnish sentiment and action to superior beings, to trace the counsels of hell, or accompany the choirs of heaven.

But he could not be always in other worlds: he must sometimes revisit earth, and tell of things visible and known. When he cannot raise wonder by the sublimity of his mind, he gives delight by its fertility.

Whatever be his subject, he never fails to fill the imagination. But his images and descriptions of the scenes or operations of Nature do not seem to be always copied from original form, nor to have the freshness, raciness, and energy of immediate observation. He saw Nature, as Dryden expresses it, *through the spectacles of books*; and on most occasions calls learning to his assistance. The garden of Eden brings to his mind the vale of *Enna*, where Proserpine was gathering flowers. Satan makes his way through fighting elements, like *Argo* between the *Cyanean* rocks, or *Ulysses* between the two *Sicilian* whirlpools, when he shunned *Charybdis* on the *larboard*. The mythological allusions have been justly censured, as not being always used with notice of their vanity; but they contribute variety to the narration, and produce an alternate exercise of the memory and the fancy.

His similes are less numerous, and more various, than those of his predecessors. But he does not confine himself within the limits of glorious comparison: his great excellence is amplitude, and he expands the adventitious image beyond the dimensions which the occasion required. Thus, comparing the shield of Satan to the orb of the Moon, he crowds the imagination with the discovery of the telescope, and all the wonders which the telescope discovers.

Of his moral sentiments it is hardly praise to affirm that they excel those of all other poets; for this superiority he was indebted to his acquaintance with the sacred writings. The ancient epick poets, wanting the light of Revelation, were very unskilful teachers of virtue: their principal characters may be great, but they are not amiable. The reader may rise from their works with a greater degree of active or passive fortitude, and sometimes of prudence; but he will be able to carry away few precepts of justice, and none of mercy.

From the Italian writers it appears, that the advantages of even

Christian knowledge may be possessed in vain. Ariosto's pravity is generally known; and though the *Deliverance of Jerusalem* may be considered as a sacred subject, the poet has been very sparing of moral instruction.

In Milton every line breathes sanctity of thought, and purity of manners, except when the train of the narration requires the introduction of the rebellious spirits; and even they are compelled to acknowledge their subjection to God, in such a manner as excites reverence, and confirms piety.

Of human beings there are but two; but those two are the parents of mankind, venerable before their fall for dignity and innocence, and amiable after it for repentance and submission. In their first state their affection is tender without weakness, and their piety sublime without presumption. When they have sinned, they shew how discord begins in mutual frailty, and how it ought to cease in mutual forbearance; how confidence of the divine favour is forfeited by sin, and how hope of pardon may be obtained by penitence and prayer. A state of innocence we can only conceive, if indeed, in our present misery, it be possible to conceive it; but the sentiments and worship proper to a fallen and offending being, we have all to learn, as we have all to practise.

The poet, whatever be done, is always great. Our progenitors, in their first state, conversed with angels; even when folly and sin had degraded them, they had not in their humiliation *the port of mean suitors*; and they rise again to reverential regard, when we find that their prayers were heard.

As human passions did not enter the world before the Fall, there is in the *Paradise Lost* little opportunity for the pathetick; but what little there is has not been lost. That passion which is peculiar to rational nature, the anguish arising from the consciousness of transgression, and the horrours attending the sense of the Divine Displeasure, are very justly described and forcibly impressed. But the passions are moved only on one occasion; sublimity is the general and prevailing quality in this poem; sublimity variously modified, sometimes descriptive, sometimes argumentative.

The defects and faults of *Paradise Lost*, for faults and defects every work of man must have, it is the business of impartial criticism to discover. As, in displaying the excellence of Milton, I have not made long quotations, because of selecting beauties there had been no end, I shall in the same general manner mention that which seems to deserve censure; for what Englishman can take delight in transcribing passages, which, if they lessen the reputation of Milton, diminish in some degree the honour of our country?

The generality of my scheme does not admit the frequent notice of verbal inaccuracies; which Bentley, perhaps better skilled in grammar than poetry, has often found, though he sometimes made them, and which he imputed to the obstrusions of a reviser whom the author's blindness obliged him to employ. A supposition rash and groundless, if he thought it true; and vile and pernicious, if, as is said, he in private allowed it to be false.

The plan of *Paradise Lost* has this inconvenience, that it comprises neither human actions nor human manners. The man and woman who act and suffer, are in a state which no other man or woman can ever know. The reader finds no transaction in which he can be engaged; beholds no condition in which he can by an effort of imagination place himself; he has, therefore, little natural curiosity or sympathy.

We all, indeed, feel the effects of Adam's disobedience; we all sin like Adam, and like him must all bewail our offences; we have restless and insidious enemies in the fallen angels, and in the blessed spirits we have guardians and friends; in the Redemption of mankind we hope to be included; in the description of heaven and hell we are surely interested, as we are all to reside hereafter either in the regions of horror or of bliss.

But these truths are too important to be new; they have been taught to our infancy; they have mingled with our solitary thoughts and familiar conversation, and are habitually interwoven with the whole texture of life. Being therefore not new, they raise no unaccustomed emotion in the mind; what we knew before we cannot learn; what is not unexpected cannot surprise.

Of the ideas suggested by these awful scenes, from some we recede with reverence, except when stated hours require their association; and from others we shrink with horror, or admit them only as salutary inflictions, as counterpoises to our interests and passions. Such images rather obstruct the career of fancy than incite it.

Pleasure and terrour are indeed the genuine sources of poetry; but poetical pleasure must be such as human imagination can at least conceive, and poetical terrour such as human strength and fortitude may combat. The good and evil of Eternity are too ponderous for the wings of wit; the mind sinks under them in passive helplessness, content with calm belief and humble adoration.

Known truths, however, may take a different appearance, and be conveyed to the mind by a new train of intermediate images. This Milton has undertaken, and performed with pregnancy and vigour of mind peculiar to himself. Whoever considers the few radical positions which the Scriptures afforded him, will wonder by what energetick operation he expanded them to such extent, and ramified them to so much variety, restrained as he was by religious reverence from licentiousness of fiction.

Here is a full display of the united force of study and genius; of a great accumulation of materials, with judgement to digest, and fancy to combine them: Milton was able to select from nature, or from story, from ancient fable, or from modern science, whatever could illustrate or adorn his thoughts. An accumulation of knowledge impregnated his mind, fermented by study, and sublimed (exalted) by imagination.

It has been therefore said, without an indecent hyperbole, by one of his encomiasts, that in reading *Paradise Lost* we read a book of universal knowledge.

But original deficience cannot be supplied. The want of human interest is always felt. *Paradise Lost* is one of the books which the reader admires and lays down, and forgets to take up again. (None ever wished it longer than it is.) Its perusal is a duty rather than a pleasure. We read Milton for instruction, retire harassed and overburdened, and look elsewhere for recreation; we desert our master, and seek for companions.

Another inconvenience of Milton's design is, that it requires the description of what cannot be described, the agency of spirits. He saw that immateriality supplied no images, and that he could not show angels acting but by instruments of action; he therefore invested them with form and matter. This, being necessary, was therefore defensible; and he should have secured the consistency of his system, by keeping immateriality out of sight, and enticing his reader to drop it from his thoughts. But he has unhappily perplexed his poetry with his philosophy. His infernal and celestial powers are sometimes pure spirit, and sometimes animated body. When Satan walks with his lance upon the *burning marle*, he has a body; when in his passage between hell and the new world, he is in danger of sinking in the vacuity, and is supported by a gust of rising vapours, he has a body; when he animates the toad, he seems to be mere spirit, that can penetrate matter at pleasure; when he *starts up in his own shape*, he has at least a determined form; and when he is brought before Gabriel, he has *a spear and a shield*, which he had the power of hiding in the toad, though the arms of the contending angels are evidently material.

The vulgar inhabitants of Pandæmonium, being *incorporeal spirits*, are *at large, though without number*, in a limited space; yet in the battle, when they were overwhelmed by mountains, their armour hurt them, *crushed in upon their substance, now grown gross by sinning*. This likewise happened to the uncorrupted angels, who were overthrown the *sooner for their arms*, for *unarmed they might easily as spirits have evaded by contraction or remove*. Even as spirits they are hardly spiritual; for *contraction* and *remove* are images of matter; but if they could have escaped without their armour, they might have escaped from it, and left only the empty cover to be battered. Uriel, when he rides on a sun-beam, is material: Satan is material when he is afraid of the prowess of Adam.

The confusion of spirit and matter which pervades the whole narration of the war of heaven fills it with incongruity; and the book, in which it is related, is, I believe, the favourite of children, and gradually neglected as knowledge is increased.

After the operation of immaterial agents, which cannot be explained, may be considered that of allegorical persons, which have no real existence. To exalt causes into agents, to invest abstract ideas with form, and animate them with activity, has always been the right of poetry. But such airy beings are, for the most part, suffered only to do their natural office; and retire. Thus Fame tells a tale, and Victory hovers over a general, or perches on a standard; but Fame and Victory can do no more. To give them any real employment, or ascribe to them any material agency, is to make them allegorical no longer, but to shock the mind by ascribing effects to non-entity. In the *Prometheus* of Aeschylus, we see *Violence* and *Strength*, and in the *Alcestis* of Euripides, we see *Death*, brought upon the stage, all as active persons of the drama; but no precedents can justify absurdity.

Milton's allegory of Sin and Death is undoubtedly faulty. Sin is indeed the mother of Death, and may be allowed to be the portress of hell; but when they stop the journey of Satan, a journey described as real, and when Death offers him battle, the allegory is broken. That Sin and Death should have shewn the way to hell might have been allowed; but they cannot facilitate the passage by building a bridge, because the difficulty of Satan's passage is described as real and sensible, and the bridge ought to be only figurative. The hell assigned to the rebellious spirits is described as not less local than the residence of man. It is placed in some distant part of space, separated from the regions of harmony and order by a chaotick waste and an unoccupied vacuity; but *Sin* and *Death* worked up a *mole* of *aggravated soil*, cemented with *asphaltus*; a work too bulky for ideal architects.

This unskilful allegory appears to me one of the greatest faults of the poem; and to this there was no temptation, but the author's opinion of its beauty.

To the conduct of the narrative some objections may be made. Satan is with great expectation brought before Gabriel in Paradise, and is suffered to go away unmolested. The creation of man is represented as the consequence of the vacuity left in heaven by the expulsion of the rebels; yet Satan mentions it as a report *rife in heaven* before his departure.

To find sentiments for the state of innocence, was very difficult; and something of anticipation perhaps is now and then discovered. Adam's discourse of dreams seems not to be the speculation of a new-created being. I know not whether his answer to the angel's reproof for curiosity does not want something of propriety: it is the speech of a man acquainted with many other men. Some philosophical notions, especially when the philosophy is false, might have been better omitted. The angel, in a comparison, speaks of *timorous deer*, before deer were yet timorous, and before Adam could understand the comparison.

Dryden remarks, that Milton has some flats among his elevations. This is only to say that all the parts are not equal. In every work one part must be for the sake of others; a palace must have passages; a poem must have transitions. It is no more to be required that wit should always be blazing, than that the sun should always stand at noon. In a great work there is a vicissitude of luminous and opaque parts, as there is in the world a succession of day and night. Milton, when he has expatiated in the sky, may be allowed sometimes to revisit earth; for what other author ever soared so high, or sustained his flight so long?

Milton, being well versed in the Italian poets, appears to have borrowed often from them; and, as every man learns (catches) something from his companions, his desire of imitating Ariosto's levity has disgraced his work with the *Paradise of Fools*; a fiction not in itself ill-imagined, but too ludicrous for its place.

His play on words, in which he delights too often; his equivocations, which Bentley endeavours to defend by the example of the ancients; his unnecessary and ungraceful use of terms of art, it is not necessary to mention, because they are easily remarked, and generally censured, and at last bear so little proportion to the whole, that they scarcely deserve the attention of a critick.

307

Such are the faults of that wonderful performance *Paradise Lost*; which he who can put in balance with its beauties must be considered not as nice but as dull, as less to be censured for want of candour than pitied for want of sensibility.

Of *Paradise Regained*, the general judgement seems now to be right, that it is in many parts elegant, and every-where instructive. It was not to be supposed that the writer of *Paradise Lost* could ever write without great effusions of fancy, and exalted precepts of wisdom. The basis of *Paradise Regained* is narrow; a dialogue without action can never please like an union of the narrative and dramatick powers. Had this poem been written not by Milton, but by some imitator, it would have claimed and received universal praise.

If *Paradise Regained* has been too much depreciated, *Samson Agonistes* has in requital been too much admired. It could only be by long prejudice, and the bigotry of learning, that Milton could prefer the ancient tragedies, with their encumbrance of a chorus, to the exhibitions of the French and English stages; and it is only by a blind confidence in the reputation of Milton, that a drama can be praised in which the intermediate parts have neither cause nor consequence, neither hasten nor retard the catastrophe.

In this tragedy are however many particular beauties, many just sentiments and striking lines; but it wants that power of attracting the attention which a well-connected plan produces.

Milton would not have excelled in dramatick writing; he knew human nature only in the gross, and had never studied the shades of character, nor the combinations of concurring, or the perplexity of contending passions. He had read much, and knew what books could teach; but had mingled little in the world, and was deficient in the knowledge which experience must confer.

Through all his greater works there prevails an uniform peculiarity of *Diction*, a mode and cast of expression which bears little resemblance to that of any former writer, and which is so far removed from common use, that an unlearned reader, when he first opens his book, finds himself surprised by a new language.

This novelty has been, by those who can find nothing wrong in Milton, imputed to his laborious endeavours after words suitable to the grandeur of his ideas. *Our language*, says Addison, *sunk under him*. But the truth is, that, both in prose and verse, he had formed his stile by a perverse and pedantick principle. He was desirous to use English words with a foreign idiom. This in all his prose is discovered and condemned;

for there judgement operates freely, neither softened by the beauty, nor awed by the dignity of his thoughts; but such is the power of his poetry, that his call is obeyed without resistance, the reader feels himself in captivity to a higher and a nobler mind, and criticism sinks in admiration.

Milton's stile was not modified by his subject: what is shown with greater extent in *Paradise Lost*, may be found in 'Comus'. One source of his peculiarity was his familiarity with the Tuscan poets: the disposition of his words is, I think, frequently Italian; perhaps sometimes combined with other tongues. Of him, at last, may be said what Jonson says of Spenser, that *he wrote no language*, but has formed what *Butler* calls a *Babylonish Dialect*, in itself harsh and barbarous, but made by exalted genius and extensive learning, the vehicle of so much instruction and so much pleasure, that, like other lovers, we find grace in its deformity.

Whatever be the faults of his diction, he cannot want the praise of copiousness and variety: he was master of his language in its full extent; and has selected the melodious words with such diligence, that from his book alone the Art of English Poetry might be learned.

After his diction, something must be said of his *versification. The measure*, he says, *is the English heroick verse without rhyme*. Of this mode he had many examples among the Italians, and some of his own country. The earl of Surrey is said to have translated one of Virgil's books without rhyme; and, besides our tragedies, a few short poems had appeared in blank verse; particularly one tending to reconcile the nation to Raleigh's wild attempt upon Guiana, and probably written by Raleigh himself. These petty performances cannot be supposed to have much influenced Milton, who more probably took his hint from Trisino's *Italia Liberata*; and, finding blank verse easier than rhyme, was desirous of persuading himself that it is better.

Rhyme, he says, and says truly, *is no necessary adjunct of true poetry*. But perhaps, of poetry as a mental operation, metre or musick is no necessary adjunct: it is however by the musick of metre that poetry has been discriminated in all languages; and in languages melodiously constructed with a due proportion of long and short syllables, metre is sufficient. But one language cannot communicate its rules to another: where metre is scanty and imperfect, some help is necessary. The musick of the English heroick line strikes the ear so faintly that it is easily lost, unless all the syllables of every line co-operate together: this co-operation can be only obtained by the preservation of every verse unmingled with another, as a distinct system of sounds; and this distinctness is obtained and preserved by the artifice of rhyme. The variety of pauses, so much boasted by the lovers of blank verse, changes the measures of an English poet to the periods of a declaimer; and there are only a few skilful and happy readers of Milton, who enable their audience to perceive where the lines end or begin. *Blank verse*, said an ingenious critick, *seems to be verse only to the eye.*

Poetry may subsist without rhyme, but English poetry will not often please; nor can rhyme ever be safely spared but where the subject is able to support itself. Blank verse makes some approach to that which is called the *lapidary stile*; has neither the easiness of prose, nor the melody of numbers, and therefore tires by long continuance. Of the Italian writers without rhyme, whom Milton alleges as precedents, not one is popular; what reason could urge in its defence, has been confuted by the ear.

But, whatever be the advantage of rhyme, I cannot prevail on myself to wish that Milton had been a rhymer, for I cannot wish his work to be other than it is; yet, like other heroes, he is to be admired rather than imitated. He that thinks himself capable of astonishing, may write blank verse; but those that hope only to please, must condescend to rhyme.

The highest praise of genius is original invention. Milton cannot be said to have contrived the structure of an epick poem, and therefore must yield (owes reverence) to that vigour and amplitude of mind to which all generations must be indebted for the art of poetical narration, for the texture of the fable, the variation of incidents, the interposition of dialogue, and all the stratagems that surprise and enchain attention. But, of all the borrowers from Homer, Milton is perhaps the least indebted. He was naturally a thinker for himself, confident of his own abilities, and disdainful of help or hindrance: he did not refuse admission to the thought or images of his predecessors, but he did not seek them. From his contemporaries he neither courted nor received support; there is in his writings nothing by which the pride of other authors might be gratified, or favour gained; no exchange of praise, nor solicitation of support. His great works were performed under discountenance, and in blindness, but difficulties vanished at his touch; he was born for whatever is arduous; and his work is not the greatest of heroick poems, only because it is not the first.

67. Blackburne on Milton's political principles

1780

Extract from Francis Blackburne, *Memoirs of Thomas Hollis, Esq.* (1780), 92–4, 148.

Francis Blackburne (1705–87) was a minister who entered a number of theological arguments. *The Confessional*, dealing with the doctrine of confession and the demands placed upon protestant ministers, was sent to Thomas Hollis (1720–74), known for his republican views, who published it in 1766. In 1780 appeared Blackburne's memoirs of his friend, which frequently present Hollis's writings and remarks on Milton as well as his own criticism and observations. Hollis was also the editor of Toland's *Life of Milton* in 1761. Blackburne's editions of *Of Education* and *Areopagitica* will be found with his *Remarks on Johnson's Life of Milton* (1780), inserted into the second part of the *Memoirs*.

We have mentioned president Holyoke's letter of thanks to Mr. Hollis for Milton's prose works, dated December 28, 1759, and given an extract from it, wherein the president says, 'Milton (his political works not at all withstanding) we esteem a great honour to the British name.'

Mr. Hollis seems to have understood from this parenthesis, that Mr. Holyoke and his associates approved of Milton's political principles with some reserve. And indeed, from the President's manner of expressing himself, one would imagine they had *real* objections to those principles. Be that as it might, Mr. Hollis in the same letter to Dr. Mayhew, after citing Mr. Holyoke's restriction, thought proper to deliver his sentiments of Milton's political principles in the following detail:

'If I understand Milton's principles, they are these; that government, at least our government, is by compact. That, a king becoming a tyrant, and the compact thereby broken, the power reverts again to the constituents, the people, who may punish such tyrant as they see fit, and constitute such a new form of government as shall then appear to them to be most expedient. It is true, indeed, that that form of government, which he and many other able honest men inclined to, on the death and punishment of the tyrant Charles, was a commonwealth, which the army, the Hydra-beast, prevented; forcing the nation thereby, against its bent, after numberless vexations, to call back that riot-prince Charles the Second. But Milton, or the warmest common-wealth man, never thought of altering the antient form of government, till Charles the First had sinned flagrantly and repeatedly against it, and had destroyed it by his violences.

'On the contrary, there are several and very fine passages in his prose works, where he commends that antient form exceedingly, and with highest justice; and it is undoubted truth, that we owe the most noble, the most happy Revolution, to his principles, and to those of his friends; principles that will uphold and cherish every honest, virtuous prince; and check only and confound (which GOD grant!) every bad prince and every tyrant. You see, dear Sir, if I have explained myself clearly, that it is to Milton, the divine Milton, and such as he, in the struggles of the civil war, and the Revolution, that we are beholden for all the manifold and unexampled blessings which we now every where enjoy; and Mr. President Holyoke for liberty and his college. But of this passage I have taken no notice in my answer to that gentleman.'

Many reflections might be made on this passage, both as it concerns Milton's political principles, and those of the writer of it. The readers of Milton's prose works in these days I believe are very few; and few of those that read them, it is probable, take the pains to understand them. He is seldom quoted in our present political squabbles, though he has said as much, and as pertinently to the purpose of the late oppositions to administration, as any English author we have: those of his prose works which have been most read of late years, are, as far as I can judge, the *Iconoclastes*, and his defences of the people of England against Salmasius and others; and because he vindicates the people for avenging their wrongs upon a particular tyrant, they take him to have been an enemy to regal government *as such*; whereas a very little attention might have convinced them, that all his authorities by which he asserts the constitutional rights of the people, are taken from books whose authors lived and wrote under the government of kings, and did not think of a legal government without a king, though their maxims might lead to that remedy when they should be oppressed by a tyrant, and when a better form could not be had. Our patriots at the Revolution, who had read Milton with a perfect comprehension of his meaning, found a better remedy against the tyrannical encroachments of the wretched James, in the substitution of king William. Thus our patriot, Mr. Hollis, understood Milton; and, whatever may have been said of his republican principles, was attached to the *mode* of the Revolution, as well as to the *principles* of it; and not less to the act settling the succession in the protestant House of Hanover; as abundantly appears by the several memorials he hath left behind him. . . .

Upon the whole, if Milton had adopted for his epic poem a political hero, as it seems he once intended; and had the plan been executed upon the principles which occur in his noble and excellent tracts of religion and government, it may be justly questioned whether either the harmony of his numbers, the greatness and justness of his invention, or the majesty of his style, would have redeemed it from the fate, which Mr. Baron informs us, befell the *Iconoclastes*, and some other prose-tracts, whenever such poem should have fallen into the like orthodox hands.

These particulars, it is apprehended, will account sufficiently for the abuse of Milton's prose-works by one sort of readers, for the neglect of them by another, and for the absolute ignorance of their contents, and even of their existence, in still more, among his own countrymen; their estimation indeed was high among the patriots of the Revolution; but seems to have gradually declined as that period became more remote from modern times; and it could not escape Mr. Hollis's observation, that the remaining stream of our antient and wholesome revolution-principles began to be diverted into a quite contrary channel a very few months after the death of the Second George. And can it be any wonder with those who knew this benevolent man, that he should endeavour to stem the pernicious current, and apprise the men of England of their danger, by referring them to those immortal geniuses Milton, Sidney, Locke, &c. for instruction upon what only solid foundation the preservation of their rights and liberties depends?

68. Hayley on Milton's epic

1782

Extract from William Hayley, 'An Essay on Epic Poetry' (1782),
lines 411–32. William Hayley, *Poems and Plays* (1788), iii, 73–4.

A poet, scholar, important biographer and editor of Milton,
William Hayley (1745–1820) was a friend of William Cowper and
of such artists as William Blake, John Flaxman, and George
Romney, all important in Milton study. His verse is understand-
ably not read today, even though he was offered the laureateship
upon Warton's death. Three of his important statements on Milton
are represented in this collection.

> Apart, and on a sacred hill retir'd,
> Beyond all mortal inspiration fir'd,
> The mighty MILTON sits—an host around
> Of list'ning Angels guard the holy ground;
> Amaz'd they see a human form aspire
> To grasp with daring hand a Seraph's lyre,
> Inly irradiate with celestial beams,
> Attempt those high, those soul-subduing themes,
> (Which humbler Denizens of Heaven decline)
> And celebrate, with sanctity divine,
> The starry field from warring Angels won,
> And God triumphant in his Victor Son.
> Nor less the wonder, and the sweet delight,
> His milder scenes and softer notes excite,
> When at his bidding Eden's blooming grove
> Breathes the rich sweets of Innocence and Love.
> With such pure joy as our Forefather knew
> When Raphael, heavenly guest, first met his view,
> And our glad Sire, within his blissful bower,
> Drank the pure converse of th' aethereal Power,
> Round the blest Bard his raptur'd audience throng,
> And feel their souls imparadis'd in song.

69. Thomas Warton on the minor poems

1785

Extract from Thomas Warton, ed., *Poems upon Several Occasions*
(1785), 'The Preface', xi, xiv–xv, and selected notes, pp. 22–3,
34–5, 93–5, 264–5, 301, 303, 587–9.

Thomas Warton (1728–90) was professor of poetry at Oxford,
professor of history, and poet laureate (in 1785). Important criticism of literature will be found in his *History of English Poetry*
(1774–81) and *Observations on the Faerie Queene of Spenser* (1754);
his views place him strongly under the label of 'pre-Romantic'.
His edition of Milton's early poems (1785; revised 1791) is a major
work of criticism both in introductions and in notes; his belief,
however, that these poems were largely neglected is not really
well founded.

An editor of Milton's juvenile poems cannot but express his concern, in
which however he may have been anticipated by his reader, that their
number is so inconsiderable. With Milton's *mellow hangings*, delicious as
they are, we reasonably rest contented: but we are justified in regretting
that he has left so few of his early blossoms, not only because they are
so exquisitely sweet, but because so many more might have naturally
been expected. And this regret is yet aggravated, when we consider
the cause which prevented the production of more, and intercepted the
progress of so promising a spring: when we recollect, that the vigorous
portion of his life, that those years in which imagination is on the wing,
were unworthily and unprofitably wasted on temporary topics, on
elaborate but perishable dissertations in defence of innovation and
anarchy. To this employment he sacrificed his eyes, his health, his
repose, his native propensities, his elegant studies. Smit with the deplorable polemics of puritanism, he suddenly ceased to gaze on *such sights
as youthful poets dream*. . . .

   In the Elegies, Ovid was professedly Milton's model for language
and versification. They are not, however, a perpetual and uniform tissue

of Ovidian phraseology. With Ovid in view, he has an original manner and character of his own, which exhibit a remarkable perspicuity of contexture, a native facility and fluency. Nor does his observation of Roman models oppress or destroy our great poet's inherent powers of invention and sentiment. I value these pieces as much for their fancy and genius, as for their style and expression.

That Ovid among the Latin poets was Milton's favourite, appears not only from his elegiac but his hexametric poetry. The versification of our author's hexameters has yet a different structure from that of the *Metamorphoses*: Milton's is more clear, intelligible, and flowing; less desultory, less familiar, and less embarrassed with a frequent recurrence of periods. Ovid is at once rapid and abrupt. He wants dignity: he has too much conversation in his manner of telling a story. Prolixity of paragraph, and length of sentence, are peculiar to Milton. This is seen, not only in some of his exordial invocations in the PARADISE LOST, and in many of the religious addresses of a like cast in the prose-works, but in his long verse. It is to be wished that in his Latin compositions of all sorts, he had been more attentive to the simplicity of Lucretius, Virgil, and Tibullus.

'Lycidas', 130

In these lines our author anticipates the execution of archbishop Laud by a *two-handed engine*, that is, the ax; insinuating that his death would remove all grievances in religion, and complete the reformation of the church. Doctor Warburton supposes, that saint Peter's sword, turned into the two-handed sword of romance, is here intended. But this supposition only embarrasses the passage. Michael's sword 'with huge two-handed sway' is evidently the old Gothic sword of chivalry, *PARAD. L.* B. vi. 251. This is styled an *Engine*, and the expression is a periphrasis for an ax, which the poet did not choose to name in plain terms. The sense therefore of the context seems to be, 'But there will soon be an end of all these evils: the *ax* is at hand, to take off the head of him who has been the great abettor of these corruptions of the gospel. This will be done by one stroke.'

In the mean time, it coincides just as well with the tenour of Milton's doctrine, to suppose, that he alludes in a more general acceptation to our Saviour's metaphorical AX in the gospel, which was to be *laid to the root of the tree*, and whose stroke was to be quick and decisive. MATT. iii. 10. LUKE, iii. 9. 'And now the AX is laid to the root of the tree: therefore every tree which bringeth not forth good fruit is hewn down,

&c.' That is, 'Things are now brought to a crisis. There is no room for a moment's delay. God is now about to offer the last dispensation of his mercy. If ye reject these terms, no others will be offered afterwards: but ye shall suffer ONE FINAL sentence of destruction, as a tree, &c.' All false religions were at once to be done away by the appearance of christianity, as when an ax is applied to a barren tree: so now an ax was to be applied to the corruptions of christianity, which in a similar process were to be destroyed by a single and speedy blow. The time was ripe for this business: the instrument was at hand. Our author has the same metaphor in a treatise written 1641. 'They feeling the AX of God's REFORMATION HEWING at the old and hollow TRUNK of popery.' PROSE-WORKS, ut supr. vol. i. 17. Where he also says, that 'the painted battlements, and gaudy rottenness, of Prelatry, want but ONE PUFF of the king's to blow them down like a paste-board house built of *court-cards*.' Ib. 18. But he is rather unhappy in his comparison, which follows, of episcopacy to a large wen growing on the head: for allowing such a wen, on his own principles, to be an excrescency and a deformity, to cut it off may prove a dangerous operation; and perhaps it had better remain untouched, with all its inconveniencies.

It is matter of surprise, that this violent invective against the church of England and the hierarchy, couched indeed in terms a little mysterious yet sufficiently intelligible, and covered only by a transparent veil of allegory, should have been published under the sanction and from the press of one of our universities; or that it should afterwards have escaped the severest animadversions, at a period, when the proscriptions of the Star-chamber, and the power of Laud, were at their height. Milton, under pretence of exposing the faults or abuses of the episcopal clergy, attacks their establishment, and strikes at their existence.

[Final note on 'Lycidas']

Addison says, that He who desires to know whether he has a true taste for History or not, should consider, whether he is pleased with Livy's manner of telling a story; so, perhaps it may be said, that He who wishes to know whether he has a true taste for Poetry or not, should consider, whether he is highly delighted or not with the perusal of Milton's 'Lycidas'.

If I might venture to place Milton's Works, according to their degrees of Poetic Excellence, it should be perhaps in the following order; *Paradise Lost*, 'Comus', *Samson Agonistes*, 'Lycidas', 'L'Allegro', 'Il Penseroso'. The three last are in such an exquisite strain, says Fenton, that though he had left no other monuments of his genius behind him, his name had been immortal. Dr. J. WARTON.

Doctor Johnson observes, that 'Lycidas' is filled with the heathen deities; and a long train of mythological imagery, such as a College easily supplies. But it is such also, as even the Court itself could now have easily supplied. The public diversions, and books of all sorts and from all sorts of writers, more especially compositions in poetry, were at this time overrun with classical pedantries. But what writer, of the same period, has made these obsolete fictions the vehicle of so much fancy and poetical description? How beautifully has he applied this sort of allusion, to the Druidical rocks of Denbighshire, to Mona, and the fabulous banks of Deva! It is objected, that its pastoral form is disgusting. But this was the age of pastoral: and yet 'Lycidas' has but little of the bucolic cant, now so fashionable. The Satyrs and Fauns are but just mentioned. If any trite rural topics occur, how are they heightened! [ll. 25–9]. Here the day-break is described by the faint appearance of the upland lawns under the first gleams of light: the sunset, by the buzzing of the chaffer: and the night sheds her *fresh dews* on their flocks. We cannot blame pastoral imagery, and pastoral allegory, which carry with them so much natural painting. In this piece there is perhaps more poetry than sorrow. But let us read it for its poetry. It is true, that passion plucks no berries from the myrtle and ivy, nor calls upon Arethuse and Mincius, nor tells of *rough Satyrs with cloven heel*. But poetry does this; and in the hands of Milton, does it with a peculiar and irresistible charm. Subordinate poets exercise no invention, when they tell how a shepherd has lost his companion, and must feed his flocks alone without any judge of his skill in piping: but Milton dignifies and adorns these common artificial incidents with unexpected touches of picturesque beauty, with the graces of sentiment, and with the novelties of original genius. It is said 'here is no art, for there is nothing new.' But this objection will vanish, if we consider the imagery which Milton has raised from local circumstances. Not to repeat the use he has made of the mountains of Wales, the isle of Man, and the river Dee, near which Lycidas was shipwrecked; let us recollect the introduction of the romantic superstition of Saint Michael's Mount in Cornwall, which overlooks the Irish seas, the fatal scene of his friend's disaster.

But the poetry is not always unconnected with passion. The poet lavishly describes an antient sepulchral rite, but it is made preparatory to a stroke of tenderness. He calls for a variety of flowers to decorate his friend's hearse, supposing that his body was present, and forgetting for a while that it was floating far off in the ocean. If he was drowned, it was some consolation that he was to receive the decencies of burial. This is a pleasing deception: it is natural and pathetic. But the real catastrophe recurs. And this circumstance again opens a new vein of imagination.

Our author has been censured for mixing religious disputes with pagan and pastoral ideas. But he had the authority of Mantuan and Spenser, now considered as models in this way of writing. Let me add, that our poetry was not yet purged from its Gothic combinations; nor had legitimate notions of discrimination and propriety so far prevailed, as sufficiently to influence the growing improvements of English composition. These irregularities and incongruities must not be tried by modern criticism.

[Note on 'L'Allegro' and 'Il Penseroso']
It will be no detraction from the powers of Milton's original genius and invention to remark, that he seems to have borrowed the subject of 'L'Allegro' and 'Il Penseroso', together with some particular thoughts, expressions, and rhymes, more especially the idea of a contrast between these two dispositions, from a forgotten poem prefixed to the first edition of Burton's ANATOMIE OF MELANCHOLY, entitled 'The Author's ABSTRACT of Melancholy, or a Dialogue between Pleasure and Pain'. Here Pain is Melancholy. It was written, as I conjecture, about the year 1600. I will make no apology for abstracting and citing as much of this poem, as will be sufficient to prove to a discerning reader, how far it had taken possession of Milton's mind. The measure will appear to be the same; and that our author was at least an attentive reader of Burton's book, may be already concluded from the traces of resemblance which I have incidentally noticed in passing through the 'L'Allegro' and 'Il Penseroso'. . . .

As to the very elaborate work to which these visionary verses are no unsuitable introduction, the writer's variety of learning, his quotations from scarce and curious books, his pedantry sparkling with rude wit and shapeless elegance, miscellaneous matter, intermixture of agreeable tales and illustrations, and perhaps, above all, the singularities of his feelings cloathed in an uncommon quaintness of style, have contributed to render it, even to modern readers, a valuable repository of amusement and information.

But I am here tempted to add a part of Burton's prose, not so much for the purpose of exhibiting a specimen of his manner, as for the sake of shewing, at one view, how nearly Milton has sometimes pursued his train of thought, and selection of objects, in various passages of 'L'Allegro' and 'Il Penseroso'. It is in the chapter entitled, *Exercise rectified both of Body and Minde*. 'But the most pleasing of all outward pastimes, is *Deambulatio per amœna loca*, to make a pretty progresse, to see cities, castles, townes: as Fracastorius, . . . To walke amongst orchards, garden, bowres, and artificiall wildernesses, green thickets, arches, groves, rillets, fountains, and such like pleasant places, like that Antiochian Daphne, pooles,—betwixt wood and water, in a faire meadow by a riuer side, to disport in some pleasant plaine, to run vp a steepe hill, or sit in a shadie seat, must needes be a delectable recreation. —To see some pageant or sight go by, as at coronations, weddings and such like solemnities; to see an embassadour, or prince, met, receiued, entertained with Maskes, shewes, &c.—The country has its recreations, may-games, feasts, wakes, and merry meetings.—All seasons, almost all places, haue their seuerall pastimes, some in sommer, some in winter, some abroad, some within.—The ordinary recreations which we haue in winter, and in most solitary times busy our mindes with, are cardes, tables,—musicke, Maskes, vlegames, catches, purposes, questions, merry tales of errant knights, kings, queenes, louers, lordes, ladies, dwarfes, theeues, fayries, &c.—Dancing, singing, masking, mumming, stage-playes, howsoeuer they bee heauily censured by some seuere Catos, yet if opportunely and soberly used, may iustly be approved.— To read, walke, and see mappes and pictures, statues, old coynes of seuerall sortes, in a fayre gallerie, artificiall workes &c. Whosoeuer he is therefore, that is overrunne with Solitarinesse, or carried away with a PLEASING MELANCHOLY and vaine conceits,—I can prescribe him no better remedie than this of study'. He winds up his system of studious recreation, with a recommendation of the sciences of morality, astronomy, botany, &c. 'To see a well-cut herball, all hearbs, trees, flowers, plants, expressed in their proper colours to the life, &c.' P. ii. 2. p. 224–234. edit. 1624.

In Beaumont and Fletcher's *NICE VALOUR* or *PASSIONATE MADMAN*, there is a beautiful Song on Melancholy, some of the sentiments of which, as Sympson long since observed, appear to have been dilated and heightened in the 'Il Penseroso'. See A. iii. S. i, vol. x. p. 336. Milton has more frequently and openly copied the plays of Beaumont and Fletcher, than of Shakespeare. One is therefore surprised, that in his panegyric on the stage, he did not mention the twin-bards, when he celebrated the learned sock of Jonson, and the wood-notes wild of Shakespeare. But he concealed his love.

'L'Allegro' and 'Il Penseroso' may be called the two first descriptive poems in the English language. It is perhaps true, that the characters are not sufficiently kept apart. But this circumstance has been productive of greater excellencies. It has been remarked, 'No mirth can indeed be found in his melancholy, but I am afraid I always meet some melancholy in his mirth'. Milton's is the dignity of mirth. His chearfulness is the chearfulness of gravity. The objects he selects in his 'L'Allegro' are so far gay, as they do not naturally excite sadness. Laughter and jollity are named only as personifications, and never exemplified. *Quips*, and *Cranks*, and *wanton wiles*, are enumerated only in general terms. There is specifically no mirth in contemplating a fine landschape. And even his landschape, although it has flowery meadows and flocks, wears a shade of pensiveness; and contains *russet* law[n]s, fallows *gray*, and *barren* mountains, overhung with *labouring* clouds. Its old turretted mansion peeping from the trees, awakens only a train of solemn and romantic, perhaps melancholy, reflection. Many a pensive man listens with delight to the milk-maid *singing blith*, to the mower *whetting his scythe*, and to a distant peal of village-bells. He chose such illustrations as minister matter for true poetry, and genuine description. Even his most brilliant imagery is mellowed with the sober hues of philosophic meditation. It was impossible for the author of 'Il Penseroso' to be more chearful, or to paint mirth with levity; that is, otherwise than in the colours of the higher poetry. Both poems are the result of the same feelings, and the same habits of thought.

[Note on 'Comus']

We must not read 'Comus' with an eye to the stage, or with the expectation of dramatic poetry. Under this restriction, the absurdity of the Spirit speaking to an audience in a solitary forest at midnight, and the want of reciprocation in the dialogue, are overlooked. 'Comus' is a suite of Speeches, not interesting by discrimination of character; not conveying a variety of incidents, nor gradually exciting curiosity: but perpetually attracting attention by sublime sentiment, by fanciful imagery of the richest vein, by an exhuberance of picturesque description, poetical allusion, and ornamental expression. While it widely departs from the grotesque anomalies of the Mask now in fashion, it does not nearly approach to the natural constitution of a regular play. There is a chastity in the application and conduct of the machinery: and Sabrina is introduced with much address, after the Brothers had imprudently suffered the inchantment of Comus to take effect. This is the first time the old English Mask was in some degree reduced to the principles and form of rational composition. A great critic observes, that the dispute between the Lady and Comus is the most animated and affecting scene of the piece. Perhaps some other scenes, either consisting only of a soliloquy, or of three or four speeches only, have afforded more true pleasure. The action is said to be improbable: because the Brothers, when their sister sinks with fatigue in a pathless wilderness, wander both away together in search of berries, too far to find their way back, and leave a helpless lady to all the sadness and danger of solitude. But here is no desertion, or neglect of the lady. The Brothers leave their sister under a spreading pine in the forest, fainting for refreshment; they go to procure berries or some other fruit for her immediate relief, and, with great probability, lose their way in going or returning. To say nothing of the poet's art, in making this very natural and simple accident to be productive of the distress, which forms the future business and complication of the fable. It is certainly a fault, that the Brothers, although with some indications of anxiety, should enter with so much tranquility, when their sister is lost, and at leisure pronounce philosophical panegyrics on the mysteries of virginity. But we must not too scrupulously attend to the exigencies of situation, nor suffer ourselves to suppose that we are reading a play, which Milton did not mean to write. These splendid insertions will please, independently of the story, from which however they result; and their elegance and sublimity will overbalance their want of place. In a Greek tragedy, such sentimental harangues, arising from the subject, would have been given to a chorus.

On the whole, whether 'Comus', be or be not, deficient as a drama, whether it is considered as an Epic drama, a series of lines, a Mask, or a poem, I am of opinion, that our author is only inferiour to his own *Paradise Lost*.

[Note on 'On Time']

Milton could not help applying the most solemn and mysterious truths of religion on all subjects and occasions. He has here introduced the beatific vision, and the investiture of the soul with a robe of stars, into an inscription on a clock-case. Perhaps something more moral, more plain and intelligible, would have been more proper. John Bunyan, if capable of rhyming, would have written such an inscription for a clock-case. The latter part of these lines may be thought wonderfully sublime: but it is in the cant of the times. The poet should be distinguished from the puritan.

[Note on 'Solemn Music', ll. 17–25]

Perhaps there are no finer lines in Milton, less obscured by conceit, less embarrassed by affected expressions, and less weakened by pompous epithets. And in this perspicuous and simple style, are conveyed some of the noblest ideas of a most sublime philosophy, heightened by metaphors and allusions suitable to the subject.

[Note on the prose]

Upon the whole, and with regard to his political writings at large, even after the prejudices of party have subsided, Milton, I believe, has found no great share of favour, of applause, or even of candour, from distant generations. His *Si quid meremur*, in the sense here belonging to the words, has been too fully ascertained by the mature determination of time. Toland, about thirty years after the Restoration, thought Milton's prose-works of sufficient excellence and importance to be collected and printed in one body. But they were neglected and soon forgotten. Of late years, some attempts have been made to revive them, with as little success. At present, they are almost unknown. If they are ever inspected, it is perhaps occasionally by the commentator on Milton's verse as affording materials for comparative criticism, or from motives of curiosity only, as the productions of the writer of 'Comus' and *Paradise Lost*, and not so much for any independent value of their own. In point of doctrine, they are calculated to annihilate the very foundations of our civil and religious establishment, as it now subsists; they are subversive of our legislature, and our species of government. In condemning tyranny, he strikes at the bare existence of kings; in combating superstition, he decries all public religion. These discourses hold forth a system of politics, at present as unconstitutional, and almost as obsolete, as the nonsense of passive obedience: and in this view, we might just as well think of republishing the pernicious theories of the kingly bigot James, as of the republican usurper Oliver Cromwell. Their style is perplexed, pedantic, poetical, and unnatural: abounding in enthusiastic effusions, which have been mistaken for eloquence and imagination. In the midst of the most solemn rhapsodies, which would have shone in a fast-sermon before Cromwell, he sometimes indulges a vein of jocularity; but his witticisms are as aukward as they are unsuitable, and Milton never more misunderstands the nature and bias of his genius, than when he affects to be arch either in prose or verse. His want of deference to superiours teaches him to write without good manners; and, when we consider his familiar acquaintance with the elegancies of antiquity, with the orators and historians of Greece and Rome, few writers will be found to have made so slender a sacrifice to the Graces. From some of these strictures, I must except the *Tractate on Education*, and the *Areopagitica*, which are written with a tolerable degree of facility, simplicity, purity, and perspicuity; and the latter, some tedious historical digressions, and some little sophistry excepted, is the most close, conclusive, comprehensive, and derisive vindication of the liberty of the press that has yet appeared, on a subject on which it is difficult to decide, between the licentiousness of scepticism and sedition, and the arbitrary exertions of authority. In the mean time, Milton's prose-works, I suspect, were never popular: he deeply engaged in most of the ecclesiastical disputes of his times, yet he is seldom quoted or mentioned by his contemporaries, either of the presbyterian or independent persuasion: even by Richard Baxter, pastor of Kidderminster, a judicious and voluminous advocate on the side of the presbyterians, who vehemently censures and opposes several of his coadjutors in the cause of church-independency, he is passed over in profound silence. For his brethren the independents he seems to have been too learned and unintelligible. In 1652, sir Robert Filmer, in a general attack on the recent antimonarchical writers, bestows but a very short and slight refutation on his politics. It appears from the 'Censure of the Rota', a pamphlet published in 1660, said to be fabricated by Harrington's club, that even his brother party-writers ridiculed the affectations and absurdities of his style. Lord Monboddo is the only modern critic who ranks Milton as a prose-writer with Hooker, Sprat, and Clarendon.

I have hitherto been speaking of Milton's prose-works in English. I cannot allow, that his Latin performances in prose are formed on any one chaste Roman model. They consist of a modern factitious mode of latinity, a compound of phraseology gleaned from a general imitation of various styles, commodious enough for the author's purpose. His *Defensio pro populo Anglicano* against Salmasius, so liberally rewarded by the presbyterian administration, the best apology that ever was offered for bringing kings to the block, and which diffused his reputation all over Europe, is remembered no more.

Doctor Birch observes of this prophetic hope in the text, that 'the universal admiration with which his Works are read, justifies what he himself says in his Ode to Rouse.' *Life*, p. lxiii. But this hope, as we have seen, our author here restricts to his political speculations, to his works on civil and religious subjects, which are still in expectation of a reversionary fame, and still await the partial suffrages of a *sana posteritas*, and a *cordatior ætas*. The flattering anticipation of more propitious times, and more equitable judges, at some remote period, would have been justly applicable to his other works; for in those, and those only, it has been amply and conspicuously verified. It is from the *ultimi nepotes* that justice has been done to the genuine claims of his poetical character. Nor does any thing, indeed, more strongly mark the improved critical discernment of the present age, than that it has attoned for the contemptible taste, the blindness and the neglect, of the last, in recovering and exalting the poetry of Milton to its due degree of cultivation and esteem: and we may safely prognosticate, that the posterities are yet unborn, which will bear testimony to the beauties of his calmer imagery, and the magnificence of his more sublime descriptions, to the dignity of his sentiments, and the vigour of his language. Undoubtedly the *Paradise Lost* had always it's [sic] readers, and perhaps more numerous and devoted admirers even at the infancy of its publication, than our biographers have commonly supposed. Yet, in its silent progression, even after it had been recommended by the popular papers of Addison, and had acquired the distinction of an English classic, many years elapsed before any symptoms appeared, that it had influenced the national taste, or that it had wrought a change in our versification, and our modes of poetical thinking. The remark might be still farther extended, and more forcibly directed and brought home, to the pieces which compose the present volume.

70. Scott on 'Lycidas'

1785

John Scott, *Critical Essays on Some of the Poems, of Several English Poets* (1785), essay ii, 'Lycidas', pp. 37–64. Some footnotes omitted.

John Scott (1730–83) was a poet, a lover of literature, and a critic. His own work was influenced by James Thomson, as seen in *The Garden* (1766), in rhymed couplets, and in *Amwell, A Descriptive Poem* (1776), in blank verse. Other poems considered in the same volume of his critical essays are 'Windsor Forest', Gray's 'Elegy', and 'The Seasons'.

On Milton's 'Lycidas'.

To controvert the common opinion is certainly less pleasing than to confirm it. Respecting the 'Cooper's Hill', I was reluctantly necessitated to oppose high authorities: respecting the 'Lycidas', I am happy to coincide with the judgment of most of my predecessors. Between the two performances there is indeed an essential difference. Denham's is dull; Milton's is spirited: the thoughts of the former are mean, and the numbers unmusical; the ideas of the latter are grand, and the verse melodious. The one can boast little that merits the name of good sense; the other is not totally clear of conceits and incongruities. The one is usually termed a Descriptive Poem, but, as I have shewn, has nothing that deserves the title of description; the other is a Pastoral, and in general well preserves the rural character.

Dr. Johnson, who, in his account of 'Cooper's Hill' concurred with the *vox populi*, has in his account of 'Lycidas', widely dissented from it. His censure is indeed sufficiently severe. He objects to the form, as that of a pastoral, easy, vulgar, and disgusting. He asserts, that 'whatever images it can supply, are long ago exhausted,' and that 'its inherent improbability forces dissatisfaction on the mind;' that 'it cannot be considered as an effusion of real passion, because passion runs not after remote allusions, or obscure opinions, rural imagery, or mythological personages;' that 'it introduces Heathen deities' 'among copses, flocks, and flowers;' that 'it combines Pagan and Christian characters;' and

326

that 'the diction is harsh, the rhymes uncertain, and the numbers unpleasing.'

This derogatory sentence seems to affect pastoral in general, and to condemn Milton's plan, as well as his execution.

The manners of antiquity differed so widely from ours, that some species of poetry, which to the ancients were just representations of nature, appear to us improbable; such poetry nevertheless does not cease to please. There is an inherent improbability in modern tragedy, and in modern pastoral; families do not discourse in blank verse, nor do shepherds converse in rhyme; yet a well written drama, and a well written eclogue, will always be read with delight. Theocrites perhaps gave a picture of genuine Sicilian rural life. Virgil introduced himself, and his friend Gallus, in a rustick character, which they never really bore; yet his first and tenth eclogues received the approbation of the Augustan age, and even now have power to command attention.

When our above-mentioned ingenious critick thinks that 'Lycidas' cannot be considered as an effusion of real grief, he seems to have mistaken the nature of the poem. There is an anxiety from apprehension of losing a beloved object; and there is a grief immediately subsequent to its actual loss, which cannot be expressed but in the shortest and simplest manner. There is a grief softened by time, which can recapitulate past pleasures in all their minutiae of circumstance and situation, and can select such images as are proper to the kind of composition, wherein it chuses to convey itself. It was no sudden impetus of passion, but this mellowed sorrow, that effused the verses now under consideration.

That Milton has introduced Heathen deities among his copses, flocks, and flowers, is perhaps not strictly fact: those personages seem rather to appear only to his supposed shepherd's imagination. That he has connected Heathen and Christian characters in the same poem, is true, but it may be deemed some merit, that he has not grouped them confusedly together; they are viewed in succession, one character is dismissed before the other is produced, and they are all sufficiently distinguished. The irregularity of the rhyme is obviously the effect of design, not of carelessness, and may not please some ears, but the numbers, or component parts of the lines, are in general so musical, that one should think they must please all.

'Lycidas' is an elegy on a deceased friend. The plan of the poem is that of a monody, or soliloquy, in which the speaker episodically introduces matter which he supposes to have heard spoken by others. The monodist begins with an apostrophe to the laurel, myrtle, and ivy, perhaps considered as funereal greens. This whatever defects it may have, is certainly poetical: [1–14]. The proper name Lycidas, repeated, has an agreeable effect, and the placing it in the same part of the line twice, and changing its position the third time, gives it additional beauty. An ingenious foreign critick has well distinguished between two modes of expression, very different in their nature, but in both of which there is a superfluity of words. The one he terms a pleonasm, the other a perissology. The first is exemplified, when the same idea, by recurring in different, but proper, language, is impressed more strongly on the mind; the second, when a profusion of unmeaning verbiage renders thought indistinct, and often unintelligible. The first is mostly of the effect of design, the second always of incapacity or negligence. The pleonasm seems properly instanced, when Lycidas is said to be dead *before his prime*, and immediately after is called *young* Lycidas; for the repetition is here advantageously emphatical [ll. 15–31].* The shepherd's wish, that in like manner as he purposes to lament his friend, he may be lamented by some other, is truly pathetick. The picture is lively, and the sentiment interesting: we see a person passing by a tomb, and suddenly turning to render his tribute of respect to the deceased, and our minds are soothed with the idea of this supposed instance of repayment of funeral eulogy. Gray has beautifully touch'd this natural circumstance in his church-yard elegy:

> For thee, who mindful of the unhonour'd dead,
> Dost in these lines their artless tale relate;
> If chance by lonely contemplation led,
> Some kindred spirit shall inquire thy fate:
> Haply, some hoary-headed swain may say, &c.

'When Cowley,' says Dr. Johnson, 'tells of Hervey, that they studied together, it is easy to suppose how much he must miss the companion of his labours, and the partner of his discoveries; but what image of tenderness can be excited by these lines,' 'We drove afield,' &c.? 'We know that they never drove afield, and that they had no flocks to batten; and though it be allowed that the representation may be allegor-

---

* [Note to l. 28:] Milton's commentators have supposed the grey fly to be a scaraboeus, viz. the common grey cockchafer, frequent in most places on summer evenings. Perhaps the poet rather intended some diurnal insect, and meant to point out the process of a whole day, from morning through noon, to evening and night; marking the first by the appearance of the lawns, the second by the hum of the grey fly, expressed by the bold epithet of Sultry Horn, and the third and fourth by the appearance and descent of the evening star. Thomson mentions the hum of insects in the woods at noon.

ical, the true meaning is so uncertain and remote, that it is never sought, because it cannot be known when it is found.'

Cowley speaks of Hervey in *propria persona*, Milton is *pro tempore* a rustick poet; one therefore must naturally draw his images from the business of the study, and the other from the business of the field. It seems not very easy to discover what idea of tenderness is excited by Cowley, the collegian, in his mention of the literary occupations of his fellow-student, which is not also excited by Milton, the supposed shepherd, in his mention of the rural occupations of his field companion. Whatever there is of pathos in either, results from the recollection of friendship terminated by death. Milton meant only to give his pastoral scene a stronger appearance of reality, by descending to the particulars of 'driving afield,' &c. There is no reason to believe that his literal sense in these respects had any allegorical one, analogous or parallel; consequently there is no occasion to guess what it could be [ll. 32–6]. Dr. Johnson has censured this passage, and it must be acknowledged to be indefensible. The mind revolts from such a positive introduction of imaginary beings. While we acquiesce in the pastoral idea in general, we start at this particular and violent extension of it. Satyrs and fauns can have no business on English ground [ll. 37–49]. The foregoing lines are remarkable for a peculiar languid melody, well suited to their subject; they seem indeed the proper language of complaint. The poetical licence by which sense is attributed to inanimate existence, should be indulged with great caution: there are some instances in which it pleases, and there are others in which it disgusts. The more important the circumstances in which it is used, the better it succeeds. On trivial occasions, if it is not designedly burlesque, it will be seriously ridiculous. Rural scenes may perhaps be properly said to mourn, because a person who was wont to frequent them is deceased; but not because a shepherdess frowns on her lover, or a lady loses her lap-dog. Milton, in the above quotation, has used this liberty to great advantage. Simplicity, indeed, is a little violated, by the conceit of flowers wearing their gay *wardrobe* [ll. 50–63]. This celebrated imitation of Virgil has great sublimity and beauty. Nothing can be more poetical, than the speaker, as it were inadvertently, adopting the ancient popular belief in the divinity of the muses, and regretting their absence, and then with sudden self-correction, observing, that no advantage could have been derived from their presence. The supposed situations assigned to the nymphs of poetry, are romantick, appropriate to them, and suited to the occasion. The mention of the fate of Orpheus, affords a kind of indirect illustrative comparison.

The Monodist now combining the characters of shepherd and poet, pathetically reflects on the pursuit of learning, rendered fruitless by the shortness of life, and with a noble abruptness of transition, intimates that he hears Phoebus, as God of verse, pronouncing praise, the recompence of virtue in heaven: [ll. 64–84]. This passage has great dignity, but is rather deficient in correctness. The diction cannot perhaps be totally exonerated from the charge of affectation and obscurity. The Latinism *Meditate the Muse*, and the word *thankless*, whose meaning seems here ambiguous, are rather exceptionable. Fame is somewhat confusedly represented, both as a motive and a reward; there should have been a distinction between the desire of applause as the *spur*, and the obtainment of it as a *guerdon*. There is a difficulty in these lines:

> Fame is no plant that grows on mortal soil,
> Nor in the glistering foil,
> Set off to the world. [70–2]

It seems doubtful whether the metaphor of a plant in the first line is continued to the second, or exchanged for another. If it is continued, what connexion can a plant have with a foil? if it is exchanged, what is it exchanged for? perhaps a conjectural emendator would read,

> Nor stone in glistering foil,
> Set off to the world—*

But most probably the metaphor of a *plant* is not varied at all. If it is quitted, it is soon resumed, for after the intervention of a superfluous negative alternative under the name of *broad rumour*; the affirmative describes fame as *living* and *spreading by* the pure eyes, that is, in the presence of all judging Jove.

Mythological machinery is managed with so much difficulty, that in modern composition it seldom fails to disgust. Milton, however, has employed it in a manner, which all Dr. Johnson's ridicule cannot degrade, when he says, 'one god asks another god what is become of Lycidas, and neither god can tell.' Milton's friend was drowned in his passage from Chester, on the Irish seas. The Monodist represents himself as listening to Triton, the herald of the sea, who comes to exculpate Neptune from occasioning the misfortune: [ll. 88–102].

The creation of fictitious persons, and the description of real ones,

---

* Foil is the appellation of a thin piece of metal, in which crystals, or other stones are set, to heighten their colour, or improve their lustre. Milton seems to use the word, generally, for any ornament. Perhaps he meant an allusion to a plant with leaves naturally variegated, or to one on some occasion artificially, or fancifully adorned with gilding.

have generally been esteemed among the principal operations of poetry. Camus, the genius of the river Cam, and St. Peter, are now introduced, and their supposed appearance forcibly painted: [ll. 103–12].*

St. Peter's speech is an animated and severe censure of the clergy of the times. This satire, however just, is certainly no necessary, nor perhaps very proper, part of the poem, and contains some imagery that is more natural and striking, than agreeable; for instance:

> V.125. The hungry sheep look up and are not fed,
> But *swoln* with *wind*, and the rank mist they draw,
> *Rot inwardly*, and foul contagion spread.

Dr. Johnson's insinuation, that there is in it a confusion of the actual feeder of sheep with the ecclesiastical pastor, seems nevertheless void of foundation. To the literal shepherd all the circumstances mentioned seem justly attributable, though there was doubtless here a correspondent allegorical meaning designed for all of them.

The poet now apostrophizes to Alpheus, and the Sicilian Muse; and as if totally forgetting the situation of Lycidas, invokes them to call the vales to strew his hearse with flowers; [ll. 131–52].† This passage is beautifully descriptive, but it is not without defects. Milton is rarely so diffuse, as to talk of 'quaint enamell'd *eyes*, purpling the ground with vernal *flowers*;' for eyes and flowers must certainly mean one thing; nor is he often so careless of his rhymes, as to place them on an unaccented syllable, as in *jessamine, woodbine,* and *violet.* Too many of the flowers, considering the occasion, are specified by name, and the blooms of spring, the primrose, cowslip, pansie, and crowfoot, &c. are injudiciously blended with the productions of summer; the pink, the rose, the amaranthus, and others abovementioned. The meaning of *every flower that sad embroidery wears,* is not obvious; and the *daffodil lies filling their cups with tears* is an unnatural and trifling conceit. The word *surmise,* in the last line, is used as we should use *supposition.*

Imagination, properly directed, will not be employed in producing impossible fictions, but in exploring real existence, and selecting from it circumstances grand or beautiful, as occasion may require. Such an imagination was that of our poet, which could accompany the drowned

---

* [Note to l. 106:] There seems some ambiguity in the point of resemblance here; but the poet probably did not mean that the bonnet's edge was sanguine or red, but that it was inscribed with symbols of woe.

† [Note to ll. 131–2:] Bishop Newton, from Richardson, has noticed Milton's poetical judgment in this passage; he had marked the superiority of the speech of Apollo, by terming it a 'strain of higher mood.' He now marks the speech of St. Peter, by the grand circumstance of its shrinking the streams of Alpheus.

body of his friend beneath the ocean, through a variety of supposed situations, in which he imagines it attended by the newly separated spirit. His apostrophe to the dolphins must however relate to the inanimate form; for the assistance of dolphins to convey an incorporeal subject, would certainly be unnecessary: [ll. 154–64].

The common conclusion of a funeral elegy, is the beatification of the deceased. Milton has not deviated from this plan, but he has executed it with unusual grandeur, both of thought and expression. But the passage, however sublime, is not wholly free from faults. The day-star is very poetically, but not correctly introduced, both as a person, repairing *his* drooping *head*, &c. and as an orb of radiance, *flaming* in the *forehead* of the morning sky. There seems also some incongruity in the scriptural idea of Lycidas having the tears wiped from his eyes, and the classical one of his becoming the genius of the shore: [ll. 165–85].

The termination of the Piece has great merit. The Shepherd elegiast, who, contrary to the general practice, has not been yet formally introduced, but only supposed present; is now set before us among his oaks and rills, warbling his Dorick lay from morning to evening. Milton, always peculiarly happy in the measurement of time, has marked the above-mentioned periods, the one by a fine prosopopoeia, the other by a picturesque natural circumstance; the Morn goes forth in her grey sandals, and the sun, after stretching out all the hills, sinks into the ocean: [ll. 186–93].

Milton has been generally supposed to have introduced in this poem, a great number of antiquated phrases. This opinion, however it came to obtain, is erroneous. On a close examination, there will not be found, in near two hundred lines, a dozen words of obsolete character.*

Whether 'Lycidas' should be considered as a model of composition, has been doubted. Some have supposed that the arbitrary disposition of the rhymes produces a wild melody, adapted to the expression of sorrow. Some have thought the couplet and tetrastick with their stated returns of chime, preferable. To decide the point by argument, might be difficult; but supposing two elegies, one of each structure, to be equally well written in other respects, probably most readers would incline to favour the regular form.

'Lycidas' is a noble poem: the author's name is not wanted to recommend it: its own enthusiasm and beauty will always make it please, and abundantly atone for its incorrectness.

* Viz. *Rathe, scrannel, self-same, swart, ruth, freakt, trick,* as a substitute for *adorn,* and perhaps two or three more.

71. Cumberland on *Samson Agonistes*

1785

Richard Cumberland, *Observer*, no. 76 (1785).

A mediocre dramatist and Sir Fretful Plagiary of Sheridan's *The Critic*, Richard Cumberland (1732–1811) also attempted other forms, including a periodical *Observer*, which contains some brief and some extended comment on Milton. His poem 'Calvary' (1792) is often imitative of Milton's epic.

In my foregoing paper, when I remarked that Jonson in his comedy of *The Fox* was a close copier of the ancients, it occurred to me to say something upon the celebrated drama of the *Samson Agonistes*, which, though less beholden to the Greek poets in its dialogue than the comedy above mentioned, is in all other particulars as complete an imitation of the ancient tragedy, as the distance of times and the difference of languages will admit of.

It is professedly built according to the ancient rule and example, and the author, by taking Aristotle's definition of tragedy for his motto, fairly challenges the critic to examine and compare it by that test. His close adherence to the model of the Greek tragedy is in nothing more conspicuous than in the simplicity of his diction: in this particular he has curbed his fancy with so tight a hand, that, knowing as we do the fertile vein of his genius, we cannot but lament the fidelity of his imitation; for there is a harshness in the metre of his chorus, which to a certain degree seems to border upon pedantry and affection: he premises that the measure is indeed of all sorts, but I must take leave to observe that in some places it is no measure at all, or such at least as the ear will not patiently endure, nor which any recitation can make harmonious. By casting out of his composition the strophe and antistrophe, those stanzas which the Greeks appropriated to singing, or in one word, by making his chorus monostrophic, he has robbed it of that lyric beauty, which he was capable of bestowing in the highest perfection; and why he should stop short in this particular, when he had otherwise gone so far in imitation, is not easy to guess: for surely it would have been quite as natural to suppose those stanzas, had he written any, might be sung, as that all the other parts, as the drama now stands, with a chorus of such irregular measure, might be recited or given in representation.

Now it is well known to every man conversant in the Greek theatre, how the chorus, which in fact is the parent of the drama, came, in process of improvement, to be woven into the fable, and from being at first the whole, grew in time to be only a part; the fable being simple, and the characters few, the striking part of the spectacle rested upon the singing and dancing of the interlude, if I may so call it, and to these the people were too long accustomed and too warmly attached, to allow of any reform for their exclusion; the tragic poet therefore never got rid of his Chorus, though the writers of the Middle Comedy contrived to dismiss theirs: and probably their fable being of a more lively character, their scenes were better able to stand without the support of music and spectacle than the mournful fable and more languid recitation of the tragedians. That the tragic authors laboured against the Chorus will appear from their efforts to expel Bacchus and his Satyrs from the stage, in which they were long time opposed by the audience, and at last, by certain ingenious expedients, which were a kind of compromise with the public, effected their point; this in part was brought about by the introduction of a fuller scene and a more active fable, but the Chorus, with its accompaniments, kept its place, and the poet, who seldom ventured upon introducing more than three speakers in the scene at the same time, qualified the sterility of his business by giving to the Chorus a share of the dialogue, who, at the same time that they furnished the stage with numbers, were not counted among the speaking characters, according to the rigour of the usage above mentioned. A man must be an enthusiast for antiquity, who can find charms in the dialogue part of a Greek Chorus, and reconcile himself to their unnatural and chilling interruptions of the action and pathos of the scene; I am fully persuaded they came there upon motives of expediency only, and kept their post upon the plea of long possession, and the attractions of spectacle and music: in short, nature was sacrificed to the display of art, and the heart gave up its feelings that the ear and eye might be gratified.

When Milton therefore takes the Chorus into his dialogue, excluding from his drama the lyric strophe and antistrophe, he rejects what I conceive to be its only recommendation, and which an elegant contemporary, in his imitations of the Greek tragedy, is more properly attentive to: at the same time, it cannot be denied that Milton's Chorus subscribes more to the dialogues, and harmonises better with the business of the scene, than that of any Greek tragedy we can now refer to.

I would now proceed to a review of the performance itself, if it were not a discussion, which the author of the *Rambler* has very ably prevented me in: respect, however, to an authority so high in criticism must not prevent me from observing, that, when he says—'This is the tragedy, which ignorance has admired, and bigotry applauded,' he makes it meritorious in any future critic to attempt at following him over the ground he has trode, for the purpose of discovering what those blemishes are, which he has found out by superior sagacity, and which others have so palpably overlooked, as to merit the disgraceful character of ignorance and bigotry.

The principal, and in effect the only, objection, which he states, is, 'that the poem *wants a middle*, since nothing passes between the first act and the last, that either hastens or delays the death of Samson.' This demands examination: the death of Samson I need not describe: it is a sudden momentary event; what can hasten or delay it, but the will of the person, who, by exertion of miraculous strength, was to bury himself under the ruins of a structure, in which his enemies were assembled? To determine that will depends upon the impulse of his own spirit, or it may be upon the inspiration of Heaven: if there are any incidents in the body of the drama, which lead to this determination, and indicate an impulse, either natural or preternatural, such must be called leading incidents, and those leading incidents will constitute a middle, or, in more diffusive terms, the middle business of the drama. Manoah, in his interview with Samson, which the author of the *Rambler* denominates the second act of the tragedy, tells him

> This day the Philistines a popular feast
> Here celebrate in Gaza, and proclaim
> Great pomp and sacrifice and praises loud
> To Dagon, as their god— [ll. 434-7]

Here is information of a meeting of his enemies to celebrate their idolatrous triumphs; an incident of just provocation to the servant of the living God, an opportunity perhaps for vengeance, either human or divine; if it passes without notice from Samson, it is not to be styled an incident; if, on the contrary, he remarks upon it, it must be one— but Samson replies—

> Dagon must stoop, and shall ere long receive
> Such a discomfit as shall quite despoil him
> Of all these boasted trophies won on me,
> And with confusion blank his worshippers. [ll. 468–71]

Who will say the expectation is not here prepared for some catastrophe, we know not what, but awful it must be, for it is Samson which denounces the downfall of the idol, it is God who inspires the denunciation; the crisis is important, for it is that which shall decide whether God or Dagon is to triumph, it is in the strongest sense of the expression—*dignus vindice nodus*—and therefore we may boldly pronounce *Deus intersit!*

That this interpretation meets the sense of the author is clear from the remark of Manoah, who is made to say that he receives these words as a prophecy. Prophetic they are, and were meant to be by the poet, who, in this use of his sacred prophecy, imitates the heathen oracles, on which several of their dramatic plots are constructed, as might be shewn by obvious examples. The interview with Manoah then is conducive to the catastrophe, and the drama is not in this scene devoid of incident.

Delilah next appears, and if whatever tends to raise our interest in the leading character of the tragedy, cannot rightly be called episodical, the introduction of this person ought not to be accounted such, for who but this person is the cause and origin of all the pathos and distress of the story? The dialogue of this scene is moral, affecting, and sublime; it is also strictly characteristic.

The next scene exhibits the tremendous giant Harapha, and the contrast thereby produced is amongst the beauties of the poem, and may of itself be termed an important incident: that it leads to the catastrophe I think will not be disputed, and if it is asked in what manner, the Chorus will supply us with an answer—

> He will directly to the Lords, I fear,
> And with malicious counsel stir them up
> Some way or other farther to afflict thee. [ll. 1250–2]

Here is another prediction connected with the plot, and verified by its catastrophe, for Samson is commanded to come to the festival and entertain the revellers with some feats of strength: these commands he resists, but obeys an impulse of his mind by going afterward, and thereby fulfils the prophetic declaration he had made to his father in the second act. What incident can shew more management and address

336

in the poet, than this of Samson's refusing the summons of the idolaters, and obeying the visitation of God's Spirit?

And now I may confidently appeal to the judicious reader, whether the *Samson Agonistes* is so void of incident between the opening and conclusion as fairly to be pronounced *to want a middle*. Simple it is from first to last, simple perhaps to a degree of coldness in some of its parts; but to say that nothing passes between the first act and the last, which hastens or delays the death of Samson, is not correct, because the very incidents are to be found, which conduce to the catastrophe, and but for which it could not have come to pass.

The author of the *Rambler* professes to examine the *Samson Agonistes* according to the rule laid down by Aristotle for the disposition and perfection of a tragedy, and this rule he informs us is, that it should have a *beginning, a middle, and an end*. And is this the mighty purpose for which the authority of Aristotle is appealed to? If it be thus the author of the *Rambler* has read the Poetics, and this be the best rule he can collect from that treatise, I am afraid he will find it too short a measure for the poet he is examining, or the critic he is quoting. Aristotle has said, 'that every whole hath not amplitude enough for the construction of a tragic fable; now by a whole (adds he in the way of illustration), I mean that, which hath beginning, middle, and end.' This and no more is what he says upon beginning, middle, and end; and this, which the author of the *Rambler* conceives to be a rule for tragedy, turns out to be merely an explanation of the word *whole*, which is only one term amongst many employed by the critic in his professed and complete definition of tragedy. I should add, that Aristotle gives a further explanation of the terms, beginning, middle, and end, which the author of the *Rambler* hath turned into English, but in so doing, he hath inexcusably turned them out of their original sense as well as language; as any curious critic may be convinced of, who compares them with Aristotle's words in the eighth chapter of the *Poetics*.

Of the poetic diction of the *Samson Agonistes* I have already spoken in general; to particularize passages of striking beauty would draw me into too great length; at the same time, not to pass over so pleasing a part of my undertaking in absolute silence, I will give the following reply of Samson to the Chorus—[ll. 547–52].

Of the character I may say in few words, that Samson possesses all the terrific majesty of Prometheus chained, the mysterious distress of Œdipus, and the pitiable wretchedness of Philoctetes. His properties, like those of the first, are something above human; his misfortunes, like those of the second, are derivable from the displeasure of Heaven, and involved in oracles; his condition, like that of the last, is the most abject, which human nature can be reduced to from a state of dignity and splendour.

Of the catastrophe there remains only to remark, that it is of unparalleled majesty and terror.

72. White on analogues to *Paradise Lost*

1786

Extract from T[homas] H[olt] W[hite], letter, *Gentleman's Magazine*, lvi (January 1786), 39–41. Most analogues omitted.

Thomas Holt White, aside from periodical comments like those included in this collection, published *A Review of Johnson's Criticism on the Style of Milton's English Prose; with Strictures on the Introduction of Latin Idiom into the English Language* (1818), and edited *Areopagitica* (1819) with extensive notes.

When it suits you, please to insert a few remarks which I have made in looking over Newton's edition of Milton. If some of them appear minute, let it be considered, that whatever gives the least light into any obscure passage in Chaucer, Shakspeare, Milton, Dryden, or Pope, should not be esteemed trivial; neither will imitations or accidental resemblances be neglected by those who are desirous of seeing in what manner different authors express the same thought. The works of these our greatest masters are growing every day darker from the shades which time gradually spreads over them, and which it is much beyond the power of any one man to clear off effectually. I therefore throw my mite occasionally into your valuable collection.

Yours, &c. T. H. W.

NOTES ON MILTON.

Paradise Lost.

Instruct me, for Thou know'st; Thou from the first
Wast present, . . . B. i. ver. 19.

Copied from Homer's invocation of the Muses: . . .

Instruct me now, O ye Muses, who have celestial mansions;
For ye are goddesses, and are present, and know all things. [*Iliad* I, 19]

That sea-beast
Leviathan, which God of all his works
Created hugest that swim th' ocean stream
Him haply slumb'ring on the Norway foam
The pilot of some small night-founder's skiff
Deeming some iland, oft, as seamen tell,
With fixed anchor in his skaly rind
Moors by his side under the lee, . . . Ver. 200.

'It sometimes falleth out, that mariners, thinking these whales to be ilands, and casting out ankers upon their backs, are often in danger of drowning. The Bishop of Breme, in old time, sent certaine legates with a coven of friers to preach and publish in the North the popish faith; and when they had spent a long journey in sailing towards the North, they came unto an iland, and there casting their anker, they went ashore, and kindled fires, and so provided victuals for the rest of their journy. But when their fires grew very hote, this iland sanke, and suddenly vanished away, and the mariners escaped drowning very narrowly with the boate that was present.' *Hakluyt's Voyages*, I. 568.

His pond'rous shield,
. . . . . . the broad circumference
Hung on his shoulders like the moon, . . . Ver. 284.

And on her shoulder hung her shield, . . .
As the fair moon in her most full aspect.
Spenser's F. Q. b. V. cant. v. st. 3.

. . . Bentley, in a note on *verse* 303 of this book [IV], is surprised that Milton, in his description of the person of Adam, should omit his beard. Newton imagines it was because the painters never represent our first parent with one. But neither the critic nor the good bishop were aware of the ignominy which the beard of man lies under. Helmont gravely asserts, that Adam was created an handsome young man, without a beard; but that his face was afterward degraded with hair, like the beasts, for his disobedience; and that Eve, being less guilty, was permitted to retain her smooth face. The fantastic philosopher also adds this extraordinary remark, that, if an angel appears with a beard, you may depend on it that he is an evil one, for no good angel ever wore a beard. . . .

> Neither various stile
> Nor holy rapture wanted they to praise
> Their Maker, in fit strains pronounc'd or sung
> Unmeditated, such prompt eloquence
> Flow'd from their lips, in prose or numerous verse,
> More tuneable than needed lute or harp
> To add more sweetness; . . . B. V. v. 146.

On the contrary, a modern writer on the *Origin and Progress of Language* [Lord Monboddo] hath laboured much to prove what Lucretius had said in fewer words, that the first men were mute, and that it was several ages before they could speak distinctly. The feelings of Lord M. would have been much hurt, if he had known that he was flatly contradicting a person of so amiable a character as *St. Hildegardis*, as well as Milton; for she tells us, that the voice of the first man was so extensively harmonious, that it contained the whole art of music, and was so powerful, that it would have been too much for degenerate ears; nay, that it was so sonorous, that when Adam began to sing, it frightened even the devil himself. But take the very words of this virgin-saint and prophetess, in the sermon which she preached in Latin to the good people of Mentz in the twelfth century. . . .

Jortin, in his note on Book XI. ver. 565, introduces the following remark: . . . *Lucret.* lib. V. v. 1240. 'These verses want emendation. Plumbi potestas is nonsense. The stop should be placed thus:

> Et simul argenti pondus, plumbique potestas
> Ignis ubi ingentes, &c.

Argenti pondus plumbique, as in Virgil, argenti pondus et auri. Potestas ignis expresses the consuming power of fire. We have potentia solis in Virgil, and potestates herbarum.' JORTIN.

If Dr. Jortin had examined the whole passage in Lucretius relating to the discovery of metals and the uses men first applied them to, he would not have thought any alteration necessary in the pointing. . . . Ver.

1267. No doubt the *potestas plumbi* in the former quotation hath the same meaning as the *potestas auri et argenti* in this. The plain import of this description of the poet is, that metals were first discovered by the burning of forests, and that men valued the different sorts, in early ages, according as they found them more or less hard, when they attempted to use them in such tools and instruments as their occasions required. . . . [Further analogues to other poems follow.]

73. White on the Sonnets

1786

Extract from T[homas] H[olt] W[hite], letter, *Gentleman's Magazine*, lvi (part 2, 1786), 1110.

The Sonnet succeeding the Ode, and the Idyllium [sonnet vii], is in Milton's best manner, which is surely the highest possible praise. Little elegies, consisting of four stanzas and a couplet, are no more sonnets than they are epic poems. The sonnet is of a particular and *arbitrary* construction; it partakes of the nature of blank verse, by the lines running into each other at proper intervals. Each line of the first eight rhimes four times, and the order in which these rhimes should fall is *decisive*. For the ensuing six lines there is more licence, and they may, or may not, at pleasure, close with a couplet.

Of Milton's English sonnets, only that to Oliver Cromwell ends with a couplet; but that single instance is a sufficient precedent. However, in three out of his five Italian ones, the two concluding lines rhime to each other.

The style of the sonnet should be nervous; and, where the subject will with propriety bear elevation, *sublime*; with which simplicity of language is by no means incompatible. If the subject is familiar and domestic, the style should, though affectionate, be vigorous, though plain, be energetic. The great models of perfection for the sublime and domestic sonnet are those of Milton's 'To the Soldier to spare his Dwelling-place,' and 'To Mr. Laurence.' The sonnet is certainly the most difficult species of all poetic composition; but difficulty well subdued is excellence. Mrs. Smith says she has been told, that the *regular* sonnet suits not the nature or genius of our language. Surely this assertion cannot be demonstrated, and therefore was not worth attention.

Out of eighteen English sonnets, written by Milton, four are bad. The rest, though they are not all free from certain hardnesses, have a pathos, and a greatness in their simplicity, sufficient to endear the legitimate sonnet to every reader of just taste; they possess a characteristic grace, which can never belong to three elegiac stanzas closing with a couplet.

74. Hawkins on Johnson's criticism of Milton

1787

Extract from Sir John Hawkins, *The Life of Samuel Johnson* (1787), 243–4.

Sir John Hawkins (1719–89), a lawyer, wrote a *History of Music* (1776), containing comments on composers and music connected with Milton's poems and his father, and a *Life* of his friend Samuel Johnson in 1787.

Johnson's talent for criticism, both preceptive and corrective, is now known and justly celebrated; and had he not displayed it in its utmost lustre in his *Lives of the Poets*, we should have lamented that he was so sparing of it in the *Rambler*, which seemed to be a vehicle, of all others the most proper, for that kind of communication. An eulogium on Knolles's *History of the Turks*, and a severe censure of the *Samson Agonistes*, of Milton are the only critical essays there to be found; to the latter he seems to have been prompted by no better a motive, than that hatred of the author for his political principles which he is known to have entertained, and was ever ready to avow. What he has remarked of Milton in his *Lives of the Poets* is undoubtedly true: he was a political enthusiast, and, as is evident from his panegyric on Cromwell, a base and abject flatterer. His style in controversy was sarcastic and bitter, and not consistent with christian charity; and though his apologists endeavour to defend him by the practice of the times, there were in his time better exemplars than he chose to follow, the writings of Jewel, Mede, Hooker, Dr. Jackson, and others, his predecessors in religious and political controversy; nor does he seem in his private character to have possessed many of those qualities that most endear men to each other. His friends were few, Andrew Marvel, Marchmont Needham, and the younger Vane; and Cyriac Skinner, Harrington, Henry Nevil, John Aubrey, and others, members of that crack-brained assembly the Rota-club, all republicans; and there is reason to suspect, from the sternness of his temper, and the rigid discipline of his family, that his domestic manners were far from amiable, and that he was neither a kind husband nor an indulgent parent. But neither these nor those other qualities that rendered him both a bitter enemy and a railing disputant, could justify the severity of Johnson's criticism on the above-mentioned poem, nor apologize for that harsh and groundless censure which closes the first of his discourses on it, that it is 'a tragedy which ignorance has admired, and bigotry applauded.'

75. Mickle on *Samson Agonistes*

1788

[William Mickle], 'A Critique on the *Samson Agonistes* of Milton, in Refutation of the Censure of Dr. Johnson', *European Magazine*, xiii (1788), 401–6.

The poet William J. Mickle (1735–88) is best remembered today for his translation of Camoens' *Lusiads* (1775), with various introductory discussions including a critical excursus on epic poetry. His work little reflects a study of Milton.

A respectable writer has some time ago, in a periodical paper, thought proper to pass a very severe sentence on that excellent tragedy, the *Samson Agonistes* of Milton. After having given *his* epitome of it, 'This is undoubtedly, (says he) a just and regular catastrophe, and the poem therefore has a beginning and an end which Aristotle himself could not have disapproved. But it must be allowed to want a middle, since nothing passes between the first act and the last that either hastens or delays the death of Samson. The whole drama, if its superfluities were cut off, would scarcely fill a single act, yet this is the tragedy which ignorance has admired, and bigotry applauded.' But confident and dogmatical as this severe censure is, we doubt not of convincing the reader that it is extremely ill-founded. The story of Samson certainly affords a proper and eligible subject for a tragedy on the Greek model, and that model Milton has preferred. To judge justly therefore of *Samson Agonistes*, we must consider the conduct of some of the most celebrated of the Greek tragedies. The different tragedies on the story of Œdipus, have, since the days of Aristotle, been esteemed the models of perfection; and the middle of every one of them consists of new light and information breaking in by degrees, which by degrees also produces an alteration of mind in Œdipus; and that alteration of mind, in the most natural and regular manner, produces the catastrophe. Exactly in the same manner is the conduct of the *Samson Agonistes*; and if it is found that the catastrophe of Milton's tragedy is dependant on, and produced by,

344

an alteration of mind in Samson, which alteration is produced by a train of circumstances and conversations, it must follow that it has a just and regular middle, in the true spirit of the Greek tragedy.

And that the *Samson Agonistes* has such a middle, will be evident from the following impartial epitome of its conduct.

The beginning.—The Philistines keep a high festival in honour of their God Dagon, to whom they ascribe the overthrow and captivity of their great enemy Samson. Samson, their prisoner, has had his eyes put out, and is a slave to grind at their public mill; but is respited from labour on this holiday. The poem here opens with Samson speaking to a guide: [1–5].

Samson having dismissed his guide, falls into a very natural soliloquy on the prophecies of his birth, that he was to deliver Israel, and describes and laments his blindness in the most pathetic manner: [12–15, 38–42].

And as the festival must have been known round the neighbourhood, nothing can be more natural than that Samson's friends should take that opportunity of his respite to visit him. And a chorus of Danites (his tribe) accordingly come to see, and converse with him. And old Manoah his father next arrives. Here ends the beginning, which, as our severe critic allows, is such as 'Aristotle himself could not have disapproved.'—The middle now commences in the true spirit and manner of the Greek tragedy. Samson's mind is worked upon by different visitors, and by extremely natural and proper gradations is brought to a determination which as naturally produces the catastrophe. Manoah laments the deplorable condition of his son, and Samson severely condemns himself. The following is strikingly pointed: [410–19].

Manoah replies, equally condemning his subjection to Philistine women, but still with a mixture of paternal tenderness: [430–47].

Samson with generous contrition acknowledges, [449–71].

> *Manoah.* With cause this hope relieves thee, and these words
> I as a prophecy receive . . . [472–3]

Progressive impressions on the mind of Samson have in the above citations been artfully delineated, and continued in just succession. Manoah informs his son that he intends to treat with the Philistine lords for his ransom, of which he expresses good hope. But this the perturbed mind of Samson at first rejects [487–90]. And with manly feeling he resents the idea of his being an useless and idle burden at home: [564–75].

> *Man.* [577–89]
> *Sam.* [590, 593–8]

The hopes with which Manoah endeavours to impress the mind of his son, and Samson's presage that his death was *nigh at hand*, in the above most beautiful speech, are truly in the spirit and conduct of the Grecian tragedy, in leading on the minds of its heroes, so as in the most natural manner to produce the catastrophe. The father thus replies: [599–605].

To say, that in these expostulations, between Manoah and his son, the Drama is advancing towards no event, is perverseness indeed. Manoah is now dismissed, and Samson and the Chorus continue preparatory discourses of the same progressive nature. And Samson's perturbation of mind and dark forebodings, like those of Œdipus, are gradually heightened by the appearance of Dalila and Harapha, a gigantic boaster.

Dalila, his wife and traitress, perfumed and richly dressed, with a damsel train approaches. She pretends remorse for betraying him, implores forgiveness, and boasts of the love and affection with which she will attend him after having obtained his deliverance. Samson's resentments of her former treachery will not trust her. After some dialogue highly characteristic, Dalila throws off the mask of affection, boasts of what she had done to her country's enemy, and basely insults him. The agitation of Samson's mind thus increased, is still farther aggravated by the boasts of the giant Harapha, who, on Samson's thrice challenging him to single combat, retires, threatening the revenge of a coward: [1242–3].

Cho. [1250–2]

Undaunted by the worst of prospects, Samson replies, [1262–7].

What Samson had before said to his father, that the contest was now between God and Dagon, expressing his confidence that God would speedily vindicate his own honour, he repeats in substance to Harapha. And his prophetic hope, just cited, strongly marks the progress of what is passing in his mind. A messenger now arrives from the Philistian lords, commanding his attendance in the temple of Dagon, to shew them feats of his strength. Samson at first absolutely refuses: [1319–21].

Samson persists, the messenger retires, and the Chorus, apprehensive that his report may produce greater evils to Samson, intimate their wish, that he had obeyed the summons. He replies, urging the impiety of

Vaunting *his* strength in honour to their Dagon: [1360]

and says, that 'not dragging' should constrain him to the temple of the idol. Yet his dark forebodings more and more agitate his mind.

To the officer's departing speech,

> I am sorry what this stoutness will produce [1346]

he had replied,

> Perhaps thou shalt have cause to sorrow indeed. [1347]

And now having mentioned how unpardonable he would be in the sight of God, were he to be *willingly* present at idol-worship, his revolving mind adds,

> Yet that he may dispense with me or thee
> Present in temples at idolatrous rites,
> For some important cause, thou needs't not doubt. [1377-9]

The middle is here pointedly drawing to a conclusion. The Chorus perceive that the agitation of his mind is about something important, that his temper is now worked up, and beg with a change of conduct. [1380-9]

After addressing himself to the messenger, who is now returned, he again assures his brethren, the Chorus [1423-6].

> *Cho.* [1427-42]

Here the middle is evidently summed up; and he who reads the *Samson Agonistes*, and cannot perceive the progressive workings of the mind of Samson, arising naturally from the incidents which follow the opening or beginning of the tragedy, must either be grossly inattentive, or prejudiced indeed. That Samson's mind is in a very different state, when he bids the Chorus farewell, from that in which they found him, is so self-evident on attentive perusal, that it is truly astonishing how a respectable critic could hazard the assertion, that 'nothing passes between the first act and the last, that either hastens or delays the death of Samson.' Every thing, on the contrary, tends to hasten it, by artfully producing, by degrees, that temper of mind which leads Samson to the temple of Dagon. The tragedy had therefore a just and true middle, on the Greek model. And strange it is, that our severe critic should have disregarded or overlooked Milton's own defence of the conduct of his own fable [in the introductory note, which is quoted].

Our critic has allowed that the *Samson Agonistes* 'has a beginning and an end which Aristotle himself could not have disapproved.' And we trust our reader is now convinced, that it has also a just and regular middle, which produces the catastrophe. The progressive change of temper in Samson is evidently the cause of his consenting to go to the temple of Dagon. The Chorus remains, and old Manoah, 'with youthful

347

steps,' almost immediately joins them, elated with the hopes of procuring his son's liberty by ransom, when he abruptly exclaims,

> What noise or shout was that? It tore the sky. [1472; 1473-80]

Old Manoah thus immediately recurring to the ransom of his son [1490-2], is finely expressive of the feelings of the father. Another shout is heard. Manoah is the first to observe it: [1508-18].

An Hebrew now arrives on speed from the city, who, as Milton himself expresses it in the Argument, 'confusedly at first and afterward more distinctly relates the catastrophe, what Samson had done to the Philistines, and by accident to himself, wherewith the tragedy ends.'

Beside an investigation of the fable and dramatic conduct of the *Samson Agonistes*, it was our first intention to point out the beauties of that performance, so truly in the Grecian model; but that task, we found, would be too tedious; we shall therefore content ourselves with pointing out a few.—As we were just talking of the catastrophe, we shall cite part of it. Samson, in the temple, had shewn the Philistine Lords several feats [1627-8].

He then desires [1632-59].

Cho. [1660-4]

The concluding speech of Manoah is truly grand, very worthy of the father of a patriot hero: [1708-24].

Manoah's dwelling on the sentiments and repeating it in other words, 'that *there was nothing for tears, nothing to wail, no weakness, no contempt, dispraise, or blame, nothing but good and fair*, in the death of Samson,' is truly characteristic of the feelings of a brave old man, on first hearing the tidings of the honourable death of an heroic son. Manoah then proposes to find the body of Samson [1729-33].

This and what follows are in the genuine spirit of the first of the Greek tragedies: [1733-44].

To say that Samson's celebrated soliloquy on blindness, with which the tragedy opens, contains wonderful merit, is saying but little. It is every way worthy of the feelings of a first-rate poet, labouring under that grievous calamity. The grief and lamentations of Manoah, and his fond hope of procuring Samson's liberty by ransom, all speak the emotions of the afflicted father contemplating a brave but fallen son. The visits of Dalila, his treacherous wife, and Harapha, the vain-boasting Philistian giant, are both most naturally characteristic. They knew that it was a high festival, and that then was the time to see and talk with him. In Dalila, the character of the unfaithful wife and female tyrant is delineated in a most masterly manner. It is natural for such character easily to forgive itself, to gloss over the crime and pretend affection, and to wish for a reconciliation with the injured husband; but such a reconciliation as implies total submission and forgiveness, on his part, and a surrender of himself to her future discretion and love. On all her arts proving ineffectual on the determined mind of Samson, who tells her,

> Love quarrels oft in pleasing concord end;
> Not wedlock treachery . . . [1008–9]

the other part of so selfish and base a character bursts forth in rage, abuse, and in glorying in what she has done. And in Harapha, the boastful coward, who comes to insult a blind and fallen enemy, is excellently displayed. And each of these visits has an evident tendency to work upon the despairing temper in which his father left him; and as we already have cited in our former mention of the giant Harapha, we find the mind of Samson labouring with dark forebodings of the approaching event. What Dr. Johnson had been pleased to say of Shakespeare (*see his preface to his edition*) may with great justice be applied to Milton in his conduct of the *Agonistes*.—'His real power is not shewn in the splendour of particular passages, but by the *progress of the fable*, and the tenor of his dialogue. The dialogue of this author is often so evidently determined by the incident which produces it, and is pursued with so much *ease* and *simplicity*, that it seems scarcely to claim the merit of fiction, but to have been gleaned by diligent selection out of common conversation and common occurrences.'

After having thus pointed out the dramatic progress of the fable of *Samson Agonistes*, and held up to view some of its many splendid and truly classical beauties, we trust the intelligent reader will join with us in lamenting that the force of prejudice (conceived, most probably, from a dislike of Milton's political creed) should have betrayed so respectable an authority as that of Dr. Johnson, into the absurd assertion, that 'nothing passes between the first act and the last that either *hastens or delays* the death of Samson;' or into the injustice and extreme petulence of the following: 'The whole Drama, if its superfluities were cut off, would scarcely fill a single act; yet this is the tragedy which *ignorance has admired, and bigotry applauded.*'

Peace to thy manes, oh Johnson! Thou hast, on the whole, deserved greatly of the Republic of Letters; but let the living improve by thy prejudices, thy weaknesses, and thy errors!

76. Neve on Milton and the poems

1789

Philip Neve, 'Milton', *Cursory Remarks on Some of the Ancient English Poets, Particularly Milton* (1789), 109–46.

Philip Neve is very important to Milton scholarship because of his discussion of the poems included in this collection and because of *A Narrative of the Disinterment of Milton's Coffin* (1790), which received a second edition in the same year. See also Cowper's poem on the disinterment, No. 77, below. Little else is known about Neve.

'Arcades'

The proper place to rank this early production of *Milton*'s pen seems, as a kind of prologue to 'Comus'. *Milton* went to live with his father at *Horton*, Bucks, in 1632. At *Harefield* in the neighbourhood of *Horton*, resided the Countess Dowager of *Derby*, at whose house this piece was first performed: and 'Comus' was acted, in 1634, at *Ludlow Castle*, before the Earl of *Bridgewater*, who had married a daughter of the Countess of *Derby*. This piece was 'presented by some noble persons of the Countess's family;' probably the children of Earl of *Bridgewater*, who were by it, as a kind of dramatic exercise, initiated to the stage, and brought to perform, the next year, in 'Comus', in characters, that required greater confidence and exertion.

It has been observed, that *Milton* not only instituted this piece upon Ben Jonson's *Entertainment of the Queen and Prince at Althorpe*, but that he has servilely copied some of his words. . . . Perhaps, upon thorough investigation, what is called servility, may be found good judgment in *Milton*. This Countess of *Derby* was daughter of the Lord *Spenser* of *Althorpe*, who had there received the Queen and Prince. She was Dowager at *Harefield*, in 1633; and *Ben Jonson*'s entertainment had been performed at *Althorpe*, as the occasion of it had been given, but thirty years before. It seems therefore a very delicate compliment in *Milton*, to apply to her the words, that had, upon a former occasion, been applied to the Queen; and to remind her, by such repetition, of scenes, very flattering to her family, in receiving the Queen and Prince on their first arrival in the kingdom; and at which scenes she had herself probably been present.

'Lycidas'

This poem appears to have been formed between *Spenser* and the early Italians. *Dryden* says, in the 'Preface' to his *Fables*, '*Milton* was the *poetical* son of *Spenser*. He has acknowledged to me, that *Spenser* was his original.' 'Astrophel' therefore probably gave rise to 'Lycidas'. And, as *Dante* has made *Cato* of *Utica* keeper of the gates of Purgatorio, *Milton* has here, in return, placed St. *Peter* in company with *Apollo*, *Triton*, *Æolus*, &c. For the intrusion of what follows, respecting the clergy of his time, the earliest Italians have, in pieces of every sort, set plentiful example. Perhaps no better reason can be given for *Milton*'s conduct here, than what some commentator gives for *Dante*'s aboved mentioned: 'Per verità è un gran capriccio, ma in ciò seque suo stile.' [In terms of truth it is extremely fanciful, but in this lies his style.]

Whoever compares this poem, towards the end, *i.e.* twenty lines from 'Weep no more, woful shepherds, weep no more,' with the conclusion of the 'Epitaphium Damonis', from 'Nec te Lethæo fas quæsivisse sub Orco,' will find them much alike.

A late writer's inference, 'that no man could ever have read "Lycidas" with pleasure, independently of the knowledge of its author,' has somewhat of the same foundation as one of *Lauder*'s replies, 'that those, who inveigh against his interpolations, would themselves not scruple to commit real forgeries, did not the fear of the laws restrain them;' for neither writer could know of whom he was judging.

'Il Pensoroso'

It would be, doubtless, in the opinion of all readers, going too far to say, that *Beaumont*'s song, in the *Passionate Madam*, deserves as much notice as the '*Pensoroso*' itself: but it so happens, that very little of the former can remain unnoticed, whenever the latter is praised.

Of that song the construction is, in the first place, to be admired. It divides into three parts. The first part displays the moral of melancholy: the second the person or figure: the third the circumstance; *i.e.* such things as encrease, or flatter the disposition. Nor is it surprizing, that *Milton* should be struck with the images and sentiments it affords; most

of which are somewhere inserted in the 'Pensoroso'. It will not, however, be found to have contributed much to the construction of *Milton's*
poem. The subjects they severally exhibit are very different: they are
alike only, as shewn under the same disposition of melancholy. *Beaumont's* is the melancholy of the swain; of the mind, that contemplates
nature and man, but in the grove and the cottage. *Milton's* is that of the
scholar and philosopher; of the intellect, that has ranged the mazes of
science; and that decides upon vanity and happiness, from large intercourse with man, and upon extensive knowledge and experience. To
say, therefore, that *Milton* was indebted to *Beaumont's* song for his
'Pensoroso' would be absurd. That it supplied some images to his poem
will be readily allowed: and that it would be difficult to find, throughout the 'Pensoroso', amidst all its variety, any more striking, than what
Beaumont's second stanza affords, may also be granted.

Milton's poem is among those happy works of genius, which leave a
reader no choice how his mind shall be affected.

In Milton's *Latin Poems* pure diction and harmonious versification
are every where observable. The *Elegies* have a perfectly classical elegance. Perhaps no scholar could succeed in forming a happy elegiac
stile, without the study of *Ovid*. Of such study these poems afford
much proof. . . . No part of *Milton's* writings contain so full account
of himself, as his Latin poems: nor are any where found so many
embryo-passages of his greater works.

Milton's six *Italian Poems* shew a very extensive skill in that language; and highly deserve the elaborate praise *Francini* has bestowed on
them in his *Ode*, where he says, with much grace,

> Dammi tua dolce cetra
> Se vuoi ch'io dica del tuo dolce canto.

The second *Sonnet*,

> Qual in colle aspro al imbrunir di sera, &c.

has great delicacy, both of sentiment and expression. It is without weakness, and without hyperbole: a medium, which seems Italian perfection.
In the *Canzone* is one of the most elegant forms, used in the language;

> *Dinne*, se la tua speme sia mai vana,
> E de pensieri lo miglior *t'arrivi*;

a mode used by the earliest, and the best Italians; . . . Even in such
trifles as Italian *Sonnets*, it is easy to discover the man, and the scale of
mind, that was composing them. . . .

Milton's language, both in prose and verse, is so peculiarly his own, that the style of no former, or contemporary writer bears any resemblance to it. From his phraseology the idiom of no learned, or foreign language is excluded. To a reader, unacquainted with the foreign and ancient-English languages, and incapable of tracing words to their parent root in the learned, the sense and spirit of *Milton's* phrase must be often unattainable. To ostentation, to a desire of frequently displaying the acquirements of study, has this copiousness of learning been by some attributed. Perhaps a more liberal and more just cause may be assigned. *Milton* was, till his thirtieth year, a laborious and uninterrupted student. When he engaged himself in the business of the world, still his occupation was learning. His familiarity with all languages is generally known: and nothing is so common an effect of perfection in, and intimate use of a language, as thinking in, and expressing the thoughts by the idiom of that language. In *Dryden's* English we find Latinisms allowed and admired; and, if *Milton* was a better scholar in all languages, than *Dryden* in Latin, the idioms of all were in common to him. Bishop *Atterbury*, an excellent judge in every part of polite literature, censures *Waller* for his total want of Grecisms, and for his few Latinisms, and infers from thence very slender scholarship. If *Atterbury's* rule be just, judge all your poets by the same rule; and let not *Milton*, who abounds with learned allusions; whose text perpetually reminds us of the Greek writers, and who has epithets and phrases without end from *Horace* and *Virgil*, and almost all the poetical turns either language could afford to his own; let not him, thus qualified and thus excelling, be blamed for what would have been praised in *Waller*, or any other poet.

The great extent of poetical imagery, allusion, and description in the *Paradise Lost*, necessarily led its author to extensive dealings with the Greek and Roman epics, and transferred much of their readings and idiom from those languages to his own: but, of all modern languages, the peculiar favorite of *Milton's* study was *Italian*. No part of his works is exempt from notices of this predilection. Wherever he has a choice, the Italian derivation is preferred. He has *sovran, ammiral, harald, perfet, tempest, v. &c. &c. &c.* And it is, perhaps, not difficult to account for this preference. Whoever is acquainted with the Italian and Greek languages, will find a strong analogy between them; and such a force in many of the Italian words, as brings the resemblance nearest, even in those very parts, where the greatest strength of the Greek lies. If the Greeks have *apodemos*, the Italians have *fuoruscito*. When the Greek indeed rises to *philapodemos*, the Italian is left; and at some point must every language be left by it; for with it, to the full extent of the composite words, none other can compare. The force of a Greek composite can never be better shown, than by the text of *Milton*, who in his 'Masque' has taken a full line and half to render one word, used by *Homer*:

—what time the labor'd ox
In his loose traces from the furrow came—

is all expressed by *Boslytus*. But the Italians, though far short of this force, have still composite words of sufficient power to make every lover of Greek love Italian. And, that *Milton*'s attachment to it arose from this affinity, seems probable, because his taste for it was greatly antecedent to his visiting *Italy*; and the kind and flattering reception, he met with there, was the consequence, not the cause of his great proficiency in it. His fondness for music too might have some influence in favour of a language, so well adapted to musical expression.

It has been observed of *Milton*, 'that he very often imitates *Scripture*, where he is thought most to follow a classic original.' A like observation may be made on his Italian Imitations; for he has often followed the poets of that language, where classic authors are referred to. In the note on *Par. Reg.* b. iii. l. 310, varior. edit.

He look'd, and saw *what numbers numberless*
The city gates outpour'd, light-armed troopes;

Æschylus is referred to: whereas *Milton* took both the expression and much of the sentiment from *Tasso, La Ger.* c. xix. st. 121:

Ma non aspettar già che di quell' oste
L'innumerabil numero ti conti.

Several other instances of this sort might be pointed out. Another note, or two, may here be added. In the 'Allegro',

Warble his native *woodnotes wild*,

is Tasso's

boscarecce inculte avene.
La Ger. c. vii. st. 6.

In *Par. Lost*, var. edit. b. ii. at l. 124,

When he, who most excels *in fact of arms*;

a change is proposed to, *facts*, or *feats*. The text is a simple Gallicism; *en fait d'armes*; as, maitre *en fait d'armes*. Same book, l. 185,

Unrespited, unpitied, unrepriev'd,

is from Shakspeare's

Unhousel'd, unappointed, unaneal'd.

Ghost, in *Hamlet.*

This seems the most obvious allusion possible. No line, or passage in *Shakspeare* appears to have made so deep impression on *Milton's* imagination, as this: he has fourteen or fifteen imitations of it. Yet, the notes refer only to the Greek tragedies in general.—The passage in *Par. Lost*, b. x. l. 296,

> —the rest his look
> *Bound with Gorgonian rigor* not to move,
> *And with Asphaltic slime*; broad as the gate,
> Deep to the roots of hell the gather'd beach
> They fasten'd—

has no small difficulty. This is the punctuation of both *Milton's* editions. About such substances and such operations it is vain to reason too physically. Perhaps some help towards an interpretation may be gained from the phraseology of *Tacitus*; who frequently couples, under the same verb, a moral subject and a material: . . . and in many other like instances. The modern editions alter the punctuation, by placing the semicolon at *move*; and only a comma at *slime*. In 'Comus', l. 380, *all to-ruffled*, the original reading of both *Milton's* editions, should be restored to the text, instead of the words now found there. This is a mode of expression very frequent in *Chaucer*, as, in the *Monkes Tale*,

> she wold kille
> Leons, lepards, and beres *al to-rent.*

i.e. *rent bears entirely to pieces.*

To metre and accent, of which many readers affect to perceive so much grace and harmony in the verse of *Milton*, he appears to have been, in general, very little attentive. Among his blank heroics are found both rhyming couplets and alexandrines. That no passages appear, throughout his books, where the position of the words, or the accents have been studied, can with no more truth be asserted, than that the generality of his verses discover marks of care. Wherever the image was to be illustrated by a pause,

> Dire was the tossing, deep the groans, Despair
> Tended the sick, busiest from couch to couch;
> And over them triumphant Death his dart
> *Shook*—but delay'd to strike.

or by an accent,

> Gambol'd before them; th' *unwieldy* elephant.

or by a burthen of the verse,

> Created *hugest, that swims th' ocean stream.*

In such cases his care was bestowed with a success, that few poets before him, except *Homer* and *Ariosto*, have equalled. In other cases he committed himself to his reader, upon his general dignity of sentiment and boldness of expression, frequently the result of such liberty of writing. The most striking character of his poetical style is formed by the turn of words,

> *Glory to him,* whose just avenging ire
> Had driven out th' ungodly from his sight
> And th' habitations of the just; *to him*
> *Glory* and praise—
>
> *Par. Lost,* b. vii.

> Servit odoriferas per opes levis *aura* Favoni,
> *Aura* sub innumeris humida nata rosis.
>
> Eleg. 3.

With these both his English and Latin poems abound. The 114th *Psalm,* which he has rendered both into English and Greek paraphrase, (of which the English was done by him at fifteen years old) appears to have attracted his notice, by a particularly beautiful turn of lines found in it. Yet *Dryden* says, in his 'Dedication of Juvenal', 'Had I time I could enlarge on the beautiful turns of words and thoughts, which are as requisite in satire, as in heroic poetry. With these beautiful turns I confess myself to have been unacquainted, till in a conversation, which I had with Sir George *Mackenzy,* he asked me why I did not imitate, in my verses, the turns of Mr. *Waller* and Sir John *Denham;* of which he repeated to me many. This hint, thus seasonably given me, first made me sensible of my own wants, and brought me afterwards to seek for the supply of them in other English authors. I looked over first the darling of my youth, the famous *Cowley;* there I found, instead of them, points of wit and quirks of epigram, even in the *Davideis.* Then I consulted a greater genius, I mean *Milton;* but I found not there neither, that for which I looked.' And, to ascertain his meaning, he concludes with examples from *Ovid*:

> Heu quantum scelus est in *viscera viscera* condi!

and from *Catullus*:

> Tum jam *nulla* viro juranti fœmina credat;
> *Nulla* viri speret sermones esse fideles:
> Nam, simul ac cupidæ mentis satiata libido est,
> Dicta *nihil* matuere, *nihil* perjuria curant.

Dryden used occasionally to visit *Milton*, who had expressed an opinion, not very favorable to him, as a poet; though he allowed him to be a rhymist. *Dryden* might be piqued at this opinion: he, more probably believed what he wrote. With his usual haste he took up *Milton*'s book, looked over a page or two, and, not finding there any turn of words, formed a general conclusion. His censure, however, seems to demonstrate, that he was, at least when he wrote this, in 1693, but a casual reader of *Milton*. And so erroneous is his opinion, that it may be doubted, even after all his study for examples, whether the ten thousand verses, which he delivered to *Tonson*, during the several succeeding years, contain as many turns of words, as the *Paradise Lost* alone, which consists of very few more lines.

Of *Milton*'s fame with posterity the measure is not yet full. That learning, science, and truth are impeded by the necessary distractions of life, and by the errors and variety of opinions, which the different limitations in the progress of our search and studies occasion, will not be more readily allowed, than that consummate knowledge itself is not alone sufficient for the establishment of truth; and that prejudice and malignity, with the highest talents, may render interpretations doubtful, or obscure facts, as certainly as ignorance, or the clouds of error.

It has been *Milton*'s fate, after a long interval of neglect and silence to his writings, to be at length brought forth and expounded by commentators of excellent taste, judgment, and erudition; by *Hume*, by *Addison, Thyer, Richardson*, and *Newton*: and, after the example of such men, illustrious some by their station, and all by their learning, a just life, at least a just history of the poetical character of *Milton*, had come with some grace from the late author of *The Lives of the Poets*. Yet, when to honor the greatest poet our annals can boast, these wreaths are gathered, the hymns composed, the altar prepared, and but the torch wanting for his apotheosis, like his own *Belial*,

> —whose tongue
> Dropt manna, and could make the worse appear
> The better reason, to perplex and dash
> Maturest counsels—

comes this avowed enemy, to forbid the rites, and oppose the claim.—
Of *Johnson*, from his great abilities, and his peculiar talent in biography,
it will probably be the fate, for many years, to be the last writer of a life
of *Milton*: yet let every reader in the mean time remember, that prejudice, envy, nay malignity, have, throughout this work, ever extinguished the candor of its author: in all cases determined his will against
his subject, and in some misled his judgment. He charges *Milton* with
vanity, in having prefixed to his juvenile Latin poems, the age, at which
they were severally written. That *Milton* did so, is certainly in itself a
proof of his modesty; 'take my poems and their apology with them.'
To construe such addition of his age a boast, you must at least allow
them to have (what is true) extraordinary excellence; and then Envy's
construction will be, 'at such an age I could make such poems.' But, how
illiberal it is to turn merit against itself, or make virtue in any way shadow
its own fame, may be judged of, without that great writer's abilities;
and will be allowed, without his prejudices. In the review of the Italian
Poems, his conduct is scarcely secure from ridicule. 'Of *Milton*'s Italian
Poems he cannot pretend to speak as a critic;' yet of every stanza of
Francini's Italian 'Ode', in commendation of them, he judges. The truth
is, that, finding in *Milton*'s Italian Poems nothing to dispraise, he would
still forbear to commend them, elegant as they are in themselves, and
the single instance of an English poet's exercise in that language. When
their perfection stood the test of his own examination, still they were to
be envied the just praise, they had received from others; and he has
fallen upon those very Italians themselves, who have celebrated them.
But with how much taste and judgment he has done this, may easily
be seen. His chief criticisms on *Francini*'s 'Ode' are, 'that the first stanza
is only empty noise,' and 'that the last is natural and beautiful.' With
respect to the first remark; whoever has passed, without admiring it,
Tasso's invocation, in his second stanza, (of which this first stanza of
Francini is a very elegant paraphrase), has probably found no one beauty
to admire, throughout the whole *Gerusalemme*. With respect to the
second remark; if *Carlo Dati* may be allowed a judge of just sentiment,
and poetical expression in Italian, the last stanza of *Francini*'s Ode is not
'natural and beautiful'; he having himself ridiculed it, in his Latin
Encomiastic-Inscription, subjoined to that *ode*: for, where he says, 'Illi, in
cujus virtutibus evulgandis ora famæ non sufficiant; *nec hominum stupor
in laudandis satis est*,' he can only allude to *Francini*'s conclusion,

> Freno dunque la lingua, e ascolto il core,
> *Che ti prende a lodar con lo stupore.*

It is also called pride in *Milton* to have printed, before his poems, the Italian testimonies in his favor. At the head of them is found a distich of *Manso*, Marchese di *Villa*, a man by birth, by letters, by military fame, fortune, and his patronage of scholars, among the most illustrious of his country, or his age. Could *Milton* then, who had received every civility and kindness from this man at *Naples*, consistently with humanity, good breeding, or any right of society, omit to print his distich, in a work published even in his lifetime, and which contained a long poem, purposely composed and presented personally to him by *Milton*, on his leaving *Naples*, in gratitude for the favors received there? If it were necessary that *Manso*'s testimony should appear, of course the others were required: and they are put forth with as much modesty, as could well be expressed concerning them, by a declaration, 'non tam de se quam supra se esse dicta.' *Milton*'s biographer has in these, and various other instances, forgotten (though he have elsewhere praised it) the best rule in Pope's *Essay on Criticism*,

> Learn then what morals critics ought to show;
> For 'tis but half a judge's task to know.
> 'Tis not enough, wit, art, and learning join;
> In all you speak let truth and candor shine.

Of this Marchese *Manso* it was the singular fate to be the common patron of both *Tasso* and *Milton*, though at the distance of forty-three years; for *Tasso* died in 1595, and *Milton* was not in *Italy* till 1638. The former poet celebrates his splendor and liberality:

> Fra 'cavalier magnanimi, e cortesi
> Risplende il *Manso*; e doni, e raggi ei versa.
> La Ger. Conq. c. xx. ed. 1593.

the latter his taste and patronage of the Muses:

> Dicetur tum sponte tuos habitâsse penates
> *Cynthius*, et famulas venisse ad limina musas.
> Carm. ad *Mansum*.

a couplet, which may, not unaptly, be applied to *Pope*.

Of the several commentators on *Milton*, Mr. *Richardson* and Mr. *Thyer* are the most conspicuous for the allusions: the former for the classical; the latter for the Italian. For the design of the poem, the conduct, and the manners, Mr. *Addison*; who points out, with great propriety, the consistency in the characters: a consistency, which is much and justly admired in *Tasso*; for which he is praised by every discerning reader, and celebrated by that fine judge of epic and dramatic excellence, *Metastasio*; who calls him 'dipintore fidelissimo de' caratteri veri e costanti.' This propriety in the Italian could not escape the observation of *Milton*, who had studied every line of *Tasso*, and whose poem has much in common with the *Gerusalemme*. The commendation of *Tasso*, however, in this particular, must not detract from *Milton*. The utmost he could derive from the example before him, was a notice, that the best critics would admire him, if he should adhere to the same consistency: and well rewarded has his care been in so good a judge of the decorum of character, as Mr. *Addison*, to point out his beauties.

The genius of *Milton*, the contemplations, the powers of intellect in invention and combination, are above example, or comparison. In proportion to the terror excited by the sublimity of his design, is the delight received by his wonderful execution. His subject, and his conduct of it, exalt him to a supreme rank; to a rank, with which all other poets compare but as a second class. *Homer's* intercourse with the gods is when they descend, as *Satan* entered *Paradise*, in mists and clouds to the earth. *Shakspeare*, though the first scholar in the volume of mankind, rises 'above the wheeling poles,' but in glances and flashes of sublimity. *Tasso* up to the heavens 'presumes;' but *Milton* 'into the heaven of heavens,' and dwells there. He inhabits, as it were, the court of the Deity: and leaves on your mind a stability and a permanent character of divine inhabitation and divine presence, of which no other poet gives you a thought: Others rise to sublimity, when they exceed; *Milton's* institution, his quality, his element is sublimity: from his height he descends to meet the greatness of others.

Mr. *Addison* has remarked, that 'perhaps never was a genius so strengthened by learning, as *Milton's*.' So true is this, that years might be spent in the examination of the *Paradise Lost*, without exhausting all its topics of allusion to ancient and modern learning. Yet the constitution of *Milton's* genius; his creative powers; the excursions of his imagination to regions, untraced by human pen, unexplored by human thought, were gifts of nature, not effects of learning. Had his studies, by any fatality, been confined to an English version of the sacred Books, *Paradise Lost* had equally come forth, though with less ornament.

By this view of the genius of *Milton* may be decided the question, Whether *Shakspeare's* powers would have been enlarged, or altered by learning? *Shakspeare*, as *Dryden* happily expresses himself, 'was naturally learned.' His learning was above the study of books; and by them he might, like *Milton*, have illustrated nature; have given variety to narration, or energy to allusion; but never have improved, through the knowledge of others, that first knowledge, which was peculiarly his own.

But the learning of *Milton*, though not the first subject of our admiration, is not to be passed over, without a degree of praise, to which perhaps no other scholar is entitled. To both the dialects of *Hebrew* he added the *Greek, Latin, Italian, French,* and *Spanish*; and these he possessed, not with study only, but commanded them in ordinary and familiar use. With these, aiding his own natural genius, he assumed a vigor of intellect, to which difficulties were temptations; that courted all that is arduous: that soared to divine counsels, without unworthiness; and met the majesty of heaven, without amazement or confusion.

The energy of his mind, upon all occasions, shews itself such, that we make no allowances (because we find none necessary) for his situation. Yet the greatest work of human genius, his *Paradise Lost*, was not begun till he was blind. Had any one, possessing all the faculties of man without impair, executed this work, who would not say he had written with all nature present to his mind; that is, within the power of his mind, by help of that reference or revision, which connects science and retrieves learning? But of *Milton*,

> —from the chearful ways of men
> Cut off, and for the book of knowledge fair
> Presented with an universal blank
> Of nature's works, to him expung'd and raz'd,
> And wisdom at one entrance quite shut out— [III, 46–50]

more must be said: he wrote with all nature present to his memory.

That the praise of *Milton* is, like that of *Cowley*, to have no thought in common with any author, his predecessor, cannot be urged. Though he thought for himself, he had a just deference for the thoughts of others; and, though his genius enabled him without helps to execute, he disdained not to consult and direct himself by the most approved examples. In his Latin elegies, *Ovid* was his master: in his first essay in masque, *Ben Jonson*: in his Italian poems, *Dante, Petrarca,* and *Fulvio Testi*. It was his peculiar study to explore the traces of genius, in whatever authors had gone with eminence before him. He read them all. He took the golden ornaments from the hands of the best artists; he considered their fashion, their workmanship, their weight, their alloy; and, storing and arranging them for occasion, he adapted them, as he saw fit, to the chalice, or the pixis, formed from the sublime patterns of his own mind. Works of exquisite and wonderful invention; which the most learned and the most ingenious are the first to admire; but which themselves can never be imitated! To form the *Paradise Lost*, what learning have the *sacred*, or the *classic* books, that has not been explored? And what are the beauties, or the excellences of either, that he has not there assembled and combined? 'Tis a temple, constructed to his own immortal fame, of the cedar of *Lebanon*, the gold of *Ophir*, and the marble of *Paros*.

77. Cowper on Milton's disinterment

August 1790

William Cowper, 'Stanzas on the late indecent Liberties taken with the Remains of the great Milton' ([August] 1790). William Hayley, ed., *The Life, and Posthumous Writings, of William Cowper* (Chichester, 1803), II, 296–7. Stanzas one and two are drawn from 'Mansus', lines 91–3.

One of the important poets of the last half of the century, William Cowper (1731–1800) clearly evidences a close study of Milton in his works, besides frequent allusions in poems and letters. His translations of the Latin, Greek, and Italian poems were published by William Hayley in 1808, and he planned a full commentary on *Paradise Lost*. These notes, published in the same volume, are given as No. 79 in this collection.

Me too, perchance, in future days,
    The sculptur'd stone shall show,
With Paphian myrtle, or with Bays
    Parnassian, on my brow.

But I, or ere that season come,
    Escap'd from every care,
Shall reach my refuge in the tomb,
    And sleep securely there.

So sang in Roman tone and stile
    The youthful Bard ere long
Ordain'd to grace his native Isle
    With her sublimest song.

Who then but must conceive disdain
    Hearing the deed unblest
Of wretches who have dar'd prophane
    His dread sepulchral rest.

Ill fare the hands that heav'd the stones
    Where Milton's ashes lay
That trembled not to grasp his bones,
    And steal his dust away.

Oh ill-requited bard! neglect
    Thy living worth repay'd,
And blind idolatrous respect
    As much affronts thee dead.

78. Burney on Milton's Greek

1790

Extract from Charles Burney, *Remarks on the Greek Verses of Milton* (1790). Henry John Todd, ed., *The Poetical Works of John Milton* (1801), 'Preliminary Observations on the Greek Verses', vi, 275–6, 277, 287.

Charles Burney (1757–1817), son of the musical scholar, whose works frequently refer to music based on Milton's texts, was a classical scholar, well known in his own day.

When it is considered, how frequently the life of MILTON has been written, and how numerous the annotations have been, on different parts of his works, it seems strange, that his Greek verses, which, indeed are but few, should have passed almost wholly without notice. They have neither been mentioned, as proofs of learning, by his admirers, nor exposed to the ordeal of criticism, by his enemies. Both parties seem to have shrunk from the subject.

To investigate the motives for this silence is not necessary, and the search might possibly prove fruitless. The present observations attempt to supply the deficiency of former Commentators, whose stores of critical knowledge have been lavished . . . merely on the English poetry of Milton.

It will, perhaps, be asserted, that the following remarks are frequently too minute. Yet it seems the duty of a commentator, *on the Greek productions of a modern*, to point out, in general, the sources from which each expression flowed, and to defend by collected authorities, what to some readers may appear incontrovertibly right, as well as to animadvert on passages, of which the errours will be discovered by those only, who have devoted a large portion of their time and attention to the study of the Ancients. Critical strictures on such works should be written to direct the judgement of the less learned, and not merely to confirm the opinions of profound scholars.

In these Remarks, the reader will find some objections stated, which

are to be considered as relating rather to point of taste, than of authority.
—In passages of which the propriety or impropriety could be decided
by appeals to the Ancients, reference has generally been made to
Euripides, in preference to all other Writers. It is well known, that he
was much studied by Milton, and he is properly termed *his favorite
poet* by Mr. Warton, in his Note on 'Comus', ver. 297.

Those, who have long and justly entertained an high idea of Milton's
Greek erudition, on perusing these notes, will probably feel disappointed; and may ascribe to spleen and temerity, what, it is hoped,
merits at least a milder title.—To Milton's claim of extensive, and,
indeed, wonderful learning, who shall refuse their suffrage! It requires
not our commendation, and may defy our censure.—If Dr. Johnson,
however, observes of some Latin Verse of Milton, that it is not secure
against a stern grammarian, what would he have said, if he had bestowed
his time, in examining part of this Greek poetry, with the same exactness of taste, and with equal accuracy of criticism. . . .

I

PSALM cxiv.

This Greek version, as Dr. Joseph Warton has justly observed, is
superior to that of Duport. It has more vigour, but is not wholly free
from inaccuracies. . . .

II

Philosophus ad Regem quendam, &c.

In this short composition, the style of the Epick Poets is imitated very
inaccurately, and is strangely blended with that of the Tragick
Writers. . . .

III

In Effigiei ejus Sculptorem.

This Epigram is far inferior to those, which are preserved in the
Greek Anthologia, on Bad Painters. It has no point: it has no [smooth-
ness]. It is destitute of poetical merit, and appears far more remarkable
for its errours than for its excellencies. . . .

79. Cowper's notes on *Paradise Lost*

1791–2

Extract from William Cowper, 'Commentary on *Paradise Lost*' (1791–2), *Latin and Italian Poems of Milton*, ed. William Hayley (1808). Selected notes for Books I–III, 'The Fragment of an Intended Commentary on *Paradise Lost*,' pp. 189–91, 197–8, 203, 211–14, 217–19, 227–8, 230–1.

[Book I] Line 26. *And justify the ways of God to men.*

Justify them by evincing, that when Man by transgression incurred the forfeiture of his blessings, and the displeasure of God, himself only was to blame. God created him for happiness, made him completely happy, furnished him with sufficient means of security, and gave him explicit notice of his only danger. What could he more, unless he had compelled his obedience, which would have been at once to reduce him from the glorious condition of a free agent to that of an animal.

There is a solemnity of sentiment, as well as majesty of numbers, in the exordium of this noble Poem, which in the works of the antients has no example.

The sublimest of all subjects was reserved for Milton, and bringing to the contemplation of that subject not only a genius equal to the best of theirs, but a heart also deeply impregnated with the divine truths, which lay before him, it is no wonder, that he has produced a composition on the whole superior to any, that we have received from former ages. But he, who addresses himself to the perusal of this work with a mind entirely unaccustom'd to serious and spiritual contemplation, unacquainted with the word of God, or prejudiced against it, is ill-qualified to appreciate the value of a poem built upon it, or to taste its beauties. Milton is the Poet of Christians: an Infidel may have an ear for the harmony of his numbers, may be aware of the dignity of his expression, and in some degree of the sublimity of his conceptions, but the unaffected, and masculine piety, which was his true inspirer, and is the very soul of his poem, he will either not perceive, or it will offend him.

We cannot read this exordium without perceiving, that the author

366

possesses more fire than he shows—There is a suppressed force in it, the effect of judgment. His judgment controuls his genius, and his genius reminds us (to use his own beautiful similitude) of

> A proud steed rein'd,
> Champing his iron curb.

he addresses himself to the performance of great things, but makes no great exertion in doing it; a sure symptom of uncommon vigor.

Line 39. *To set himself in glory above his peers.*

Dr. Pearce needed not perhaps to have gone so far as he did in his note on this line for a key to the true meaning of it. A single word in the next verse but one seems sufficiently to explain it—the word *ambitious.* It imports plainly an opposition not of mere enmity, but of enmity that aspired to superiority over the person opposed. Satan's aim, therefore, was in Milton's view of it, to supplant the Most High, and to usurp the supremacy of Heaven; and by *Peers* are intended, not only those, who aided him in his purpose, but all the Angels, as well the faithful as the rebellious.

Line 300. *Of that inflamed sea.*

Milton sometimes cuts off the last syllable of the participle in *ed,* and sometimes, as here, allows its complete pronunciation. It were to be wished, that the practice of incorporating it with the preceding syllable by the absorption of the intermediate *e*—as in *thrash'd, advanc'd, wreck'd,* and other words of the like kind, had not so universally obtained, as it has. For the consequence is often a clutter of consonants with only a single vowel to assist their utterance, which has a barbarous effect, both in the sound, and in the appearance.

Line 315.

Of all the harrangues, that either history, or poetry, has invented for commanders rallying their routed armies, none was ever better conceived than this. Satan seems himself astonished in the begin[n]ing of it, but it is at their astonishment, which, though he sees it, he can hardly believe. Next affecting ignorance of the real cause of their inactivity, he imputes it to sloth and indolence, as if to stimulate them by derision. In the third place, to provoke and rouse them still more, he pretends to suppose it possible, that they may be at that moment employed in worshipping and doing homage to the conqueror. Lastly he uses solid argument, reminding them of the danger, to which they expose themselves by such supineness, and finishes his exhortation with a line detached from the rest, and therefore so emphatical, that while he utters it, we seem to hear the vaults of Hell re-echo.

Line 663. *He spake: and to confirm his words.*

This is another instance (see the note on line 589) in which appears the advantage, that Milton derives from the grandeur of his subject. What description could even he have given of a host of human warriors insulting their conqueror, at all comparable to this? First, their multitude is to be noticed. They are not thousands but millions; and they are millions not of puny mortals, but of mighty Cherubim. Their swords flame not metaphorically, but they are swords of fire; they flash not by reflexion of the sunbeams like the swords of Homer, but their own light, and that light plays not idly in the broad day, but far round illumines Hell. And lastly, they defy not a created being like themselves, but the Almighty.

It was doubtless a happiness to have fallen on a subject that furnished such scenery, and such characters to act in it, but a happiness it would not have been to a genius inferior to Milton's; such a one on the contrary would have been depressed by it, and in what Milton reaches with a graceful ease, would have fallen short, after much, and fruitless labour.

[Book II], line 370.
> *and with repenting hand*
> *Abolish his own works.*

It seems highly probable, that Satan was prompted to the seduction of our first parents by some such expectation. An expectation which must have been gratified, but for the interposition of the Son of God, of whose intended incarnation he was undoubtedly ignorant. No slighter consequence than the destruction of the earth, by the hand that formed it, could otherwise have followed the revolt of man, since to have continued, and multiplied, a species called into existence only to be miserable for ever, would have been a mode of punishment more dishonourable to God, than the sin itself, for which it was inflicted.

Line 488. *As when from mountain tops* . . .
The reader loses half the beauty of this charming simile, who does not give particular attention to the numbers. There is a majesty in them not often equalled, and never surpassed even by this great poet himself; the movement is uncommonly slow; an effect produced by means already

hinted at, the assemblage of a greater proportion of long syllables than usual. The pauses are also managed with great skill and judgment; while the clouds rise, and the heavens gather blackness, they fall in those parts of the verse, where they retard the reader most, and thus become expressive of the solemnity of the subject; but in the latter part of the simile, where the sun breaks out, and the scene brightens, they are so disposed as to allow the verse an easier, and less interrupted flow, more suited to the cheerfulness of the occasion.

Line 496. *O shame to men!*

It has been observed by the critics, and by Aristotle, the chief of them all, that in an Epic work the poet should be hidden as much as possible, and ought but seldom, in the way of reflection, or remark, to obtrude himself on the notice of the reader. The observation was, no doubt, at first suggested by the practice of Homer, who rarely shows himself, except when he invokes the Muse, or would rehearse the terrors of a battle by seeming to shudder at his own description of it. Virgil is also very temperate in this particular, and if Milton be less reserved than either, it should be considered that there is more real worth and importance in a single reflection of his, than in all those of his heathen predecessors taken together; and that in a poem, like that of *Paradise Lost*, where the subject could not fail continually to suggest the most interesting and valuable remarks, it was almost a duty not to suppress them. Milton, however, must in fact have suppressed a multitude, and instead of being blamed for excess, deserves to be admired for his moderation.

Line 618. . . . *Through many a dark and dreary vale.*

The poet seems to have contemplated the horrid scene, till, as in a dream or vision, he saw it. His description of Hell is not only a map, but a natural history of it, and the Hells of Homer and Virgil are even comfortable compared with this.

A reader of taste cannot fail to observe how the colouring deepens, and darkens, from the beginning to the finishing of this dreadful picture, and that there is a frightful solemnity in the numbers of the whole period wonderfully adapted to the subject.

Line 672. . . . *what seem'd his head.*

The indistinctness of this phantom-form is admirably well preserved. First the poet calls it a shape, then doubts if it could properly so be called; then a substance; then a shadow; then doubts if it was either; and lastly, he will not venture to affirm, that what seemed his head, was such in reality, but being covered with the similitude of a crown, he is rather inclined to think it such. The dimness of this vague and fleeting outline is infinitely more terrible than exact description, because it leaves the imagination at full liberty to see for itself, and to suppose the worst.

Book III *Hail holy light, &c.*

Certainly, as Dr. Newton intimates, there can be no need to apologize for lines like these, nor is there any room to question their propriety. If Epic poetry can possibly disclaim so rich and noble an ornament, we may then fairly say, that Milton has given us something better than an Epic poem. But while we admire, and are charmed with the diction, and the melody of the numbers, we cannot but feel, that there is something in this passage still more captivating than even these, something, which not only pleases the ear, and the fancy, but that wins the heart also, and endears the writer. It is that vein of unaffected piety, which winds through it, and occasionly discovers itself, as he proceeds. When in the opening of this fine exordium he addresses himself to the Light, considering it as in some sort an attribute of God, he evidently speaks under an impression of such awe and reverence, as could only be felt by a mind habituated to divine contemplation. When afterward, alluding to his constant and regular study of the divine writers, he says so musically—[ll. 29-32] knowing that this was not a *gratis dictum* for embellishment-sake merely, much less the language of ostentation, and that Milton was in truth, as he professed himself to be, frequently occupied in the study of Scripture, we respect and honour him for the just and manly avowal of it, and taking this acknowledged fact with us, are convinced that when, in the close of all, he prays for spiritual illumination, he asks it, not because it suited his poetical occasions to finish with a prayer, but because he really wished it, and hoped also to obtain it.

It ought likewise to be observed for the honour of the Bible, that to his firm belief of it, and his familiar acquaintance with it, this divine poet, and truly such, was in a great measure indebted as well for the beauty of the stile and sentiments, as for the matter of his poem.

Line 134. *But mercy first and last.*

The words *first* and *last* may either refer to the promise of a Saviour given in the garden, and to the consummation of all things, or they may respect the original purpose of God to show mercy, and the subsequent application of it.

We have in this speech, not the divinity of the schools, but that of the Scripture. Here are no subleties to puzzle the reader, no webs of sophistry to entangle him. The fore-knowledge of God in Milton's opinion of it, fetters not the will of man. Man is not represented here as the blind and impotent slave of an ir[r]esistible destiny, but as endowed with that high and rational privilege of option, which alone renders him an accountable creature, and which is therefore the very basis of God's right to judge him.

With respect to the composition of this speech, it is as unexceptionable as the matter of it! The expressions are nervous, and notwithstanding the abstruseness of the subject, beautifully clear. The lines are also harmonious, nor is the great poet less apparent in such a passage as this, than in the most flowery description. Let it be tried by Horace's rule; divest it of measure, cast the words into their natural order, do what you please with it, you can never make it prose.

It is impossible to close this short comment upon it, without adverting for a moment to a line of Mr. Pope's, which for the flippancy of it, considering whom it censures, it might be wished that he had never written; that line in which he charges Milton with making—

God the Father turn a school divine.

The doctrines here agitated, and in the other speeches which Milton ascribes to the two first persons in the Trinity (as Mr. Addison well observes) naturally grow up in a poem on the fall of man, and Mr. Pope must have been very little acquainted with the schoolmen, to have asserted that in Milton's manner of handling those doctrines, there is any thing that resembles theirs.

80. Godwin on Satan

1793

Extract from William Godwin, *An Enquiry concerning Political Justice* (Dublin, 1793), I, 241–2 (book iv, appendix i).

A dissenting minister, atheist, and anarchist, William Godwin (1756–1836) is read today for his views as well as for his important novel *Adventures of Caleb Williams*. He is often remembered, moreover, as Shelley's father-in-law and step-father of Claire Clairmont, mother of Byron's daughter Allegra. The *Enquiry concerning Political Justice* emphasized reason and man's ability to rationalize and to act accordingly; thus laws and authoritarian institutions are not needed for rational men. His comments on Milton's Satan state succinctly the attitude toward that figure which has been associated with the Romantics.

It has no doubt resulted from a train of speculation similar to this, that poetical readers have commonly remarked Milton's devil to be a being of considerable virtue. It must be admitted that his energies centered too much in personal regards. But why did he rebel against his maker? It was, as he himself informs us, because he saw no sufficient reason for that extreme inequality of rank and power which the creator assumed. It was because prescription and precedent form an adequate ground for implicit faith. After his fall, why did he still cherish the spirit of opposition? From a persuasion that he was hardly and injuriously treated. He was not discouraged by the apparent inequality of the contest: because a sense of reason and justice was stronger in his mind, than a sense of brute force: because he had much of the feelings of an Epictetus or a Cato, and little of those of a slave. He bore his torments with fortitude, because he disdained to be subdued by despotic power. He sought revenge, because he could not think with tameness of the unexpostulating authority that assumed to dispose of him. How beneficial and illustrious might the temper from which these qualities flowed have proved with a small diversity of situation!

. . . Upon the whole it appears, that great talents are great energies, and that great energies cannot flow but from a powerful sense of fitness and justice. . . . A man of quick resentment, of strong feelings, and who pertinaciously resists every thing that he regards as an unjust assumption, may be considered as having in him the seeds of eminence. Nor is it easily to be conceived that such a man should not proceed from a sense of justice to some degree of benevolence; as Milton's hero felt real compassion and sympathy for his partners in misfortune.

81. Dunster's notes on *Paradise Regain'd*

1795

Extract from Charles Dunster, ed., *Paradise Regained, a Poem, in Four Books, by John Milton* (1795).

Charles Dunster (1750–1816) produced two very important contributions to Miltonic scholarship: his edition of *Paradise Regain'd* (1795) with extensive variorum notes and *Considerations on Milton's Early Reading* (1800), in which he showed Milton's debt to Guillaume Du Bartas through the translation of Joshua Sylvester. His other miscellaneous writings range from an edition of John Philips' Miltonic *Cider* to pamphlets on the gospels. A contributor to the notes included here was Robert Thyer (1709–81), a scholar in the circle of Newton, Warton, Dunster, and Todd. His remarks on Milton appear only in their editions. Dunster tells us that his comments on *Paradise Regain'd* were lost in transit and reproduced therefore only from memory. Thyer is perhaps best known for his edition of Samuel Butler's *Remains* (1759).

Preface, pp. i–ii

The present publication originates in an opinion, (which perhaps begins to prevail,) that the *PARADISE REGAINED* of our great English poet has never had justice done it either by critics or commentators. As it has been generally and unjustly under-rated, so it has been negligently and scantily illustrated. . . .

To rescue in some degree from neglect and oblivion, (by more ample illustration than it has hitherto received,) a poem, of which the great Author himself thought so highly, is the object of the present attempt; which, it is hoped, may not be unacceptable, at least to the admirers of Milton. At all events the pains of the Editor have not been without their recompense, in the very great pleasure which he has found from a closer examination of a poem replete with that species of intrinsic beauty, which, though it may not allure and fascinate at the first glance, is certain, when attentively considered, to engage and rivet the admiration.

Notes

I, 3 [p. 3]

It may seem a little odd, that Milton should impute the recovery of

Paradise to this short scene of our Saviour's life upon earth, and not rather extend it to his agony, crucifixion, &c. But the reason no doubt was, that Paradise, *regained* by our Saviour's resisting the temptations of Satan, might be a better contrast to Paradise, *lost* by our first parents too easily yielding to the same seducing spirit. Besides he might, very probably, and indeed very reasonably, be apprehensive, that a subject, so extensive as well as sublime, might be too great a burden for his declining constitution, and a task too long for the short term of years he could then hope for, even in his *Paradise Lost* he expresses his fears, lest he had begun too late, . . . and surely he had much greater cause to dread the same now, and to be very cautious of launching out too far.

Thyer.

I, 358 [pp. 40–1]

Satan's instantaneous avowal of himself here has a great and fine effect. It is consistent with a certain dignity of character which is given him in general, through the whole of the *Paradise Lost*.—The rest of the speech is artfully submissive.

It may not be improper in this place, to consider the conduct of the Poet, and the reason of it, respecting the Arch-Fiend's appearance and demeanour here, and, in a part of the *Paradise Lost*, where his situation may be considered as in some degree similar.—In the FOURTH Book of the *PARADISE LOST*, Satan is represented sitting, in an assumed shape, 'close at the ear of Eve;' in order to inspire such dreams and ideas as might render her a more apt subject of temptation. Being discovered in this situation, on the touch of Ithuriel's spear, he resumes his own proper form; and, on being questioned by the Angels concerning the purpose of his being there, he answers in scornful and indignant terms. —In the instance before us, Satan is also in an assumed shape, under which he is immediately known to our blessed Lord; whose power to discover him, through that disguise, he does not seem to have been at all aware of, until his declaration,

> Knowing who I am, as I KNOW WHO THOU ART. [356]

Satan, on finding himself discovered, makes here no vaunt of his power or rank, as he had done in the other instance; but, having acknowledged who he is, returns only apologies and flattery to the 'stern' rebukes of our Saviour, not withstanding that he was at the same time

> —inly stung with anger and disdain.

The conduct of our author, on both these occasions, is highly proper and admirable. . . .

Milton's different representations of the conduct of Satan, in these two different exigencies, may be considered as meant to elucidate and exalt the character of our Lord, whom the Almighty had before directed all the angels of Heaven to adore and honor as himself, [PL III, 343–4]. Neither are his glory and honor confined to the celestial mansions; but even the infernal spirits are involuntarily led to pay him the same homage.—We may observe, as a further circumstance of the marked superiority of our Lord's character over that of the blessed angels, that Ithuriel and Zephon, on Satan's resuming his own proper shape, knew him not, until he informed them who he was. . . . But our Lord here is acquainted with all the wiles and intentions of his adversary, and knows him under all his disguise, and at his first approach. . . . This discovery of Satan then may be considered as an intended proof of our Lord's divine character, in his discerning what was invisible, except *to God alone*; and the submiss and crouching behaviour of the Arch-Fiend, so different from what it was upon all other occasions, amounts to a further attestation of it.

II, I [p. 61]

The greatest, and indeed justest, objection to this Poem is the narrowness of its plan, which, being confined to that single scene of our Saviour's life on earth, his Temptation in the Desert, has too much sameness in it, too much of the reasoning, and too little of the descriptive part; a defect most certainly in an epic poem, which ought to consist of a proper and happy mixture of the instructive and the delightful. Milton was himself, no doubt, sensible of this imperfection, and has therefore very judiciously contrived and introduced all the little digressions that could with any sort of propriety connect with his subject, in order to relieve and refresh the reader's attention. The following conversation betwixt Andrew and Simon upon the missing of our Saviour so long, with the Virgin's reflections on the same occasion, and the council of the Devils how best to attack their enemy, are instances of this sort, and both very happily executed in their respective ways. The language of the former is cool and unaffected, corresponding most exactly to the humble pious character of the speakers; that of the latter is full of energy and majesty, and not inferior to their most spirited speeches in the *Paradise Lost.*   *Thyer.*

[Concluding comment, pp. 266–7]

It has been observed of almost all the great epic poems, that they fall

off, and become languid, in the conclusion. The six last books of the
ÆNEID, and the twelve last of the ODYSSEY, are inferior to the
preceding parts of those poems. In the PARADISE LOST the two
last books fall short of the majesty and sublimity of the rest. . . . Perhaps the two concluding books of the PARADISE LOST might be
defended by other arguments, and justified in a more effective manner,
than has been done by Mr. Addison; but it is certainly fortunate when
the subject and plan of an epic poem are such, that in the conclusion
it may rise in dignity and sublimity, so as to excite to the very last the
attention and admiration of the reader.—This last book of the PARA-
DISE REGAINED is one of the finest conclusions of a poem, that
can be produced. The Book of Job, which I have before supposed to
have been our Author's model, materially resembles it in this respect,
and is perhaps the only instance that can be put in competition with
it.—It has been remarked that there is not a single simile in the first
Iliad: neither do we meet with one in the three first Books of the
PARADISE REGAINED. In the beginning of this FOURTH Book the
poet introduces an Homeric cluster of similes; which seems to mark an
intention of bestowing more poetical decoration on the conclusion of
the poem, than on the preceding parts of it.—They who talk of our
Author's genius being in the decline when he wrote his second poem,
and who therefore turn from it, as from a dry prosaic composition, are,
I will venture to say, no judges of poetry. With a fancy, such as Milton's
it must have been more difficult to forbear poetic decorations, than to
furnish them; and a glaring profusion of ornament would, I conceive,
have more decidedly betrayed the *poeta senescens* [the aging poet], than
a want of it. . . . The PARADISE REGAINED has something of the
didactic character; it teaches not merely by the general moral, and by
the character and conduct of its hero, but has also many positive precepts every where interspersed. It is written for the most part in a style
admirably condensed, and with a studied reserve of ornament: it is
nevertheless illuminated with beauties of the most captivating kind. Its
leading feature throughout is that 'excellence of composition', which,
as Lord Monboddo justly observes, so eminently distinguished the
writings of the Ancients; and in which, of all modern authors, Milton
most resembles them.

82. Hayley on the last poems

1796

Extract from William Hayley, 'Life of Milton' (1796, reprinted 1797, 1799). William Hayley, *The Life of John Milton with Conjectures on the Origin of the Paradise Lost* (1799), 214–16, 252–5.

In 1671, the year after the first appearance of his history, he published the *Paradise Regained*, and *Samson Agonistes*.

Many groundless remarks have been made on the supposed want of judgment in Milton to form a proper estimate of his own compositions. 'His last poetical offspring (says Johnson) was his favorite; he could not, as Ellwood relates, endure to have *Paradise Lost* preferred to *Paradise Regained*.' In this brief passage, there is more than one misrepresentation. It is not Ellwood, but Phil[l]ips, who speaks of Milton's esteem for his latter poem; and instead of saying that the author preferred it to his greater work, he merely intimates, that Milton was offended with the general censure, which condemned the *Paradise Regained* as infinitely inferior to the other. Instead of supposing, therefore, that the great poet was under the influence of an absurd predilection, we have only reason to conclude, that he heard with lively scorn such idle witticism as we find recorded by Toland, 'That Milton might be seen in *Paradise Lost*, but not in *Paradise Regained*.' His own accomplished mind, in which sensibility and judgment were proportioned to extraordinary imagination, most probably assured him what is indisputably true, that uncommon energy of thought and felicity of composition are apparent in both performances, however different in design, dimension, and effect. To censure the *Paradise Regained*, because it does not more resemble the preceding poem, is hardly less absurd than it would be to condemn the moon for not being a sun, instead of admiring the two different luminaries, and feeling that both the greater and the less are visibly the work of the same divine and inimitable power. . . .

There is one characteristic of Milton, which ought to be considered as the chief source of his happiness and his fame; I mean his early and perpetual attachment to religion. It must gratify every Christian to reflect, that the man of our country most eminent for energy of mind, for intenseness of application, and for frankness and intrepidity in asserting whatever he believed to be the cause of truth, was so confirmedly devoted to christianity, that he seems to have made the Bible, not only the rule of his conduct, but the prime director of his genius. His poetry flowed from the scripture, as if his unparalleled poetical powers had been expressly given him by Heaven for the purpose of imparting to religion such lustre as the most splendid of human faculties could bestow. As in the *Paradise Lost* he seems to emulate the sublimity of Moses and the prophets, it appears to have been his wish, in the *Paradise Regained*, to copy the sweetness and simplicity of the milder evangelists. If the futile remarks that were made upon the latter work, on its first appearance, excited the spleen of the great author, he would probably have felt still more indignant, could he have seen the comment of Warburton. That disgusting writer, whose critical dictates form a fantastic medley of arrogance, acuteness, and absurdity, has asserted, that the plan of *Paradise Regained* is very unhappy, and that nothing was easier than to have invented a good one.

Much idle censure seems to have been thrown on more than one of Milton's poetical works, from want of due attention to the chief aim of the poet:—if we fairly consider it in regard to *Paradise Regained*, the aim I allude to, as it probably occasioned, will completely justify, the plan which the presumptuous critic has so superciliously condemned. Milton had already executed one extensive divine poem, peculiarly distinguished by richness and sublimity of description; in framing a second, he would naturally wish to vary its effect; to make it rich in moral sentiment, and sublime in its mode of unfolding the highest wisdom that man can learn; for this purpose it was necessary to keep all the ornamental parts of the poem in due subordination to the preceptive. This delicate and difficult point is accomplished with such felicity, they are blended together with such exquisite harmony and mutual aid, that instead of arraigning the plan, we might rather doubt if any possible change could improve it; assuredly, there is no poem of epic form, where the sublimest moral instruction is so forcibly and abundantly united to poetical delight: the splendor of the poet does not blaze, indeed, so intensely as in his larger production; here he resembles the Apollo of Ovid, softening his glory in speaking to his son, and avoiding to dazzle the fancy, that he may descend into the heart, His dignity is not impaired by his tenderness. The *Paradise Regained* is a poem, that deserves to be peculiarly recommended to ardent and ingenuous youth, as it is admirably calculated to inspire that spirit of self-command, which is, as Milton esteemed it, the truest heroism, and the triumph of christianity.

It is not my intention to enter into a critical analysis of the beauties and the blemishes that are visible in the poetry of Milton, not only because Addison and Johnson have both written admirably on his greatest work, but because my most excellent friend, the poet (whose spirit I esteem most congenial to that of Milton) is engaged in such illustration of his honored predecessor; I shall therefore confine myself to a single essay, detached from this narrative, under the title of 'Conjectures on the Origin of the *Paradise Lost*.'

I must not, however, omit to speak here, as I have engaged to do, of the character bestowed by Johnson on the principal performance of the poet; the greatest part of that character is, perhaps, the most splendid tribute that was ever paid by one powerful mind to another. Aristotle, Longinus, and Quintilian, have not spoken of their favorite Homer with more magnificence of praise; yet the character, taken altogether, is a golden image, that has lower parts of iron and of clay. The critic seems to prepare a diadem of the richest jewels; he places them, most liberally, on the head of the poet; but in the moment of adjusting his radiant gift, he breathes upon it such a vapor of spleen, as almost annihilates its lustre.

After displaying, in the noblest manner, many of the peculiar excellencies in the poem, he says, 'its perusal is a duty rather than a pleasure; we read Milton for instruction, retire harassed and over-burdened, and look elsewhere for recreation; we desert our master, and seek for companions.'

Injurious as these remarks are to the poet, let us ascribe them, not to the virulence of intended detraction, but to the want of poetical sensibility in the critic. . . .

83. Hayley on the origin of *Paradise Lost*

1796

Extract from William Hayley, 'Conjectures on the Origin of the *Paradise Lost*' (1796, reprinted 1797, 1799). William Hayley, *The Life of John Milton with Conjectures on the Origin of the Paradise Lost* (1799), 314–16.

But whatever may be thought of the heathen bard, Milton, to whom a purer religion had given great purity, and I think greater force of imagination, Milton, from a long survey of human nature, had contracted such an abhorrence for the atrocious absurdity of ordinary war, that his feelings in this point seem to have influenced his epic fancy. He appears to have relinquished common heroes, that he might not cherish the too common characteristic of man—a sanguinary spirit. He aspired to delight the imagination, like Homer, and to produce, at the same time, a much happier effect on the mind. Has he succeeded in this glorious idea? Assuredly he has:—to please is the end of poetry. Homer pleases perhaps more universally than Milton; but the pleasure that the English poet excites, is more exquisite in its nature, and superior in its effect. An eminent painter of France used to say, that in reading Homer he felt his nerves dilated, and he seemed to increase in stature. Such an ideal effect as Homer, in this example, produced on the body, Milton produces in the spirit. To a reader who thoroughly relishes the two poems on Paradise, his heart appears to be purified, in proportion to the pleasure he derives from the poet, and his mind to become angelic. Such a taste for Milton is rare, and the reason why it is so is this:—To form it completely, a reader must possess, in some degree, what was superlatively possessed by the poet, a mixture of two different species of enthusiasm, the poetical and the religious. To relish Homer, it is sufficient to have a passion for excellent verse; but the reader of Milton, who is only a lover of the Muses, loses half, and certainly the best half, of that transcendent delight which the poems of this divine enthusiast are capable of imparting. A devotional taste is as requisite for the full

381

enjoyment of Milton as a taste for poetry; and this remark will sufficiently explain the inconsistency so striking in the sentiments of many distinguished writers, who have repeatedly spoken on the great English poet—particularly that inconsistency, which I partly promised to explain in the judgments of Dryden and Voltaire. These very different men had both a passion for verse, and both strongly felt the poetical powers of Milton: but Dryden perhaps had not much, and Voltaire had certainly not a particle, of Milton's religious enthusiasm; hence, instead of being impressed with the sanctity of his subject, they sometimes glanced upon it in a ludicrous point of view.

Hence they sometimes speak of him as the very prince of poets, and sometimes as a misguided genius, who has failed to obtain the rank he aspired to in the poetical world. But neither the caprices of conceit, nor the cold austerity of reason, can reduce the glory of this pre-eminent bard.—It was in an hour propitious to his renown, that he relinquished Arthur and Merlin for Adam and the Angels; and he might say on the occasion, in the words of his admired Petrarch. . . .

> I bless the spot, the season, and the hour,
> When my presumptuous eyes were fix'd so high.

To say that his poem wants human interest, is only to prove, that he who finds that defect wants the proper sensibility of man. A Work that displays at full length, and in the strongest light, the delicious tranquillity of innocence, the tormenting turbulence of guilt, and the consolatory satisfaction of repentance, has surely abundance of attraction to awaken sympathy. The images and sentiments that belong to these varying situations are so suited to our mortal existence, that they cannot cease to interest, while human nature endures. The human heart, indeed, may be too much depraved, and the human mind may be too licentious, or too gloomy, to have a perfect relish for Milton; but, in honor of his poetry, we may observe, that it has a peculiar tendency to delight and to meliorate those characters; in which the seeds of taste and piety have been happily sown by nature. In proportion as the admiration of mankind shall grow more and more valuable from the progressive increase of intelligence, of virtue, and of religion, this incomparable poet will be more affectionately studied, and more universally admired.

84. Anonymous discussion of Milton's similes

1796-8

J. A., 'The Similes of Homer, Virgil, and Milton, Examined and Compared', *Monthly Magazine*, i (1796), 284–7, 380–3; ii (1796), 546, 714; iii (1797), 428–9; iv (1797), 112–3; v (1798), 188–9. The author may have been John Aiken.

I shall not begin this Paper with attempting to lay down any rules for the construction or application of similes in poetry: for upon what *speculative* principles could they be founded so securely, as upon a view of the *practice* of the greatest masters of the art, compared as to the several purposes designed, and effects produced? Remarks of this kind, will, therefore, properly accompany or succeed the intended display of what has been performed by the three eminent epic poets, whose names are prefixed; and considering the celebrity of all the three, with the different ages in which they lived, and languages in which they wrote, it may be fairly supposed, that the subject of similes will receive a very complete illustration from the specimens they afford. These I shall arrange under several classes, according to the objects from which the comparisons are drawn. And first, as to those taken from

THE HEAVENLY BODIES.

It will appear extraordinary, that amidst the numerous objects in nature which caught the eye of Homer, the noblest of all, *the sun*, should be so little applied by him to poetical use. I can find but one instance in which this luminary is made, in its proper character, a subject of comparison; and this is comprized in a single line. Achilles, shining in arms, is said to be 'like the sun in its ascension.' *Il.* xix. 398.

Unaided by the example of Homer, it would seem that the genius of Virgil found itself unequal to the management of so grand and dazzling an object: but our Milton has ventured, and nobly succeeded, in his attempt to paint it; not, indeed in meridian splendour, but with its glory dimmed and obscured: [*PL* I, 594–600].

This sublime simile has an excellence, which may generally be met with in those of Milton, and, indeed, is necessary to constitute the perfection of this figure—its resemblance consists not only in sensible properties, but in character. Thus, it is not only the *form* of Satan, still retaining its brightness, though obscured, which is compared to that of the sun behind a mist; but his malignant *character* is also expressed by the ominous nature of an eclipse, according to the superstitious notions so universally received concerning that phenomenon.

Sun-shine, though not the sun himself, is the subject of two other similies in Homer and Milton. When Patroclus repels the hostile fire from the Grecian ships, the interval of returning repose and safety to the Greeks, is expressed in the following simile: [*Il*. xv, 297–302].

The similitude here consists in the *effect*, not in the *objects* themselves; for in these there is rather an opposition, *fire* being *extinguished* in one instance, and *light restored* in the other. But the effect of these circumstances on the mind is the same in both cases: joy and hope are restored. Mr. Pope, indeed, contrary to all the commentators, and to the poet's own explanation of his simile, supposes the likeness to consist solely in obvious and sensible appearances; and that the *clearing away the smoke* after the extinction of the fire is meant to be resembled to the *dispersion of the cloud*. But nothing appears to support this explanation. It may be added, that in the poetical language of the Jewish scriptures, *light* and *joy* are used almost synonymously; and there are examples of the same imagery in the language of Homer himself.

Milton, in his imitation of this simile, has applied it to the same purpose. After Satan has taken upon himself the perilous exploratory voyage, which was to free the diabolic host from their terrible prison, their returning hope and joy are expressed in this beautiful similitude: [*PL* II, 488–95].

The moon is likewise the subject of two similar comparisons in Homer and Milton; but the Greek poet only touches upon what our countryman improves into a noble picture. Of Achilles, it is said,

> And next he raised his ample ponderous shield,
> Whence beam'd from far a lustre, like the moon's. *Il*. xix, 73[–4]

The shield of Satan is thus represented: [*PL* I, 284–91].

This is an example, of which we shall find many others in this poet, and in Homer, whom he imitates, of that kind of simile, in which, besides the circumstances on which the resemblance depends, others are introduced, merely for the sake of improving the picture. Thus, the figure of the Tuscan artist viewing the moon through his telescope, and the imagined rivers and mountains descried in its *spotty* surface, have no direct reference to the shield of Satan; but only serve to render the appearance of this luminary more picturesque. Some fastidious critics have censured this exuberance as a vicious excess, derogating from the simplicity and unity requisite in every piece of art; and the French have ridiculed such similes by the appellation of *long-tailed similes*. But if it be considered that the use of similes in poetry is perhaps rather to enliven and diversify, than to elucidate or enforce a subject, and that such is the versatility of the mind as to enable it with great ease to range from one object to another, and back again to the first, without perplexity; we shall be inclined to regard with indulgence, or rather with applause, every attempt to increase our pleasures by varying agreeable images. He who would rigorously lop off every circumstance in a simile which has not its exact counterpart in the original object, would better consult his genius by the study of mathematics or philosophy, than of poetry. . . .

In *sublimity of conception*, Milton has, by copying this simile, surpassed both his originals; and, indeed, the superior grandeur of his personages allowed him, without fear of offensive exaggeration, to employ the loftiest images his great mind could suggest to him. He has judiciously confined his resemblance to the comet: [*PL* II, 706–11].

What can be imagined more terribly sublime, than the figure of the comet filling the whole space of a vast constellation, and shaking plagues from his locks?

The fancied form of Orion, in the heavens, has afforded Virgil a simile of extraordinary grandeur; but somewhat hyperbolical and injudicious in its application to one who is only a second-rate hero in his poem: [*Aen.* x, 763–6].

Milton has again employed a simile derived from the celestial bodies, as the only objects capable of inspiring adequate ideas of his angelic heroes. Michael and Satan join in conflict, [*PL* VI, 310–15].

The meteor commonly called a falling star, is probably intended by Homer as the object of similitude to the descent of Minerva: [*Il.* iv, 75–8].

This is imitated, and, as usual, much heightened, by Milton, in his description of Uriel's descent: [*PL* IV, 555–60].

The same poet uses the image of a meteor in his magnificent description of the great Satanic standard: [*PL* I, 535–7].

The last Paper insensibly brought me into what I meant to make the second division of similes, those from

METEORS, LIGHTNING, THUNDER, AND CLOUDS.

To proceed with the first of these appearances: Milton has a striking and highly wrought simile, derived from the *ignis fatuus*: [*PL* IX, 634–43].

This simile has, in an eminent degree, that union of moral with natural resemblance, which constitutes the perfection of this kind of figure. The attendant *evil spirit,* the *delusive light misleading* the *wanderer* to *danger* and *destruction, far from succour,* have as much reference to the *character* and *situation* of the Serpent and Eve, as the *glittering light* of the meteor has to the *shining skin* of the snake. This exactness of adaptation is only to be expected from the poet of a cultivated and critical age, and is, therefore, seldom found in Homer, nor is it frequently remarkable in Virgil.

Another meteorous phænomenon, the *aurora borealis,* could only have escaped the notice of the ancient poets, from its great uncommonness in their ages or countries. Virgil, indeed, alludes to it in his account of the prodigies at the death of Cæsar; but an appearance so unusual as to be a prodigy, could scarcely be applied as a simile. Even Milton speaks of it as portentous, when he describes it as an object of similitude to the martial exercises of the fallen angels: [*PL* II, 533–8].

Poets whose genius and subject led them to search for images of terror and sublimity, could not possibly overlook the aweful occurrence of thunder and lightning; in which, solemnity of sound, brilliancy of appearance, swiftness of motion, and vehemence of action, all unite to impress the imagination. One of the earliest similes in Homer, is a noble one, derived from this source. After his minute catalogue of the Grecian army, the effect of which is to inspire a high idea of its force, he sustains the image of grandeur he had excited, by thus describing their march to the enemy; [*Il.* ii, 781–5].

Milton, in like manner, compares the sound of a great assembly, to distant thunder. When the council of Pandemonium is dissolved, he says,

> Their rising all at once was as the sound
> Of thunder heard remote. [*PL* II, 476–7].

. . . Milton, in a simile derived from the same objects [lightning and clouds], has, by his original and unequalled sublimity of invention, as greatly surpassed in grandeur the two preceding poets, as the actors in his story are superior to their's. Satan and Death, those mighty and terrible combatants, preparing to engage, are thus represented: [*PL* II, 713–18].

As it was necessary for the comparison, that the clouds should move in opposite directions, he has properly made them thunder-clouds, in which such a circumstance is common; besides, that the 'artillery' with which they are fraught, renders their shock a peculiarly striking image of battle.

We proceed to similes more directly drawn from

WIND, STORM, AND TEMPEST,

the sensible effects of which are more striking and terrible, considering their frequency, than those of any other phenomena of nature.

The awful *sound* of wind is one of the circumstances attending it, most obviously fitted for poetical application. Homer has properly joined it with the roaring of the waves, and the rattling of fire, as a comparison for the noise and tumult of battle. . . .

Our great countryman, who never borrows without such improvements as give him all the merit of originality, has a beautiful passage founded on this similitude [Vergil's use of the noise of wind to represent the sound of the gods' assent]. It is at the close of Satan's noble speech to his peers: [*PL* II, 284–90]. This simile is truly Homeric, but in Homer's best manner. The scenery, into which the description wanders, is highly picturesque, and, though somewhat digressive from the main purpose of the simile, yet is in perfect harmony with it. . . .

Milton has a simile of uncommon beauty derived from the same natural object [the meteor]: [*PL* XII, 627–32].

The airy form and smooth motion of these celestial beings are finely imaged by the comparison here suggested; and the Homeric prolongation of the simile is highly picturesque.

The same poet gives a short, but very poetical simile taken from the *dew*, which will close our examples on this head: [*PL* V, 745–7]. The subject of this comparison is the host of fallen angels; and the point of resemblance is not only their *number*, but their *brilliancy*. Yet it may, perhaps, be thought that the resembling object is of too gay and pleasing a nature for a parallel with an infernal troop, agitated by the blackest emotions.

THE SEA, SHIPS SAILING, &C.

. . . It may seem extraordinary, that MILTON has not yet been introduced, as making use of a store of imagery, apparently so well suited to his genius. But where he could not improve, he scorned to borrow; and HOMER and VIRGIL had anticipated him in all the most striking phenomena relative to the sea, afforded by nature. The improvements of art, however, greater, perhaps, in maritime affairs, than in any other department, afforded him a source of novelty, which he has not neglected. Thus, Satan flying through hell, upon his exploratory voyage, suggests the following comparison: [PL II, 636–43].

This simile is purely of the ornamental kind, for it has too little affinity with the subject of comparison to enforce or illustrate it. Nay, the ideas it excites are rather of an opposite nature, and too gay and pleasing to correspond well with the gloomy being and his dark purpose, which the poet is then describing. However, the intrinsic merit of the picture may apologize for such a defect.

In another passage of the same poet, where sailing is also introduced in a simile, it is entirely a foreign and ornamental part of the piece, and has no counterpart in the narration: [PL IV, 159–65].

It is true, he immediately adds,

So entertain'd these odorous sweets the fiend; [IV, 166]

but it is obvious, that the only real comparison is that of the fragrance of Paradise to the Arabian gales. The passage is, however, in an exquisite strain of poetry, and its scenery most agreeably varies the delicious prospects of the garden of Eden.

Another more exactly applied simile, in which the sailor's art is almost technically described, is that in which the winding and circuitous track of the serpent, in his cautious approach to Eve, is resembled to the working of a ship: [PL IX, 513–16]. Nothing can be more perfectly illustrative of the thing intended, than this similitude; which, however, cannot, I think, be considered as original. In Dr. Newton's edition of Milton, a quotation is given from the Latin poems of a Scotch writer, Andrew Ramsay, published in 1633, in which the same image is given in words so nearly similar, and applied to a similar subject, that I see not how it is possible to reject such striking *marks of imitation*. The poet is treating of Christ's temptation, and the only difference in the application of the simile is, that it refers not to the corporeal motion, but to the wiles of the serpent. . . .

MILTON has another simile in which a ship is introduced, as a comparison for a woman richly dressed and adorned, the fair and wanton Dalila: [SA, 710–19].

The easy motion and graceful figure of a fine woman could not be more happily illustrated, than by the image here painted.

FROM ROCKS AND MOUNTAINS.

These noble and striking objects have afforded fewer images of similitude to the epic poets than might have been expected. The *want of motion* was probably the cause of their being found so little applicable to the purposes of heroic action; and this idea seems confirmed by the circumstance that, among the few similes from this source to be met with, the greater share have motion artificially, as it were, introduced into them. . . .

The English poet appears with his accustomed dignity and originaality after these great masters, taking, at most, a hint from them, expanded into much superior grandeur. When Satan recoils from the stroke of Abdiel, it is

> —As if on earth
> Winds underground, or waters, forcing way,
> Sidelong had pushed a mountain from his seat
> Half sunk with all his pines. *Par. L.* vi. 195[-8]

He is more of a copyist in his imitation of one of the most sublime and highly wrought similes in Virgil, where Eneas moves triumphant to the combat with Turnus: [*Aen.* xiii, 700–4].

Milton did not require the same variety of imagery for his purpose, which was only to give a striking idea of strength and stability [*PL* IV, 985–9].

The sublimity of description is here expended upon the figure of Satan himself, and the mountains are only allusively, as it were, introduced, like well-known and familiar objects. Indeed, considering the superior magnitude of the real figure, the resembling one could only be employed for illustration.

FROM WILD BEASTS

. . . The *Tiger* a congenerous animal, amid a flock of sheep, affords Virgil a simple comparison, without any description, to Turnus having burst his way into the Trojan camp. But Milton has derived a very characteristic simile from the same terrible beast, in which its manner of seizing its prey is pointed with much picturesque exactness. [*PL* IV, 403–8].

The application is to Satan, watching the actions of Adam and Eve in Paradise.

The *Wolf*, a more ignoble beast of prey, but one, which from its bloody and savage character, would suggest fit comparisons to the painter of war-scenery, has been introduced by Homer with his usual truth and spirit. . . .

Milton could be no more than an imitator in chusing the Wolf for an object of comparison; but the application in the following simile is new, and the resemblance very perfect. It refers to Satan, leaping with a bound over the wall of Paradise [*PL* IV, 183-7]. . . .

85. Godwin on Milton's prose style

1797

Extract from William Godwin, *The Enquirer. Reflections on Education, Manners, and Literature* (1797). Essay xii, 'Of English Style', section iii, 'Milton and Clarendon', pp. 402-12.

The age which, next after that of queen Elizabeth, has obtained the suffrage of the critics, is that of Charles the second. This was a period adorned with the writings of Milton, Dryden, Butler and Otway; and perhaps deserves above all others to be styled the golden age of English poetry. Fanciful observers found a certain resemblance between it and the age of Augustus, the literary glory of which has sometimes been represented as owing to this circumstance, that its wits were bred up in their youth in the lap of republican freedom, and afterwards in their riper age received that polish which is to be derived from the splendour and refinement of a court. Just so, the scene amidst which the wits of King Charles's days passed their boyish years, was that of civil war, of regicide, or of unrestrained republican speculation; which was succeeded by the manners of a gay and licentious court, grafting the shoots of French refinement, upon the more vigorous and luxuriant plant of English growth. It is indeed easy to trace in the adventurous sallies of the authors of this period, the remnant and tincture of republican audaciousness. The principle however here intended to be established is, that, if our poetry never appeared to greater advantage, our prose at least was yet unformed and rude.

We will begin with Milton, the oldest of those writers, by whom the reign of Charles the second has been made illustrious. Milton was more than fifty years old at the period of the Restoration, and, though most of his poetry was written subsequently to that event, his prose is almost entirely of an earlier date.

The style of Milton, unlike that of most of our older writers, has by a few modern critics been treated with particular harshness. Among the foremost of these is Dr. Johnson [quotation from *Lives of the Poets*].

After reading the extracts that have been given from writers under queen Elizabeth, it will be suspected that this censure of Milton's style is too strong and disproportionate. If Addison were somewhat misled by his veneration for Milton, Johnson has erred in the other extreme. The former will probably be found at least as near to the truth as the latter.

The fact seems to be, that Milton was dissatisfied with the shapeless chaos in which our language appeared in former writers, and set himself, with that ardour which always distinguished him, to reform it. His success indeed is not entitled to unlimited encomium. The gigantic structure of his genius perhaps somewhat misled him. He endeavoured to form a language of too lofty and uniform a port. The exuberance of his mind led him to pour out his thoughts with an impetuosity, that often swept away with it the laws of simplicity and even the rules of grammatical propriety. His attempt however to give system to the lawless dialect of our ancestors, was the mark of a generous spirit, and entitles him to our applause.

If we compare the style of Milton to that of later writers, and particularly to that of our own days, undoubtedly nothing but a very corrupt taste can commend it. But the case is altered, if we compare it with the writings of his predecessors. An impartial critic would perhaps find no language in any writer that went before Milton, of so much merit as that of Milton himself.

As a specimen of Milton's style, it may be worth while to select that passage from his *Reason of Church-Government urged against Prelaty*, published more than twenty years before the *Paradise Lost*, in which he speaks, in little less than a prophetic spirit, of what he purposed to execute, to give substance to his own talent, and for the ornament of his country. . . .

The *Areopagitica* of Milton, or a *Speech for the Liberty of Unlicenced*

Printing, notwithstanding the occasional stiffness and perplexity of its style, is one of the most eloquent prose compositions in this or any other language. To give the reader an adequate idea of its beauties, it would be necessary to insert one third of the performance. Let us content ourselves with the following admirable description of the person over whom the licenser will occasionally be called to exercise his jurisdiction. . . .

From these specimens every impartial reader will pronounce, that Milton wrote a style superior to that of the most celebrated authors that went before him.

It is however singular, and deserves to be noticed, as a proof of the state of the English language, that, with all his profound and indefatigable scholarship, and his evident solicitude upon the question of style, Milton is often glaringly ungrammatical, and his periods broken off abrupt and unfinished. Instances of this last frequently occur in his *Paradise Lost*. One that ought to be singled out, is in perhaps the finest passage of the whole poem; Satan's speech to his companion in the opening of the work, before he has yet raised himself from off the burning lake. The speech begins with a hypothetical clause, 'If thou beest he;' but the hypothesis is finally left without a consequence. The sentence is suspended through the whole speech, interspersed with parenthesis upon parenthesis, and left imperfect at last. So possible is it to convey the noblest sentiments, and the finest flights of poetry, amidst the most flagrant violation of the rules of grammar.

86. Todd on 'Comus'

1798

Henry J. Todd, 'Origin of Comus', *Comus, A Mask* (Canterbury, 1798), 50–62. The first section (to p. 397) was written by Thomas Warton: Todd printed 'Origin of *Comus*' from *Poems Upon Several Occasions* (1791), pp. 135–6, into which he inserted 'Appendix to the Notes on *Comus*', pp. 591–3 of the 1785 edition, and then added his own discussion.

Henry John Todd (1763–1845) edited 'Comus' in 1798 with accounts of the Bridgewater family and the Bridgewater MS. of the mask; his five variorum editions of the poems were published in 1801, 1809, 1826, 1842, and posthumously in 1852, and *Some Account of the Life and Writings of John Milton*, part of the edition, was issued separately in 1801. Todd's edition became standard for the greater part of the nineteenth century despite its many textual errors. It accumulated notes and essays from previous editions and commentators. The biographical account has a bibliography appended, which is still the best for the dates covered, though woefully inadequate.

In Fletcher's *FAITHFUL SHEPHERDESS*, an Arcadian comedy, recently published, Milton found many touches of pastoral and super-stitious imagery, congenial with his own conceptions. Many of these, yet with the highest improvements, he has transferred in 'Comus'; together with the general cast and colouring of the piece. He catched also from the lyric rhymes of Fletcher, that *Dorique delicacy*, with which Sir Henry Wotton was so much delighted in the Songs of Milton's drama. Fletcher's comedy was coldly received the first night of its performance. But it had ample revenge in this conspicuous and indisputable mark of Milton's approbation. It was afterwards represented as a Mask at court, before the king and queen on twelfth-night, in 1633. I know not, indeed, if this was any recommendation to Milton; who in the *PARADISE LOST* speaks contemptuously of these interludes, which had been among the chief diversions of an elegant and liberal monarch. B. iv. 767.

—Court-amours,
Mix'd dance, and wanton MASK, or midnight ball, &c.

And in his *Ready and easy Way to establish a free Commonwealth,* written in 1660, on *the inconveniencies and dangers of readmitting Kingship,* and with a view to counteract *the noxious humour of returning to Bondage,* he says, 'a King must be adored as a demigod, with a dissolute and haughty court about him, of vast expence and luxury, MASKS and *Revels,* to the debauching our prime gentry, both male and female, not in their *pastimes* only, &c.' *PR. W.* i. 590. I believe the whole compliment was paid to the genius of Fletcher. But in the mean time it should be remembered, that Milton had not yet contracted an aversion to courts and court-amusements; and that in 'L'Allegro', MASKS are among his pleasures. Nor could he now disapprove of a species of entertainment, to which as a writer he was giving encouragement. The royal Masks, however, did not, like 'Comus', always abound with Platonic recommendations of the doctrine of chastity.

The ingenious and accurate Mr. Reed has pointed out a rude outline, from which Milton seems partly to have sketched the plan of the fable of 'Comus'. See *BIOGRAPH. DRAMAT.* ii. p. 441. It is an old play, with this title, '*THE OLD WIVES TALE,* a pleasant conceited Comedie, plaied by the Queenes Maiesties players. Written by G. P. [i.e. George Peele.] Printed at London by John Danter, and are to be sold by Ralph Hancocke and John Hardie, 1595.' In quarto. This very scarce and curious piece exhibits, among other parallel incidents, two Brothers wandering in quest of their Sister, whom an Enchanter had imprisoned. This magician had learned his art from his mother Meroe, as Comus had been instructed by his mother Circe. The Brothers call out on the Lady's name, and Echo replies. The Enchanter had given her a potion which suspends the powers of reason, and superinduces oblivion of herself. The Brothers afterwards meet with an Old Man who is also skilled in magic; and by listening to his soothsayings, they recover their lost Sister. But not till the Enchanter's wreath had been torn from his head, his sword wrested from his hand, a glass broken, and a light extinguished. The names of some of the characters, as Sacrapant, Chorebus, and others, are taken from the *ORLANDO FURIOSO.* The history of Meroe a witch, may be seen in 'The xi Bookes of the Golden Asse, containing the Metamorphosie of Lucius

Apuleius, interlaced with sundrie pleasant and delectable Tales, &c.
Translated out of Latin into English by William Adlington, Lond.
1566.' See Chap. iii. 'How Socrates in his returned from Macedony to
Larissa was spoyled and robbed, and how he fell acquainted with one
Meroe a witch.' And Chap. iv. 'How Meroe the witch turned divers
persons into miserable beasts.' Of this book there were other editions,
in 1571, 1596, 1600, and 1639. All in quarto and the black letter. The
translator was of University College. See also APULEIS in the original.
A Meroe is mentioned by Ausonius, *EPIGR*. xix.

Peele's Play opens thus.

Anticke, Frolicke, and Fantasticke, three adventurers, are lost in a
wood, in the night. They agree to sing the old Song,

> Three merrie men, and three merrie men,
> And three merrie men be wee;
> I in the wood, and thou on the ground,
> And Jacke sleeps in the tree.

They hear a dog, and fancy themselves to be near some village. A cottage appears, with a lantern: on which Frolicke says, 'I perceiue the
glimryng of a gloworme, a candle, or a cats-eye, &c.' They intreat him
to shew the way: otherwise, they say, 'wee are like to wander among
the owlets and hobgoblins of the forest.' He invites them to his cottage;
and orders his wife to lay a crab in the fire, 'to rost for lambes-wool,
&c.' They sing

> When as the rie reach to the chin,
> And *chopcherrie, chopcherrie ripe* within;
> Strawberries swimming in the creame,
> And schoole-boyes playing in the streame, &c.

At length, to pass the time *trimly*, it is proposed that the wife shall
tell 'a merry winters tale', or, 'an old wiues winters tale', of which sort
of stories she is not without a *score*. She begins, There was a king, or
duke, who had a most beautiful daughter, and she was stolen away by a
necromancer, who turning himself into a dragon, carried her in his
mouth to his castle. The king sent out all his men to find his daughter;
'at last, all the king's men went out so long, that hir Two Brothers
went to seeke hir.' Immediately the two Brothers enter, and speak,

> 1 *Br*. Vpon these chalkie cliffs of Albion,
> We are arriued now with tedious toile, &c.
> To seeke our Sister, &c.—

A soothsayer enters, with whom they converse about the lost lady. '*Sooths.* Was she fayre? *2Br.* The fayrest for white and the purest for redde, as the blood of the deare or the driven snowe, &c.' In their search, Echo replies to their call. They find too late that their Sister is under the captivity of a wicked magician, and that she had tasted his cup of oblivion. In the close, after the wreath is torn from the magician's head, and he is disarmed and killed, by a Spirit in the shape and character of a beautiful page of fifteen years old, she still remains subject to the magician's inchantment. But in a subsequent scene the Spirit enters, and declares, that the Sister cannot be delivered but by a Lady, who is neither maid, wife, nor widow. The Spirit blows a magical horn, and the Lady appears; she dissolves the charm, by breaking a glass, and extinguishing a light, as I have before recited. A curtain is withdrawn, and the Sister is seen seated and asleep. She is disinchanted and restored to her senses, having been spoken to THRICE. She then rejoins her Two Brothers, with whom she returns home; and the Boy-spirit vanishes under the earth. The magician is here called 'inchanter vile', as in 'Comus', v. 907.

There is another circumstance in this play, taken from the old English *APULEIUS*. It is where the *Old Man* every night is transformed by our magician into a bear, recovering in the daytime his natural shape.

Among the many feats of magic in this play, a bride newly married gains a marriage-portion by dipping a pitcher into a well. As she dips, there is a *voice*:

> Faire maiden, white and red,
> Combe me smoothe, and stroke my head,
> And thou shall haue some cockell bread!
> Gently dippe, but not too deepe,
> For feare thou make the golden beard to weepe!
> Faire maiden, white and redde,
> Combe me smooth, and stroke my head;
> And euery haire a sheaue shall be,
> And euery sheaue a golden tree!

With this stage-direction, '*A head comes up full of gold; she combes it into her lap.*'

I must not omit, that Shakespeare seems also to have had an eye on this play. It is in the scene where '*The Haruest-men enter with a Song.*' Again, '*Enter the Haruest-men singing with women in their handes.*' Frolicke says, 'Who have we here, our amourous haruest-starres?'—*They sing,*

> Loe, here we come a reaping a reaping,
> To reape our haruest-fruite;
> And thus we passe the yeare so long,
> And neuer be we mute.

Compare the Masque in the *TEMPEST*, A. iv. S. i. where Iris says,

> You sun-burnt sicklemen, of August weary,
> Come hither from the furrow, and be merry;
> Make holy-day: your rye-straw hats put on,
> And these fresh nymphs encounter every one
> In country footing.

Where is this stage-direction, *Enter certain Reapers, properly habited: they join with the nymphs in a graceful dance.* The *TEMPEST* probably did not appear before the year 1612.

That Milton had his eye on this ancient drama, which might have been the favourite of his early youth, perhaps it may be at least affirmed with as much credibility, as that he conceived the *PARADISE LOST*, from seeing a Mystery at Florence, written by Andreini a Florentine in 1617, entitled *ADAMO*.

In the mean time it must be confessed, that Milton's magician Comus, with his cup and wand, is ultimately founded on the fable of Circe. The effects of both characters are much the same. They are both to be opposed at first with force and violence. Circe is subdued by the virtues of the herb Moly which Mercury gives to Ulysses, and Comus by the plant Haemony which the Spirit gives to the Two Brothers. About the year 1615, a Masque called the *INNER TEMPLE MASQUE*, written by William Browne author of *BRITANNIA'S PASTORALS*, which I have frequently cited, was presented by the students of the Inner Temple. See Notes on 'Com.' V. 252. 636. 659. It has been lately printed from a manuscript in the Library of Emanuel College: but I have been informed, that a few copies were printed soon after the presentation. It was formed on the story of Circe, and perhaps might have suggested some few hints to Milton. I will give some proofs of Parallelism as we go along. . . .

Doctor Newton had also observed, that Milton formed the plan of 'Comus' very much upon the episode of Circe in the *Odyssey*. And Doctor Johnson, in his Life of Milton, says, that the fiction is derived from Homer's Circe. But a learned and ingenious annotator on the *Lives of the Poets* is of opinion, notwithstanding the great biographer's assertion, that 'it is rather taken from the "Comus" of ERYCIUS PUTEANUS, in which, under the fiction of a dream, the characters of "Comus" and his attendants are delineated, and the delights of sensualists exposed and reprobated. This little Tract was published at Louvain in 1611, and afterwards at Oxford in 1634, the very year in which MILTON's "Comus" was written.' Note signed H. in Johnson's *LIVES OF THE POETS*. vol. i. p. 134 ed. 1790. and p. 123. ed. 1794.

In *Remarks on the Arabian Night's Entertainments* by RICHARD HOLE, L. L. B. Lond. 1797, this observation has been confirmed by various extracts from Puteanus's work. But, before I present the reader with the correspondencies in the Dutch and British 'Comus', which this acute and entertaining writer has exhibited, it should be remarked, that the first edition of Puteanus is not that which was printed at Louvain in 1611; although it is said to be the *first* by Mr. Hole, p. 232, and implied to be the *first* in the preceding information of the annotator on Johnson. Mr. Watson refers to Puteanus, in his note on v. 58. of 'Comus', whose work, he says, was *written* in 1608. It was probably *published* at Louvain in the same year. The edition of 1611 has the following title, 'ERYCI PUTEANI "Comvs" SIVE, PHAGESIPOSIA CIMMERIA. SOMNIVM: Secundò jam et accuratius editum. LOVANII, Typis GERARDI RIVII. [MDXI].' Dan. Heinsius has prefixed a copy of verses to Puteanus in this edition.

'Milton certainly read this performance with such attention, as led, perhaps imperceptibly, to imitation. His "Comus"

> Offers to every weary traveller
> His orient liquor in a crystal glass.

In Puteanus, one of his attendants discharges that office. . . . From the following passage Milton seems to have derived his idea of the mode, in which he first introduces the voluptuous enchanter. . . . These figurative personages recall to our minds

> Meanwhile welcome Joy and Feast
> Midnight Shout and Revelry,
> Tipsy Dance, and Jollity.

In the same speech our Poet evidently has in view a lively Anacreontic Ode, which the Comus of Puteanus likewise addresses to his dissipated Votaries.' Hole's REMARKS &c. pp. 233, 234.

The lines, which Mr Hole has extracted from this Ode, are given as 'resemblances which can hardly be considered accidental;' and he adds, 'whoever chooses to compare farther the poetical address of Comus in each author, will find a similar spirit and congeniality of thought, though the Dutch Muse in point of chastity is very inferior to the British.' REMARKS &c. p. 236. . . .

'It may naturally indeed be supposed,' says Mr. Hole, 'that Milton had perused the description of Comus by Philostratus, as well as the Dutch author, who evidently borrowed and expanded several of his ideas; but Milton judic[i]ously avoids some traits of character, which Puteanus adopts in their full spirit.' REMARKS, &c. p. 238.

The description of the figure of Comus in Puteanus is entirely taken from Philostratus, and is introduced as an illustration of Comus's PICTURE, which, among the most famous productions of Painting and Statuary, Puteanus and Aderba behold in the palace of Comus. See pp. 39. 40 ed. supr.

The Comus of Puteanus carries a torch in one hand, and in the other his intoxicating cup . . . p. 17. ed. supr. Compare the entry of Milton's Comus and his attendants after verse 92. *Stage-Direction.*

Milton, however, in his imitations of Puteanus, has interwoven many new allusions and refined sentiments. Puteanus, it must be acknowledged, is often sprightly as well as poignant. But in HIS 'Comus' we shall search in vain for the delicacy of expression and vigour of fancy, which we find in the 'Comus' of MILTON. From the indecencies also in Puteanus the reader will turn away with disgust; but to the jollities in Milton he can listen 'unreproved,' because his 'invitations to pleasure are so general, that they excite no distinct images of currupt enjoyment, and take no dangerous hold on the fancy.'*

* Dr. Johnson, in his *Life of Milton.*

87. Penn on *Samson Agonistes*

1798

Extract from John Penn, *Critical, Poetical, and Dramatic Works* (1798), 'Preliminary Observations' [to *Samson Agonistes*], ii, 213–14 and note, ii, 263.

John Penn (1759–1834) was a lawyer and a Member of Parliament, whose biography is mainly concerned with political activities, particularly in connection with the American colonies. *The Battle of Eddington: or, British Liberty; a Tragedy* (1792) was much criticized in the periodicals. In the collected volume of 1798 he printed Milton's drama in scenes, with some notes and various deletions which he attempted to justify.

Milton's tragedy may appear to be much curtailed in the following pages; but it acquires, by such means, that rational as well as theatrical rapidity of march which the example of the managers, in shortening our finest plays for representation, justifies us in communicating to it, for the purpose of showing the true nature of the drama. It might, in nearly this form, be acted as an interlude, without danger of being ill received. The choruses would not only give it variety, but desirably prolong it in the representation. I have excluded from them every thing that has not quite the appearance of song; so that there is no more left of that confused mixture of song and dialogue, which I had been the first to forbear introducing in a choral play.

I will make one remark upon my alteration of this tragedy. There are very often speeches of a single line in the Greek tragedies, continuing for a long time together, and a single piece of information, which the mind is eager to obtain, is splintered into several of these speeches by the means of question and answer. Whether it was from the example of Shakespeare, or from his own unbiassed judgment, Milton has not imitated the ancients much in this respect, I have only had occasion in the last scene to form one speech of several, which will be there perceived. Unity requires, that what is asseverated of one thing should be confined to one speech, unless its division gives extraordinary force to the composition.

. . . I think Johnson's excellent criticism on this work only severe in supposing, that it contained no more than the substance of one act. I might have shortened, but have left it of the length of two. I must confess, I think it inferior both to 'Lycidas', and the 'Allegro' and 'Penseroso', though still one of Milton's valuable works. Those literary men who see 'Comus' acted with greater pleasure from owing their amusement to the mind of Milton, might on that account, as well as from the merits of this drama, wish to see its effect in representation.

88. Green on the three major poems

1799–1800

Extract from Thomas Green, *Extracts from The Diary of a Lover of Literature* (1799–1800), (Ipswich, 1810), 126, 192, 198.

Thomas Green (1769–1825) was a lawyer who gave up his profession upon inheriting money in 1794, thereafter devoting himself to literature. The main result of this study was his *Diary*, published in extract in 1810.

March the 1st.
Finished the *Paradise Regained*. Milton has been most unhappy in the choice of his subject,—an inexplicable and suspicious legend; unconnected with the narrative where it appears; easily feigned; and incapable of contradiction:—but he has worked it up with wonderful ability; nor am I surprised at his partiality for an offspring, so naturally sickly in its constitution, and which he must have reared with such surpassing pains and assiduity.—Milton has been extolled for the exquisite delicacy of his ear; but what shall we say to such lines as these

And made him bow to the Gods of his wives.   B.2.v.171.

And with these words his temptation pursued.   B.2.405.

From that placid aspect and meek regard.   B.3.217.

No wonder, for though in thee be united.   B.3.229.

How are they to be recited? To my ears 'lay your knife and your fork across your plate', sounds just as *numerous*.—Newton's note on v.245.B.4.

The Attic Bird trills her thick warbled notes,

explains what, I have been asked, Gray means by the 'Attic Warbler', in his Ode on Spring. Philomela, the Daughter of Pandion, King of Athens, was changed into a Nightingale; which was thence in Latin called Atthis.—Milton in 16 lines from v. 293 to 308. B.4, gives a good summary of the systems of the different moral Philosophers of Greece.

March the 8th.

Read Milton's *Samson Agonistes*;—a noble Poem, but a miserable Drama. 'Comus', though a much earlier, is surely a much finer composition:— after all, however, give me the *Gothic* Architecture of Shakespear.— 'Lycidas', though highly poetical, I agree with Johnson, breathes little sincere sorrow, and is therefore essentially defective as a Monody.

February the 2nd.

Finished the perusal of the First Six Books of Milton's *Paradise Lost*. The scene betwixt Satan, Sin, and Death, in the 2d. Book, is transcendantly sublime: the Allegory, to which Addison objects, is lost amidst such force and vividness and majesty of description, as, I think with Atter- bury, renders the grandest passages in Homer and Virgil comparatively feeble and dwarfish.—In the 3d Book, not all the powers of Milton's skill and genius, though vigorously exerted for the purpose, can palliate the monstrous absurdities, or reconcile the glaring inconsistencies, of the orthodox faith: they rather stare out in higher and more offensive relief, from the strength with which he has brought before us, the personages, and the state of being, to which they attach.—Relieved from these shackles, in the 4th. Book, Milton once more towers into native excellence, and 'is himself again'.

Feb. the 7th.

Finished the remaining Six Books of *Paradise Lost*. The Battle of the Angels, in the 6th. Book,—a most daring effort of invention,—is sup- ported with wonderful force, fire, and sublimity; and rises to the last:—

nor do *I*, myself, when warmed with the subject, object to the taunting jeers, and scornful puns, of Satan and Belial.—In the 9th. Book, Milton naturalises the Fall of Man, with admirable address.—The interest of the Poem, no doubt, in some measure declines as it advances; but, upon the whole, my opinion of this astonishing effort of genius, is greatly raised by this review of it. Compare the slender and unpromising *stamina* on which Milton had to work, with the stupendous production which he has formed upon them:—this is the way to estimate his powers of Invention, the great characteristic of a Poet.

89. Dunster on Milton's use of Du Bartas

1800

Extract from Charles Dunster, *Considerations on Milton's Early Reading, and the Prima Stamina of His Paradise Lost* (1800), pp. 5–7, 11–17, 25, 119.

The folio edition of Sylvester's Du Bartas was published in 1621; when Milton was just at the age of thirteen. . . . I would suppose that Milton, who was an early and passionate reader, became acquainted with this edition of Sylvester's Du Bartas on its first publication; and that he then perused it with the *avidity* of a young poetical mind; hence, perhaps, that the true *origin* of *PARADISE LOST* is, in this respect, to be traced primarily to SYLVESTER'S DU BARTAS. . . .

Nothing can be farther from my intention than to insinuate that Milton was a plagiarist, or servile imitator; but I conceive, that, having read these sacred poems of very high merit, at the immediate age when his own mind was just beginning to teem with poetry, he retained numberless thoughts, passages, and expressions therein, so deeply in his mind, that they hung inherently on his imagination, and became, as it were, naturalized there. Hence many of them were afterwards insensibly transfused into his own compositions. . . .

The versification of our translator, Joshua Sylvester, has in it, it must be confessed, numerous highly obsolete and vulgarised expressions; frequent discordant and disgusting rhymes; and, very often, a most offensive jingle of adjunct rhyming, or similarly sounding words. It has also some passages so highly bombastic, as to be most completely ludicrous. In spite of all this, his language is at times admirably condensed, and it abounds in passages which, I conceive, cannot but reclaim our most unbounded admiration; and which, I firmly believe, made a forcible appeal to the finely-tuned ear of Milton.

The earliest pieces of poetical composition, published by the author of *Paradise Lost*, are his versification of the 114th and 136th Psalms, written when he was only fifteen; in which Mr. Warton has pointed out several *foreshewings* of future poetical eminence. The archetypes of several of these, (or at least something that materially contributed towards them), I fancied that I found in Sylvester's Du Bartas; the folio edition of which had been published by Humfrey Lownes, only two years before. This induced me to make the experiment, how far I could trace Milton, in these and some others of his early poems, to the publication of his neighbour.

The result of that experiment I now submit to your better judgement.—I must apprise you that the passages, which I cite as parallel, or in some respect strikingly similar, must not be expected all to have equal force. Some, I think, will speak for themselves with strong claims; others with less powerful ones. On the whole, they may *jointly* go *near* to prove the point, which I have fancied myself able to shew.

. . . [Parallels and discussion of lines of Psalm 114.] In this psalm, Milton's first-avowed poetical attempt, the style of versification, (being heroic rhime, which he has not often attempted) seems to have been adopted from Sylvester. Two years after, when he wrote his 'Verses on the Death of a Fair Infant', he was palpably become acquainted with Spenser; who is there his model. Hence I suppose the *priority* of his acquaintance with *Sylvester's Du Bartas*; which I would consider as his *primary attachment*.

. . . [Parallels and discussion of other early poems through 'Lycidas', plus various sonnets.] I much fear . . . that I may have fatigued you by my too abundant citation, of supposed *parallel*, or in some respects *similar*, passages from Milton's JUVENILIA and Sylvester's DU BARTAS, and *other poems*.—I submit them to your accurate and tasteful judgment. —*Futile* and *irrelevant*, as some of them may appear *singly* considered, when taken altogether, I cannot but think, they *go near* to evince, that the author of *PARADISE LOST* had made an early acquaintance with his predecessor in Sacred Poetry. This might be strongly corroborated, and a much larger extent of obligation might be pointed out from various parts of his two great Poems. . . .

90. Todd on various poems

1801

Extracts from Henry J. Todd, ed., *The Poetical Works of John Milton* (1801), IV, xvii–xix, 335, 497; V, 55–6, 416–17; VI, 396–7.

['The Origin of *Paradise Regain'd*']
The origin of this Poem is attributed to the suggestion of Ellwood the quaker. Milton had lent this friend, in 1665, his *Paradise Lost*, then completed in manuscript, at Chalfont St. Giles; desiring him to peruse it at his leisure, and give his judgement of it. On returning the Poem, Milton asked him what he thought of it: 'which I modestly, but freely told him,' says Ellwood in his Life of himself; 'and, after some further discourse about it, I pleasantly said to him, "Thou hast said much of *Paradise Lost*, but what hast thou to say of *Paradise Found?*" He made me no answer, but sat some time in a muse; then broke off that discourse, and fell upon another subject.' When Ellwood afterwards waited on him in London, Milton showed him his *PARADISE REGAINED*; and, 'in a pleasant tone,' said to him, '*This is owing to you*; for you put it into my head by the question you put me at Chalfont; which before I had not thought of.'

On this subject the Muses had not been before silent. In our own language, Giles Fletcher had published *Christ's Victorie and Triumph*, in 1611; an elegant and impressive poem in four parts, of which the second, entitled 'Christ's Triumph on Earth', describes the Temptation. To this poem, however, the *Paradise Regained* owes little obligation. Perhaps the Italian Muse might afford a hint. In the following sacred poem, consisting of ten books, 'La Humanita del Figlivolo di Dio. In

ottaua rima, per Theos filo Folengo, Mantoano. Venegia, 1583,' 4.°, the
fourth book treats largely of the Temptation: from which I will cite
the descriptive scene, after the Devil has tempted our Lord, and has been
rebuked with the reply 'Thou shalt worship the Lord thy God, &c.'
. . . There had been published also at Venice, in 1518, 'La Vita et
Passione di Christo, &c. composta per Antonio Cornozano. In terza
rima.' The subject of the sixth chapter of the first book is the Temptation: to which is prefixed a wooden cut, wherein Satan is represented
as an old man with a long beard, offering bread to our Lord. The
Tempter indeed is an *aged man* like the Tempter of Milton, in Vischer's
cuts to the Bible, as noticed by Mr. Thyer; and in Salvator Rosa's fine
painting of the Temptation, as noticed by Mr. Dunster. See the 'Life
of Milton' in the first volume. The Devil is also represented in a
monastick habit by Luca Giordano, in a picture of the Temptation,
which made a part of the Dusseldorp collection. But poetry likewise
seems to have painted, not seldom, the *gray dissimulation* of the Tempter
in the same colours. Milton draws him in the habit of an aged Franciscan
in his admirable verses 'In Quint. Novembris'. There is a poem, entitled
'Monachos mentiti Daemones,' in Wierus *De Præstigiis Dæmonum*,
Basil. 1583, p. 84. in which the assumed disguise is somewhat similar:
. . . In Ross's description of the Temptation, *Christiados* lib. viii. ed.
1638. p. 178, he is also thus painted, by the adaptation of Virgilian
phrases: . . .

  There is an Italian poem, which I have not seen, entitled *Il Digiuno di
Christo nel Deserto* by Giovanni Nizzoli, dated in 1611. And I observe
also among the works of P. Antonio Glielmo (who died in 1644),
enumerated by Crasso in his 'Elogii d' huomini letterati' *Il Calvario
Laureato, Poema*: a kindred subject perhaps with that of *Paradise Regained*;
the mention of which Italian title induces us to acknowledge with
gratitude, the existence of a *Calvary* in our own poetry [by Richard
Cumberland]: of which the plan is the faultless plan of a Paradise
regained; the spirit is truly Miltonick; and the language at the same
time, original.

[Note to *Paradise Regain'd*]
Doubtless the *Paradise Regained*, like the mild and pleasing brightness of
the lesser luminary, will ever obtain its comparative admiration. The
fine sentiments, which it breathes; the pure morality, which it incul-
cates; and the striking imagery, with which it is frequently embellished;
must commend the Poem, while taste and virtue are respected, to the

grateful approbation of the world. The versification indeed wants the variety and animation, which so eminently distinguish the numbers of *Paradise Lost*. And it cannot but be acknowledged that the plan is faulty: For, to attribute the Redemption of Mankind solely to Christ's triumph over the temptations in the wilderness, is a notion not only contracted, but untrue. The gate of everlasting life was opened, through the Death and Resurrection of our Lord. Dr. Bentley's remark has not yet been controverted: See the note on *Paradise Lost*, B. x. 182. I do not, however, think, that *Paradise Regained* is without 'allusions to poets either ancient or modern,' as is insinuated in a preceding remark: It exhibits, on the contrary, several elegant imitations, interwoven with Milton's original graces, both of the classical and the romantick Muses.

[Note to *Samson Agonistes*]
Mr. Penn has printed, in the second volume of his valuable *Critical, Poetical, and Dramatick Works*, 1798, an abridgement of Milton's *Samson*; in nearly which form he thinks it might be acted as an interlude, without danger of being ill received. The abridgement is formed with much ingenuity. Yet the classical reader will not perhaps accede to the absence of some splendid, and some affecting, passages. Mr. Penn also remarks, that Dr. Johnson's criticism on this tragedy is severe only in supposing, that it contained no more than the substance of one act; and that, though still one of Milton's valuable works, *Samson* is inferiour both to 'Lycidas', and the 'Allegro' *and* 'Penseroso'. I agree in preferring the earlier poems of Milton to his tragedy; But I may be permitted not to subscribe to the assertion in Dr. Johnson's criticism that 'nothing passes between the first act and the last, that either hastens or delays the death of Samson;' which, Mr. Cumberland observes, is not correct. See before, p. 356. On the contrary, I admire the art and judgement with which the poet has delineated the various circumstances that, from the first entrance of Manoah to the last appearance of Samson, progressively affect the mind of the hero, and finally produce the resolution which hastens the catastrophe. *Samson*, as an oratorio, is divided into three acts: Mr. Penn's abridgement exhibits the length of two.

It has been observed by Goldsmith, that *Samson* is a tragedy without a love-intrigue, as the *Athalie* of Racine also is, which appeared not many years after *Samson*; and that Maffei, instructed by these examples, has formed his *Merope* without any amorous plot.

[Note to 'Lycidas']
I wish indeed that the fictions of heathenism had not here been mingled

with what is sacred; particularly that, after the sublime intimation from Scripture of Angels *wiping the tears for ever from the eyes of Lycidas*, Lycidas, thus beautified, had not been converted into the classical *Genius of the shore*. It had been observed, that, 'as Dante has made Cato of Utica keeper of the gates of Purgatory, Milton has here, in return, placed St. Peter in company with Apollo, Triton, Æolus, &c. For the intrusion of what follows, respecting the clergy of his time, the earliest Italians have, in pieces of every sort, set plentiful example. Perhaps no better reason can be given for Milton's conduct here, than what some commentator gives for Dante's above mentioned: *Per verità e un gran capriccio, ma in ciò seque suo stile.'* See Cursory Remarks on some of the ancient English poets, particularly Milton, 1789, p. 112.

The rhymes and numbers, which doctor Johnson condemns, appear to me as eminent proofs of the poet's judgement; exhibiting, in their varied and arbitrary disposition, an ease and gracefulness, which infinitely exceed the formal couplets, or alternate rhymes, of modern Elegy. Lamenting also the prejudice which has pronounced 'Lycidas' to be vulgar and disgusting, I shall never cease to consider this monody as the sweet effusion of a most poetick and tender mind; entitled, as well by its beautiful melody, as by the frequent grandeur of its sentiments and language, to the enthusiasm of admiration.

[Note to 'Comus']
Perhaps the conduct and conversation of the Brothers, which Mr. Warton blames, may not be altogether indefensible.

They have lost their way in a forest at night, and are in 'the want of light and noise.' It would now be dangerous for them to run about an unknown wilderness; and, if they should separate, in order to seek their Sister, they might lose each other. In the uncertainty of what was their best plan, they therefore naturally wait, expecting to hear perhaps the cry of their lost Sister, or some noise to which they would have directed their steps. The Younger Brother anxiously expresses his apprehensions for his Sister. The Elder, in reply, trusts that she is not in danger, and, instead of giving way to those fears, which the Younger repeats, expatiates on the strength of Chastity; by the illustration of which argument he confidently maintains the hope of their Sister's safety, while he beguiles the perplexity of their own situation.

It has been observed, that 'Comus' is not calculated to shine in theatrick exhibition for those very reasons which constitute its essential and specifick merit. The *Pastor Fido* of Guarini, which also ravishes the *reader,* and *The Faithful Shepherdess* of Fletcher, could not succeed upon the *Stage.* However, it is sufficient, that 'Comus' displays the true sources of poetical delight and moral instruction, in its charming imagery, in its original conceptions, in its sublime diction, in its virtuous sentiments. Its few inaccuracies weigh but as dust in the balance against its general merit. And, in short, (if I may be allowed respectfully to differ from the high authority of a preceding note,) I am of opinion, that this enchanting Poem, or Pastoral Drama, is both gracefully splendid, and delightfully instructive.

[Note on Latin style]
[T]here are various passages in the English prose, besides the *Tractate on Education* and the *Areopagitica,* which seem entitled to the praise of the most impressive eloquence. Nor, in his Latin performances are there wanting examples of pure as well as animated style. The accurate scholar seldom ceases to be visible either in the politician, in the controversialist, or in the secretary. Perhaps his English style is, in general, too learned. Of his *History of England* Warburton has said, that 'it is written with great simplicity, contrary to his custom in his prose-works; and is the better for it. But he sometimes rises to a surprising grandeur in the sentiment and expression, as at the conclusion of the second book, *Henceforth we are to steer* &c. I never saw any thing equal to this, but the conclusion of Sir Walter Raleigh's *History of the World.*' That Milton may be found virulent in these civil and religious speculations, will not, perhaps, be denied: His pen, dipped, as it sometimes is, in the gall of puritanism, hurries him into the violence of rage; and he then condemns without mercy, as he judges without candour. But, at other times, his pages breathe the sweetest language of sensibility; the abusive spirit, which the turbulence of the times excited, sinks into calmness; and, without subscribing to his political sentiments, we are led to admire the uncommon felicity of his expression.

91. Boyd on the fallen angels

before 1809

Henry Boyd, 'Observations on the Characters of the Fallen Angels in *Paradise Lost*'. From Henry J. Todd, ed., *The Poetical Works of Milton* (1809), ii, 259–71.

Henry Boyd, who died in 1832, was a minor poet and translator, his Dante (1802) being well praised. His notes on this major issue of *Paradise Lost* were put together apparently between Todd's first variorum in 1801 and their publication in the second in 1809.

The characters of Satan and his associates in this wonderful poem, are by the generality of readers merely considered as noble efforts of imagination. But it may probably contribute to illustrate the genius of the Poet, if we consider them merely as pictures of human nature, or at least of human passions, personified with aggravated features indeed, but still preserving their original lineaments. If this contributes to develope in any degree the origin and progress of certain propensities in our nature, it may at least, point out the mode of reading the Poets with profit as well as pleasure.

The sentiments that Satan is made to express in the very first speech, are such, Addison observes, as might be expected from the most exalted and most depraved of beings.

Besides the depravity of the Arch-fiend, which appears on his first address to his associate, the most prominent feature is that obstinacy which it displays, and which in man is by flattery, both from himself and others, called firmness of character. This, when properly founded, and under the direction of right reason, is the basis of every thing dignified and magnanimous.

> By this, the mercury of man is fixt;
> Strong grows the virtue with his nature mixt;
> The dross cements what else were too refin'd,
> And in one interest body acts with mind.

But its perversions are as eminently conspicuous in the characters of Sylla, Borgia, and many other names of great celebrity in ancient and modern times, but in none more than in certain literary characters, some of which have persevered to the last in the profession and publication of dogmas of the most fatal tendency to virtue and religion. This spurious fortitude, as it affects the vulgar observer, has the semblance of worth, not substance; abstracted from its motives and tendency, it operates with no less fallacious effect on the mind where it is entertained; especially, when combined with pride, such effects are produced as the Poet means to expose. It is observable, that the most depraved characters make some effort to palliate their own vices to themselves, by something which, at least to them, has the appearance of *moral* approbation. So strong is the voice of natural conscience in the very worst, that they endeavour to substitute for themselves one which may be called artificial. Thus Satan pleases himself with the picture of 'the *unconquerable* will,' and the 'courage' of his enterprize, though unfortunate, and it is produced as a sort of apology, both to *himself* and his associate. It shews also what support this spurious conscience, this unfounded self-approbation, derives from the sophistry of the passions. *Things ill begun make strong themselves in ill*; thus pride begets false zeal, and *that*, in its turn, generates persecution. Under a similar influence, we find the enemy of God and man renders himself more obdurate, by this sort of palliation. This appears in his reply to the speech of his companion [I, 159–65]. This is the natural language of malignity, *as such*, whether it appears in human characters, or is exhibited in that of other beings. This speech therefore must be allowed to be too just a picture of the nature of man, when depravity becomes habitual. Passions and dispositions operate according as they are directed. If man has such principles as lead him to do good to his fellow-creatures, he also has some which, under certain impulses, lead to the commission or the excessive retaliation of injury real or supposed. Ungoverned passion will be gratified at all hazard, even of evil to one's self. There is, it is true, properly speaking, no self-hatred, but there is a degree of hatred and revenge, which effectually overpowers self-love. There is probably no ill-will of any person to another, if he feels no emulation or resentment towards that other. But envy is the corruption of emulation, as emulation is merely the desire and hope of equality with, or superiority over, others with whom we compare ourselves. But when this becomes envy, and envy of course produces resentment, both must have their gratification. In the natural passion there appears to be no pain, but the want implied in the desire; but its corruption envy, is attended with acute pain, which impels it to seek its end with eagerness, in the depression of others: but in its progress to maturity, the doing mischief to others (as we say *for mischief's sake*), appears to be the prime motive and chief gratification. In the vices that arise from the strength of mere animal propensities, though so degrading in themselves, and pernicious to our fellow creatures, that they are justly described *as warring against the soul*, yet mischief to *others* is not their immediate purpose, but a semblance of good;—but the direct object of envy, malice, and revenge, is *to injure others*; this is the vital food on which they live, and their only source of enjoyment. It is the criterion which distinguishes them from all other passions, and gives them a characteristick which may be truly termed *diabolical*. This is more conspicuous, when those in whom this passion is predominent know and acknowledge, that the result of their course of action, or their machinations against others, must be accumulated misery to themselves. Satan, in the Poem, is often made to acknowledge this; but even when this consequence is not so immediately foreseen, these passions, at least in the extreme, bear a stamp, and answer to a description, which seems scarce compatible with humanity, without some infusion of supernatural malignity. At least the gratification of such passions, by such means, is like the relief obtained (as is supposed) by a rabid animal, when he communicates that pain, which he feels, to others. A disposition to calumny, is in Milton represented as a principal ingredient in the character of Satan; a common effect of pride, which we are taught to believe was his original vice. To suppose we exalt ourselves by degrading the character of others, is its necessary consequence. We rise, at least in our own esteem, and as we are apt to imagine, in the opinion of others, by indulging this propensity; as we flatter ourselves, that the vehemence of our invective may be thought to proceed from a sort of moral indignation. The human calumniator, indeed, does not designedly hazard his own safety to gratify his revenge, but he is at least insensible of his greatest danger, viz. the light in which he must appear to the Searcher of Hearts.

But to return, this spirit appears predominant in the Speech of Satan on his escape from the burning lake, and his contemplation of his future destination. He had before attributed *Tyranny* to the Almighty; 'here he expresses his hope, *that the Almighty hath not built* HERE *for his envy*'. Calumny, we know, among men, contributes to the self-deception of the calumniator, with regard to his own merit; how far in this light it could impose upon the Arch-rebel we cannot judge, only so far as we know that pride and other passions darken the understanding. But we see, in the address to his infernal host, the effects of his unsatisfied ambition, and vindictive spirit, and we acknowledge the skill with which he suits his topicks to inflame the pride, the vengeance, and the hopes of his followers, for the purpose of hardening them in their impious obstinacy.

As the origin of Satan's rebellion is represented to be an ardent desire to rise above his equals, by whatever means he could devise, if we turn our observations to mankind, it is incalculable what mischief has been done, by a similar principle of action in those, who have endeavoured to render their names illustrious, regardless of the means: to exemplify this in the ambition of warriours, and to detail their pretexts for publick good, by which they have imposed upon mankind, and led them on to slaughter, would be to transcribe a great part of the annals of the world. But this spirit is no less conspicuous, perhaps equally destructive, in these who have toiled to propagate opinions either pernicious, or at least, calculated to render established tenets less beneficial; and this, merely to obtain what the Poet calls *the whistling of a name*.

These observations apply to the Speeches of Satan in the second Book, in which his character, as represented above, appears more manifest. But in his soliloquy in the fourth Book, the Poet has represented him in somewhat of a new light, and, I think, very judiciously, as there appears a novelty in his situation. He seems here at first to have lost much of that ferocious pride and obdurate spirit, which distinguished him at his first introduction; he had, since that, been engaged in the contemplation of the works of the Almighty, and the proofs of his beneficence. This seems to have made an impression on his mind, transient indeed, but so far, at least, conducive to the ends of poetry, as that by *reflection*, we may say it enhances the impression made on us by the objects presented to us. (This observation also may be applied to his speech in the ninth Book.)

> O thou, that, with surpassing glory crown'd,
> Look'st from thy sole dominion like the God
> Of this new world, &c. [IV, 32–4]

Led by the marks of power and goodness in the creation, to acknowledge them in the Creator, he feels for a moment something like remorse; speaking of his rebellion and ingratitude, he exclaims:

> Ah, wherefore! He deserv'd no such return
> From me, whom he created what I was . . . Lifted up so high,
> I 'sdein'd subjection, &c. [IV, 42–50]

His reflection upon the consequences of his ambitious wickedness, raises a conflict of passions, natural in some degree, to even a bad mind, in such a state of inward torture. The pain incident to such a condition, continually prompts it to vent its fury on any thing that depraved fancy may represent as the cause of its intolerable anguish. Thus Satan attributes his torments even to the love or long suffering of God.

> Be then his love accurs'd, since love or hate,
> To me alike, it deals eternal woe. &c. [IV, 69–70]

But immediately with a violent recoil, natural to that tumultuous state of mind, he vents his rage upon himself.

> Nay, curs'd be thou; since against his *thy* will
> Chose freely what it now so justly rues, &c. [IV, 71–2]

This brings on a more acute paroxysm of misery:

> Which way I fly is Hell; myself am Hell;
> And, in the lowest deep, a lower deep
> Still threatening to devour me opens wide, &c. [IV, 75–7]

Under this dreadful pressure he seems inclined to seek relief, even by submission and supplication for mercy; but his dormant pride soon revives, and exerts itself in one of its most powerful modifications; in that, in fact, which produces half the moral evils of the world, viz. *the dread of being despised by those on whose suffrage we place a value, whether that estimation be made on just grounds or otherwise.* Contempt is a punishment even harder to be borne by a proud spiirt than pain; for 'contempt', as Aristotle observes, 'implies hatred without fear'.[1]

He seems again to make a faint effort against the depraved bias of his mind, when he reasons thus:

> But say I could repent, &c. [IV, 93]

He, however, concludes like a confirmed *Fatalist*, that his *nature cannot be changed.* A sentiment that sometimes encourages the Sensualist, and sometimes inspires the Fanatick; which some writers have the effrontery to support in publick, and which, it is to be feared, is too often employed in excuse for vice; at least, so far as it serves as a secret palliation. It will not be necessary to dwell at any length on the circumstances of the Temptation, in the ninth Book; it will be only necessary to remark how judiciously the Poet has managed, in making the Tempter

[1] *Rhetoric*, Bk. 2, Ch. 7.

excite, in a new created being of inferiour order, a love of knowledge. It had been before observed, by Addison, that Eve's Vision, in the fifth Book, was skilfully introduced, to prepare her mind for the full effects of Satan's Temptation.

As to the rest, the influence which the tempter obtains over the mind of Eve, is so far from being incredible, that, supposing a mere mortal in the situation of the serpent, he, in order to accomplish his designs, would begin with flattery; the self-complacency which that would probably produce, would easily be perceptible to the eye. In a soil so prepared, Pride would quickly vegetate, nor would Envy fail to find a place there, particularly if conveyed in the vehicle of curiosity: this, operating with Ambition, might bring about all the natural consequences recorded in the narrative, supposing the characters not exalted above the standard of humanity.

The foregoing observations on the character of Satan, are in some degree applicable to his associates, as the first impulse came from him, and he may be said to have given them all a certain tincture of his own character: this similarity will enable us to apply, in a certain sense to *him*, what we shall further remark with regard to *them*.

The character of Moloch, in the second book, is remarkable for extravagance and fury. There are some traits in it which would lead one to conjecture that the poet had Jonson's Cethegus in his eye. However that may be, there appears a sublimity and spirit in his speech, which equals it with any thing in the poem. At first sight his sentiments appear very extravagant, as he seems to conclude that *Omnipotence* could be subdued by *power*. We indeed cannot easily conceive how in this case, and in that of Satan, excess of passion may cloud the intellect of beings so much superiour to man. But, as observed before, Milton could only draw his ideas from human characters, and *there*, we know, transcendent superiority of parts, is by no means a security against the most extravagant absurdity of theory, to say nothing of practice. Of this the more immediate cause may be vanity, perhaps some more malignant passion. But the remote origin is pride, the source of almost every malignant passion. To give an example of this, when Hume denied that we can have any knowledge of *cause* or *effect*, and by inference, *none* of the first cause, he had been led into this opinion first by literary vanity, but his pride would not allow him to recant or to confess a feeling of the ridicule with which he must have been stung, by the simple case put by Beattie, (in his 'Essay on Truth',) of *a book being found on a table in an apartment where none had access but himself, which* HE *had not left there, and which, however, could not have grown there, i.e. come without a cause.* It is hardly conceivable, that such a man should believe his own position. It is scarce less extraordinary if he did *not* believe them, that he should venture to give currency to doctrines so pernicious to society, at the *risque* at least of incurring guilt of a very deep dye. Yet so great was the pride of this man, that it must have been the source of that factitious firmness of character, which induced him to persevere in contriving to bestow on these opinions as much celebrity as possible, when he himself should be mouldering in the dust. This is certainly carrying human criminality to the utmost degree of extravagance equal to that of Moloch, if Moloch could be supposed to represent an human character. The most striking instance of the predominance of pride and revenge in this vindictive spirit is, his enjoying the thought, that *though reduced to this side nothing*, yet *revenge*, even a series of vindictive attempts, would be to him full compensation.

In many of these characters, from the greatest to the more subordinate, the art of the poet appears conspicuous, in giving them extensive powers of ratiocination, and yet keeping them clear of any expressions of compunction or remorse, or any approximation to that virtue which they had lost. This skill however seems most apparent in the character of Belial, who is described as *in act more graceful and humane*; yet he is as far as the rest from expressing any sentiment which would entitle even him to compassion, though he is not represented as equal to some of the others in malignity.

What has been observed of the skill of Homer in diversifying the principle of *courage*, according to the characters of his several warriours, seems equally true of the management of Milton, with respect to pride and envy, the reigning vices of his pandemonian heroes. We can, for instance, easily suppose the contradiction of Belial to Moloch to have been meant as a secret gratification of those passions in the former, particularly as he turns the ferocious warriour into ridicule, a talent which he exerts on another occasion. He is described as a sensualist, with many epicurean lineaments of character, particularly in his predilection for *indolence*, or the abscence of pain. His opinions are supported with great plausibility. His abhorrence of non-existence, seems copied from that dread of death, exhibited by some of that sect of old. In all his character there appears a species of pusillanimity, yet it is remarkable how careful the poet is to keep this perfectly clear from any infusion of tenderness or sympathy; it is no less remark[a]ble, that, of all men in the world, sensualists have less of that fellow-feeling than any other description of men; in other words, they are the most *selfish* of all mankind; witness the ruin they bring on their own families, and that of others', without any visible compunction. In some instances also, like Belial, such characters exhibit a very extraordinary sophistical acuteness; this too is natural, for it is an habit they must have acquired in devising palliations for their hateful enormities. Two remarkable portraitures of this sort occur in Shadwell's play of the *Libertine Destroyed*, and in the character of Pandarus in Chaucer's *Troilus and Cressida*.

In the character of Mammon, it would have been highly improper to have introduced those elevated sentiments, where grandeur and depravity are so conspicuously united, as they appear in the speeches of his associates. This combination would have been incongruous to the natural train of ideas in one who was accustomed to admire *the riches of heavens pavement, trodden gold*. From him who is described as the least *erected spirit that fell from heaven*, we could not expect those ardent excursions of fancy, which we meet with from others in the course of the debate, and which fill the mind with a mixture of delight and horrour. In Mammon, therefore, we contemplate the passions of the infernals, envy and revenge in all their native deformity, without any rhetorical decorations, except in one instance, which seems better adapted to the style of Belial: [II, 262–8].

But in the course of his argument, he makes a supposition that shows the depravity of these fallen spirits in a very striking light: [II, 237–49].

It is remarkable that he exhibits in his speech an opinion which has since made no small figure in some noted systems of morality, viz. that utility is the standard of every thing laudable. This has been carried so far by Aristotle, Hume, and others, that every accomplishment, mental and bodily, has been dignified by the name of VIRTUE, and consequently, if what we now from old prejudice denominate crimes, such as adultery, fraud, &c. can be in any way subservient to publick utility, they become duties, or at least are not deserving of either punishment or censure!

The character of Beelzebub is distinguished from the rest by more extensive views, and more deliberate wickedness. In malignity he resembles his master, but his mind is less ardent. In his first speech, his sagacity had at once perceived that their misery was irremediable. On this topick he expatiates, here, and enforces his opinion from the character under which he represents the Supreme Being. Him he describes as powerful, vindictive, and arbitrary. He arraigns, by implication, the justice of the Deity, yet without expressing any regard to that attribute; for he represents the Sovereign of the Universe, as acting on a system which he himself would have adopted in a like situation.

As the poet's ideas are drawn *ab intimis recessibus mentis* [from the secret recesses of the mind], we are here naturally led to observe the gradations by which the mind is led *to judge of others by itself*.* Sympathy was bestowed upon us, that by our own, we should judge of the feelings of others, that we might be taught, not only by precept, but by sentiment, *to rejoice with those that rejoice*, and *to weep with those that weep*. But as Pope observes of the RULING PASSION, *this* also may be perverted, and often produces the most baneful consequences, when this happens; as often is the case with the most precious gifts of nature. It would detain us too long to account for this, or to show by what degrees selfishness, aided by pride, acquires the preponderance in the moral balance, though they are designed by Providence to counteract each other. Selfishness is the handmaid of many vices: yet corrupt as the heart may be, pride still flatters the fancy by all the arts of self-adulation. It is not necessary here to analyse those arts which will be found amply detailed in the works of many moralists and divines. But with this pride, a spurious sort of sympathy is often found to combine, if it may be called sympathy which consists, not in *fellow feeling*, properly so called, but in viewing all characters *through its own medium*, and judging of their principles, motives, and actions, by its own. It therefore draws this conclusion, that where the motives are the same, the actions must be similar. The language of the true philanthropist is 'I will put myself in *that* person's situation, and act towards him as I might *reasonably* expect he would act with regard to me in like circumstances.' The secret language of the selfish man, who attributes to all mankind his own disposition, is, 'I will mal-treat or defraud that man, for, had he it in his power, he would act the same part by me; *for are not all men alike?*' There is the more necessity of guarding against this, and no less against that self-deception which induces mankind to palliate their faults to themselves; as, whether sympathy operates as it ought or not, there is always something like it at work in the mind. This is that sort of plastick power in the fancy, by which every person, I believe, when figuring to himself an absent person, whom he has not seen, but expects to see, always gives the picture a sort of resemblance to himself, both in outward lineaments and disposition. If we could combine the idea of high intellectual powers, joined with the utmost depravity, we might conceive a mixture of malignity and pride, which might presume to attribute its own hideous

* i.e., to impute its own vices to others.

character to the Supreme Being. In fact, this often has been the case in some degree in the ancient world, and still is where idolatry and *fanaticism* prevail. This, or somewhat like it, seems to be what the poet means to represent in the characters of Beelzebub and of Satan himself; it may at least probably account for the seeming extravagance of some of the sentiments expressed here and in other parts of the poem where these characters are introduced; or, if it even shows the origin and progress of some pernicious habits in the mind, from the prevalence of *one* grand source of moral evil, the observation may not be quite useless.

It is observable, that not only at *this* period of their misery, but at first, the supposed tyranny or arbitrary government of the Supreme Being, is assigned first as a sufficient excuse for ingratitude and rebellion; and, after their overthrow, it is pleaded as a just reason for retaliation and revenge. In the same manner here, a fancied slight, even from a benefactor, is often, to a depraved mind, made a plea for the most bitter and persevering resentment.

Appendices

(*a*) SELECTED SECONDARY REFERENCES

Dowden, Edward. 'Milton in the Eighteenth Century (1701–1750)'. *Proceedings of the British Academy*, 1908.

Good, John W. *Studies in the Milton Tradition*. University of Illinois Press, 1915; reprinted, New York, 1967.

Havens, Raymond D. *The Influence of Milton on English Poetry*. Harvard University Press, 1922; reprinted, New York, 1961.

Mackail, J. W. 'Bentley's Milton'. *Proceedings of the British Academy*, 1924.

Oras, Ants. *Milton's Editors and Commentators From Patrick Hume to Henry John Todd (1695–1801): A Study in Critical Views and Methods*. Tartu, 1938.

Robertson, J. G. 'Milton's Fame On The Continent'. *Proceedings of the British Academy*, 1908.

Sensabaugh, George. *Milton in Early America*. Princeton University Press, 1964.

Shawcross, John T., ed. *Milton: The Critical Heritage* [1628–1731]. London, Routledge & Kegan Paul, 1970.

Sherburn, George. *The Early Popularity of Milton's Minor Poems*. University of Chicago Press, 1920. Originally published in *Modern Philology*, 17 (1919–20), 259–78, 515–40.

Thorpe, James, ed. *Milton Criticism: Selections from Four Centuries*. New York, 1950; reprinted, London, Routledge & Kegan Paul, 1966.

Wittreich, Joseph A., Jr, ed. *The Romantics on Milton: Formal Essays and Critical Asides*. The Press of Case Western Reserve University, 1970.

(*b*) ADDITIONAL SIGNIFICANT CRITICISM OMITTED IN THIS SELECTION

[Anonymous]. 'Fragments by Leo. No. XIII'. *European Magazine*, xiii (1788), 401–6.
Critique of *Samson Agonistes* in refutation of Johnson.

[Anonymous]. Letter. *Gentleman's Magazine*, lvi (1786), 557–9. Signed 'Catul. Nemesius'. Strictures on Johnson's criticism of Milton's Latinity.

Barry, James. *An Inquiry into the Real and Imaginary Obstructions to the Acquisition of the Arts in England*. London, 1775.
Milton's pictorial imagination in *Paradise Lost*, pp. 109–20.

Beyträge zur critischen Historie der deutschen Sprache, Poesie, und Beredsamkeit. Leipzig: Bernhard Christoph Breitkopf. Vol. 24 (1740), 652–68.
Criticism of Bodmer and comparison with Addison as a critic of *Paradise Lost*.

[Blackburne, Francis]. *Remarks on Johnson's Life of Milton. To which are added, Milton's Tractate of Education and Areopagitica.*
Reissued in *Memoirs of Thomas Hollis, Esq.* (1780).

Bodmer, Johann Jacob. *Joh. Jacob Bodmers critische Abhandlung von dem Wunderbaren in der Poesie und dessen Verbindung mit dem Wahrscheinlichen in einer Vertheidigung des Gedichtes Joh. Miltons von dem verlohrnen Paradiese; der Bengefüget ist Joseph Addisons Abhandlung von den Schönheiten in demselben Gedichte.* Zurich, 1740.
Full discussion of *Paradise Lost* and criticism (e.g., Addison's, Voltaire's).

Bodmer, Johann Jacob. *Critische Betrachtungen über die poetischen Gemählde der Dichter mit einer Vorrede von Johann Jacob Breitinger.* Zurich, 1741.
Concerned with influence, style, and prosody; *passim*.

Breitinger, Johann Jacob. *Johann Jacob Breitingers Fortsetzung der critischen Dichtkunst worinnen die poetische Mahleren.* Zurich and Leipzig, 1740.
Discussions of the character of *Paradise Lost*, of translations, and of language; *passim*.

Gottsched, Johann Christoph. *Versuch einer critischen Dichtkunst vor die Deutschen.* Leipzig, 1730; revised, 1742, 1751.
Discussion of prosody, translations, mythological elements in *Paradise Lost*, etc.; *passim*.

[Johnson, Samuel, the Dancing Master]. *Court and Country: A Paraphrase upon Milton. By the Author of Hurlo-Thrumbo.* London [1780].
Supposedly the second part of a play with two characters who discuss Milton's beliefs in *Paradise Lost* satirically.

Kirkpatrick, J[ames]. *The Sea-Piece, A Narrative, Philosophical and Descriptive Poem.* London, 1750.
Defence of Milton against Lauder; preface, pp. xxii–xxvi.

[Macaulay, Aulay]. *Essays on Various Subjects of Taste and Criticism.* London, 1780.
'A Critique on the First Book of *Paradise Lost*; with some preliminary observations on the poem in general', pp. 42–108.

Masenio, Jacobo. *Sarcotis. Carmen. Auctore Jacobo Masenio S. J. Editio altera cura & studia J. Dinouart.* Coloniae Agrippinae: Parissiis, 1757.
Latin and French texts, plus discussion and reprints of various documents concerned with the Lauder controversy (e.g., from *Le Journal Étranger* and *Gentleman's Magazine*).

Massey, W[illiam]. *Remarks upon Milton's Paradise Lost. Historical, Geographical, Philological, Critical, and Explanatory.* London, 1761.

[Mitford, William]. *An Essay upon the Harmony of Language, Intended Principally to Illustrate that of the English Language.* London, 1774.
The verse of *Paradise Lost* and 'Comus' discussed, pp. 101–33.

Murphy, Arthur. *An Essay on the Life and Genius of Samuel Johnson, LL.D.* London, 1792.
Discussion of Lauder controversy, pp. 59–67; comment on Milton's governmental relationship and political ideas, pp. 180–6.

Das Neueste aus der anmuthigen Gelehrsamkeit. Leipzig: Bernhard Christoph Breitkopf, 1752.
'Ein Versuch von Miltons Gebrauche . . .', pp. 260–75. Review and discussion of Lauder's charges.
'Fortsetzung des Auszuges, von Miltons Gebrauche neuerer Dichter, in seinem verlohrnen Paradiese', pp. 41–52. Further remarks.
'Fortsetzung des Auszuges aus Hrn. Lauders Abhandlung von Miltons Gebrauche der neueren Dichter im verlohrnen Paradiese', pp. 438–45. Additional remarks.
'Fortsetzung von Miltons Gebrauche neuerer Dichter in seinem verlohrnen Paradiese', pp. 620–6, 831–9. Further discussion of Lauder as well as of Bentley.
'Beschlusz des Auszuges, von Miltons Gebrauche der Neuern in seinem verlohrnen Paradiese', pp. 913–23. Additional comments on Milton's alleged sources.

Das Neueste aus der anmuthigen Gelehrsamkeit. Leipzig: Bernard Christoph Breitkopf, 1755.
'Nachricht von der Aufnahme der französischen Christiade . . .', pp. 688–90. Comparison of Satan and Christ.

[Neve, Philip]. *A Narrative of the Disinterment of Milton's Coffin, in the Parish-Church of St. Giles, Cripplegate, on Wednesday, 4th of August, 1790; and of the Treatment of the Corpse, During that and the Following Day.* London, 1790.
Ed. 2 (1790) expands the first edition by fifteen pages.

Racine, Louis. *Le Paradis perdu de Milton, Traduction Nouvelle, Avec des Notes, la Vie de l'Auteur, un discours sur son poëme, les remarques d'Addisson; & à l'occasion de ces remarques au discours sur le poëme épique.* Paris, 1755. 3 vols.
See *Life of Milton, Together With Observations on Paradise Lost,* translated by Katherine Johns (London, 1930).

Richardson, R[ichard]. *Zoilomastix: or, a Vindication of Milton, from all the Invidious Charges of Mr William Lauder. With several new remarks on Paradise Lost.* London, 1747.

Milton's Paradise Lost. A New Edition, By Richard Bentley, D. D. London, 1732.
Revised text with notes.

Johann Miltons verlust des Paradieses. Ein helden Gedicht. In ungebundener Rede übersetzet. Frankfurt and Leipzig, 1732.
Translated into German prose and edited by Johann Jacob Bodmer. With introduction.

Areopagitica. London, 1738.
With unsigned preface by James Thomson. First separate edition since 1644.

A Complete Collection of the Historical, Political, and Miscellaneous Works of John Milton: Correctly printed from the Original Editions. With an Historical and Critical Account of the Life and Writings of the Author; containing several Original Papers of His, Never before Published. London, 1738.
2 vols. The prose works edited by Thomas Birch, including Joseph Washington's translation of *Defensio prima* and John Phillips's *Responsio ad Apologiam Anonymi*. Introduction records poetic readings from the Trinity MS. Revised in 1753 by Richard Baron.

Comus, A Mask: (Now Adapted to the Stage) as Alter'd from Milton's Mask.
John Dalton's version, employing a portion of 'L'Allegro'. Includes non-Miltonic prologue and epilogue. Text only.

Paradise Lost. A Poem, in Twelve Books. . . . A New Edition, with Notes of Various Authors, by Thomas Newton, D. D. London, 1749.
2 vols. Variorum edition with 'The Life of Milton', an index, and a word index.

An Essay on Education. London, 1751.
First separate English edition since 1644.

Paradise Regain'd. A Poem, in Four Books. To which is added Samson Agonistes: and Poems Upon Several Occasions. . . . A New Edition, with Notes of Various Authors, by Thomas Newton, D. D. London, 1752. Variorum edition.

Eikonoklastes . . . Now First Published from the Author's Second Edition, Printed in 1650: With many Enlargements: by Richard Baron. With a Preface shewing the Transcendent Excellency of Milton's Prose Works. To which is added, an Original Letter to Milton, Never Before Published. London, 1756.
First separate edition since 1650. The letter, dated 26 May 1659, is from John [i.e., Moses] Wall.

An Old Looking-Glass for the Laity and Clergy . . . Being Considerations Touching the Likeliest Means to Remove Hirelings out of the Church of Christ . . . With the Life of Milton: also Large Extracts from His Works, Concerning Bishops. Philadelphia, 1770.

First American edition of Milton. Elijah Fenton's 'Life'; extracts from *Animad-versions, Of Reformation*, and *Apology*.

Paradise Lost. A Poem, in Twelve Books. The author John Milton. With the Life of Milton. By Thomas Newton, D. D. Philadelphia, 1777.

Vol. I: I–XI. 'Life' is a brief abstract. Title page for vol. II: *Paradise Regain'd. A Poem, in Four Books. To which are added, Samson Agonistes: and Poems on Several Occasions.* Philadelphia, 1777.

Book XII of *PL* given in vol. II. First American edition of Milton's poetry.

The Tenure of Kings and Magistrates . . . Originally written by the Celebrated John Milton. Now Corrected, and Re-published with Additional Notes and Observa-tions; and Particularly Recommended, at this time, to the Perusal of the Men of Ireland. Dublin, 1784.

Abbreviated text, primarily through omission of testimonials and quotations. Notes aimed at contemporary Irish audience.

Poems Upon Several Occasions, English, Italian, and Latin, with Translations . . . With Notes Critical and Explanatory, and Other Illustrations, by Thomas Warton. London, 1785.

Revised and enlarged 1791; it includes Charles Burney's 'Remarks on the Greek Verses of Milton'.

Sur la liberté de la presse, imité de l'Anglois de Milton. Londres [i.e., Paris], 1788.

French imitation of *Areopagitica* by Honoré Gabriel Riquetti, Comte Mira-beau.

Théorie de la Royauté d'Après la Doctrine de Milton. [Paris], 1789. *Defensio prima*, translated and adapted by J. B. Salaville, with preface entitled 'Sur Milton et ses ouvrages', perhaps by Mirabeau.

Paradise Regain'd: A Poem in Four Books. Philadelphia, 1790. First separate edition.

A Treatise of Civil Power in Ecclesiastical Causes. London, 1790. First separate edition since 1659.

The Ready and Easy Way to Establish a Free Commonwealth. London, 1791. First separate edition since 1660.

Paradise Lost. A Poem in Twelve Books. . . . The Original System of Ortho-graphy Restored; the Punctuation Corrected and Extended. With Various Readings: and Notes, Chiefly Rhythmical. Bury St Edmunds, 1792.

Edited by Capel Lofft. Book I only. Second edition, 1793, gives Books I and II. No more published.

The Poetical Works of John Milton. With a Life of the Author, by William Hayley. London, 1794–7.

3 vols. Illustrated, includes George Romney's 'Milton and His Daughters'.

Paradise Regained, a Poem, in Four Books. London, 1795.

Edited by Charles Dunster, with variorum notes.

Samson Agonistes. A Dramatick Poem. Written on the Model of the Antient Greek Tragedy. London, 1796.

First separate edition in English. Bell's Library. With Fenton's 'Life' and remarks on the character of the drama.

Comus, a Mask Presented at Ludlow Castle . . . With Notes Critical and Explanatory by Various Commentators, and With Preliminary Illustrations; To Which is Added a Copy of the Mask from a Manuscript belonging to His Grace the Duke of Bridgewater. Canterbury, 1798.
Edited by Henry John Todd.

The Poetical Works of John Milton. London, 1801.
6 vols. Edited by Henry John Todd. Variorum notes and various essays.

Select Bibliography

Bond, Richmond P. *English Burlesque Poetry, 1700–1750*. Harvard University Press, 1932; reprinted, N.Y., 1964.

Darbishire, Helen, ed. *The Early Lives of Milton*. London, 1932.

Diekhoff, John S. *Milton on Himself*. Oxford University Press, 1939; reprinted, N.Y., 1958. Contains extensive excerpts from Milton's work, dealing with aims, plans, and self-criticism, *passim*.

Dowden, Edward. 'Milton in the Eighteenth Century (1701–1750)'. *Proceedings of the British Academy*, 1908.

Dowling, John, ed. *Testimonies and Criticism Relating to the Life and Works of John Milton*. St Austell, 1903. A similar collection with some connective discussion and emphasis on nineteenth-century materials.

French, J. Milton, ed. *The Life Records of John Milton*. Rutgers University Press, 1949–58. Five vols. A chronological listing, with notes, of all known documents relating to Milton or discussions of him during his lifetime, and to his immediate relatives before his birth and after his death.

Gillespie, Edgar B. '*Paradise Regained*: A History of the Criticism and an Interpretation.' Unpublished doctoral dissertation, Duke University, 1966.

Good, John W. *Studies in the Milton Tradition*. University of Illinois Press, 1915; Reprinted, N.Y., 1967.

Graham, James J. G., ed. *Autobiography of John Milton*. London, 1872. Prints items dealing with aims and inspiration.

Grewe, Eugene F. 'A History of the Criticism of John Milton's *Comus*, 1637–1941.' Unpublished doctoral dissertation, University of Michigan, 1964.

Havens, Raymond D. *The Influence of Milton on English Poetry*. Harvard University Press, 1922; reprinted, N.Y., 1961. A list of poems which were influenced by Milton's works, categorized by year and types, is appended.

Keeley, Gracie Lee. 'Milton's Reputation in the Eighteenth Century as Reflected in the *Gentleman's Magazine* and the *Monthly Review*.' Unpublished master's thesis, University of Georgia, 1940.

Mackail, J. W. 'Bentley's Milton.' *Proceedings of the British Academy*, 1924.

Manuel, M. *The Seventeenth-Century Critics and Biographers of Milton*. Trivandrum, India: University of Kerala, 1962.

Moore, C. A. 'Miltoniana (1679–1741).' *Modern Philology*, XXIV (1926–7), 321–39.

Oras, Ants. *Milton's Editors and Commentators From Patrick Hume to Henry John Todd (1695-1801): A Study in Critical Views and Methods.* Dorpat Universitet, Acta, XX (1930).

Parker, William Riley. *Milton's Contemporary Reputation.* Ohio State University Press, 1940. Contains a list of printed allusions, dated from 1641 to 1674.

Plunkett, Frank W. 'The Miltonic Tradition in One of Its Phases. The Criticism of Milton as Found in Leading British Magazines of the Pre-Romantic and Romantic Periods (1779-1832).' Doctoral dissertation, Indiana University. 1931, printed in summary form by Arkansas State College Press, 1934.

Robertson, J. G. 'Milton's Fame On The Continent.' *Proceedings of the British Academy,* 1908.

Shawcross, John T., ed. *Milton: The Critical Heritage.* London, Routledge & Kegan Paul, 1970. Covers the period 1628 to 1731.

Sherburn, George. *The Early Popularity of Milton's Minor Poems.* University of Chicago Press, 1920. Originally published in *Modern Philology,* 17 (1919-20), 259-78, 515-40.

Spingarn, J. E., ed. *Critical Essays of Seventeenth Century.* Oxford, 1908-9, reprinted, Indiana University Press, 1957. Three vols. Essays and remarks. *passim.*

Thorpe, James, ed. *Milton Criticisms: Selections from Four Centuries.* New York, 1950; reprinted, London, 1966. Contains Marvell's and Dryden's commendatory poems; excerpts from Dryden, Toland, Dennis; the first six papers on *Paradise Lost* by Addison; and excerpts from Pope, Richardson, Johnson's *Life,* and Thomas Warton. The introduction presents a brief history of Milton criticism.

Select Index

I

CRITICS REPRINTED IN THIS VOLUME

429

II

MILTON'S WORKS

III

TOPICS

IV

GENERAL

THE CRITICAL HERITAGE SERIES

GENERAL EDITOR: B. C. SOUTHAM

Volumes published and forthcoming

Continued